LAW, CRIME AND DEVIANCE SINCE 1700

LAW, CRIME AND DEVIANCE SINCE 1700

MICRO-STUDIES IN THE HISTORY OF CRIME

Edited by Anne-Marie Kilday and David Nash

Bloomsbury Academic
An imprint of Bloomsbury Publishing Plc

B L O O M S B U R Y
LONDON · OXFORD · NEW YORK · NEW DELHI · SYDNEY

Bloomsbury Academic

An imprint of Bloomsbury Publishing Plc

50 Bedford Square	1385 Broadway
London	New York
WC1B 3DP	NY 10018
UK	USA

www.bloomsbury.com

BLOOMSBURY and the Diana logo are trademarks of Bloomsbury Publishing Plc

First published 2017

British Library Cataloguing-in-Publication Data
A catalogue record for this book is available from the British Library.

ISBN: HB: 978-1-4725-8527-1
PB: 978-1-4725-8528-8
ePDF: 978-1-4725-8530-1
ePub: 978-1-4725-8529-5

Library of Congress Cataloging-in-Publication Data
Names: Kilday, Anne-Marie, editor. | Nash, David (David S.), editor.
Title: Law, crime and deviance since 1700 : micro-studies in the history of crime / edited by Anne-Marie Kilday and David Nash.
Description: London ; New York : Bloomsbury Academic, 2016. | Includes bibliographical references and index.
Identifiers: LCCN 2016010856 (print) | LCCN 2016017273 (ebook) | ISBN 9781472585288 (pbk.) | ISBN 9781472585271 (hardback) | ISBN 9781472585295 (epub) | ISBN 9781472585301 (epdf)
Subjects: LCSH: Crime–History–Case studies. | Criminology–Case studies.
Classification: LCC HV6251 .L39 2016 (print) | LCC HV6251 (ebook) | DDC 364.9–dc23
LC record available at https://lccn.loc.gov/2016010856

Cover design: Sharon Mah
Cover image © The Illustrated Police News, 9th August 1879, Issue 808

Typeset by Integra Software Services Pvt. Ltd.
Printed and bound in India

For Dr Carol Beadle on her retirement,

with thanks and much love.

CONTENTS

Contents

LIST OF ILLUSTRATIONS

NOTES ON CONTRIBUTORS

Adrian Ager is Associate Lecturer in the Department of History, Philosophy and Religion at Oxford Brookes University, UK. He has extensive research experience of crime in Britain during the early modern period. His specialisms include the impact that changing socio-economic conditions and legislative reforms had on criminal behaviour.

David J. Cox is Reader in Criminal Justice History at the University of Wolverhampton and a Fellow of the Royal Historical Society. He has published several books concerning the criminal justice system of the eighteenth and nineteenth centuries and is particularly interested in the field of pre-Metropolitan Police history.

Neil Davie is Professor of British History at Université Lumière Lyon 2, France. He is the author of *Tracing the Criminal: The Rise of Scientific Criminology in Britain, 1860–1918* (2005) and *The Penitentiary Ten: The Transformation of the English Prison, 1770–1850* (2015). He is currently working on a history of Parkhurst children's convict prison.

Barry Godfrey is Professor and Associate Pro Vice Chancellor (Research) in the Faculty of Humanities and Social Sciences at the University of Liverpool. He has authored or co-authored fourteen books on the history of crime. His research interests include private policing, desistance, biographical historical methods, digital methodologies, longitudinal studies of sentencing, ethics and historical research, and changes to the operation of criminal justice in the nineteenth and twentieth centuries.

Rachael Griffin is a historian of English criminal justice and earned her doctorate from The University of Western Ontario in 2015. Her doctoral thesis 'Detective Policing and the State in Nineteenth-century England' explored the development of the country's first police detective force at Scotland Yard and the close relationship between Metropolitan Police detectives and the Home Office.

Anja Johanson is Senior Lecturer in History at the University of Dundee. Her research is focussed on the relationship between police and the public in France, Germany and Britain during the nineteenth and twentieth centuries. Her current research project 'Quarrelsome Citizens: Emerging Police Complaints Cultures in London, Paris and Berlin, 1880–1914' compares the ways in which individual citizens challenged police violence and malpractice. She is also interested in the development of civil liberties activism in the late nineteenth and early twentieth centuries, and how individual citizens sought to challenge public authorities – including the police and the judiciary.

Helen Johnston is Senior Lecturer in Criminology at the University of Hull. Her most recent book is *Crime in England, 1815–1880: Experiencing the Criminal Justice System*, published by Routledge in 2011.

Anne-Marie Kilday is Professor of Criminal History at Oxford Brookes University. She has published widely on the history of violence and the history of female criminality in Britain, Europe and North America from 1600 to the present. She is currently working on two monograph projects: one on the history of homicide in Britain and another on the history of violence in Scotland.

Vivien Miller is Associate Professor of American Studies at the University of Nottingham. She is the author of *Hard Labor and Hard Time: Florida's 'Sunshine Prison' and Chain Gangs* (2012), which merited an honourable mention in the BAAS Book Prize 2013, and co-editor of *Transnational Penal Cultures: New Perspectives on Discipline, Punishment, and Desistance* (2015). She has written several articles on Florida crime and punishment, including murder, kidnapping and theft, convict leasing, chain gangs and prisons, and is currently working on the history of the death penalty in the twentieth-century American South.

David S. Nash is Professor of History at Oxford Brookes University. He has written and published on the secular movement in Britain, the history of blasphemy, the history of secularization and the history of shame. He has given expert advice on the issue of blasphemy to the British, Australian and Irish governments as well as the European Parliament. He is currently researching for a book on the history of hate crime.

Helen Rogers is a lecturer in English and Cultural History at Liverpool John Moores University. Her main teaching and research interests lie in the nineteenth century. She has published books on women and radical culture and on gender and fatherhood. Currently Helen is working on a study of crime, punishment and rehabilitation based on the work of the prison visitor Sarah Martin with inmates at Yarmouth Gaol. She is also part of a group working to establish a digital archive of working-class writing to be hosted by Liverpool John Moores University.

Jo Turner is Senior Lecturer in Criminology at the University of Chester. Her research interests and publications lie primarily in the history of crime and punishment. More particularly, she is interested in female offending, imprisonment and aftercare.

Katherine D. Watson is Senior Lecturer in the history of medicine at Oxford Brookes University and a Fellow of the Royal Historical Society. Her research focusses on areas where medicine, crime and the law intersect. She is the author of *Poisoned Lives: English Poisoners and Their Victims* (2004) and *Forensic Medicine in Western Society: A History* (2011), and the editor of *Assaulting the Past: Violence and Civilization in Historical Context* (2007). She is currently working on a monograph on medico-legal practice in England and Wales 1700–1914, based on a project funded by the Wellcome Trust.

Clifford Williamson is Senior Lecturer in Contemporary British and American History at Bath Spa University. His research interests and publications include work on 'The Teddy Boys', the development of private practice in the NHS in the 1950s and 1960s and the religious history of contemporary Scotland. He is currently working on a monograph on deviance and disorder in popular music.

Sarah Wilson is Senior Lecturer in Law at York Law School. After completing her LLB at Cardiff Law School she gained an MA and PhD at the School of History, University of Swansea. Her key research is undertaken in Financial Regulation and Financial Crime, and also in 'Law and History', which seeks to combine legal scholarship with modern history. Her recent monograph *The Origins of Modern Financial Crime: Historical Foundations and Current Problems in Britain* (2014) was shortlisted for the 2015 Wadsworth Prize awarded by the Business Archives Council.

ACKNOWLEDGEMENTS

The editors would like to thank the numerous people who have helped in the writing of this book. Firstly, we would like to express our thanks to staff at the Archives Nationales and the Archives of the Préfecture de Police both in Paris, the National Archives at Kew, the National Archives of Scotland and the Bodleian Library, Oxford, for their patience and helpful advice. We would also like to thank each of the contributors to this volume for their hard work and, in particular, their patience and grace when dealing with our many queries. Special and grateful thanks also go to Richard Craven and his colleagues at OBIS for rescuing one of the chapters from a computer problem which would otherwise have consigned it to oblivion.

We would also like to thank those involved at Bloomsbury Publishing in the production of this book from embryonic idea to published work. Thanks go to our commissioning editor Claire Lipscomb and to our editorial contact Emma Goode. We would also like to thank our anonymous reviewers for their helpful and important contributions.

INTRODUCTION

David S. Nash and Anne-Marie Kilday

I

As scholars interested in the history of law, crime and criminals there are various questions we ask ourselves when we encounter sources which reveal the experiences of our criminal ancestors. What did countless individuals in the historical past think of the criminal justice system of their age as they stood in the dock awaiting a gloomy sentence or a hoped-for acquittal? How did individuals conceive of how the law was going to operate? How criminal and 'immoral' did individuals perceive their deviant behaviour to be when it was both covert and private or public and vilified? How far were criminals and villains 'made' and 'unmade' by the exposure of their story to the media of various historical periods? How far could such 'making' of the reputation of criminals and individual cases continue long after the deaths of all the protagonists? How far did identities (associated with race, gender, age or nationality) affect how criminals were treated by systems of justice and the populace at large?

We might also consider that whilst prisons and incarceration systems may have had their respective 'regimes', how did inmates negotiate their way through these and react to their apparent philosophy? From the other side of the fence, we might ask how did those charged with implementing such philosophies conceive of their role and how did they make decisions about the 'right' and 'wrong' way to run such regimes? In the world at large, how did populations regard the function and purpose of policing in its many forms and how did authorities cope when such policing failed to garner a favourable reputation? Consideration of questions such as these potentially opens up the world of the history of crime to a broader range of insights and, using the narratives of individuals, we can explore new themes about how humans have interacted with the systems associated with law, crime, deviance and punishment through time and across cultures.

After many years of working with secure paradigms within the historical investigation of both law and crime, historians and social scientists are increasingly trying to wrestle new insights and ways of interpreting a range of historical evidence. This often occurs when scholars are in pursuit of unanswered questions or alternatively are seeking more satisfying answers to existing or past ones. This is particularly true where such scholars are seeking to relate the history of these areas to wider social and cultural developments.[1] Investigative paradigms of the criminal past have often included a sustained interest in the power of criminal statistics and their analytical application. These have been used to indicate variously the importance of micro changes in behaviour, in policing and in the application of justice. Another, but obviously related, use of such statistics has been the attempt to trace and follow long-term trends associated with specific offences or aspects of criminal behaviour. Generally speaking, these are concerned with the pursuit of overarching long-term patterns and seek to reach wider and deeper conclusions from these.[2]

However, some well-established paradigms of analysis also include amongst their number some species of grand explanatory theory, which are quarried to produce insights which explain the long-term history of crime, law and human behaviour. These are teleological theories and paradigms which are really in the business of describing processes of change such as modernization, and they have a number of specifically distinct variations. Amongst these we must include the insights of Foucault, who has sought to analyse the history of criminality in relation to the structures modernizing society and how they have evolved in various ways, to deal with it as a specific problem. This has shaped consideration of issues such as the history of incarceration and has also produced a history of the specialist professions which include psychiatry, criminology and penology. These were invented by the long-term urge to classify individuals caught in the arena of law and crime – thereby turning them from autonomous subjects into oppressed objects.[3] Alongside this theoretical paradigm, there is also the equally process-led, teleological analysis offered by Norbert Elias. In constructing the so-called Civilizing Process, Elias created a surprisingly durable template for process-led teleological models associated explicitly with behaviour. This latter paradigm is still remarkably influential in the study of law and crime and is quite regularly restated.[4] This also highlights modernization as an ideological motif driving the decline of violence and the development of manners and politeness. This has led many historians to write almost with that paradigm specifically in mind.[5]

Other ways of writing law and crime history have focussed on specific aspects of legal and judicial practice as self-sustaining entities within themselves.[6] This means that history written in this vein has attempted to show the interplay between legislative, cultural, ideological and technological development and the application of practices to somehow 'modernize' and transform the experience of crime and the law for modern populations. Generally speaking, this has been done through the articulation of a perceptively different past. Very often, descriptions of individual crimes, policing methods or the application of justice come to be homogenized and try to produce analyses of general trends and changes.[7] One upshot of this has been an undue (and sometimes unconscious) reliance upon many of the process-led models as categories of explanation. It is interesting to speculate why this should persist around the study of law and crime. In other areas of social and cultural history, forms of postmodern analysis gained a significant foothold and, at least for a time, genuinely offered some alternative ways of seeing subjects such as radicalism, gender, class and identity. Likewise, it has impacted upon the history of secularization, another area where process-led models had previously strongly influenced the history that has been written about religion.[8]

Yet postmodernism has notably made comparatively little inroad into the history of law and crime. In this respect, the models of rationality, progress and modernization are far more durable and have lasted much longer in this area than metanarratives such as class identity were ever likely to. Whilst the impact of postmodernism on these other areas can scarcely said to have been wholly beneficial, it did at least introduce many otherwise sceptical historians to the idea of using discourses, narratives and representation as ways of exploring the previously dark corners and silences of their respective subject areas.

II

A shift away from considering the history of crime and deviance as phenomena to be encountered through collective or abstract conceptual study has also served to enhance the importance of individual stories. Sometimes the act of piecing these together allows the historian to see the breadth of connections that protagonists moved through and also allowed them to realize that encounters with crime or deviance were but one facet of their lives. This also provided a tacit method of locating such methods and activities firmly within their historical and cultural context, where 'connections' (in all sense of that term from interpersonal alliances right through to relationships with events and other social processes and phenomena) became clear and apparent. Given the advantages of looking at individual instances, and our clear espousal of these, in this volume, we would like to further promote the value of an approach within crime history that we have endeavoured to call the 'micro-study' approach to crime and legal history.

In some respects the connection between these is more obvious than we often realize. Crimes and criminals, as well as their policing and detection, are themselves rooted firmly in narrative. This appears in the conceptualization of them by police and legal authorities as 'cases' for investigation, interpretation and resolution – in some respects the same actions and desires that historians of crime seek to do and achieve. Likewise crimes, their detection and commodification so often take the form of narrative and 'case study' creation at the hands of the various media involved and again in the act of their consumption by the public at large. This occurs not simply through apparent reporting of the 'facts' of the case, but also through a range of other genres that elide these 'facts' into 'true crime' right through to the creation of the wholly fictional detective and crime fighter. Terms of imprisonment or other forms of incarceration are also themselves clearly micro-histories of individuals suffering punishment. Thus protagonists and subsequent historians engage with this concept in the shape of prisons, transportation ships and chain gangs. The evidence generated by these occurrences often shape themselves into narrative structures and micro-history case studies.

Sometimes the way historical evidence manifests itself for the crime and legal historian can be seen as an open invitation to utilize the micro-history method. Court cases are themselves micro-histories of the law at work in individual instances and for individual people. When they are drawn out and contested, they constitute rich evidence of social and cultural expectations and how the management and negotiation of these have failed. Equally they offer historical insight into the preoccupations of past societies and how the law itself dealt with these. As such they provide evidence of what Geoffrey Elton, whilst introducing his own excursion into the genre, described as the opportunity of 'testing some of the generalisations that we necessarily apply to historical writing, and of correcting misconceptions only too likely to occur when history becomes divorced from knowledge of detail'.[9]

Given this craving for detail, we would also seek the opportunity to make it work still harder for the historian. We would especially argue for the benefits produced, by actively linking such studies or narratives together. This method looks at a specific narrative case or incident closely in context and works outwards to provide both 'thick description' and analysis of the case in relation to the wider history of crime, law and society. In the past, some successful previous book-length attempts have been made to self-consciously use micro-history to study conflict and areas that might be considered related to the history of crime. Though a little dated now, Robert Darnton's *The Great Cat Massacre* remains something of a trailblazer in this respect, with its evocation of eighteenth-century Parisian episodes of conflict and exploration of cultural transactions and meanings.[10] However, the studies within this book are very disparate and scarcely any of the stories relate to the single theme of law and crime – perhaps readily apparent in the book's subtitle 'Episodes in French Cultural History'. A similar volume covering English Tudor history is David Cressy's *Agnes Bowker's Cat,* which again sought to uncover individual stories and episodes about deviance.[11] Yet the examples chosen were quite diverse, even if nonetheless sporadically interesting precisely because of this. From this range and variety, Cressy was merely able to demonstrate the multiplicity of forms of conflict, protest and social negotiation that occurred at a time of upheaval. Once again these strayed from a few central areas of concern to embrace a widely disparate range of subjects. Perhaps the very closest, most sustained and most academically successful use of the micro-study to investigate the history of law and crime is Richard Evans's *Tales from the German Underworld.* Whilst this volume did successfully target the history of criminality and the law, once again the issues described are quite fragmented, so that the overarching theme drawn from these concerned the rather obvious rise, professionalization and bureaucratization of the German state.[12]

The approach that we are advocating here has been practised in a recent volume which will soon be augmented by two further works. This has not been a significant feature of work on crime and deviance in Britain up to this point. Although case studies have been a feature of scholarly work on crime in America, generally speaking, these are case studies which themselves are considered self-contained. The reasons for these two situations are not hard to find. Britain's relatively unified systems of justice, policing and punishment often encourage histories which count, classify and approach their subject, seeking to write the history of policy and practice evolving over time. America's more obviously fragmented systems have generally driven their historians to embrace the detailed case study, generally as a substitute for the almost impossible task of creating anything that resembles national histories of crime, policing and incarceration. Nonetheless, these case studies carry with them both opportunities and pitfalls that are a consequence of the other writing genres that they (self-consciously or otherwise) borrow from. Beyond crime history itself, some of these works display attributes acquired from the genre of biography, whilst others owe much to the 'unsolved mystery' genre. Certainly, almost all find themselves closer to the phenomenon of 'true crime' writing than historians this side of the Atlantic would be used to.[13]

Our approach hopes to speak to both the situations described above. By showcasing the value of comparing and linking together micro-histories to American scholars, it is hoped that new approaches that seek to illuminate similarities and differences might well emerge. Similarly, the new approaches inherent in micro-histories of crime might well assist British crime history to broaden and diversify from its roots in producing the history of systems and how they operate. The micro-history approach we used in an earlier work of British history was linked by the desire to examine issues associated with one aspect of legal and behavioural history. This approach was used to put forward a closely argued thesis, which employed in-depth micro-studies to illuminate analysis around specific issues associated with the theme of shame and how it changed over time.[14] Although in our now extant work individual cases predominated in each chapter, the opportunity to unpack the wider historiographical issues involved in each episode and thematic area enabled discussion of the wider context and implications for the history of this particular manifestation of deviance and social relations. This meant that the whole monograph was thus also chronologically and theoretically linked together.

Six of the eight chapters of this previous work were built around the micro-study of 'crimes' (or forms of behaviour) to which society attached or imposed some measure of shame as an observable social emotion. However, importantly, each of these chapters was also a single episode in the ongoing history of shame and was less obviously free standing as many genres of micro-history are. These chapters were likewise juxtaposed with two discursive chapters; the first of which demonstrated the origins, prehistory and use of shame in the eighteenth century. The second illuminated how the early nineteenth century investigated and characterized shame and thought again about its purposes and value within legal and punishment systems.

The benefits offered by this approach would seem to be considerable. The use of the narrative self-contained micro-history structure is able to look at an aspect of any area of study, related to the social history of crime and the law, at a specific moment in time. However, collecting these together (alongside the analysis offered by contextual and theoretical chapters) also constitutes a map of how an area of study altered within society over this time. This is a valuable method which usefully synthesizes reactions to crime, punishment and the responses of individuals caught in socially and culturally perilous situations. It encourages and sustains systematic archive-based investigation of the vital question of how individuals used written and unwritten law within their families and localities. It also offers the capacity for insight into the less well known and less understood crimes such as blasphemy, bestiality, infanticide and domestic violence. This provided an especially amenable way into the otherwise dimly lit corners of the cultural history of law, crime and deviance.

Importantly, this approach effectively forges links with other aspects of cultural history. It also manifestly brings real incidents to life to produce a deeper and enhanced understanding of what the law meant to real people in real situations. In this respect it can effectively illuminate how law is often part of much wider negotiation within the arena of conflict. We see that the law is not always by definition the first port of call for protagonists ensnared by adverse circumstances. Micro-studies are also an opportunity to investigate some of the mainstream theories associated with behaviour and the formation of the self without using the traditional 'top down' approach. Such traditional approaches can too readily find themselves homogenizing and generalizing experience, unwittingly accommodating other agendas which determine, classify and categorize.

Relating such incidents to their wider society also readily illuminates the power and activities of both the media and other institutions that seek to create and voice their own opinions on such matters. These are frequently in the business of constructing, portraying and advocating norms, and the micro-study approach often allows the historian the chance to see this building process in action. This is an invaluable insight when many studies of behaviour and morality often work with perceived and already 'established' norms. The micro-study approach also concentrates much more on the issue of motive and displays this interaction with the law and thus its interface with cultural expectations. In this we see the mechanisms that establish, promote and police them – as well as ways and reasons explaining how they come to be transgressed. Thus the chance to present a history of popular contact with forms of good and bad behaviour and how this is essential to social relations, cultural practice and even consumption and entertainment becomes realized through this method. Similarly this methodological approach is good at exposing and illuminating the cracks and fissure points where law is seen by its producers and/or consumers as functioning to only a limited and sometimes unsatisfactory degree. Likewise it is an especially useful tool in evaluating and exposing aspects of legal and cultural thinking self-consciously or otherwise, in the acts of both construction and transition, something the homogenization of law in other paradigms tends to gloss over or neglect.

III

This current volume is, unlike our work on shame, not a closely sustained use of micro-history to elaborate one theme, as it has a different purpose. It has three 'looser' thematic sections which indicate broad areas that the micro-histories themselves address. Although less tightly connected, laying such studies side by side also offers valuable chronological, geographical and contextual comparison. The collection and investigation of significant numbers of micro-studies potentially presents the opportunity to envisage a rounded and fully nuanced history that really addresses the issues of less homogenous and individual experience unanswered by the generalized process and modernization models. This nuanced picture would also therefore be more flexible in accommodating the mounting challenges, or at least realistic qualifications, to the directional thrust of such generalized models – be they pessimistic or optimistic.

The inherent value of micro-studies is their illumination of human motivation as an important factor which influences the outcomes of many procedures and mechanisms. This enables the scholar to empathize and contemplate each individual stage of a character's interaction with the process of criminality and the law. At each of these stages, the number of prospective behavioural choices becomes more manifest than ever before. As readers with a clear interest in people realize, the micro-history method better enables them to more readily relate to characters and situations in comparison with a simple examination of bare facts. It becomes actively possible to 'wear the shoes' of the individual protagonist in any study – and to contemplate one's own hypothetical actions if confronted with a wholly similar situation. This reintroduces an important degree of empathy within historical scholarship, which enables the appreciation of real dilemmas confronting protagonists in the historical past. Wider interest in this has increased lately with the growth and development of historical fiction. This has, perhaps unwittingly, heightened interest in some aspects of historical writing, such as characterization, previously perhaps neglected by positivist and homogenizing approaches. In doing so an attempt is made within these chapters to investigate the gaps in historical knowledge where these are more readily glossed over in macro-style theories and approaches. As such they are often the antithesis of statistical data, but the experience they tell can be seen as potentially both unique and a starting point for building their status as representative of wider experience. This becomes especially pertinent when they are put together with what we know from the wider history of institutions and processes.[15]

Micro-studies also enable, and often actively encourage, a greater understanding of context with investigative research involving knowledge of a range of attendant social, cultural, political and economic factors. Knowledge of this extra context also potentially inspires the researcher to explore other creative connections and insights provoked by this knowledge, alongside the imperative to look at the operation of these contextual factors upon the protagonists within the fully realized micro-study. The application of this approach also potentially widens the scope and potential reach of both theoretical and historiographical insights that might be used by the researcher in investigating the history of crime. Micro-studies are also an important way of reacquainting the researcher with the importance of causality – a factor reinforced by the ability to 'weigh up' the behavioural choices that each incident presents its protagonists with – alongside their potential motives. Focussing upon this aspect also invites the researcher to contemplate such choices and potentially indulge in exploration of the counterfactual which can add further nuances to understanding.[16]

The appreciation of the context within such studies offers the chance to contemplate different species of action which would have led to alternative outcomes for protagonists. In weighing these up, issues of motive, behaviour and self-image become more readily apparent than they would otherwise have done. Such studies are also a particularly good way of capturing such aspects of the everyday history of behaviour that are so frequently hidden from view. This valuable opportunity is particularly evident around crime histories where the reader routinely gets a snapshot of life in the 'lower orders' – something which is often difficult to retrieve from more 'traditional' sources and methodological approaches.[17] Micro-studies are also capable of inspiring researchers to make better informed and sustained use of techniques associated with record linkage. In other words the micro-study encourages scholars to systematically use a variety of sources, and to methodically piece them together, to build up a detailed picture of a given character, incident or situation. In this way, micro-studies are very useful in building up 'full' histories of different locations and issues. Thus the micro-study and its related stories can yield and involve a multitude of perspectives which can readily allow us to hear the voice of individual and community opinions and perspectives on a given subject. They can also reveal an array of opinion relating to class, gender, age, race/ethnicity, religious persuasion, as well as offering a range of contrasts between establishment and non-establishment viewpoints.

The application of the micro-study has, moreover, also proved especially valuable in the classroom as a method of engaging students in the wider context in which crime history is situated. We, and other contributors to this volume, have discovered that such studies regularly appeal to the creative side of history students, and they often warm to the opportunities within these to explore and assess the impact of the various behavioural choices on offer. In this area micro-histories teach the next generation of citizens how such choices are, and have been, prescribed and proscribed by past societies with different agendas. However, they also importantly teach that such changes never occur overnight, nor as comfortably as some more conventional histories of crime, law and policing are still prepared to argue. When students engage with these in number, they similarly prove useful in deriving and fully appreciating comparative commentaries, where students compare one set of circumstances with those of another culture, time, context or country.[18]

IV

Obviously it is now worth considering the future application of the micro-study and the value of them when collected together. This micro-case study approach potentially proves especially useful when applied to geographical areas where justice is fragmented, overlapping and in some instances actively contradictory. More modern American law and justice also appears to be especially amenable to the application of this mode of study because of its frequently uneasy combination of devolved and centralized justice where local and federal perceptions and imperatives conflict with notable regularity. This sometimes enabled criminals to exploit the possibilities of conflicting jurisdictions, differing technological infrastructures and different policy imperatives driving the local, state and federal perceptions of justice and its purpose.[19] In this, the perceived 'borders' of law and crime (in every sense of this term) become important. These are borders of understanding and comprehension as much as they are the physical borders of judicial systems, or those separating counties or individual states of the union. Indeed several other research possibilities remain intriguing and we intend to pursue a volume investigating these issues in the very near future.

It also becomes possible to conceive that the micro-study approach is better able to foreground and draw more meaningful relationships with adjacent areas of interest and study. Social history, cultural history, gender history, the history of material culture and the history of mentalities all have much to gain from such insights. Likewise economic history, political history and the history of identities may also be enriched by the discoveries lying in wait within the law and its application. The micro-study format also reminds us quite powerfully that the human psyche and the self have to interact very frequently with the law, even if only in the act of passive and mute observance. This, and more active interactions with the law, often happen in ways that are sometimes unexpected, unplanned and unusual. Similarly the reaction of those plunged into this can be both rational and irrational in some wholly unpredictable ways. Could it be said in fact that only here within the micro-study, do we fully encounter and perceive the individual in the historical past coping with their own encounter with forms of legal apparatus, the law, crime and criminality? Through the use of the micro-study, we are also capable of investigating such individuals grasping the law and then harnessing it for their own purposes and motives. In short, the role, history and impetus behind human agency is far more likely to appear in such micro-studies than in many more generalized homogenizing histories of process-based modernization and change.[20] As such, the micro-study is particularly appealing and relevant since it contains an inescapable ability to put the human individual, and the power of their narrative, back into the history of law and crime – creating a place where they become agents rather than passive actors and the otherwise helpless victims of processes.

With an acknowledgement that, more than many other areas of historical study, the phenomenon of law and crime attracts public attention, there is important scope for an agenda which actively addresses this phenomenon of history's wider accountability. The micro-study approach is also potentially better able to engage the wider public in the history of crime and the law and is perhaps more readily in tune with how archives and museums frequently present the history of crime and those who perpetrate it – although we should note particularly that this has its own in-built problem. The fact that the portrayal of such individuals follows a 'criminal or victim of the month' style format too readily contemplates the law and crime significantly, and perhaps unhelpfully, after the fact.

In Britain and elsewhere, the micro-study approach has also been important in showcasing related and analogous experience from the Celtic fringe, and other marginal contexts which are otherwise apt to be ignored, unhelpfully homogenized or in some ways left the victim of significant condescension.[21] Thus it offers ways of more fully incorporating the marginal and forgotten (in many senses of this term) who so often prove both simultaneously illusive and interesting within the study of law and crime history. Thus the micro-study may yet be the perfect tool for moving towards a total history of crime, the law and its application mediated through the act of experiencing it. In this respect it may truly illuminate the contention that when individuals conceptualize their interactions with the social world, the law *really* is the theory for those who otherwise have no theory. As such it is seen to shape their lives, mentalities, modus operandi and modes of behaviour. Thus we venture to suggest that the micro-study approach to law, crime and deviance is an holistic method that contributes to a wide, deep and nuanced understanding of these areas and the societies in which they occur.

v

This book is divided into three sections. The first of these is entitled 'Criminality, State and Society' and this shows the ways that criminality and criminals make states and cultures take decisions about how to construct norms and apply laws. Moreover it also highlights the long tradition of these decisions never being allowed to be above comment, criticism or censure. This section begins with David Nash's examination of the Thomas Aikenhead blasphemy case of 1696–7. Aikenhead was a student at Edinburgh University whom some saw as an adolescent hothead voicing blasphemous opinions. Others saw him as a serious sceptic voicing a species of bottom-up religious dissent that has been hidden from history. All agree that Aikenhead's trial and execution was a grotesque overreaction which had considerable implications and consequences. As befits a volume on micro-histories, this chapter is not so much about the story itself but instead demonstrates that micro-history has been consciously and unconsciously used by individuals from as far back as the early eighteenth century. This particular case has had a life of its own as a story made to convey a considerable range of narratives that speak about injustice, oppression and national history. As such, it is a useful primer in analysing how cultural weeds and foliage grow and flourish around landmark cases which have significance and reach into the twentieth and twenty-first centuries.

The second chapter by Sarah Wilson is a micro-historical examination of financial fraud. This chapter notes a perceived 'silence' about financial crime that simultaneously reflects an almost axiomatic failure of the public to understand its nature and a failure of academic interest in its perpetration and wider implications. It displays a belief that micro-history can bridge the gap between historians and criminologists, for the mutual benefit of both. Building upon the revelations about financial crime exposed by the John Sadleir case, and those against Strahan, Paul and Bates, Sarah Wilson investigates the frauds committed by Joseph Windle Cole and latterly Ernest Saunders. These micro-histories allow us to discover the enduring fraud-laden themes of respectability and trust alongside their relationship with social structures and how these develop. We also learn the considerable importance of the images that such individuals self-consciously create for public consumption and how these potentially alter over time. As Wilson argues, micro-history is wholly capable of supplying some of the parts that are currently missing from both the established historical and criminological approaches to financial crime.

Chapter 3, by Adrian Ager, is an investigation of the well-known Caroline Wybrow case which became a *cause célèbre* in the debates around the Victorian period's Contagious Diseases Acts, since Wybrow was arrested and detained under suspicion that she was a prostitute in need of compulsory inspection. Wybrow was a victim of guilt by association and the chapter investigates both Caroline's history as well as the milieu she moved in that undoubtedly assisted in the construction of her unwarranted reputation. Although the case is well known to historians, the examination in this chapter also investigates the case as a micro-history of how such stories of the mistreatment of an innocent woman can be grasped and used by pressure groups to forward the politics of a deeper and wider policy issue.

The fourth chapter by Clifford Williamson investigates the 'cleft chin' murder which was a wartime sensation that took place in London in the autumn of 1944 involving the folk devils of the age – an American serviceman named Gustav Hulten and an ambitious delinquent stripper named Elizabeth Jones. As such it illuminates the shady world of what Williamson calls the *demi-monde* of the wartime cities' glamour spots that attracted soldiers and 'good time' girls alike and, indeed, the murder appears to be a precise product of this very world. The case is also noteworthy for the unusual use of British law to prosecute an American serviceman and the discretionary use of the Prerogative of Mercy which spared the female felon whilst ensuring the male went to the gallows. The chapter also notes the power of micro-history to describe a moment as a unity of time, place and context as well as providing deeper insight into the power of agency in both criminal acts and the application of justice.

The book's second section, 'Violence and the Violent', begins with Katherine Watson's chapter on vitriol throwing in late nineteenth-century Britain. This chapter looks at the case of Emilie Foucault who threw vitriol over her erstwhilst lover André Delombre in a paroxism of jealousy. This chapter shows how a micro-narrative can help understand the personal nature of relationships within a crime and a criminal situation. Through our investigation of this, we also start to discover aspects of Victorian/Edwardian crime reporting and how this both borrows and reinforces ideas to convey aspects of culpability, emotion and criminal behaviour. In this particular case, the female protagonist cast herself successfully as the courtroom victim, which in turn strongly influenced the press reaction to her plight. As such, the story became a vehicle for the press to tell and reinforce stories of gender and the behavioural norms which clustered around this.

In contrast to the outcome of Chapter 5, the sixth chapter by Anne-Marie Kilday investigates what happens when criminal justice and society turn against a female defendant. Kate Webster, an Irish domestic servant in nineteenth-century England, was accused of killing her mistress. In her defence Webster hastily blamed others and began to alter her account of the story which in turn spun out of her control and irreparably damaged her character, her potential to attract pity and indeed clemency from her peers. She thus emerged as an untrustworthy woman and this realization was increasingly linked in the public mind with stereotypes of the duplicitous Irish. The chapter also focusses upon the growth of public fascination with individual murder stories to eventually spawn the phenomenon of 'dark' tourism.

Section III, entitled 'Police and Policing', contains three chapters. These illuminate some unknown corners of the history of policing. In particular they demonstrate that in the nineteenth century it was a slowly evolving practice which may have caught all participants in this process somewhat by surprise. As such the stories partly explain why its known history is more fragmented than it should be, how its performance was influenced by its human raw material and by the choices made by institutional structures in creating discipline within policing, and lastly how the public and policemen at all levels of the service adapted to the use of practices and mechanisms that many felt intrusive and alien. The first chapter by David Cox draws upon the fact that there is no official history written of the Bow Street Runners and that precious few fragments remain to enable us to understand their development and place in early nineteenth-century society. This chapter shows the ingenuity that historians have to display in piecing together the narrative history of individuals and institutions by blending together fact and fiction from close observation. As is to be expected, this has advantages and pitfalls, yet this chapter demonstrates the occasional necessity of this unusual approach to constructing the micro-history of policing and criminal law.

The second chapter in this section by Anja Johansen uses micro-history to investigate complaints against the police. This focusses on the ignominious career of a Parisian policeman, Léon Kien, who was active in the French capital between 1897 and 1918. Kien's career is a micro-history of everything that can go wrong with policing – corruption, ill-judged actions, overzealous conceptions of 'duty' and performance levels at odds with the expectations of both public and police authorities – all provide a litany of complaints about a spectacularly poor officer. However, this micro-history also unwittingly tells us about the growing public expectations of policemen and their duties, the survival of older 'practices' in resolving problems and how these were increasingly at odds with growing standards of policing professionalism. The chapter also highlights the issue of police management and discipline and how this is conceptualized and implemented, if only episodically and sometimes indifferently. Sometimes the will to act is absent amongst senior officers, yet also institutions can change their tone, structure and attitude with 'regime change' at senior levels.

Rachael Griffin's last chapter in this section focusses upon the policing of vice in Victorian England through the use of plain-clothes police officers. It investigates what micro-histories of undercover policing can tell us about the use and misuse of both police power and wider authority alongside the public reaction to this. Plain-clothes policemen were used as an anonymous way of targeting illegal drinking, gambling and other vices. Yet both police commissioners and the general public, spurred by both a belief that the practice was despotic and the infamy of *agents provocateurs*, widely derided the practice. Despite this, the growing imperative to combat illegal drinking, gambling and Sabbath breaking, pushed all into accepting the use of plain-clothes officers as a necessary evil. This micro-history shows this practice evolving and likewise demonstrates that the coherence imposed on some areas of policing by more generalized accounts of it as a process of development need to accept the findings of this more nuanced approach. The use of plain-clothes officers was episodic and had to mediate between the strong feelings of the police, and policed, alongside the pressures that dictated their presence within specific contexts.

The final section of the volume, entitled 'Stories of Confinement', is an examination of systems of imprisonment and incarceration. This is an especially fertile area for the use of micro-history since it can really get at the history of how criminals are 'made' and how 'successful', or otherwise, the punishment/rehabilitation regime they are exposed to can actually be in practice. Criminals here display self-knowledge and a series of reactions to the system they find themselves within, thus lending a profoundly human dimension to what too frequently are described as penal 'systems'. This section commences with a chapter by Helen Johnson, Barry Godfrey and Jo Turner. This looks in considerable detail at the criminal career of the chronic serial offender Julia Hyland. Hyland was recalcitrant, disobedient and periodically violent whilst numerous strategies to contain her behaviour were tried without success – resulting in the epithet uttered about her at the head of this chapter. The creation of a micro-history around this difficult woman uncovers the nuanced richness of information and record linkage that can shed light upon some aspects that conventional histories gloss over. We hear about the family left behind and the prison conversion of Hyland alongside its subsequent impact on her life reflections upon her erstwhile criminal career.

The second chapter in this section from Helen Rogers focusses upon the life histories of two brothers, William and Abraham Jenkins, who were young offenders imprisoned at Great Yarmouth gaol in the 1840s. This chapter recreates their biographical history right through to their transportation to the colonies in Australia. It discusses their interactions with the criminal justice system and its institutions, noting how this interplayed with both expressions of adolescence and manhood. This created their respective personas amongst the prison population as well as partially determining the social implications of their offence and punishment. As such it sheds considerable light on the nineteenth century's attitudes to young offenders and their treatment but, innovatively, also uses both quantitative and qualitative evidence to do so.

Vivien Miller's penultimate chapter in this section discusses prison narratives from members of prison chain gangs in the US penal system during the interwar period up until 1950. This uses the autobiographies of six prisoners to reveal the day-to-day life of prisoners in the American South. It conveys their stories of the misery of prison and chain gang conditions and how inmates endured and minimized the impact of these during the Jim Crow era. We follow them from prison to life on the outside where we also encounter their struggle with the post-prison world. Here they reflect upon the effectiveness of such punishment regimes and the pitfalls of society allowing them to function imbued with corruption or benevolence. The autobiographies themselves had different afterlives and their impact blended with Hollywood portrayals to create and shape public opposition to penal practices in the southern states.

The very last chapter in the work by Neil Davie is the micro-history of a prison chaplain in 1840s England. Joseph Kingsmill's papers outline his struggles to engage, implement and occasionally nullify prison policies that keep evolving and changing. Kingsmill is equivocal about his role and anxiously seeks ways to perform both vocation and responsibility. This leads him into dilemmas about his role and the ideals of his calling to help prisoners in the face of consistent changes to the prison regime. Kingsmill's story tells of an archetypal ideological conflict between the desire to reform through humane treatment or to punish as example and deterrent. All of these set against the contexts of budgets, interpersonal relationships and varying standards of professionalism.

Thus in this volume there is an array of micro-histories that investigate many different corners of the history of law, crime and deviance. We believe and hope such stories will convince readers that micro-history is an intrinsic and evolving part of investigating and studying the history of this area. Likewise we hope that such explorations and the insights that they offer can inspire all researchers, both inside and outside academe, to create linked micro-histories of their own and thus reap the benefits that we now hope the following stories showcase.

Notes

1. See S.G. Magnússon and I.M. Szijártó (2013) *What Is Microhistory? Theory and Practice* (London: Routledge), pp. 6–7.

2. See, for example, C. Coleman (1996) *Understanding Crime Data: Haunted by the Dark Figure* (Buckingham: Open University Press); T.R. Gurr (1991) 'Historical Trends in Violent Crime: A Critical Review of the Evidence', *Crime and Justice: An Annual Review of Research*, Vol. 3, pp. 295–353; M. Eisner (2001) 'Modernisation, Self-control and Lethal Violence – The Long-term Dynamics of European Homicide Rates in Theoretical Perspective', *British Journal of Criminology*, Vol. 41, pp. 618–38; J.M. Beattie (1974) 'The Pattern of Crime in England 1660–1800', *Past and Present*, No. 62, pp. 47–95; J.S. Cockburn (1991) 'Patterns of Violence in English Society: Homicide in Kent', *Past and Present*, No. 130, pp. 70–106; V. Gatrell (1980) 'The Decline of Theft and Violence in Victorian England' in V. Gatrell, B. Lenman and G. Parker (eds) *Crime and the Law* (London: Europa Publications), pp. 238–370; C. Hammer (1978) 'Patterns of Homicide in Early Modern Europe', *Past and Present*, No. 78, pp. 3–23; K.I. Wolpin (1978) 'Capital Punishment and Homicide in England: A Summary of Results', *American Economic Review*, Vol. 68, No. 2, pp. 422–7 and L. Zedner (1991) 'Women, Crime and Penal Responses: A Historical Account', *Crime and Justice*, Vol. 14, pp. 307–62.

3. See M. Foucault (1991) *Discipline and Punish: The Birth of the Prison* (Harmondsworth: Penguin); M. Foucault (2001) *The Order of Things: Archaeology of the Human Sciences* (London: Routledge) and M. Foucault (2006) *Madness and Civilisation* (London: Vintage Books).

4. See, for example, P. Spierenberg (2004) 'Punishment, Power and History: Foucault and Elias', *Social Science History*, Vol. 28, pp. 607–36. See also Eisner, 'Modernisation, Self-control and Lethal Violence', *passim*.

5. See J. Carter Wood (2004) *Violence and Crime in Nineteenth-century England: The Shadow of Our Refinement* (London: Routledge) and E. Foyster (2002) 'Creating a Veil of Silence? Politeness and Marital Violence in the English Household', *Transactions of the Royal Historical Society*, Vol. 12, pp. 395–415.

6. For examples of this, see C. Brooks (1997) *Communities and Courts in Britain, 1150–1900* (London: Bloomsbury); J.S. Cockburn and T.A. Green (eds) (2014) *Twelve Good Men and True: The Criminal Trial Jury in England, 1200–1800* (Princeton: Princeton University Press); P. King (2000) *Crime, Justice and Discretion in England, 1740–1820* (Oxford: Oxford University Press); P. King (2004) 'The Summary Courts and Social Relations in Eighteenth Century England', *Past and Present*, No. 183, pp. 125–72; N. Landau (2002) *Law, Crime and English Society, 1660–1830* (Cambridge: Cambridge University Press) and A. May (2006) *The Bar and the Old Bailey, 1750–1850* (Chapel Hill: University of North Carolina Press).

7. For examples of this, see V. Bailey (ed.) (1981) *Policing and Punishment in Nineteenth Century Britain* (London: Croom Helm); J.M. Beattie (2001) *Policing and Punishment in London 1660–1750: Urban Crime and the Limits of Terror* (Oxford: Oxford University Press); E. Carrabine, P. Cox, M. Lee and N. South (2002) *Crime in Modern Britain* (Oxford:

Oxford University Press); T.A. Critchley (1978) *A History of the Police in England and Wales* (Edinburgh: Constable); C. Emsley (1983) *Policing and Its Context 1750–1870* (London: Macmillan); C. Emsley (1996) *The English Police: A Political and Social History* (London: Routledge); D. Hay (ed.) (1989) *Policing and Prosecution in Britain 1750–1850* (Oxford: Oxford University Press); D. Philips (1980) 'A New Engine of Power and Authority: The Institutionalisation of Law Enforcement in England, 1750–1850' in V.A.C. Gatrell, B. Lenman and G. Parker (eds) *Crime and the Law: The Social History of Crime in Western Europe since 1500* (London: Europa Publications), pp. 155–89 and D. Taylor (1997) *The New Police: Crime, Conflict and Control in Nineteenth Century England* (Manchester: Manchester University Press).

8. For an example of this around the themes related to secularization, see C. Brown (2001) *The Death of Christian Britain: Understanding Secularisation 1800–2000* (London: Routledge).

9. G. Elton (1958) *Star Chamber Stories* (London: Methuen), p. 9. Elton's interest in these cases stemmed directly from his work on Tudor politics, yet he remained adamant that one purpose behind choosing particular cases was that they 'were good stories'.

10. R. Darnton (1985) *The Great Cat Massacre and Other Episodes in French Cultural History* (London: Vintage Books).

11. D. Cressy (2001) *Agnes Bowker's Cat: Travesties and Transgressions in Tudor and Stuart England* (Oxford: Oxford University Press).

12. R. Evans (1998) *Tales from the German Underworld: Crime and Punishment in the Nineteenth Century* (Yale: Yale University Press).

13. See, for example, G. Hoeper (1995) *Black Bart: Boulevardier Bandit – The Saga of California's Most Mysterious Stagecoach Robber and the Men Who Sought to Capture Him* (Fresno, CA: Craven Street Books); E.J. Gorn (2011 edition) *Dillinger's Wild Ride: The Year That Made America's Public Enemy Number One* (Oxford: Oxford University Press); B. James (2011) *Popular Crime: Reflections on the Celebration of Violence* (New York: Simon & Schuster); P. Collins (2013) *Duel with the Devil: The True Story of How Alexander Hamilton and Aaron Burr Teamed Up to Take on America's First Sensational Murder Mystery* (New York: Crown Publishers); R. Montillo (2015) *The Wilderness of Ruin: A Tale of Madness, Fire and the Hunt for America's Youngest Serial Killer* (New York: Harper Collins) and R.E. Murphy (2015) *The Three Graces of Raymond Street: Murder, Madness, Sex, and Politics in 1870s Brooklyn* (Albany: State University of New York Press).

14. D.S. Nash and A.-M. Kilday (2010) *Cultures of Shame: Exploring Crime and Morality in Britain, 1600–1900* (Basingstoke: Palgrave).

15. See Magnússon and Szijártó, *What Is Microhistory?* pp. 106–7.

16. Although it is not practised here, it is worth considering the experiments in creating multiple 'endings' for historical stories advocated by Peter Burke; see ibid., p. 24.

17. This was recognized by the Italian pioneers Carlo Ginzburg and Carlo Poni; see ibid., p. 19.

18. For the apparent power of micro-histories as a pedagogical model, see ibid., pp. 154–5.

19. See, for example, J. Guinn (2009) *Go Down Together: The True Untold Story of Bonnie and Clyde* (London: Simon & Schuster).

20. We would argue this is an important factor in creating the micro-history of crime and policing since it is clearly about interaction. The failure to portray this adequately has been a recurring criticism of Darnton – see Magnússon and Szijártó, *What is Microhistory?*, pp. 42–3 and 74–5.

21. See the discussion of this in respect of remote nineteenth-century communities in Iceland recaptured in ibid.

SECTION I
CRIMINALITY, STATE AND SOCIETY

CHAPTER 1
THE USES OF A MARTYRED BLASPHEMER'S DEATH: THE EXECUTION OF THOMAS AIKENHEAD, SCOTLAND'S RELIGION, THE ENLIGHTENMENT AND CONTEMPORARY ACTIVISM

David S. Nash

I

This book showcases the value and use of the micro-narrative in uncovering and elaborating on the context of a specific crime or group of 'deviant' individuals. It is thus perhaps appropriate that we commence with the narrative that is the most remote in time. This remoteness alongside its proximity from the present enables us to see how, over time, one story accumulated a vast number of significant meanings which self-consciously 'used' the narrative to tell different wider stories displaying some very diverse ideas and motives. As such, this history of a single narrative itself illuminates how historians, politicians, broadcasters and even ordinary individuals have made use of the micro-narrative. In this case, they have also harnessed the power of this narrative to influence and perhaps change opinion about culture, religion, the law, civilization and even Scotland itself.

The investigation of these different stories not only provides a history of the use of narrative, but it also demonstrates that the world at large has always used micro-histories of crimes and deviance to tell future generations about the lessons and insights they can learn from delving into the past. Thus, this is not the history of an individual crime but a history of how a particular narrative of a particular crime has its own history. Thus it is a story which seems to be a simple collection of apparent 'facts' which have been interpreted in a number of ways to carry distinct messages to local, national and professional audiences alike. This chapter explores the precise nature of some of these interpretations and retellings and shows how these are also motivated by the ideological demands of a precise historical context. It also explores wider questions of how narratives about crime also regularly invoke some very similar conflicting tropes of justice/injustice, civilization/barbarity, backwardness/enlightenment, punishment/mercy and familiarity/otherness.

II

The facts of the case in question are generally well known, with very little in the way of major dispute about their veracity and the consistency of accounts. Nonetheless, they repay telling once again in brief detail, since they record incidents and the responses of individuals that have been useful tools for subsequent commentators.[1] Thomas Aikenhead's career began in a relatively quiet and unassuming manner. He enrolled to study at Edinburgh University in the mid 1690s and appeared enthusiastically devoted to his studies – arguably looking forward to being eventually able to study medicine if he was successful in his preliminary studies. This would have been a major step to alleviate the poverty that his family had fallen into from comparative prosperity two generations earlier. However, it was precisely this scholarly diligence and serious devotion to philosophy that led to his downfall when he began to voice unorthodox religious opinions in front of his fellow students. If he believed the views he was expressing, then Aikenhead had rejected conventional established religion and declared himself a deist – a belief which discarded churches and established religion to instead believe solely in an intelligence that had created the universe. Deists thus had no time for ministers of religion or the authority that they claimed over the cultural and intellectual lives of the population, a view which was to be important in this group's own reaction to Thomas Aikenhead and his actions.

Deism had become quietly fashionable in elite circles during the seventeenth century, but its appearance amongst the young, scholarly and impressionable was a serious cause for concern for authority of various kinds. Aikenhead was to be especially unfortunate as a victim of this panic when five witnesses were found who confirmed that he had denied the existence of the Trinity and had questioned the validity of the Bible. This led inevitably to his arrest and imprisonment in late 1696 on a charge of blasphemy.[2] His crime was considered serious enough for him to face the Lord Barons, the highest criminal court in Scotland at the time that was especially concerned with the maintenance of social order. But before this would happen, Aikenhead had much thinking to do.[3] Whilst he was in prison in St. Giles Tollbooth he was visited by several religious ministers who appeared to have been simultaneously appalled by the views he held and curious about how he had acquired them. One of these ministers, William Lorimer, held especially strong opinions about the evils of dangerous beliefs and rapidly equated deism with blasphemy – the scoffing and disrespectful treatment of religious doctrine. Lorimer later even went so far as to preach an uncompromising sermon on this subject with ultimately influential results.[4]

There is no doubt that Thomas Aikenhead at some point came to his senses and realized the danger he was in and the possible fate that might await him if he did not renounce his opinions. In both England and Scotland during the latter half of the seventeenth century, the crime of blasphemy became linked with the security and cultural peace of the state. In this, both legal opinion and actual parliamentary statutes (such as those of 1661 and 1695) linked sacred religious doctrine with respect for authority, morality and the law.[5] Those who broke these statutes were considered enemies of the state and liable to the harshest penalties. It was certainly thoughts like these which focussed the mind of

Thomas Aikenhead. When he finally appeared before the judges he did his best to portray himself as a naïve young man unfortunately led astray by unwise company, damaging reading habits and the hasty zealousness of youth. In admitting this he was prepared to publicly renounce the error of his ways and may even in his own mind have thought his experiences would serve as a useful warning and example to others. He loudly declared to those present who would listen, that he once again hated the errors of religious thought he had been led into and went out of his way to embrace the central element of the Christian doctrine including the sacraments, the Trinity and the truth of the Old and New Testaments. In desperation, he tried to convince the judges that others had misunderstood him and had taken his discussion of the opinions of the authors he had read as representing his own views. This last point was disputed by some, such as Lorimer, who considered him to be an obstinate blasphemer during his confinement in prison.

Ultimately he was hoping that his profession of orthodox faith would demonstrate that he had renounced the dangerous opinions ascribed to him. However he had not reckoned on a change in the legal climate which had made deluded unfortunates into dangerous enemies of the state whose presence threatened to unravel the social peace of seventeenth-century Scotland, particularly in the strained circumstances of 1696–7. Moreover his decision to suggest he had spoken the opinions of others that he had gleaned from books merely highlighted in the minds of the judges that print and discussion, especially in university circles, could spread and ferment a lack of respect for religious and civil authority.

These attitudes, alongside an unhealthy level of fear, were to influence the responses that Aikenhead found himself confronted with in court. Aikenhead addressed a formal petition to the court in which he offered his recantation and public embrace of orthodoxy and demonstrated himself to be a reformed individual.[6] But he was no match for an especially able and ultimately determined prosecuting counsel, the Kings Advocate, Sir James Stewart who, with hindsight, appeared intent upon exposing the defendant to the full force of the law and its punishments. The remorse and penitence shown by Aikenhead would have got him off in many circumstances and before many judges and prosecutors since the relevant statutes required obstinacy and repeat offences to invoke the death penalty. But Stewart deliberately focussed upon the fact that Aikenhead's offence contained a further unforgivable dimension and this was to prove crucial to his fate. Whilst a heretic seriously holds unorthodox religious beliefs, Stewart maintained that Aikenhead had uttered his opinions not with solemnity but in a manner intended to ridicule and scoff at the central core of Christian belief, a crucial element in the new 1695 statute.[7] Such views made religion a subject of coarse humour rather than something that commanded respect, and attacking it in this way was seen as dissolving its power to control morality in partnership with the state. Potentially, this had serious repercussions for those at the top of a hierarchy who inevitably saw themselves as vulnerable to such attacks. Most importantly of all for Aikenhead, it was *this* accusation and this alone that carried the death penalty for a first offence under the new statute.

Despite the seriousness of such a charge it initially appeared as though all was not necessarily lost for Aikenhead. Four of the witnesses did confirm that he had spoken the opinions he was accused of, but none of them confirmed that he had done so in an irreverent manner, nor that he had sought to ridicule religion. Unfortunately, however, the fifth man, Mungo Craig, confirmed when pressed that Aikenhead had cursed and ridiculed the Christian religion although it was also clear that he had a vested interest.[8] Craig had lent Aikenhead the books that had helped form his deistical opinions and he must have feared the taint of complicity in Aikenhead's mental wanderings. The frightened (or perhaps cynical) testimony of this witness and his actions proved crucial, and his decision to renounce his own wayward beliefs and turn King's evidence ensured that Aikenhead would be convicted and that he would receive the death sentence.

Even at this stage in the proceedings, a glimmer of hope remained for Aikenhead. His remorse, his passionate expressions of orthodox religious belief and his desire to reform himself had not gone unnoticed in the courtroom. These provoked the influential Sir William Anstruther into action and he was the foremost figure in organizing a petition to see Aikenhead reprieved from the death sentence.[9] Unfortunately however, Anstruther discovered that any appeal for clemency really needed the full backing of the clergy and that without this nothing could be done. Evidently in the days before the execution some of these ministers had a distinct change of heart and one of them, George Meldrum, tried to obtain a full pardon for Aikenhead. When this was rejected, he requested a reprieve of his capital sentence instead.[10] All this activity stirred the judiciary into action and the day before the execution, the petition for the reprieve of the death sentence was taken to the Privy Council.[11] After a protracted debate, the judges came down in favour of upholding the sentence by the margin of one vote and their views emphasized just how deeply some considered Aikenhead's expression of his opinions as a real danger to contemporary society.[12] In their own earnest fear, these judges believed they were halting the spread of ideas that would ultimately damage society, probably irreparably.

Thus, the following day, the distraught and unfortunate Thomas Aikenhead went to the gallows still protesting his innocence, still seeking forgiveness from a God whom, at worst, he probably only denied for a very short period of an otherwise blameless and devout life. His deep sorrow, penitence and repeated confessions of faith even to the last had a profound effect upon the otherwise determined and pious Lorimer, who later claimed to have been involved in the unsuccessful Meldrum petition.[13] Thus ended the life of Thomas Aikenhead. However, his fame and more importantly the fame of his story were to live on beyond his fateful end in a complex variety of different ways.

III

Thomas Aikenhead's story has waited a long time to receive detailed scholarly coverage from a modern historian and this duly arrived in the excellent volume produced by Michael F. Graham in 2008.[14] Graham himself built upon the essence of Aikenhead's story by himself describing his book as a 'microhistorical' study. This realized that

Aikenhead's story has been pulled about and disfigured by its subsequent tellings and its full understanding could only come from its contextual restoration. This served to wrest the story, at least partly, away from the ideological capital that commentators made of it during the period between the actual events and the arrival of Graham's study. Fundamental to Graham's micro-history of the Aikenhead case is an analysis which argues that what transpired was the specific outcome of its own time and context. In other words, the eventual fate of Aikenhead was neither a surprise nor an unnecessarily harsh reaction. Graham suggests 'Aikenhead's execution was the final scene in a drama that had been building for more than year, and would be a defining moment in the providential story of Scotland as God's Covenanted Kingdom.'[15] Graham saw Aikenhead's fate as an unhappy convergence of the internal and external factors that made his convictions and execution not simply likely, but inevitable and, as we shall see, necessary.

As Graham notes, Presbyterianism in the capital felt threatened to an unprecedented degree during the 1690s. It was still effectively reeling from regime change and felt seriously besieged from an, at least, lukewarm government further south. Part of this feeling was a sense that the heady days of the covenant were simultaneously being unravelled by both the incoming tide of Episcopalian sentiment and a number of internal disagreements amongst the city's Presbyterian elite.[16] This was further compounded by the dangerous permeation of naturalistic and deist views that circulated discreetly in Edinburgh's coffee houses. The latter threat was more visible in the fact that the library of Edinburgh University, as Graham demonstrates, had access to a range of the controversial works which were fuelling this spirit of enquiry.[17] Standing out against deist and quasi-materialist ideas was certainly one comparatively easy way of seeking to unite Edinburgh's Presbyterian elite.[18]

The government south of the Tweed was unenthusiastic about the convention of the General Assembly of the Church of Scotland and resisted this successfully until March 1694. As an act of self-assertion, the members rehearsed all the moral ills that were besieging the kingdom and focussed upon blasphemy in particular – seeking a revival of the 1661 Act and a programme of its application to dangerous miscreants.[19] Moral issues and their link to questions of security also preoccupied the Scottish Parliament of 1695 and, as Graham suggests, one imperative of all early modern governments faced with blasphemy in their midst was that they saw 'staving off God's wrath as one of the most critical issues in public security'.[20] Thus, amidst its general clampdown on immorality that offended the Almighty, it was no surprise to see the Scottish Parliament focus upon blasphemy especially and pass a new act which was made more workable than the 1661 Act with graduated punishments for first and subsequent offences. What made this act exceptional beyond its predecessor, was a specific element which would move straight to dispensing the punishment of execution if the blasphemy were specifically intolerable.[21] The especially heightened sensitivity about this offence resulted in further restrictions upon even deist opinions and to eradicate what William Lorimer described as a 'plague'.[22] This threat from deist ideas very readily appeared to be a conspiracy against the godly state and its citizens.[23]

Graham suggests these were internal threats not only in Edinburgh, but arguably across the whole Presbyterian settlement of Scotland, which shuddered at the potentially explosive power of a further number of potential external threats. The mid-1690s witnessed a considerable trade slump after the Darien fiasco which undermined Scotland's ability to feed its population, especially when bad harvests struck over the same period.[24] This linkage of economic misfortune appeared to be part of divine judgement upon a land that was questioning the power of God and scoffing at powers that seemed to be evidently on display from day to day. Graham demonstrates that this feeling was further reinforced when the country fell under more immediate threats. The French for instance posed a sudden threat of invasion which necessitated a sudden mobilization of troops and militia within the Edinburgh area.[25] Early November 1696 also witnessed a catastrophic fire in Edinburgh's Canongate which seemed further proof, as the year began to draw to a close, that God was dispensing providential punishment upon a city which had turned away from him in spectacular ways.[26]

Thus, in terms of Graham's interpretation, Aikenhead was thoroughly a victim of his own context as well as the fact that he lacked status, influence and powerful friends. Edinburgh at the end of 1696 was a city besieged with problems which required a considerably desperate remedy. As Graham suggests, 'here was someone whose punishment could unite a fractured nation, reaffirming its allegiance to covenant principles whilst also placating an angry God'.[27] The appearance of Graham's account of this has done much to bring the story full circle and to place the unfortunate Thomas Aikenhead in the context which was responsible for his untimely death. However in the years since his death, right up to the publication of Graham's book in 2008 and beyond, Aikenhead's story has had a considerable number of 'lives'. This has meant that the narrative of his fate has been put to use by those who have subsequently told it and many of these people have used it to justify some very different views.

Ironically, perhaps the first individual to make use of his story was Thomas Aikenhead himself. On the way to his execution, Aikenhead presented copies of two letters to members of the crowd as well as reading their contents aloud. The sentiments of these two letters, when taken together, served to provide material that would ensure Aikenhead's own story could be construed in two separate directions. The first of these was not so much a recantation, but an impassioned plea to the vulnerable, to avoid the dangerous speculations which had led him to this sorry end.[28] This was very close to the familiar last dying speech which was to be especially popular under the eighteenth-century Bloody Code.[29] This challenge to morals was emphasized by the fact that this period also witnessed the genesis of a wide campaign of moral reform which was to become something of a national movement and eventually a belief was adopted that threatening infractions on a large scale could be stamped upon by a campaign against smaller ones – a species of 'bloody code lite'.[30]

Nonetheless Aikenhead's last dying testament was something of a collector's item because, unlike most dying speeches which were constructed by clergymen anxious to put words into the mouths of the condemned, Aikenhead alone was responsible for his.

As a blasphemer who demonstrated a reasonable grasp of his own religious faculties, his recantation alluded to a considerable range of didactic literature that warned against the perils of doubting and scoffing at Christian doctrine. Not simply this but his own personal recantation had added value because it was self-constructed. Whilst this literature was used to scare the wayward and the ignorant, its effect generally remained insufficient to placate those authorities who were anxious about the spread of blasphemy in their midst.[31] What Aikenhead had to say was encountered first-hand by the community whose ruling elite believed they were about to step off the straight and narrow into sin and perdition.

Aikenhead's didactic outline of his life concluded with an intense meditation upon his own folly and how such questioning left him distraught and unsatisfied. From the perspective of a man walking to his own death, such speculations only really left him with the opportunity to warn others and to throw himself upon God's mercy.[32] In this respect, his story found a number of ways to placate the threatened Presbyterian establishment of 1697. He was in all senses a genuine scapegoat whose death would appease God and save the community. That is, he genuinely accepted the need to atone for his sins before a God that the community believed had already decided to severely punish them all unless restitution was forthcoming. His repentance and the heavily didactic nature of his progress towards his own death proved that the Calvinist interpretation of the universe, and the place of even condemned sinners within its confines, functioned both effectively and visibly. In this respect, Aikenhead's death might ironically be seen, amidst the internal and external threats to Presbyterian in the capital, as a highpoint of the Calvinist Covenant in Scotland. The community had found its scapegoat and he had performed the task assigned to him and arguably his own sorrow and repentance were wholly necessary for the drama which unfolded before the eyes of the Edinburgh populace. In this, Thomas Aikenhead's visible and comparatively didactic, erudite repentance meant that he found himself at the pinnacle of Scottish Presbyterian Calvinism – he was, ironically in the actions of that January day in 1697, both its heir and its martyr.

Although there was little sustained justification of the magistrate's actions in the case, this was substantially because this high Presbyterian and Calvinist moment was indeed only a moment. The intensity of the emotions and fears it created did dissipate in the years that followed. Not least of the reasons for this was the fact that the following year saw the construction of the 9 & 10 William III c. 32 Blasphemy Statute south of the border. This gave England's northern neighbours a clear and welcome sense that blasphemy and the security of the land were not only taken seriously but were also, as Calvinists conceived, linked in terms of public order.[33] Thus from the perspective of members of the Presbyterian Edinburgh elite, Thomas Aikenhead's death was scarcely an act of malice, but instead a wholly logical and necessary action which soon after appeared entirely justified as the gathered sense of crisis ebbed away. This element was something that appeared to be lost in the subsequent versions of the story which had trouble seeing past malice, inhumanity and barbarity in Aikenhead's conviction and execution. Given this, it is worth recovering the context of those who pushed for his death fervently believing the welfare of the whole community depended upon this action and its visibility before God and the wider populace.

Nonetheless Aikenhead's account of his struggles for understanding have provoked another reading of his story which focusses upon seeing him as a milestone, however frail, in the history of deism's presence in Britain – although some scholars also link him with pantheism.[34] Indeed Michael Hunter was prepared to see Aikenhead's blend of pantheism, eternalism and a desire to relativize morality as wholly coherent and robust enough to be considered a system. Aikenhead and his intellectual narrative was a way to 'make sense of a facet of orthodox perceptions of heterodoxy at the time that to us may seem strange, namely, why contemporaries attached such significance to a bantering approach to Christianity, usually orally expressed.'[35] One aspect of investigating this whole area led Michael Graham to undertake a speculative investigation of Aikenhead's reading habits that itself resembled the digging that Carlo Ginzburg undertook in the preparation for his work, *The Cheese and the Worms*.[36] From these investigations, Graham was able to discern the potential influence of the freethinker John Toland (1670–1722) and more obviously how Aikenhead's questions and realizations could be readily associated with the writings and scepticism of Charles Blount (1654–93). The spread of these deist ideas was also the basis of an accusation against a more fortunate Edinburgh blasphemer, John Fraser (or Frazer), who escaped punishment on the grounds that his offence did not include the key offence of cursing and scoffing foregrounded in the 1695 strengthening of the law.[37] It also appears that Fraser's connections to Edinburgh's polite and commercial society, when combined with his penitent humility in court, ensured that he would escape significant punishment.[38]

IV

Aikenhead's story does not end here; word of his fate spread and gradually became a byword for intolerance, selective reading of the law and miscarriage of justice. The famous philosopher John Locke took an especial interest in the case and concluded that the inexperience and fears of a confused young man were opposed by the might of the finest legal brains in the kingdom. His dissatisfaction with the outcome even led Locke to conclude that the jury responsible for the conviction had perjured themselves.[39] Aikenhead's fate however was to achieve lasting fame when it was included in Thomas Babbington Macauley's five-volume *History of England*, where it was cited as an episode in which the clergy had participated in an instance of judicial murder.[40] Thereafter liberal reformers, particularly in the nineteenth century, were able to cite the case as an example of what was possible if obscurantist, hysterically fearful or unscrupulous clerics exercised the power of the law and legal decisions. Moreover, the persistence of blasphemy laws beyond the nineteenth century meant that the only individual to die for such an offence remained a lingering talking point.

The unusual nature of the Aikenhead case, and indeed for the British Isles its unusual outcome, have often meant that it has attained an almost iconic and central part in narratives created by historians of blasphemy and religious tolerance. In some respects this is really unsurprising, but equally it could be said that it often has a role in such histories beyond its simple uniqueness. Looking backwards from the story, it functions as a coda to many heresy trials initiated in the period leading up to the Reformation and beyond, through to the period of quasi-religious wars which followed it in both Europe and the three kingdoms of Britain. Aikenhead's execution, from this perspective, looks like the last gasp of these trials and their unfortunate outcome for those deemed guilty.[41] However, viewed from a perspective looking forward, its uniqueness sometimes persuades that the case was instrumental in bringing such attitudes to an end and the unfortunate outcomes that went with them.

Historians in particular have also focussed on the case as being notably indicative of poor procedure and process, describing the event as an ideological and political act – and one in which many of the people involved were to later repent of their actions. Leonard Levy's almost encyclopaedic history of blasphemy passes through the Aikenhead case linking it in a chapter in which the narrative leads on to the 1697 Blasphemy Statute. Levy accepted the verdict that Aikenhead suffered from having no adequate defence counsel and was a clear instance 'when pious shock, bigotry, and the lack of assistance by counsel work against a defendant'.[42] Levy then linked the Aikenhead case to the fate of a similar defendant Patrick Kinnymount who was tried by the same bench and was acquitted precisely *because* he had an adept and clever lawyer.[43] Levy also noted the William Lorimer and George Meldrum narratives which supposedly demonstrated both guilt and subsequent repentance.[44] Although Levy's account differs from others (particularly the fuller and more nuanced account offered by Graham) he nonetheless draws some clear conclusions which have become part of the historiography of blasphemy. For Levy the Aikenhead case was a miscarriage of justice which indicted the crudity of legal systems which hasten themselves into expedient trials and verdicts, running roughshod over more obvious and more modern conceptions of rights and justice. In a wider and chronologically longer broad-brush history of blasphemy, this is also clearly a conclusion that spoke with some resonance to the contemporary history of the offence. The attempt to use the Aikenhead case as a milestone, against which to judge other events associated with the arrival of religious tolerance, was accomplished by David Allan in his description of later attempts to indict David Hume for heresy.[45] This is given an even sharper tinge with a tone of incredulity by T.C. Smout's description of the case as 'the more shocking because it came at a time when most European countries were moving towards greater toleration'.[46]

This author's own two histories of blasphemy, one covering the history in Britain and one covering the history of the 'Christian World', also fit the Aikenhead case into wider perspective.[47] The latter in particular saw the Calvinist city state as a European-wide path not taken and Aikenhead was 'a naïve student whose recantation fell upon deaf ears and whose death influenced a generation of jurists against wholesale religious involvement in this area of justice. If this was the theocratic state, jurists were sure they did not want it, at least not on Calvinism's terms'.[48] Whilst historians do have different purposes in their writing – Nash and Levy were constructing broad-brush histories covering many centuries – it is noticeable how far these have pulled the Aikenhead story away from its own context. The critical may well prefer the more detailed and sensitive history constructed by Michael Graham. This work has successfully put Thomas Aikenhead and his story back into context so that we can far more readily appreciate the circumstances that led to his execution. Individuals felt driven and compelled by logical and justified beliefs and a malevolent context which persuaded them that a genuine scapegoat was necessary. If the purpose of history is to thoroughly investigate evidence to fully understand what happened in the past, then for a detailed and full history the Graham account is somewhat preferable. Nonetheless the difference between the purposes of these accounts still remains worth noting and gives an insight into how the same particular landmark case narrative can slot into different scholarly histories at different places and in different ways.

V

One important aspect of the Thomas Aikenhead story is that it exists as an extremely individualized and self-contained narrative. As such, there is almost an invitation for it to be dramatized and fictionalized. Thus it is no surprise to learn that Aikenhead's story has been dramatized twice – once for radio and once for the stage. The former was George Rose's *The Blasphemer* directed by the renowned Scottish playwright and author Stewart Conn. The latter was a stage play *I Am Thomas*, which, at the time of writing, is set to be revived for an Edinburgh audience. Both versions dwelled closely upon Aikenhead himself and tried to inject elements of humanity into the story. This, as we know, had been a story which was a dark legacy associated with Scotland's reputation and in some respects it is being commemorated not simply because it was a Scottish story, but because its enduring malevolent presence was perhaps a ghost to be laid by Scottish culture and society.

Certainly we should not have to look far for ways in which Thomas Aikenhead's story was used to batter Scottish sensibilities and to shape its history as an emphatically Whig progressive one, where enlightenment inevitably led from this one barbarous event. *Education Scotland*'s web page for schoolchildren on the Scottish Enlightenment commences with the prehistory of this phenomenon for which Scotland's contribution to Western culture is renowned. After a brief five-paragraph description of the Aikenhead case, this teaching resource suggests that the story 'haunted eighteenth-century Scotland'. Moreover, the account goes further to suggest that Scotland's universities reacted by commencing a role focussed upon changing society and its cultural outlooks. Crucial to this, as *Education Scotland*'s web page suggested, was an almost inevitable modernization and, by definition liberalization, of Calvinist theology. The central figure in accomplishing this was Frances Hutcheson whose ascension to the role of Moderator of the Church of Scotland meant that the 'harsh Calvinist ministers lost their grip on power as the moderate party within the Kirk gradually changed the Church of Scotland ... The foundations were laid for the Age of Enlightenment'.[49]

Similarly in 2002 an edition of Melvyn Bragg's *In Our Time* radio programme on the Scottish Enlightenment noted that progress had occurred rapidly in the sixty years since Aikenhead's demise:

> In 1696 the Edinburgh student, Thomas Aikenhead, claimed theology was 'a rhapsody of feigned and ill invented nonsense' (and) was hanged for his trouble – just one victim of a repressive religious society called the Scottish Kirk.[50]

Similarly, the online *Companion to Eighteenth Century Britain* written by the distinguished historian Harry Dickinson noted that the Aikenhead case (alongside the last execution for witchcraft in Scotland – that of Janet Horne in 1727) were two incidents which demonstrated that the tide had turned in Scotland against hard line uncompromising Calvinism. The nature of this Calvinism was also emphasized by Christopher Harvie in his *Short History of Scotland* which used the treatment of Aikenhead as a means of demonstrating Calvinism's heterogeneity. The so-called bigots who executed Aikenhead in this history are contrasted strongly with those progenitors of the Scottish Enlightenment who indulged in the new learning coming out of the medical and the legal professions.[51] These four references to one of the most celebrated cases in Scottish and British legal history indicate how it has become an important cultural and historical reference point for attitudes to Scottish law and to the history of Scottish religion.[52] This narrative contrasts with some of the other versions of the Aikenhead narrative that we have already encountered in this chapter. Where Aikenhead's execution had appeared in some of these as a Calvinist providential moment, in this narrative it was responsible for the long-term disabling of this same religious outlook. From apogee of Calvinism's response to godless infamy, the longer-term story outlined by *Education Scotland*'s web page places it as defining factor in Calivinism's longer-term discredit. In succeeding years it was to become supposedly powerless in the face of the enquiry that Aikenhead's scepticism and intellectual explorations seemed to champion.[53]

The *Executed Today* web site, genuinely interested in simply recording famous executions throughout the calendar year, opted to be slightly more scathing of the Aikenhead case in which he was subjected to

> an already-archaic punishment inflicted for what reads like headstrong youthful atheism of a decidedly garden variety … Said authorities scarcely elevated the dignity of the temporal throne in their own eagerness to swing a sledgehammer against a fly, trying the young hothead for his life under a Restoration law which by its own letter should not have lodged him in mortal peril until his third offense.[54]

Despite the fact that this is obviously an erroneous reading of what precisely happened at the trial, the tone of indignation is obvious. It also conveys that, amidst the web site's other stories of legitimate convictions, there are also apparently grave injustices to be noted and remembered.[55] Echoing the *Education Scotland* line, the account offered by *Executed Today* pushed the idea that the Aikenhead case had considerable long-term ramifications: 'The singular punishment meted out this day – the last hanging for blasphemy throughout the United Kingdom – cast a long shadow into the coming century's remarkable Scottish renaissance and lingers even today as a suggestion to some just how near the menace of theocracy might yet remain.'[56] This final suggestion at the end of this opinion is followed by a comment about the pending repeal of England's blasphemy laws (which eventually did occur in 2008) and an implied need to prevent the possibility of future theocratic tyranny.

VI

This last suggestion leads us on to perhaps the final way in which the Thomas Aikenhead case has been used in the years after his execution. In a sense this is a hybrid of the attempts to describe the case as both the last gasp of mediaeval heresy and a precursor to a world allegedly now filled with toleration and reason. The Thomas Aikenhead case has been used as an integral part of humanist and secularist campaigns against what had been the prevailing blasphemy legislation in England and Scotland. Very obviously the execution of Thomas Aikenhead appears here as a singular and isolated incident which is a warning of what can happen when theocratic visions overwhelm previously neutral and secular states. As such, it is a potent memory with considerable power that the context constructed by Graham arguably enhances. The Humanist Facebook page repeated Aikenhead's errant opinions but, with an eye on more contemporary situations, also strongly emphasized that his pleas for mercy were in vain.[57]

In January 2008 the *Freethinker* web site used the first week of January to actively remember Thomas Aikenhead in the midst of discussions about the repeal of England's law of blasphemous libel and the, then, Labour government's statement of an intention to proceed with repeal.[58] However, the spectre of theocratic involvement in government was also cited as still likely to be lingering after such appeal because 'Prime Minister Gordon Brown's spokesman said this week that ministers may table amendments to the Criminal Justice and Immigration Bill in the House of Lords. But he added: "We do believe it necessary to consult with the churches, particularly the Anglican Church, before coming to a final decision, and that's what we are doing."'[59]

Another secular and humanist commemoration of Aikenhead's death, this time by the American Freedom of Religion Foundation, firmly took the story out of the context of English and Scottish cultures and laws. Borrowing from Aikenhead's own phrase from his recantation, this web site used his words: 'it is a principle innate and co-natural to every man to have an insatiable inclination to the truth, and to seek for it as for hid treasure.'[60] Carrying this story across the Atlantic also acted as a further memorial to worldwide activism and emphasizes the often repeated sense of free speech under siege that sometime afflicts secular and secularist organizations in both historical and contemporary contexts that they deem to be unfriendly.

The Aikenhead case is also so malleable that it has been brought to bear in other debates that have entered the contemporary world. His status as a victim of religious persecution is often cited as analogous to events in the modern world alongside evidence that his narrative has become a background noise in Scottish culture and society. Ian Bell writing in the 23 September 2012 edition of *heraldscotland* stridently defended the right to blaspheme. Bell brought the issue of protecting free speech in Scotland very close to home with what amounted to a measured flippancy which would have persuaded his readers to feel amused and deeply uncomfortable about religious fundamentalism in equal measure:

> Scotland might still have a blasphemy law – no one is entirely sure – but the risks are minimal even on Leith Walk. Martyred Thomas died for all our sakes.
>
> Presbyterian nutters did away with the youth pour encourager les autres. You will have met the sort. They believed they could stop other people from thinking bad thoughts if, with pomp and ceremony, they murdered a kid who had been a bit daring, as students sometimes are, possibly after having had a few.
>
> They killed young Aikenhead because of the words that came out of his mouth. It's an aspect of faith and revealed truth that I still can't grasp. Who, being truly faithful, could possibly have their certainty, never mind their soul, put at risk by a dismal unbeliever? Which version of God – eternal, omniscient, omnipotent: the full card could be harmed by a kid mouthing off? And which version of any God answers impertinence with executions?[61]

Bell's parting shot linked Aikenhead's suffering into a much wider pantheon of all who had suffered for debating and questioning religious doctrine right into the contemporary world.

> Jokes won't comfort a gay Iraqi. A Scottish journalist attempting droll remarks won't help a Pakistani child persecuted by corrupt clerics and her country's still-potent blasphemy laws. Aikenhead would be denounced by believers of all stripes even today.[62]

Vigilance, so at least one Scottish journalist implied, needed to be constant and probing and the results of this would occasionally resurface. In January 2015 Liz Davis, a correspondent also writing to the *heraldscotland* web site, nonchalantly argued for an extension of laws against religious incitement and religious hate crime. Her comments resulted in a reply from Jim Meikle, writing from Killearn, who reminded the readership of the dangers of censoring religious opinion. He cited the Aikenhead execution as occurring 'with the full support of the Church of Scotland General Assembly'.[63] This was reinforced by the analogy with a contemporary case in Saudi Arabia where a defendant, Raid Badawi, was facing a sentence of 1,000 lashes for allegedly insulting Islam. This then turned into a defence of free speech and open debate where 'offence was unavoidable'.[64] This exchange was all grouped under the heading of 'No Place for Blasphemy Law' and the subtext simultaneously suggested that religious oppression of rights was still rife in the contemporary world. Nonetheless the allusion to Aikenhead and the now benign

General Assembly was a reminder of past persecution uncomfortably closer to home. It was also a veiled suggestion that without vigilance, contemporary religious persecution could occur in Scotland as anywhere.

After Badawi received the first instalment of his punishment, the case began to provoke international outcry with the USA, Canada, Norway and Germany issuing public condemnations. One subsequent report, like Bell's article, sought to emphasize that in Aikenhead's case the Lord Advocate had expressly mentioned that his punishment was to be 'to the example and terror of others'.[65] In recognition of the implications of this case, the Scottish Secular Society instigated the Thomas Aikenhead Award which it chose to bestow on Badawi as its first recipient.[66] In announcing the award the Scottish Secular Society's Secretary Garry Otton declared: 'It was 318 years ago a twenty year old student was hanged in Leith for expressing opinions the Kirk didn't like. It is beyond belief that we should be trying to defend a man for a similar offence today.'[67]

VII

Thus the lifecycle of the Thomas Aikenhead case rolls onwards and, it could be argued, will continue to roll onwards in climates where religious persecution and blasphemy claw back a prominent place in the world and in the conduct of relationships both within societies and between them. As we have learned, the story itself and its relatively easily understood and assimilated messages have made it amenable to historians of blasphemy. These writers have placed it within their differing interpretations and wider historiographies. In this respect the Aikenhead story has been shaped to look both forwards in time and backwards to see it as a specific outcome of some other historical events. However, what is of far greater interest is the prolonged and vibrant life that Thomas Aikenhead's story has had in the wider public sphere. It has informed perceptions of pre-modern Scotland; it has been used to contrast Enlightenment Scotland with what preceded it and perhaps even to make the Scots feel a lingering sense of submerged cultural guilt, albeit assisted by a small degree of English smugness and disdain.[68] Yet Aikenhead's unfortunate fate has also been utilized to provide context and an enduringly painful memory about persecution, in the hope that it will galvanize, inspire and actively celebrate contemporary activism.

Likewise, the range of simple messages that can be construed from what happened to a wayward Edinburgh student indicates the lasting importance of what are seen as 'classic', 'seminal', 'indicative' and very often repeated case studies in the history of crime and deviance. Scholars and readerships should thus both be aware of the 'baggage' that attaches itself to precisely these 'classic', 'seminal', 'indicative' cases. As such their retelling and the effect of the 'baggage' that attaches to them shapes and distorts the meaning and significance of such cases. Thus it is worth thinking more deeply about the history of how and why criminal narratives are told and 'used'. In our own time this has happened more quickly with instances like the Ruth Ellis case, the James Hanratty case, the

Damilola Taylor case and the Stephen Lawrence case. Historians, contemporary social commentators and journalists who do the weaving of such narratives play a central role in our perception, interpretation and use of such 'micro-histories' and it is incumbent upon any culture to be acutely aware of this and to react accordingly.

Notes

1. The most thorough listing of the primary sources for Aikenhead's story is in M.F. Graham (2013 edition) *The Blasphemies of Thomas Aikenhead: Boundaries of Belief on the Eve of the Enlightenment* (Edinburgh: Edinburgh University Press), pp. 163–9.

2. L. Levy (1993) *Blasphemy: Verbal Offense against the Sacred from Moses to Salman Rushdie* (New York: Knopf), p. 232.

3. C. Whatley (2000) *Scottish Society 1707–1830: Beyond Jacobitism, Towards Industrialisation* (Manchester: Manchester University Press), p. 28.

4. W. Lorimer (1713) *Two Discourses: The One Setting Forth The True and Only Way of Attaining Salvation. The Other Shewing Why and How All Ought to Reverence Jesus Christ, the Son of God and Saviour of Men* (London: John Lawrence).

5. The relevant two acts are 1661 c. 21 and 1695, c. 11.

6. National Records of Scotland, Process Papers, MSS JC26/78/1/12-13.

7. *Acts of the Parliaments of Scotland, 1124–1707* (Twelve Volumes) (London: HMSO), Volume IX (1814–75), pp. 386–7.

8. See Mungo Craig's account in M. Craig (1697) *A Lie Is No Scandal, Or a Vindication of Mr Mungo Craig form a Ridiculous Calumny Cast upon Him by T.A. Who Was Executed for Apostasy at Edinburgh, the 8 of January, 1697* (Edinburgh: W. Bell).

9. A. Pitcairn (ed.) (1843) *Acts of the General Assembly of the Church of Scotland, 1638–1842* (Two Volumes) (Edinburgh: Ritchie), Volume I, pp. 258–61.

10. W. Cobbett and T.B. Howell (eds) (1809–26) *A Complete Collection of State Trials* (Thirty-four Volumes) (London: Hansard), Volume XIII, p. 928.

11. Pitcairn, *Acts of the General Assembly*, pp. 258–61.

12. Ibid.

13. W. Lorimer, *Two Discourses*, p. 3.

14. Ibid.

15. Ibid., p. 4.

16. Graham, *The Blasphemies of Thomas Aikenhead*, p. 28.

17. Ibid., pp. 87–92.

18. Ibid., p. 28. See also W. Ferguson (1990) *Scotland 1689 to the Present* (Edinburgh: Mercat Press), pp. 102–9.

19. Graham, *The Blasphemies of Thomas Aikenhead*, pp. 35–7.

20. Ibid., p. 39.

21. Ibid., pp. 41–2.

22. Quoted in ibid., p. 47.

23. Ibid., p. 48.

24. Ferguson, *Scotland 1689 to the Present*, pp. 78–9; Whatley, *Scottish Society 1707–1830*, pp. 31–2 and T.M. Devine (1999) *The Scottish Nation 1700–2000* (London: Penguin), pp. 5–6.

25. Graham, *Blasphemies of Thomas Aikenhead*, pp. 54–6.

26. Ibid., p. 58.

27. Ibid., p. 61.

28. See Cobbett and Howell (eds), *A Complete Collection of State Trials*, pp. 930–4.

29. See J.A. Sharpe (1985) '"Last Dying Speeches": Religion, Ideology and Public Execution in Seventeenth Century England', *Past and Present*, Vol. 107, No. 1, pp. 144–67 and J. Kelly (2001) *Gallows Speeches from Eighteenth Century Ireland* (Dublin: Four Courts Press).

30. See D.S. Nash (2010) 'Moral Crimes and the Law since 1700', in A.-M. Kilday and D.S. Nash (eds) *Histories of Crime in Britain 1600–2000* (Basingstoke: Palgrave), pp. 17–38 at pp. 18–20.

31. See D.S. Nash (ed.) (2012) *Blasphemy in Britain and America 1800–1930* (London: Pickering and Chatto) especially Volume I, which contains many example of the didactic literature that would have actively circulated during the late seventeenth and eighteenth centuries.

32. Graham, *The Blasphemies of Thomas Aikenhead*, pp. 117–20.

33. For accounts of the 9 & 10 William Statute, its substance and importance, see Levy, *Blasphemy: Verbal Offense*, pp. 99, 224, 274, 278, 287 and 288; D.S. Nash (1999) *Blasphemy in Britain 1789 – Present* (Aldershot: Ashgate), pp. 32, 36, 85, 195, 197 and 239 and D.S. Nash (2007) *Blasphemy in the Christian World* (Oxford: Oxford University Press), 60–1, 161–2 and 193–4.

34. D.G. Mullan (2010) *Narrative of the Religious Self in Early-modern Scotland* (Farnham: Ashgate), p. 306. In this work Mullan makes use of Aikenhead as a method of questioning what narratives of early modern atheists would look like if we could unearth them.

35. M. Hunter (1992) '"Aikenhead the Atheist": The Context and Consequences of Articulate Irreligion in the Late Seventeenth Century', in M. Hunter and D. Wootton (eds) *Atheism from the Reformation to the Enlightenment* (Clarendon Press: Oxford), pp. 221–54 at p. 253.

36. The similarity had been noticed earlier on by Michael Hunter. This suggests that the episode very readily invokes micro-history-style reading as well as the almost standing invitation to view Aikenhead as a heterodox archetype. See ibid., p. 222.

37. Ibid., pp. 240–1.

38. Graham, *The Blasphemies of Thomas Aikenhead*, p. 73.

39. E.S. De Beer (1976–89) *The Correspondence of John Locke* (Eighth Volumes) (Oxford: Clarendon Press), Volume IV, pp. 17–19.

40. Thomas Babbington Macaulay (1849–65) *The History of England* (Five Volumes) (London: John Wilson), Volume IV, pp. 781–4.

41. For a version of this narrative, see J.K. Cameron (1982) 'Theological Controversy: A Factor in the Origins of the Scottish Enlightenment' in R.H. Campbell and A.S. Skinner (eds) *The Origins and Nature of the Scottish Enlightenment* (Edinburgh: John Donald), pp. 116–30 at pp. 117–18.

42. Levy, *Blasphemy: Verbal Offense*, p. 232.

43. Ibid., p. 234.

44. Ibid., p. 233.

45. D. Allan (2002) *Scotland in the Eighteenth Century: Union and Enlightenment* (Harlow: Pearson Education), p. 67.

46. T.C. Smout (1969) *A History of the Scottish People – Volume I* (London: Collins), p. 510.

47. Nash, *Blasphemy in Britain 1789 – Present*, p. 36 and Nash, *Blasphemy in the Christian World*, pp. 164–5.

48. Ibid.

49. *Education Scotland (Foglam Alba)*, 'Scottish Enlightenment', http://www.educationscotland.gov.uk/scottishenlightenment/before/index.asp (accessed 6 September 2015).

50. See BBC Radio Four, *In Our Time*, 5 December 2002 found at http://www.bbc.co.uk/programmes/p00548ln and http://www.bbc.co.uk/radio4/history/inourtime/inourtime_20021205.shtml.

51. C. Harvie (2014) *Scotland a Short History* (Oxford: Oxford University Press), p. 130.

52. BBC Radio Four, *In Our Time*, 5 December 2002 found at http://www.bbc.co.uk/programmes/p00548ln.

53. This conclusion from Aikenhead's story is also evident in the material which was prepared for a summer school staged at his own *alma mater*. See http://www.summerschool.ed.ac.uk/content/thomas-aikenhead-last-person-hanged-blasphemy-united-kingdom (accessed 25 August 2015).

54. *Executed Today:* Thomas Aikenhead found at http://www.executedtoday.com/tag/thomas-aikenhead/ (accessed 6 September 2015).

55. Ibid. Although, to some extent, *Executed Today* demonstrates some sympathy for the victim, it is noteworthy how the description of the fate of the executed Luddites remembered on the same day (8 January) as Thomas Aikenhead appears more balanced. See http://www.executedtoday.com/2013/01/08/1813-yorkshire-luddites-william-horsfall/ (accessed 6 September 2015).

56. *Executed Today:* Thomas Aikenhead.

57. See https://www.facebook.com/notes/global-secular-humanist-movement/the-persecution-of-thomas-aikenhead/301376626567998 (accessed 25 August 2015).

58. See http://freethinker.co.uk/2008/01/10/a-week-in-which-to-remember-thomas-aikenhead-the-last-man-in-britain-to-be-hanged-for-blasphemy/ (accessed 25 August 2015).

59. Ibid.

60. See https://ffrf.org/news/day/dayitems/item/14133-thomas-aikenhead1 (accessed 25 August 2015).

61. http://www.heraldscotland.com/opinion/13074159.We_must_defend_the_right_to_blaspheme/ (accessed 9 September 2015).

62. Ibid.

63. http://www.heraldscotland.com/opinion/letters/13197484.No_place_for_blasphemy_law/ (accessed 9 September 2015).

64. Ibid.

65. http://www.heraldscotland.com/news/13196246.Saudi_dissident_wins_award_commemorating_last_Scots__blasphemer__to_be_executed/ (accessed 9 September 2015).

66. http://www.heraldscotland.com/news/13197267.Saudi_dissident_s_wife_warns_her_husband_might_not_survive_next_public_flogging/ (accessed 9 September 2015).

67. http://www.heraldscotland.com/news/13196418.Saudi_dissident_to_be__lashed_severely__today/ (accessed 9 September 2015).

68. For more on this, see Graham, *The Blasphemies of Thomas Aikenhead*, pp. 157–9.

CHAPTER 2
HISTORY, NARRATIVE AND ATTACKING CHRONOCENTRICISM IN UNDERSTANDING FINANCIAL CRIME: THE SIGNIFICANCE OF MICRO-HISTORY

Sarah Wilson

I

There are numerous factors making the study of financial crime fascinating for historians. Some of these are properly regarded as part of the current structural architecture of the historiography of modern Britain, whilst others lie beyond this, with points at which these internal and external influences also come together. Firstly, lying within the framework of historical study there is the importance of 'micro-history' as a vital thread for the historiography of 'crime and society' and also the tradition of silence within crime history itself concerning modern Britain's encounters with 'a whole new world and vocabulary of ingenious crime, which could only be perpetrated by business men …'.[1] In looking at external influences, this contribution also explores how these silences in the historiography of crime and society might coexist with, and indeed even reflect, trends in criminological scholarship where criticism is made that criminologists continue to focus disproportionately on the 'conventional forms of crime and delinquency' which dominate academic scholarship.[2] This contribution engages with intellectual spheres of history and criminology and also looks to respond to calls from within both disciplines to communicate much more comprehensively with one another.[3]

The history of financial crime is an excellent reference point for encouraging greater discourse between history and criminology. It illustrates the importance of criminology for crime historians, and it shows saliently how criminologists *can* glean historical enrichment for key intellectual problematics underpinning their interest in 'law breaking' and that they *should* consider whether these problematics are themselves historically rooted. More will be said on criminologists' interest in financial crime throughout, with this being situated closely alongside its treatment from historians, and more particularly, historians of crime. Moreover challenging criminologists to engage with crime history provides an invitation, and indeed actually a mandate, to engage with current debates on the meanings of history and the role of history within arts, humanities and social science scholarship. At points it becomes difficult to isolate how examining financial crime is influenced from traditions and patterns within historical scholarship rather than by external factors. It is also the case that the global financial crisis is also a powerful influencing force for understanding both the challenges presented by financial crime in the twenty-first century and also the perceived importance of history for moving forward from a 'once-in-a-lifetime'[4] period of immense significance.

Focussing on financial crime itself, there is increasing acknowledgement amongst scholars and also beyond the academic community of an analytical 'conscious coupling' of financial crime with the financial crisis.[5] Here the global financial crisis is being identified as a turning point for financial crime enforcement,[6] itself associated with a new aggressive era of response, characterized by new tough and intrusive institutions and policies.[7] More normatively, it is being hailed as a 'transformative'[8] point for financial crimes and their perpetrators to receive opprobrium properly reflecting these activities' hugely damaging capabilities.[9] At the same time, this strong future-oriented view of financial crime is also occurring alongside UK regulators' increasing interest in how the events of the past could and indeed *should* guide the search for new post-crisis approaches to regulating the financial sphere, including calibrating new and 'transformative' responses to financial crime.[10]

II

From the above, it should now be apparent that presenting a historical case study of financial crime is a complex exercise. It must embrace the current 'spotlight' on financial crime itself in the post-crisis regulatory environment, as well as matters which might arise more obviously from historical writing. It must also be concerned with how historians have traditionally responded to its presence in the emergence of modern Britain and with how this might well tap into conventional criminology, where the study of 'white-collar crime' is an established and respected distinctive sphere of considerable volume, and yet illustrates criminology's 'chronocentric' tradition and its disproportionate concern with 'traditional' crime. Taking the latter, criticism of criminologists' characteristic adherence to 'presentism', embodied in configuring 'new times' as ones requiring 'new approaches' – and evident in a small but burgeoning body of 'historical criminology' – *is* highly pertinent for this crime history case study of financial crime. This is so on account of the perceived benefits of adopting extended time frames for study and utilizing historical methodology amongst criminologists.[11] However, there is little scope for exploring this methodologically herein. In contrast, more is said about criminologists' interest in white-collar and more traditional deviance, with most attention being paid to the acknowledged importance of micro-history within crime historiography. Additionally, this highlights the comparative absence of financial crime from established historical studies of crime and society – and actually what might be meant by 'financial crime' for these purposes.

The scope of this chapter is very strongly influenced by how, for historians of crime, the importance of undertaking research in financial crime remains to be demonstrated to a very significant degree. From this, showcasing individual case studies has to sit alongside actually making the case for why crime history should indeed embrace the history of financial crime. The selected case studies are drawn from extensive study which asserts that it was during the nineteenth century that social attitudes and legal responses to 'financial crime' started to take shape. As it was during this time when linkages between 'impropriety' and 'business people' and 'business environs' started to crystallize in British legal and wider societal consciousness in ways which are recognizable today,[12] these cases and their contextualization attest to the need for crime history to embrace the history of financial crime. Suggestion that this occurred through revelations of extensive perpetration of 'ingenious crime' accessible only by prominent businessmen from the 1840s, runs contrary both to the presentist approach of white-collar crime criminology and also to the dominant narrative of crime historiography. For criminology, its chronocentrism is readily apparent in how 'financial crimes' are presented and analysed as artefacts of 'Twentieth Century Crisis'[13] and even as 'modern crime *par excellence*',[14] with this manifested in different ways. Whilst some studies show no engagement whatsoever with times predating the twentieth century, most will suggest that misconduct worthy of the labels of 'Twentieth Century Crisis' and 'modern crime *par excellence*' is not actually 'new'[15] and is in many respects as 'old as Ancient Egypt'.[16] Both positions are grounded in the technologizing influences of the twentieth century[17] with the latter showing how presentism and chronocentrism can be associated with the distinctiveness of the present in the vein of 'new times requiring new approaches', rather than with complete denial that issues associated with 'law breaking' have a history.

In terms of what this body of work regards as 'financial crime', this can commonly be found referenced closely alongside the terminology of 'fraud' to denote some type of non-violent means of 'obtaining some economic advantage or causing some economic loss'.[18] The location of academic studies of financial crime within 'white-collar crime' scholarship reflects how the ground-breaking work of Edwin Sutherland gave rise to this distinctive strand of criminology during the 1930s and 1940s. Whilst Sutherland's seminal definition of a white-collar crime as one which is 'committed by a person of respectability and high social status in the course of his occupation'[19] *is* highly salient for this case study of financial crime. Of greater significance for illuminating scholars' use of the terminology of 'financial crime' is Sutherland's classification of two types of 'business crime'. Alongside duplicity and the manipulation of power (crimes of corruption), Sutherland located infractions involving misrepresentations of asset values, which 'approximated with fraud or swindling'.[20] For the latter, although an extensive social and economic spectrum of financial crime offending is recognized – with such activities being committed by the blue-collar community and 'elite insider dealers' alike,[21] and for some scholars even includes social security/welfare offenders – this is a study of 'crime in the commercial sphere'.[22]

III

What interested American sociologist Edwin Sutherland about white-collar crimes in the early twentieth century continues to shape today's criminology very strongly. For Sutherland, as it remains for a number of his followers, law enforcement priorities ensured that the criminal courts dealt primarily with those who committed 'traditional' or 'ordinary crimes',[23] whilst other offending remained unenforced and unpunished on account of a matrix of factors clustering around lack of effective law-making and unorganized societal opprobrium.[24] For Sutherland and his followers, this arose from how many highly profiled, extensive and high-value infractions involve some of the most powerful individuals or corporations in society.[25] However, the scholarship is also deeply divided, with the alleged legal system bias in favour of respectable business people being forcefully challenged in some quarters,[26] and where views are also expressed that such activities are properly regarded as legal violations of a more technical *mala prohibita* nature than 'serious crime'.[27] Moreover, from the observation that the terminology of 'white-collar' crime has migrated from academic study into popular discourse,[28] popular opinions on activities regarded as such appear to mirror these deep divisions within the academic community.[29] This seductive notion of white-collar crime as a 'public lexicon' as well as scholarly construct[30] is clearly a powerful draw for criminologists especially in the context of controversy and divisions in viewpoints concerning whether activities are 'less criminal'/not real crime or 'more criminal' than crime as more ordinarily understood and encountered.[31] In a setting where such perceptions of 'financial crimes' have been effectively captured in the trope (for white-collar crime more broadly) of 'crime of ambiguity',[32] these activities are regarded as 'among the most difficult crimes for the legal system to deal with, let alone control'.[33]

The attraction of analysing financial crime as white-collar crime for criminologists is clearly manifest, and the reasons set out above go a long way to explaining why this might be the case. This raises the question of why historians have not been more interested in financial crime in uncovering the emergence of modern Britain. Not only did Victorian contemporaries document the appearance of 'ingenious crime' by business men, but accompanying the observation of 'high art' crime as a novelty of the 1840s was a consciousness that financial crimes were deeply embedded in British society. This is evident in *The Times'* financial commentator David Morier Evans's direct reference to forgery and embezzlement, and allusion to the South Sea Bubble of 1719/20 in his recording of the 1840s and 1850s as a particularly 'dark page' in the 'commercial history of this country'.[34] In addition, commentary in 1841 also documented the British nineteenth-century consciousness of the seventeenth-century Dutch Tulipmania.[35] Perkin's conceptualization of 'ingenious crime'[36] illustrates how historians have not ignored nineteenth-century encounters with financial crime, but brief references from David Jones and Clive Emsley excepted,[37] historians' interest in this has come largely from those within the business and economic tradition rather than from crime history *per se*. This *has* started to change.[38] Moreover, in arguing that the history of financial crime belongs properly to crime history as much as to business history if not more so,[39] it has been suggested that effecting this requires crime historians to appreciate criminologists' approaches to the very complex relationships appearing to subsist between financial crime and society in Britain.[40]

Although it is the case that many of the most recent historical studies of financial crime continue to come from business history, these *are* embracing both crime history and criminology.[41] The challenge remains to encourage crime historians to follow suit. For this, these case studies are very significant, and they do of course also speak to what historians of crime have chosen to embrace rather than elude. We have already seen in this volume that the central remit for crime history – to uncover and understand relationships subsisting between crime and society through studies of continuity and change in the occurrence of crime and responses to it – has given much importance to micro-history. The burgeoning literature on crime and society, policing, punishment and law is of course the history of macro investigations. Here nineteenth-century developments in the criminal law and its administration during what contemporaries themselves recognized as the 'Century of Law Reform'[42] documented extensively in Parliamentary Papers, debates and other official reports *have* been painstakingly and dutifully examined by historians.[43] Contemporary appetite for improvement, standardization and centralization across a wide sweep of 'social life'[44] ensured that law-making and law reform were key preoccupations for Victorian society.[45] Thus, it is right and proper that the 'great historical questions'[46] arising from the sphere of crime and society *have* been the subject of investigations of 'nations, states, or social groupings' using the historian's *telescope*.[47] Crime history also demonstrates how use of the historian's *microscope*[48] can provide new fresh perspectives on eponymous 'great historical questions', which are themselves associated with 'grand narratives'.[49]

IV

From this, the attractiveness of micro-history for crime history follows the broad trajectory of the attraction of micro-history for historians generally. Its purveyors celebrate its potential and have carved out an ambitious agenda going forward.[50] In building on a veritable tradition, it is said to have a bright future, in being capable of bringing social and cultural history together as an approach which can both supply the explanations of social history and grasp the meanings of cultural history.[51] Micro-history has its critics, most notably pointing to an inherent limitation in 'trying to discover big things with microscopes'[52] and questioning the individual as a historical phenomenon.[53] It is also said that micro-history cannot alone serve the needs of the past as it cannot be assumed that materials used will have wider application; and indeed that if historical transformations are embedded in individual actions, it is almost impossible to infer anything about large-scale phenomena.[54] From this, micro-history has gained a reputation in some quarters for being interesting but lacking in depth, and its studies are more readily dismissed as lacking meaning and significance in comparison with other historical scholarship.[55]

Notwithstanding, much crime history attests to the effectiveness of micro-history's focus on small incidents, insignificant in themselves, from which larger structures can be revealed. It also supports views that concentrations on local or individual experiences are highly effective when conducted by those who do not lose sight of broader historical and political contexts and even that such concentration on localized experiences enables generalizations to be tested.[56] In addition, the view that the micro-historical method cannot by itself serve the needs of delivering ambitious research into the past[57] is consistent with understanding that *any* historical research can always only ever be a piece of the puzzle. For its supporters, micro-history is capable of enabling the investigation of narrowly defined subjects without the risk of oversimplifying the past, and even that it is only on this level that there is no risk of 'losing the complexity of the relationships that connect any individual to a given society'.[58] In its emphasis of the individual, micro-history is seeking to recognize high levels of individual freedom of actions within the broader social framework, by regarding people as conscious historical actors making decisions which help to produce social forms observed by historians. Although this is open to criticism, the proposition that finding' individuals in different social contexts can encourage exposures of the complexities of everyday life is clearly an exciting one.[59]

At the heart of micro-history is the idea that a small unit of study (an individual or small community) can reflect a larger whole, highlighting the importance of these small units and demonstrating their importance for historical debate.[60] In taking on board criticisms levelled at micro-history alongside the views of its supporters, these case studies of nineteenth-century financial crime are consistent with the position that the purpose of micro-history is not to eschew answering 'great historical questions', but to elucidate historical causation at the level of small groups where most of life takes place.[61] It embraces the view that 'changing the scale' of observation and investigation can glean fresh insight from different organizing principles for broader interpersonal and systemic interaction, whereby changing the scale seeks to assist in the identification of (systems of) context and social interaction.[62] In focussing on a different type of causal connectedness from macro-study, changing scales for enquiry 'reflects that social actors appear in different contexts, micro- and macro-, at the same time'.[63] From this a dynamic cartography can arise: a variety of maps 'each of which corresponds to a social terrain', and one where there is no hierarchy, where 'macro and micro no more or less real than one another'.[64]

Financial crime case studies make meaningful contributions to crime history firstly by embodying that any historical research can only be a 'piece of the puzzle' and that history is always subject to individual interpretations and properly regarded as an 'inventory' of plausible readings of the past.[65] They also uphold the importance of contextualization – that is placing the small unit of study in a broader context. Without this, such studies are commonly regarded as lacking meaning,[66] thereby acknowledging historical context as an irreducible given for any historical enquiry.[67] Arguably the nineteenth-century recalibration of the 'economy of deterrence' not only provides 'great historical questions' but actually some of the most significant ones for historians arising in the shaping of modern Britain. This construct can be used to explain the relations subsisting between crime and society which would change dramatically in the early years of the nineteenth century,[68] putting in place a new framework of criminal law, and precipitate 'revolutions' in policing and penal policy.

Crime history has diligently documented the forces for change as *pragmatic* ones relating to a declining belief in the efficacy of the Bloody Code, combined with population increase and changing demography. These were brought about by increasing urbanization on account of industrialization, the influence of mass demobilization following the end of the Napoleonic Wars and an *ideological* retreat from punishment of the body to reformation of the mind rooted in Enlightenment philosophy. This was assisted by strong metanarratives of 'pressure for change'[69] and an increasingly scientific approach towards managing progress and the externalities of progress borne from a pervasive confidence and exuberance and appetite for innovation.[70] Putting in place this new suite of responses to crime was one of the most ambitious projects for a society convinced that the 'common law combined with an extensive legislative programme would provide the basis for meeting the social, economic and political dynamics'.[71] It is thus unsurprising that historians have taken such an extensive and long-standing interest in this and have been very conspicuous in their use of micro-historical case studies, with many persuasive illustrations of how 'controlled multiplication of the scales of observation is likely to produce additional knowledge'[72] to be found within crime history itself. Despite the silences on financial crime in crime history, the same metanarratives which have served crime historians well for several decades also underpin the history of financial crime.

It is suggested that the case studies of John Sadleir MP, bankers Strahan, Bates and Paul and City merchant Joseph Windle Cole, when combined with criminological study, can help to explain what is missing from crime history itself and what history might have to offer for current and future-oriented reflections on the 'problem' of financial crime. These cases are likely to be highly persuasive for crime historians, even if they might compound the puzzle of why there has been so little intellectual engagement with financial crime from them. The manifest imbalances between crime history and business history in engaging with financial crime may be attributable in part to 'barriers' in familiarity and even perceived expertise in matters of business and economy on the part of crime historians.[73] However, there are other powerful influences at work. From little more than a glance at crime history a clear overarching thread emerges. This is from works of first- and second-generation crime history, as historians' interest has been captured firstly with configuring crime alongside class struggle[74] and thereafter channelling a 'crime and society' approach for analysing the embedding of 'new' approaches pursued through reforms to the criminal law and revolutions in policing and punishment.[75]

Here modern crime history's manifest interest in crimes of violence and street crime, and antisocial behaviour, can be seen to track closely the very orientation of the nineteenth-century reforms themselves. Here contemporary emphasis on the threats presented by 'one great criminal profession' to which 'Thieves, prostitutes, &c, seem to belong',[76] which dominated the reform agenda, ground an orthodoxy amongst crime historians of a politicization of crime and deviance. In this politicization process, the threat was not simply presented by crime *per se*, but arose from particular types of crime – types of crime increasingly associated with the conceptualization of a 'criminal class', those considered 'antithetic of every respectable community'.[77] This has been analysed as having ensured that the new ideological orientation and structures put in place would principally target 'fundamentally unsophisticated … sheep stealers and poachers … and … thieves',[78] in turn helping to foster perceptions that the emergence of the modern criminal law and its administration sought to preserve 'the illusion that socially dangerous and unacceptable activity was predominantly the province of the lower orders'.[79] In view of this, it is not surprising perhaps that crime historians' interest has been so strongly shaped by certain types of crime in preference to others, with this also being crime which criminologists now term 'ordinary' crime, 'common' crime or 'traditional' crime.[80]

V

In this regard, criminology does usefully provide 'labels' to attach to what has interested crime historians and what has not. However, in suggesting that crime historians have not placed much emphasis on deviance not fitting the conventional crime paradigm, it is also significant that criminology is itself criticized for being far too concerned with crimes associated with persons from lower social orders. Moreover, this criticism has come from within criminology *itself* and subsists notwithstanding that there *is* a sizeable criminology of white-collar crime. It has been suggested that criminologists' (continuing) disproportionate concern with ordinary deviance runs contrary to the comparatively low costs to society arising from such activities, and helps to reinforce an embedded reluctance to recognize the very significant social harm arising from crimes emanating from business sectors.[81] Whilst it is the case thus that even criminologists are said to require encouragement to focus more extensively on financial crime, it is also true that the criminology of white-collar crime is invaluable for opening up channels for crime historians. This can be illustrated through case studies arising from the 'inauguration, development, and rapid progress' of 'High art' crime.[82]

Whilst many works within white-collar criminology do acknowledge that it predates the twentieth century, the *phenomena* of white-collar crime are strongly associated with this point in time. As well as this being on account of criminology's strongly chronocentric and presentist tendencies, it is also linked with Edwin Sutherland's ground-breaking work. This arose from Sutherland's contention that neither Marxist nor traditional criminology – attributing crime respectively to class conflict and poverty and social dysfunction – could account satisfactorily for unlawful acts committed by respectable persons in the pursuit of their occupations, which *were* either criminal activities or *should* be. For Sutherland, equality before the law required this type of deviance to be analysed and enforced alongside other more usual types within a 'unified criminological theory'.[83] Yet at the same time, he appreciated that obstacles to this were considerable. For as long as business people did not 'conform to the popular stereotype of "the criminal"',[84] generating effective criminal responses to their deviance would remain problematic, on account of circular relationships subsisting between law enforcement and social mores.[85]

Seventy-five years later, Sutherland's work continues to inspire criminologists and also divide them, with this very effectively captured in the seminal construct of 'crime of ambiguity', and acceptance that 'distinctiveness' surrounds how white-collar crimes are perceived, and perhaps especially 'enforced', continues to prevail amongst scholars, legal system actors and policymakers. What is contentious, is whether this *should* happen with wide disagreement evident on whether financial crimes are *qualitatively* different from other types, or whether alleged distinctiveness is instead socially constructed and reinforces *perceptual* differences.[86] In seeking to explore the complexities surrounding views that financial crimes are seen to lack 'immediate moral outrage' associated with many crimes,[87] case studies are able to show that even seventy-five years earlier than Sutherland, connections immortalized by him between status and class, business and criminality were becoming embedded into the British psyche. This emerges through revelations of 'ingenious crime' which could 'only be perpetrated by business men'.[88]

Much contemporary comment suggests that for those bearing witness to activities termed '"High Art" crime' and also 'commercial crime' and even 'financial crime',[89] this amounted to an entirely new alliance forged between dishonesty and financial sophistication whereby 'without any great violence, all the incentives to commercial crime may be brought under the one common rubric – the desire to make money easily and in a hurry'.[90] This unified the unlawfulness of the apprentice robbing a few shillings from his employer or master, and also the gigantic forger and swindlers of the age, as well as the 'reckless speculator' who 'would risk everything in the hope of sudden gain, rather than toil safely and laboriously for a distant reward', but who whilst naturally eschewing wrongdoing would move ever closer to this in the face of adverse fortune.[91] In acknowledging the contemporary suggestion that the 'modern age' of speculation marked by the 1840s railway boom had concretized the seriousness of impropriety in financial dealings,[92] Victorian reactions to impropriety can be seen as swift and determined, notwithstanding a dominant trend within the sparse historiography regarding Victorian Britain as a 'haven' for white-collar criminals.[93] In the very early aftermath of the boom, many company directors found their conduct being investigated with a view to bringing criminal charges as early as 1846.[94] By the early 1850s, the move 'from toleration to criminalisation'[95] was firmly in place. This was readily apparent in legislation, with the Punishment of Frauds Act 1857 seeking to classify a 'broad spectrum … of actions' exhibiting 'varying degrees of intent … and wrongfulness'.[96] Earlier still than this, willingness to respond to the 'bad, moral atmosphere'[97] manifested in wrongdoing in business with *criminal* enforcement was apparent in the appearance of the criminal *cause célèbre* trial. During the 'early phase' of these criminal trials from the 1850s to the 1880s,[98] numerous prominent Victorian businessmen were called upon to answer criminal changes resulting from their professional affairs. These were the first very public demonstrations that the very worst occurrences on the 'spectrum' of misconduct in *business* amounted to conduct injurious to *social* interests.[99]

Like Sutherland sometime later, those involved in the earliest criminal trials for 'financial crime' appreciated that respectable people can and did commit crimes which were more ordinarily recognizable as 'crime'.[100] Indeed, the discoveries of 'new' types of misconduct during the nineteenth century which implicated the respectable in criminality on an unprecedented scale, included poisoning and blackmail alongside 'financial' crime.[101] Whilst John Sadleir MP and bankers Strahan, Paul and Bates occupied similar spheres to one another within Victorian Britain's highly stratified but also evolving social structure, which were different from that of Joseph Windle Cole, all their stories illustrate contemporary awareness of novel interactions between social status occupation, and criminality. From this, they also help to explain the discomforts generated for those bearing witness to it, with this appearing to be in ways recognizably associated with the 'problem' of financial crime today over 150 years later.

VI

Boyd Hilton's seminal account of acute anxiety about investment and speculation in commerce during the 'Age of Atonement' and its aftermath, identified John Sadleir MP alongside fellow parliamentarian George Hudson with 'fraudulent roguishness',[102] feeding contemporary discomfort in times of economic and social upheaval.[103] Interestingly, and without reference to modern criminology's understandings of the 'ambiguities' associated with financial crime, Hilton's account is one of how 'rogues' such as Hudson and Sadleir were regarded in a 'romantic and almost an heroic' light.[104] Hilton's hypothesis is identifiable within the seminal *criminological* construct of the 'paradox of lenience and severity' which highlights tensions underpinning sentencing decisions on offending by those who have commonly led exemplary lives as community 'pillars', but with this making violations of reposed trust particularly heinous.[105] Sentiments captured in Hilton's classic *historical* study can also be found in *contemporary* reflection on those engaging in 'High Art' crime. Views that such persons exhibit 'an amount of individual courage which, turned in any other direction, would almost constitute heroism'[106] might seem particularly poignant as Sadleir's story ends in his death, at his own hand. However he was also considered 'one of the greatest, if not the greatest, and at the same time the most successful, swindler that this or any other country has produced'.[107]

Sadleir's downfall was inextricably part of the 1856 scandal involving the Tipperary Bank, established by his grandfather, but was also attributable to his occupation of elite commercial and political circles. Sadleir entered Parliament at the general election of 1847, and it was at this point that his prominence in English consciousness started to take hold. Prior to this, this Irish Catholic solicitor from a legal and banking family was known in his homeland, largely on account of enjoying a 'respectable and lucrative legal practice' through a family business.[108] This was how his reputation in matters of business came to be forged, particularly through his work on Irish encumbered estates, where the latter also proved to be particularly lucrative.[109] Notwithstanding, this line of work and Sadleir's 'ordinary middle-class' family background were considered likely to do little more than enable Sadleir 'with industry and perseverance' to 'earn his own living, and maintain his station as a professional man'.[110] But Sadleir's ambitions outstripped these rather modest aims, and it was actually the 1840s 'railway mania' which brought him to England. By its height in 1846, his reputation as a Parliamentary agent – and for providing protection for numerous Irish schemes and antagonism for rival ones – was well established[111] and paved the way for his election to Parliament the following year.

This perseverance, ambition and high levels of self-belief enabled Sadleir to transcend his ordinary middle-class respectability[112] and penetrate Parliamentary circles – firstly as an agent and then as a Member – and it would also consolidate his reputation in business. Like many contemporary parliamentarians, numerous 'directorships and chairmanships … were pressed upon him', but aided by extensive testaments to his 'great financial ability … special business aptitude … and administrative capacity' Sadleir forged 'a high reputation in the financial and commercial world almost before he took oaths at the table of the House of Commons'.[113] In financial and commercial circles his name at the head of a board was widely reputed to be 'equivalent to a rise of at least one per cent in the market value of shares'.[114] His appointment as chairman of the London and County Bank in 1848 was considered a reflection of his talents and zeal and was also a role which 'gave him status as a financial authority'.[115] It was from the latter that his burgeoning reputation in political as well as in commercial circles could grow, and that he started to acquire the eye and indeed ear of ministers.

As talk grew of him as 'one who might someday fill the office of Chancellor of the Exchequer',[116] he was appointed as a junior Lord of the Treasury by Lord Aberdeen in 1853.[117] This came at a cost, as his 'desertion from the standard of ultra-Romanism' necessary to take up this position led to the loss of his Parliamentary seat,[118] but he was apparently un-phased by finding himself as a 'politician whom no political party would trust', which for many would be a position too 'hazardous' to contemplate.[119] However, by 1856, this 'flattering appointment', which could have led to the prize of the Exchequer post, was beset with disquiet about Sadleir's commercial dealings. These were not thought to be consistent with 'the honour of a high government official' especially one involved in Treasury business,[120] and led to his resignation from the Cabinet and to City-wide questioning of his finances.[121] These were underpinned by contemporaneous forgeries and frauds such as the dishonouring of the Tipperary Joint Stock Bank's drafts in the City in February 1856, which ensured that discovery of Sadleir's misdeeds was somewhat inevitable.[122]

Although the 'Tipperary scandal' precipitated Sadleir's suicide, it was a much less shocking occurrence for contemporaries than many other notable episodes of the 1850s. The bank whose drafts were ultimately dishonoured in the City amidst rumour of fraud and forgery was Sadleir's 'creation', as he was instrumental in increasing the profile of the small bank established by his grandfather, which had traditionally enjoyed a sound reputation and conducted its business on a 'very limited' scale.[123] Clearly it was not, as represented by report and balance sheet published in 1856, 'in the most flourishing condition' and the amount of misery caused by Sadleir's dishonesty was said to be 'incalculable'.[124] But the bank lacked the wide customer base of private and commercial clients found elsewhere. It was the latter which ensured that when the 'barely contemplated' event of 'suspension of a metropolitan joint-stock bank' *did* transpire in the collapse of the Royal British Bank (also in 1856), the consequences were catastrophic.[125]

The shock generated by the collapse of the Royal British Bank arose from how its management, which had 'most widely digressed from the prudent path of banking business' and even 'honesty and honour',[126] was widely publicized as inflicting 'serious loss upon a very considerable body of customers', many of whom were considered 'least able' to bear a loss, by virtue of being 'small traders and private individuals of limited means'.[127] There were clearly parallels between how the Royal British Bank board were – amongst other alleged wrongdoing – helping themselves to 'the contents of the till as it suited them'[128] and how private bankers Strahan, Paul and Bates had used customer deposits to cross-subsidise other enterprises they were involved in. Clearly 'The Delinquencies of Messers. Strahan, Paul, and Bates'[129] *was* deeply shocking for London society, and those more accustomed to being beside them in 'high office', including the presiding judge for their criminal trial.[130] These bankers lacked any antecedent 'reputation for extravagance' and were instead associated with 'elegances of life' and 'a liberality of expenditure' which appropriately reflected the 'station of society in which they moved'.[131] This was certainly the case for Strahan and Sir John Dean Paul. Bates alone amongst the partners could not 'boast of private means', but his service within the bank was long-standing and he was well-acquainted with and highly trusted by customers, many of whom were drawn from the social spheres occupied particularly by Strahan and Paul – 'chiefly members of the aristocracy, and wealthy commoners'.[132] This, combined with how all partners were 'men of business',[133] ensured that it was 'almost impossible to imagine an establishment pressing in the main elements of success to a more marked degree'.[134]

It was their involvement with other enterprises and commercial ventures which meant that, notwithstanding all outward appearances to the contrary, the 'reprehensible practice of borrowing from the bank-till for their own personal wants' transpired to be 'followed by all partners in this bank'.[135] This led, in 1855, to a sentence of fourteen years' transportation, a sentence which in turn was considered a year later to have been 'justly and wisely' handed down.[136] These reflections on the sentence passed for Strahan *et al.* are interesting, particularly as they were made during a House of Commons debate on transportation, and thus at a time when transportation itself was falling out of favour, as this debate makes clear. This commentary, located within a debate on transportation, stands out amongst many others which occurred in Parliament referencing the delinquent bankers. Their affairs were more typically discussed in the context of banking itself, both contemporaneously and also for a decade or more thereafter.[137] Furthermore, it is readily apparent that what became a mid-century trend towards bank incorporations was strongly influenced by their misconduct, and their nefarious activities did much to highlight the perceived core strengths of joint-stock principles for undertaking business ventures.

Increasingly generalized benefits pointing to greater capitalization capabilities, scrutiny of management decision-making and auditing, and public disclosure requirements associated with joint-stock business, became applied to banking specifically in the aftermath of the incidents described above. And it would be the collapse of the Royal British Bank, rather than Sadleir's Tipperary Bank, which cast doubt on the superiority of joint-stock business alongside the alternative traditional partnership model. In ways befitting how the alleged mismanagement of the Royal British Bank amounted to a particularly 'gross and most distressing exhibition' of misconduct which had become apparent 'to the opprobrium of the country',[138] and promoted public outrage and demands for responses, this scandal generated very considerable Parliamentary discussion.

This included placing great pressure upon the Government to take responsibility for bringing a criminal prosecution,[139] at a time where the culture of private prosecution still predominated.[140] However, notwithstanding the differences in the origins and perceived shock value of the alleged criminality of the Royal British Bank directors, Strahan *et al.*, together with John Sadleir, all are stories of how 'it requires the labour of a whole life to build up a character of honour and virtue, which in one fatal and unguarded moment may be entirely destroyed'.[141] Clearly for Sadleir at least his 'swindling' appeared to reflect multiple unguarded moments rather than 'a moment of temptation'.[142] However, all are narratives of a fall from grace experienced by those who were 'well educated' and 'moving in positions' within society[143] and who were persons of 'unquestioned integrity and honour'.[144]

VII

The same 'rogues' gallery'[145] of nineteenth-century financial infractions recounting John Sadleir's epic swindling and spoke at length on the 'delinquencies of Strahan, Paul and Bates' included Joseph Windle Cole's audacious dock warrant fraud scheme and security frauds underpinning multiple accusations of criminality during the 1850s. Cole differed from Sadleir in that had the latter stood trial, his would almost certainly have attracted courtroom observation of being 'well educated' and moving in 'a position of society'. This was said about Strahan, Paul and Bates in their trial in 1855, with such sentiments being expressed across courtroom agendas, thereby being central to prosecutorial cases, addresses being made by defence counsel, and ones from presiding judges. The trial of Strahan, Paul and Bates illustrates saliently how for those responsible for prosecutions and defence, references to respectability and social standing sought respectively to accentuate the gravity of criminal accusations for such persons, or to distance those on trial from being tainted with criminality, by insisting that respectable people did not and would not commit crime. For judges, such statements sought to capture the realities of persons in 'high office' being convicted as criminals.[146] All articulations of 'respectability' and 'criminality' embodied a strong normative disjunction between them where those on trial were drawn from the Victorian elite.[147]

Joseph Windle Cole had not moved in such circles by virtue of being a 'general merchant'.[148] He was widely regarded as having 'great business capacity',[149] despite the fact that a business with which he was previously associated had failed, leaving a 'doubtful reputation' as well as 'indifferent assets'.[150] Although his 'limited means' and 'the degree to which he thought it important to be able to avail himself of increasing and obvious advantages'[151] could be identified with a nascent Victorian 'entrepreneurial spirit',[152] Cole's background as a clerk in the City meant that he lacked key trappings of the social elite and even a growing and rapidly changing commercial 'elite'. In the course of one of his trials it was remarked that he experienced a long-standing precarious financial existence,[153] but it was also suggested that his frauds were motivated by enthusiasm for opportunities and affirmation attendant to being embedded in the City as much, if not more so, than by financial reward.[154] Cole's ability to execute frauds over a lengthy time frame was thought to be closely connected with his reputation as a 'first-class man of business' garnered from being highly successful in his enterprises.[155] He also appeared to have a personal *reputation* and even *respectability* by virtue of being considered 'generally honourable in his dealings',[156] but his narrative suggests this was respectability acquired from his business dealings rather than arising from his background. There is also strong intimation that this arose from connections made with City Houses through his dealings, rather than from his more immediate business associates (centrally his 1864 co-defendants Davidson and Gordon), where associations with prominent City stalwarts like Overend, Gurney and Co facilitated him in carrying on business 'successfully, in good reputation' as well as 'with fair credit'.[157]

Cole's 'respectability by association' appears to have been a different type from that arising from more conventional paths of social background and access to elite commercial and professional circles, as was so with Sadleir and many others whose respectability became a public focal point. Although it was arguably a more diluted and less stable species of respectability, Cole's reputation was a feature of the criminal proceedings brought against him. Furthermore, it appears that his respectability acquired through his reputation and particularly his associations assisted him in operationalizing his criminal activities, as it helped him to conceal the unlawful aspects of his dealing. Here it is interesting that the proposition of criminality being concealed by occupational legitimacy is a mainstay within white-collar crime criminology, with this commonly captured in the juxtapositioning of crimes within 'suites' rather than the 'streets'.[158] However, we must bear in mind that once again scholars are divided on whether occupational environs are more effective or less so than conventional 'crime scenes' for ensuring that criminality remains uncovered.[159] What is less contentious is the perception that occupational environments help to convey and actually confer legitimacy to many '[financial] crime scenes', and where this is also commonly attributed to respectability attaching to these environments themselves, as well as to the persons occupying them.[160]

This reference to *persons* who commit financial crimes is central to understanding how Sutherland's work has been criticized since its bold introduction. Many, who are divided over being broadly supportive of his key propositions or dismissing his postulations on under-enforcement where unlawful acts and their perpetrators do not conform to popular conceptions of 'crime' and 'the criminal', are unified in the belief that Sutherland's preoccupation with *persons* 'of respectability and high social status' has ensured that far too little attention has been paid to the activities themselves.[161] Within this, for some, Sutherland put too great an emphasis on respectability and high social status, thereby taking too little account of the actor (as well as activity) spectrum of offending.[162] Whether findings of significance attached to offenders' respectability in nineteenth-century Britain will provide a 'corrective' for applying Sutherland's work to twenty-first century Britain is likely to be a further point of contention and division amongst scholars. Indeed it might properly be argued that whatever its significance for nineteenth-century contemporaries, 'respectability' and 'standing' have little currency and import in the relatively flat social structure of twenty-first century Britain.

VIII

What is interesting in the light of such views is how important standing and reputation and even 'respectability' continue to be in twenty-first-century discourses on financial crime. Certainly it is associated with interferences with the proper course of criminal justice, where those standing accused of activities which do not necessarily attract 'moral outrage' are not perceived as being 'real criminals' or even criminals at all, by sitting juries or even criminal justice process actors themselves.[163] It is also noteworthy that those accused of financial crimes are said to lack criminal self-image,[164] not simply because their activities are not 'really wrong' but on account of having middle-class (or higher) status.[165] That respectability clearly *does* still matter for those who lack 'criminal self-image' is evident in the case of Ernest Saunders who was convicted of fraud and false accounting in 1990 as part of the highly profiled trial of the 'Guinness Four'. Saunders attributed his 'nightmare' fall from grace – occurring even prior to his conviction and imprisonment[166] and continuing long after – to not being part of 'the Establishment' by virtue of background as well as religion. Clearly, this one-time respected and successful Cambridge-educated businessman has not experienced the 'rehabilitation' and reintegration into upper echelons enjoyed by fellow 'Guinness Four' convict Gerald Ronson, which was considered to be complete within weeks of his release from serving a six-month prison sentence. At the time, this was famously sealed with a handshake from the Queen Mother,[167] and twenty-two years later this 'great survivor of the Guinness share-trading scandal' received a CBE for services to charity in the 2012 New Year Honours list.[168]

Ernest Saunders has attributed his rather different fortunes to his 'outsider' background as the son of a Jewish immigrant, whilst other accounts attach this to scepticism surrounding his (apparently) miraculous recovery from dementia.[169] But his self-image is that of 'outsider' and had he lived, perhaps John Sadleir too might have spoken of his 'nightmare' and how scrutiny of his affairs reflected his lack of belonging to the elite (incorporating also his Catholicism). The Guinness story of 'cross-class alliance of the respectable poor with the elite'[170] is complex given that whilst Saunders lacked the pedigree of fellow Guinness defendant Sir Jack Lyons, he was not like Ronson and Anthony Parnes who were 'classic self-made entrepreneurs'.[171] In this regard, the very recent tale of former JP Morgan banker Ian Hannam might be instructive. Following a successful non-criminal insider dealing enforcement against him, Hannam retained his licence to trade amidst findings that he had acted honestly and with integrity, with his financial penalty of £450,000 reflecting a serious error of professional judgement.[172] But Hannam, like Saunders, speaks of continuing social and occupational ostracization, attributing this to being an 'outsider' and not 'in the club', by virtue of growing up on a council estate and not being 'officer class' during his military career.

Both cases suggest that responding to misconduct in business is highly complex and that research into the 'problem' of financial crime for society in Britain needs to continue. That this should include historical research can be illustrated by UK regulators' current enthusiasm for the importance of the past for configuring current challenges for law-making and law enforcement in the 'commercial sphere'.[173] In turn, this very highly profiled attention being paid to history's value is a very significant development given views that, notwithstanding historians' expertise in understanding temporalities of social change, history has barely hitherto featured in social science debate.[174] This is of course an embodiment of the hypothesis of a social journey linking past and present and indeed future,[175] and this must be borne in mind when suggesting that the continuing significance of respectability within financial crime discourse can be traced to Victorian responses to 'High Art' crime.[176] This ensures that we will not mistakenly blame Victorian pioneers for the difficulties experienced today in ensuring that 'individuals who commit financial crime should be treated like the criminals they are',[177] and the perceived importance of avoiding 'soft options' enabling 'chaps' to receive 'punishment over lunch'.[178] These case studies show that during the nineteenth century, notions of respectability were articulated to highlight the gravity of being considered 'the criminal' for respectable persons. In other words to highlight the repugnance of those drawn from the elite falling to the position of 'common felons' as was said of Strahan *et al.*,[179] and to serve as stern warnings to those who lacked extenuating forces of 'poverty, want, bad education, and worse example' that commission of crime by them would be visited with utmost severity, as channelled through the trial of Joseph Windle Cole.[180]

Thus, in situating micro-history methodologically, the history of financial crime illustrates its usefulness in exploring the history of class and social structure alongside other neglected studies of minority groups, race, ethnicity and gender.[181] Crime history is concerned with social structure, and it is manifestly important for it to acknowledge that Victorian society was prepared to channel accusations of violating highly prized norms of reputation and reposed trust against its most esteemed through criminal enforcement, and to support this with sentences of imprisonment and even transportation.[182] As history should be a central part of social science debate, perceptions that perpetrators of financial crime are not being treated as the 'criminals they are' should concern crime historians as much as it does criminologists. Crime historians are uniquely placed to explain that something has clearly happened through our societal journey[183] from the mid-nineteenth century to the present. Moreover, for helping to explain what has happened and why, micro-history case studies provide an important piece of this fascinating puzzle.

Notes

1. H. Perkin (1969) *Origins of Modern English Society, 1780–1880* (London: Routledge and Kegan Paul), p. 442. On the silence of crime history regarding financial crime, see S. Wilson (2014) *The Origins of Modern Financial Crime: Historical Foundations and Current Problems in Britain* (London: Routledge).
2. D.O. Friedrichs (2012) 'Wall Street: Crime Never Sleeps', in S. Will, S. Handelman and D.C. Brotherton (eds) *How They Got Away With It: White Collar Criminals and the Financial Meltdown* (New York: Columbia University Press), pp. 3–25 at pp. 4–5.

3. For the former, see P. King (1999) 'Locating Histories of Crime: A Bibliographical Study', *British Journal of Criminology*, Vol. 39, No. 1, pp. 161–74 at p. 161 and the latter J.P. Locker and B. Godfrey (2006) 'Ontological Boundaries and Temporal Watersheds in the Development of White-Collar Crime', *British Journal of Criminology*, Vol. 46, No. 6, pp. 976–92 at p. 976.

4. A. Haldane and V. Madouros, 'The Dog and the Frisbee' (Federal Bank of Kansas Economic Policy Symposium, Jackson Hole, Wyoming, 31 August 2012), pp. 22–3, available at http://www.bankofengland.co.uk/publications/Pages/speeches/2012/596.aspx.

5. See S. Wilson (2016) 'Financial Crises and Financial Crime "Transformative Understandings" of Crime – Past Present and Future', in N. Ryder, U. Turksen and J. Tucker (eds) *The Financial Crisis and White Collar Crime – Legislative and Policy Responses* (Abingdon: Routledge), forthcoming.

6. See R. Tomasic (2011) 'The Financial Crisis and the Haphazard Pursuit of Financial Crime', *Journal of Financial Crime*, Vol. 18, No. 1, pp. 7–31 at p. 7, and N. Ryder (2014) *The Financial Crisis and White Collar Crime – The Perfect Storm?* (Cheltenham: Edward Elgar).

7. Tomasic, 'The Financial Crisis', p. 7.

8. Friedrichs, 'Wall Street', *passim*.

9. Ibid., p. 20, and indeed dwarfing the costs of conventional crime; see also key policy initiatives such as the (now replaced) National Fraud Authority's 'Fighting Fraud Together' focus launched in 2011.

10. See examples drawn from the Bank of England, the House of Commons Treasury Committee and the Financial Services Authority discussed in Wilson, *The Origins of Modern Financial Crime*.

11. For key literature, see P. Rock (2005) 'Chronocentrism and British Criminology', *British Journal of Sociology*, Vol. 56, No. 3, pp. 473–91 at p. 473, and P. Lawrence (2012) 'History, Criminology and the "Use" of the Past', *Theoretical Criminology*, Vol. 16, No. 3, pp. 313–28 at p. 313.

12. This is the core argument of Wilson, *The Origins of Modern Financial Crime*.

13. See for example A. Bequai (1978) *White-Collar Crime: A Twentieth Century Crisis* (Massachusetts: Lexington Press).

14. M. Levi (1987) *Regulating Fraud: White-Collar Crime and the Criminal Process* (London: Tavistock Press), p. 1.

15. Ibid.

16. Bequai, *White-Collar Crime*, p. iii.

17. As evident in both works from Bequai (*White-Collar Crime*) and Levi (*Regulating Fraud*) referenced above.

18. D. Kirk and A. Woodcock (1996) *Serious Fraud: Investigation and Trial* (London: Butterworth), p. 1.

19. E.H. Sutherland (1949) *White-Collar Crime* (New York: Dryden Press), p. 9.

20. E.H. Sutherland (1940) 'White Collar Criminality', *American Sociological Review*, Vol. 5, No. 1, pp. 1–12 at p. 3.

21. M. Levi (2002) 'Suite Justice or Sweet Charity? Some Explorations of Shaming and Incapacitating Business Fraudsters', *Punishment and Society*, Vol. 4, No. 2, pp. 147–63 at pp. 147 and 149.

22. Law Commission (1999) *Fraud and Deception: A Consultation Paper*, CP No. 155 (London: HMSO), para 1.4.

23. E.H. Sutherland (1945) 'Is "White Collar Crime" Crime?' *American Sociological Review*, Vol. 10, pp. 132–9 at p. 132.

24. Ibid., especially pp. 137–9.

25. Ibid., p. 139. For a more recent account of this perspective, see Friedrichs, 'Wall Street', *passim*.

26. S. Wheeler, D. Weisburd and N. Bode (1982) 'Sentencing the White-Collar Offender: Rhetoric and Reality', *American Sociological Review*, Vol. 47, No. 5, pp. 641–59 at p. 641.

27. For a comprehensive and balanced summary of key perspectives and works, see D. Nelken (1994 edition) 'White-Collar Crime', in M. Maguire, R. Morgan and R. Reiner (eds) *The Oxford Handbook of Criminology* (Oxford: Oxford University Press), pp. 355–92, at p. 355.

28. M.L. Benson and S.S. Simpson (2009) *White-Collar Crime: An Opportunity Perspective* (London: Routledge).

29. This is a recurrent theme within Wilson, *The Origins of Modern Financial Crime*.

30. S.M. Rosoff, H.N. Pontell and R. Tillman (2010) *Profit without Honor: White-Collar Crime and the Looting of America* (New Jersey: Prentice Hall), p. 3.

31. See generally Nelken, 'White-Collar Crime', *passim*.

32. V. Aubert (1952) 'White-Collar Crime and Social Structure', *American Journal of Sociology*, Vol. 58, pp. 263–71 at pp. 263 and 266.

33. Tomasic, 'The Financial Crisis', p. 7.

34. D.M. Evans (1968 edition) *Facts, Failures and Frauds Revelations: Financial Mercantile Criminal* (New York: Augustus M Kelley), especially pp. 1–5.

35. C. MacKay (1955 edition) *Extraordinary Popular Delusions and the Madness of Crowds* (London: Wordsworth Editions), p. 80.

36. Perkin, *Origins of Modern English Society*, p. 442.

37. Respectively in D.J.V. Jones (1982) *Crime, Protest, Community and Police in Nineteenth Century Britain* (London: Routledge and Kegan Paul) and C. Emsley (2010 edition) *Crime and Society in England: 1750–1900* (Abingdon: Routledge).

38. As evident in the emphasis on criminal aspects of financial crime from business historians in J. Taylor (2013) *Boardroom Scandal: The Criminalization of Company Fraud in Nineteenth-Century Britain* (Oxford: Oxford University Press) and more recently, M. Hollow (2014) *Rogue Banking: A History of Financial Fraud in Interwar Britain* (London: Palgrave).

39. See Wilson, *The Origins of Modern Financial Crime*, Epilogue.

40. Ibid.

41. As shown in the works of Taylor (*Boardroom Scandal*) and Hollow (*Rogue Banking*) referenced above.

42. See (1901) *A Century of Law Reform: Twelve Lectures on the Changes in the Law of England During the Nineteenth Century* (London: Council of Legal Education).

43. See for example, Emsley, *Crime and Society in England, passim*.

44. E.L. Woodward (1938) *The Oxford History of England: The Age of Reform 1815–1870* (Oxford: Clarendon Press); see especially, p. 426 and *passim*.

45. C. Stebbings (2012) 'Benefits and Barriers: The Making of Victorian Legal History', in A. Musson and C. Stebbings (eds) *Making Legal History: Approaches and Methodologies* (Cambridge: Cambridge University Press), pp. 72–87 at pp. 72–3.

46. S.G. Magnusson and I.M. Szijarto (2013) *What Is Microhistory? Theory and Practice* (Abingdon: Routledge), p. 5.

47. Ibid., p. 4.

48. Ibid.

49. Ibid., p. 31.

50. Ibid., especially pp. 4–6.

51. Ibid., p. 7.

52. Ibid., p. 127.

53. Ibid., p. 125.

54. Ibid., p. 148.

55. Ibid., pp. 16–17, and pp. 127–8.

56. Ibid., p. 125.

57. Ibid., p. 149.

58. Ibid., p. 7.

59. Ibid., pp. 16–17.

60. Ibid., pp. 7–10.

61. Ibid., p. 17.

62. Ibid., p. 31.

63. Ibid., embodying the idea that history is 'multi-scopic', with the authors citing Paul-Andre Rosental as an authority for this.

64. Ibid., p. 31.

65. J. Tosh (2010 edition) *The Pursuit of History: Aims, Methods and New Directions in the Study of Modern History* (Harlow: Longman), p. 33.

66. Magnusson and Szijarto, *What Is Microhistory?* p. 125.

67. Alongside historical difference and historical process, see Tosh, *The Pursuit of History*, especially pp. 8–12.

68. As coined in D. Eastwood (1993) *Governing Rural England: Tradition and Transformation in Local Government 1780–1840* (Oxford: Clarendon Press), pp. 225–60.

69. J. Black and D. McRaild (2002) *Nineteenth-Century Britain* (Basingstoke: Palgrave), p. xvii.

70. See Stebbings, 'Benefits and Barriers', pp. 72–3 and also Woodward, *The Oxford History of England*, p. 426.

71. Ibid.

72. Magnusson and Szijarto, *What Is Microhistory?* p. 31.

73. As proposed in the Epilogue for Wilson, *The Origins of Modern Financial Crime*.

74. See e.g. R.D. Storch (1975) '"The Plague of Blue Locusts": Police Reform and Popular Resistance in North England 1840–1857', *International Review of Social History*, Vol. 20, No. 1, pp. 61–90 at p. 61 and D. Philips (1977) *Crime and Authority in Victorian England* (London: Croom Helm).

75. As illustrated in Emsley, *Crime and Society in England, passim.*

76. *Parliamentary Papers*, Report of the Royal Commission on the Constabulary Force (Constabulary Force Report), Cmnd. 169, Vol. XIX (1839), p. 15.

77. U. Henriques (1972) 'The Rise and Decline of the Separate System of Prison Discipline', *Past and Present*, No. 54, pp. 61–93 at pp. 61 and 84.

78. Ibid., pp. 82–3.

79. A. Norrie (1993) *Crime Reason and History: A Critical Introduction to Criminal Law* (London: Wiedenfeld and Nicolson), pp. 85–6.

80. See Wilson, *The Origins of Modern Financial Crime.*

81. Friedrichs, 'Wall Street', p. 5.

82. Evans, *Facts, Failures and Frauds*, p. 1.

83. Sutherland, 'Is "White Collar Crime" Crime?' p. 132.

84. Ibid., p. 136, with this sentiment also reflected on in T.M. Ashe and L. Counsell (1993) *Insider Trading* (Croydon: Tolley), pp. 178–9.

85. Ibid., p. 139.

86. With both viewpoints explained in Nelken, 'White-Collar Crime', *passim.*

87. Particularly crimes against persons involving violence: see M. Cole 'The FSA's approach to insider dealing', Speech, American Bar Association, 4 October 2007.

88. Perkin, *Origins of Modern English Society*, p. 442.

89. Evans, *Facts, Failures and Frauds*, pp. 1–5.

90. Ibid., p. 1.

91. Ibid., pp. 1–2.

92. Ibid., pp. 1–5.

93. See Taylor, *Boardroom Scandal*, especially pp. 1–7.

94. D.M. Evans (1970) *The Commercial Crisis 1847–1848* (1848, reprinted New York: Burt Franklin), p. 33.

95. See Taylor, *Boardroom Scandal*, pp. 187–212.

96. Friedrichs, 'Wall Street', p. 6.

97. Evans, *Facts, Failures and Frauds*, p. 5.

98. See Wilson, *The Origins of Modern Financial Crime.*

99. For lawyers this is what discerns crime from other types of wrongs recognized by law: see G. Williams (1983) *Textbook of Criminal Law* (London: Stevens and Son).

100. As Benson and Simpson explain in *White-Collar Crime*, p. 5, Sutherland excluded 'many crimes of the upper classes' such as ones associated with violence and intoxication.

101. M. Wiener (1990) *Reconstructing the Criminal, Culture, Law, and Policy in England 1830–1914* (Cambridge: Cambridge University Press), p. 244.

102. B. Hilton (1986) *Age of Atonement: The Influence of Evangelicalism on Social and Economic Thought 1785–1865* (Oxford: Clarendon Press), p. 123.

103. For the latter, see ibid. and the former M. Lobban (1996) 'Nineteenth Century Frauds in Company Formation: *Derry v Peek* in Context', *Law Quarterly Review*, Vol. 112, No. 2, pp. 287–334 at pp. 287–8.

104. Hilton, *Age of Atonement*, p. 123.

105. Wheeler, Weisburd and Bode, 'Sentencing the White-Collar Offender', p. 645.

106. Evans, *Facts, Failures and Frauds*, p. 391.

107. Ibid., see the account of Sadleir's story, at pp. 226–67 and p. 235.

108. Ibid., p. 227.

109. Ibid.

110. Ibid., p. 128.

111. Ibid., pp. 227–8.

112. Ibid.

113. Ibid., p. 228.

114. Ibid.

115. Ibid., pp. 229–30.

116. Ibid., p. 230.

117. Ibid.

118. Ibid.

119. Ibid., p. 231.

120. Ibid. p. 232.

121. Ibid.

122. Ibid., pp. 230–1.

123. Evans, *Facts, Failures and Frauds*, p. 229. See also the affairs of the Royal British Bank collapse and subsequent criminal trial of its directors in 1858 reported in the same work at pp. 268–390.

124. Ibid., p. 235.

125. Ibid., pp. 269–70.

126. Ibid., pp. 270 and 278.

127. Ibid., p. 269.

128. Ibid., p. 269.

129. Ibid., p. iii. This is the heading used by Evans to present his commentary on the criminal trial and the events leading to it in the annotated contents section at the front of his text.

130. Ibid., pp. 106–53 documenting the downfall of Strahan, Paul and Bates, especially at p. 145.

131. Ibid., pp. 108–9.

132. Ibid., p. 111.

133. Ibid.

134. Ibid., pp. 110–11.

135. Ibid., p. 112.

136. Hansard, House of Commons (HC) Debates, 141, 3 April 1856: 414 (Sir John Parkington).

137. See for example Hansard, House of Lords (HL) Debates, 153, 24 March 1859: 686 (Lord Stanley) and Hansard, HC Debates, 178, 1 May 1865: 1286 (Mr Cave).

138. Hansard, HC Debates, 146, 8 June 1857: 1372 (Sergeant Kinglake).

139. See reflections from Attorney-General Sir Richard Bethell at Hansard, HC Debates, 145, 15 May 1857: 310–11.

140. See Wilson, *The Origins of Modern Financial Crime*.

141. See the account of Strahan, Paul and Bates' downfall in Evans, *Facts, Failures and Frauds*, pp. 106–53, especially at p. 133.

142. Ibid.

143. Ibid., p. 145.

144. Ibid., p. 137.

145. See M. Robbins (1998) *The Railway Age* (London: Mandolin Press), p. 26.

146. See extensive discussion of this in Wilson, *The Origins of Modern Financial Crime*.

147. Ibid.

148. See the account Joseph Windle Cole in Evans, *Facts, Failures and Frauds*, pp. 154–225 at p. 157.

149. Ibid., p. 158.

150. Ibid., p. 157.

151. Ibid.

152. See Wilson, *The Origins of Modern Financial Crime*.

153. Ibid., pp. 156–7.

154. Evans, *Facts, Failures and Frauds*, pp. 208–9.

155. Ibid., p. 166.

156. Ibid.

157. Ibid., p. 212.

158. Levi, 'Suite Justice or Sweet Charity?' p. 147.

159. See perspectives from Nelken, 'White-Collar Crime', *passim* and S. Shapiro (1985) '"The Road Not Taken": The Elusive Path to Criminal Prosecution for White Collar Offenders', *Law and Society Review*, Vol. 19, No. 2, pp. 179–217 at 179.

160. See for example Friedrichs, 'Wall Street', *passim*.

161. For example, see S. Shapiro (1990) 'Collaring the Crime, not the Criminal: Reconsidering the Concept of a White-Collar Crime', *American Sociological Review*, Vol. 55, pp. 346–65 at p. 346.

162. See discussion in Nelken, 'White-Collar Crime'.

163. As suggested in works referenced above in this chapter by Sutherland, Ashe and Counsell and Cole.

164. See D.O. Friedrichs (2004) *Trusted Criminals: White-Collar Crime in Contemporary Society* (Belmont, CA: Wadsworth), p. 5.

165. S. Karstedt and S. Farrall, 'Law-abiding Majority? The Everyday Crimes of the Middle Classes', Third Briefing, Centre for Crime and Justice Studies, June 2007.

166. Indeed this is how this 'most dramatic personal turn-around in fortunes in recent British commercial history' was titled: see J. Saunders (1989) *Nightmare: the Ernest Saunders Story* (London: Hutchinson).

167. M. Levi (1991) 'Sentencing White-Collar Crime in the Dark? Reflections on the Guinness Four', *Howard Journal of Criminal Justice*, Vol. 30, No. 4, pp. 257–79 at pp. 257 and 269.

168. *Daily Mail*, 24 May 2012.

169. *The Independent*, 30 December 1994.

170. Levi, 'Sentencing White-Collar Crime in the Dark?' p. 260.

171. Ibid.

172. *Hannam v FCA* [2014] UKUT 0233 (TCC).

173. See Wilson, *The Origins of Modern Financial Crime*.

174. W.H. Sewell Jr. (2005) *Logics of History: Social Theory and Social Transformation* (Chicago: University of Chicago Press), especially pp. 6–18.

175. Tosh, *The Pursuit of History*, pp. 45–7.

176. See Wilson, *The Origins of Modern Financial Crime*.

177. Rt Hon George Osborne MP, Mansion House Speech (London), 10 June 2015.

178. R. Wright, 'The Investigation and Prosecution of Serious and Complex Fraud towards the Twenty-first Century', ISRCL Commercial and Financial Fraud Conference, 12 July 1999.

179. Trial of Strahan, Paul and Bates (1855) found in Evans, *Facts, Failures and Frauds*, especially p. 117.

180. Ibid., p. 209 setting out judicial reflections on Windle Cole's 1864 conviction.

181. Magnusson and Szijarto, *What Is Microhistory?* p. 154.

182. Wilson, *The Origins of Modern Financial Crime*.

183. See Tosh, *The Pursuit of History*, especially pp. 45–7.

CHAPTER 3
THE LIMITS OF GOVERNMENT INTERVENTION: CAROLINE WYBROW AND THE SCANDAL OF THE CONTAGIOUS DISEASES ACTS
Adrian Ager

I

This chapter pieces together a brief episode in the life of seventeen-year-old Caroline Wybrow who was detained in the Chatham Lock Hospital in north Kent early in 1875. Her experience was used by the repeal movement to further their cause to have the Contagious Diseases Acts abolished (hereafter CDA). Three successive Acts were introduced during the 1860s, to control the spread of venereal diseases in towns and cities like Chatham, where there was a large maritime and military presence. In brief, they allowed for the inspection and detention of diseased prostitutes.[1] In the 1880s, Caroline was also the subject of a parliamentary enquiry into the operation of the Acts. The micro-history of this episode is used here as a backdrop to examine the interplay between the administration of the CDA, government intervention and attitudes towards prostitution during the second half of the nineteenth century.[2]

Over the last half century, the administration of the CDA has been examined from a variety of standpoints. This interest was triggered by Judith Walkowitz's influential 1970s enquiry into the links between prostitution, state regulation and socio-economic conditions. Although it is still an important touchstone, its relevance to the present survey is somewhat reduced because it was based on findings for London and the south coastal towns of Portsmouth and Southampton.[3] The same is true of Stefan Anthony Slater's more recent investigation into street prostitution in London between 1918 and 1959. This time frame also means that it sits outside of the period covered by this chapter.[4] Similar remarks apply to Maria Luddy's excellent Irish study and Julia Laite's well-regarded examination of commercial sex in London in the period 1885–1960.[5]

Consequently, much can still be learned about the relationship between prostitution and socio-economic change in the south-eastern regions during the latter part of the nineteenth century. In the late 1970s, Margaret Hamilton included a brief footnote about Caroline's experience in her article about opposition to the CDA.[6] Likewise, Brian Joyce incorporated a short summary of her story in his 1990s monograph. However, the academic credentials of his investigation are undermined because he failed to properly identify many of his source documents.[7]A more recent survey of prostitution in Kent was published by Catherine Lee in 2013.[8] Lee's sixth chapter, entitled 'The Contagious Diseases Acts in Kent', is particularly relevant to the present study. Here, she adopted a 'top-down' approach with a 'bottom up viewpoint' to trace 'the trajectory' of Caroline Wybrow, 'through the machinery of the CD Acts['] system'.[9] Because this work concentrated on a specific set of sources, it sometimes offers a limited interpretative and occasionally misleading analysis of this case. For example, Lee stated that Chatham fell under the auspices of the CDA in 1864.[10] However, a shortage of hospital space meant that the town was only partially covered by the Acts at this stage. This continued until Chatham's newly erected Lock Hospital admitted its first patients in 1870.[11]

The present work uses a more holistic methodology of record linkage to reconstruct the micro-history of Caroline Wybrow in order to ascertain the extent of the influence of her 'story' on the history of the CDA in Victorian Britain. In this instance, personal information and details relating to the key individuals involved in this case are drawn together from a variety of primary sources, including Parliamentary Reports and police documents, as well as newspapers and periodicals. This type of record linkage allows greater insights into the motives of those concerned with the above episode than one that depends on a 'more conventional methodology'.[12]

In order to reconstruct a more accurate and nuanced life history for Caroline Wybrow, this chapter centres on three main areas of interest. First, it examines the circumstances surrounding Caroline's detention in the Chatham Lock Hospital. Second, we look at how the repeal movement manipulated Caroline's experience with the authorities to further their cause against the CDA. Finally, Caroline's treatment at the Lock Hospital from the perspective of the constabulary and medical staff will be explored. Together, these strands of micro-history offer fresh interpretations of the policing of the CDA in Chatham and place their administration in context with the wider literature on the limits of state control during the Victorian era.

To achieve these aims, this investigation draws on a wide selection of primary sources, including government records, contemporary brochures and newspapers. Annual reports produced for Captain William Harris, the Assistant Chief Commissioner of the Metropolitan Police, form the cornerstone of this enquiry. Harris was ultimately responsible for the administration of the CDA in all of the subjected districts.[13] His reports published between 1881 and 1882 contain valuable data about the activities of prostitutes in these districts. They also include witness testimonies from the Select Committee's investigation into the Wybrow affair. This information offers a clearer impression of the circumstances surrounding Caroline's confinement. Yet historians need to be mindful that documents like this may reflect particular lines of questioning and/or the conditions under which the enquiries were held. Questions and responses may also have been calibrated by social status or relationships between the interlocutors. Due consideration also needs to be given to the impact that inconsistencies or gaps within datasets can have on research outcomes. To offset these difficulties, record linkage has been used wherever possible to cross-reference and validate the research findings. In the process, this chapter revisits many of the documents used by Joyce and

Lee in their analyses of the Wybrow affair. Needless to say, the provenance of all of the sources is properly explained. In a further departure from their approach, this study also emphasizes why key events or individuals are important to this case. Thus, it expands on Joyce and Lee's findings and highlights the significance of Caroline's experience to the wider literature on the administration of the CDA in the subjected districts.

II

On 31 January 1875, the radical lawyer and social campaigner Mr William Shaen wrote to the Home Secretary to complain about Caroline Wybrow's treatment at the hands of the Chatham authorities. Shaen headed a firm of London solicitors. For thirty years, he had also been actively involved with an association that lobbied to improve the laws protecting women and children.[14] Clearly a contrarian, Shaen also had extensive experience of working with the police to prosecute 'dozens' of brothel keepers.[15] In this instance, he acted as the chairman of the Executive Committee of the National Association for the Repeal of the Contagious Diseases Act (hereafter NARCDA).[16] The organization was amongst a proliferation of repeal movements that emerged in response to growing concerns about the CDA. The NARCDA was established in the north of England but soon saw its interests spread throughout the country. In 1870, it moved its power base to London, with Shaen at the helm.[17] The organization and its members will be discussed in more detail shortly. However, for the moment it is fair to say that its aims were clearly summed up by its epithet.[18] In his letter, Shaen alleged that Caroline Wybrow had been unlawfully:

> imprisoned in the Lock Hospital at Chatham and had been subjected to personal examination by the local surgeon, although she had never been guilty of any kind of immorality.[19]

Shaen addressed his letter to the Home Secretary, the Right Hon. R. A. Cross MP. His correspondence also included affidavits made by Caroline and her widowed mother, Rachel. Both were signed in the presence of E.R. Coles, a Justice of the Peace for the County of Kent.[20] The Quaker, repeal activist and retired grocer, Mr Frederick Wheeler delivered the paperwork to the Home Office in person.[21] Wheeler's involvement with the repeal movement dated back to 1870. It will not be lost on the reader that this overlapped with the opening of the Chatham Lock Hospital.[22] Throughout the nineteenth century, radicals and nonconformists, like Shaen and Wheeler, used their professional expertise to support many humanitarian initiatives. For instance, Wheeler was also a member of the British and Foreign Anti-slavery Society in the 1860s.[23] Shaen noted in his letter that Wheeler had interviewed the Lock Hospital staff and 'understood from them that, at all events, the main facts of the case could not and would not be disputed'. He wanted 'an open examination of every witness in the presence of both parties, and before an impartial tribunal'.[24]

Shaen was outraged at the improper treatment that Caroline supposedly received under the terms of the CDA. The first of these Acts was introduced in 1864, in response to growing concerns that the health of soldiers and sailors was undermined by a 'prevalence of venereal disease'. It 'was limited to military stations and seaport towns' in eleven areas. In 1866, the Act was repealed and new legislation was introduced.[25] In 1869, the CDA were scrutinized further by another Select Committee and additional amendments were made. These allowed suspected prostitutes to be detained 'for up to one year and to regular fortnightly inspections … [they] had no right of appeal and no recourse to habeas corpus'.[26]

Judith Walkowitz noted that 'in the early 1860s government officials did not concern themselves with providing elaborate defences against the acts because there was no significant challenge to their legitimacy'.[27] This situation altered because inspections on women in the 'protected districts' increased after the introduction of the 1869 Act. Societies also agitated for the Acts to be allowed in non-subjected districts. This attracted the attention of groups who objected to the inspection regimes and campaigned for the Acts to be repealed.[28]

Chatham's inclusion (albeit partially) in the first wave of CDA districts underscores not only its importance as a naval and garrison town, but also the problems that it experienced with prostitution. Throughout the nineteenth century, the dockyard was continually upgraded.[29] This expansion coincided with a period of industrial development across the Medway basin.[30] Consequently, the region's population grew exponentially. The area around the subjected district of Chatham was estimated to have 70,000 inhabitants, shortly after Caroline was detained in the Lock Hospital.[31] There was a darker side to this economic activity. Chatham and the neighbouring area had an enduring reputation for vice. This was partly because social ties in large towns were often much looser than in the countryside. F.M.L. Thompson has observed:

> The intimate nature of country society, its lack of openings for anonymity, its necessary exposure to the public eye … called forth … virtues which made for good feelings, neighbourliness and absence of friction.[32]

The bulk of the region's single females also derived their livelihoods from low-paid occupations like domestic service or seasonal work in the garment industry.[33] This presented them with difficult choices, especially during economic downturns. For some, prostitution offered a degree of financial independence and allowed them to stave off the constant threat of hardship. Yet the transient male population and servicemen stationed at Chatham also provided prostitutes with easy pickings. In 1861, around 27 per cent of the population of Chatham and nearby Old Brompton was made up of military personnel. There were nearly 4,000 servicemen stationed in the town by 1881.[34] Their presence created a volatile environment for the authorities. As Joyce observed:

> With such a high number of young, high-spirited and often drunken, men on the streets there was an ever-present threat to law and order.[35]

This exacerbated the difficulties that the town experienced with prostitution. In the late 1820s, magistrates drew up plans to prosecute alehouse keepers who harboured prostitutes on their premises. A decade or so later, a consortium of concerned citizens paid 'discharged London police officers' 25 shillings to conduct covert operations in suspected brothels.[36] Some of the blame for this can be apportioned to the area's outdated policing arrangements and rapid economic growth. The County and Borough Police Act 1856 was supposed to ease this situation, however, the ambitions of the new law were thwarted by practicalities on the ground.[37] Chatham was appended to the 'Rochester division', which had thirty-nine officers. Despite this, just nine men covered all day and night duties in the most densely populated town in the region.[38]

This explains why plain-clothes officers from the Metropolitan force were drafted into places like Chatham after the introduction of the CDA. When Caroline was detained at the Lock Hospital, Inspector William Capon was responsible for the administration of the Acts in the town. He was well-suited to this role being raised in a military family and achieving the rank of police inspector at the relatively young age of thirty-five. In all, he spent about ten years of his police career in Kent.[39] Clearly, he was an extremely capable officer, with a good working knowledge of the region and a solid grounding in military procedures. Capon was assisted by three or four constables from the Metropolitan force, with one of these officers usually stationed at the Lock Hospital.[40] Police Constable Charles Clark visited the home that Caroline shared with her widowed mother, on 22 January 1875. Six months later, on 16 June, he recalled this meeting:

> With reference to the woman Caroline Wybrow, of Denton-court, Brook-street, Chatham. I beg to state that, previous to the 22nd of January 1875, I have very frequently seen this woman in the company with soldiers and prostitutes, sometimes in the Chatham Barracks, and on the Chatham Lines, also in other parts of the districts.[41]

The long interval between Clark's visit, the date of his statement and the point at which Shaen stepped into the arena is partly explained by the time that Wheeler needed to conduct his preliminary investigations.[42] These will be discussed in more detail shortly. For the moment, several other points from Clark's statement warrant further discussion. First, that he referred to Caroline as a woman, despite the fact that she was 17 and below the age of majority.[43] This may have been a slip. Alternatively, he might have been trying to use Caroline's association with the prostitutes to establish her guilt. It is also evident that the Wybrow's address was located in one of the poorer and less salubrious parts of Chatham.[44] Speaking to the Select Committee on 21 March 1882, Wheeler described how publicans in this district erected huts for prostitutes just beyond their property boundaries in order to circumvent the law. Wheeler also said that with companions, he frequently observed 'indecent' behaviour between soldiers and women in the thoroughfares leading to the Lock Hospital.[45] This impression was not shared by Adam Stigant, the long-serving chairman of Chatham's Board of Guardians and Local Health Board. Stigant was a native of Chatham and knew the area well. In June 1881, he acknowledged that the streets had once been in a 'shocking state'. However, he also thought that the CDA had resulted in 'a decided' and 'very striking improvement'.[46] Stigant believed that the Acts fostered better behaviour from the town's citizens. He observed:

> Before the passing of the Acts there had been a great deal of unabashed profligacy in the place, a degree of lewdness in the conduct of the women that has since passed.[47]

Clearly, Wheeler and Stigant pursued very different agendas. However, together, their statements suggest that vigorous controls on vice drove the more obvious signs of prostitution from Chatham's public areas into the shadows of the backstreets. The same happened in other subjected districts. Chief Constable Frederick Wreford described how Plymouth was improved by tighter controls on alcohol and better policing of drunken or unruly behaviour. In contrast, Head Constable Mr John Lynn thought that the CDA and the Metropolitan Police had done little to reduce disorderly conduct on the streets of Devonport. Instead, he reasoned that 'whatever improvement has taken place in the order of the streets is attributable to the ordinary police, acting under their own powers'.[48]

Clark's statement also indicates that Caroline's companions were from the lower orders of society. Previously, it was noted that the Wybrows shared their abode with three other women known to the police as prostitutes.[49] This situation was not unusual and certainly goes against any notions that prostitutes were social outcasts.[50] Instead, they often lived cheek by jowl with 'respectable residents' in the poorer districts of towns and cities.[51] Perhaps unsurprisingly, Clark's observations about Caroline's poor conduct were repeated in his fellow officers' testimonies. On 16 June 1875, Constables Henry Chapman and John Armstrong made a joint statement alleging that they had 'seen Caroline Wybrow nightly in company with different soldiers and prostitutes' and that on 'several occasions' she had been found 'in brothels with prostitutes'.[52] They also reported that:

> on the 20th of January last at 7 p.m. she was in company with two soldiers and a prostitute in the High-street, Chatham, and went into the Golden Cross beerhouse, a house frequented by soldiers and prostitutes ... [at] 8.45 p.m ... they all came out together, and immediately they saw us the prostitutes covered Caroline Wybrow's face over with her handkerchief to hide her face from us, she being the worse for drink at the time.[53]

The constables informed Caroline that they would speak to Inspector Capon about the incident. Constable Edward Green also condemned Caroline's behaviour in his statement from 16 June.[54] Although the evidence against her appeared overwhelming, Capon did not act immediately. Instead, Caroline was placed under surveillance. Capon then visited her at home, again, underscoring his professionalism.

In his report, Capon noted 'at that time I found her in a brothel with two prostitutes' and 'directed her to attend for medical examination'.[55] Caroline went to the Chatham Lock Hospital on 22 January 1875, accompanied by her mother. Here, the contents of the Voluntary Submission Form H were purportedly explained to her, in the presence of her mother and Constable Clark.[56] Capon stressed that she signed the form, after acknowledging that she understood its contents. She then saw the visiting inspecting surgeon, Dr Jardine. Caroline informed him that she was menstruating. He postponed the inspection and issued Caroline with a Form J, which covered routine matters like this, and she was required to return a week later.[57] Speaking to the Select Committee, Dr Jardine indicated that such excuses were common and highlighted the difficulties of separating genuine cases from attempts to delay inspections, especially if the women were diseased.[58]

All of the above appeared to go against Caroline. Several members of the CDA constabulary alleged that she regularly associated with prostitutes and their clients. Suspicions about her conduct dated back several years. Despite considerable provocation, Inspector Capon appears to have behaved in a manner that was commensurate with his social standing. The medical staff and the constables also appear to have followed due process. Suspicions about why their statements were made on the same day and contained similar language might be mitigated by the fact that Caroline was discussed at a public repeal meeting, the evening before. At this event, 'both of the doctors' names were mentioned 'on the platform'.[59] This may have prompted the officials to close ranks, in anticipation of a gathering storm.

III

The repeal campaigners launched a three-pronged attack on the administration of the CDA at Chatham. First, they refused to accept that Caroline was guilty because she socialized with prostitutes.[60] In actuality, the term 'prostitute' was not easily defined in law.[61] Prostitutes were regarded in 'terms of being' as well as in 'terms of acting'.[62] The Vagrancy Act 1822 was meant to address this dichotomy by categorizing 'prostitutes' as 'offenders' for the first time.[63] The law was updated in 1824 and afterwards, prostitutes faced imprisonment for 'riotous or indecent behaviour'.[64] David Minto has noted:

> Although buying and selling sex were not in themselves illegal, the law did target the circumstances of prostitution, and if it stopped short of prohibiting the transaction, the effect was still to criminalize those who offered the service. By applying the label 'common prostitute' the law implied that such women were degraded, self-evidently, and an affront to moral citizens.[65]

The 1824 Act only partly resolved the problem, since the sanctions targeted behaviour beyond social norms in a rather ambiguous manner, without clearly defining the social subgroup that it affected. Susan Mumm observed that 'many fallen women were prostitutes, but the category also encompassed groups other than sexual deviants: female thieves, tramps, alcoholics' and the 'feeble-minded'.[66]

In short, late Victorian society was unable to establish a solid definition for women who solicited sex for money. In a second line of defence, the repealers refused to accept that Caroline was involved in prostitution because of where she lived. They accepted that the Wybrow's garret was in 'a very poor vicinity, and in very poor lodgings'. However, they argued that the pair had no 'control over the reception of tenants in other parts of the house'.[67] The Wybrow's accommodation reflected the distressed state of many similar makeshift households. Caroline's mother, Rachel, earned her living through nursing and char-work. Caroline was also employed as a cleaner and sometimes as a field labourer. For quite some time, the pair received 'out-door-relief' of '1s. a week and some bread'. Wheeler agreed that they 'were in extremely poor circumstances'.[68] Although Caroline was found in a room belonging to a prostitute, he argued that it was situated on the floor beneath the Wybrow's apartment. Moreover, he emphasized that Caroline was engaged in 'scrubbing' for the woman and was not involved in any illicit activities.[69] Wheeler's explanation seems plausible enough, when considered alongside remarks made by scholars Judith and Daniel Walkowitz. They noted:

In at least two South England dock towns … women accused of being 'common prostitutes' left a record of protest against the Contagious Diseases Acts … They were no dehumanized vagabonds, but rather poor women trying to survive in bustling dock towns that offered them limited employment opportunities.[70]

The dividing line between the proper enforcement of the CDA and their over-policing was extremely fine. Wrong decisions could have tragic consequences for vulnerable individuals. In 1881, Shaen was questioned by the Select Committee about Mrs Percy, a widowed professional music hall singer, who lived with her three children in Aldershot. She was instructed to attend the town's examining centre, with her sixteen-year-old daughter, in March 1875. Shortly afterwards, she was dismissed from her job. Later, her body was recovered from the canal. At the inquest, witnesses testified to the family's good character and the jury returned an open verdict.[71] In March 1881, the Kentish press reported that seventeen-year-old servant girl Elizabeth Burley was confronted by two CDA constables in Dover. Orphaned at a young age, Burley spent her formative years in the workhouse. She had been out of situation for about three weeks, when she was stopped. Burley fled from the officers, but they pursued her through the town's streets. She eventually made her way to the docks and threw herself into the water. The police supposedly left the scene, without attempting her rescue. Thanks to passers-by, she was saved from a watery grave.[72]

As well as claiming that Caroline was wrongfully accused of prostitution, the repealers also challenged her treatment at the Lock Hospital. She kept her second appointment with Dr Jardine on 29 January 1875. However, Jardine stated that once inside his surgery, she refused to allow the examination to proceed. After receiving Capon's assurance that Caroline was a prostitute, Jardine admitted her into the hospital on Form L. This sanctioned the compulsory confinement of women who were thought to be 'diseased'. Jardine later said that he had to do this to determine the true state of Caroline's health.[73] Shaen and Wheeler were unhappy with his judgement. In their estimation, Caroline signed the Form H under duress, believing that she faced imprisonment if she refused. Consequently, Shaen and Wheeler argued that Jardine had misinterpreted the law and overreached his authority. In their eyes, a magistrate should have settled the inspection dispute, since they contended that Caroline's detention in the Lock Hospital amounted to false imprisonment.[74]

Undoubtedly, Shaen and Wheeler wanted to wrong-foot the CDA administrators. Walkowitz argued that the NARCD's executive board was made up of a 'small clique of freethinkers and Unitarians' who were mostly unsuited to increasing popular support for the organization in London and other parts of the country. She also noted that even in good years 'most branches rarely had more than a handful of subscribers'.[75] However, research carried out for this chapter suggests that its footprint was much larger. In fact, the organization was part of a wider movement that operated at a local, national and trans-national level.[76]

Wheeler heard about Caroline's experience, soon after she left the Lock Hospital. However, he did not speak to the Wybrows until 17 May 1875. The 1882 Select Committee was curious about this delay and also why Caroline waited until 30 November to make her statutory declaration.[77] Wheeler explained that he had been occupied with business and that he had spent a lot of time sifting through and investigating the various statements before officially raising his complaint.[78] Consequently, a year passed between Caroline's brief detention and the moment when Shaen's opening salvo landed on the Home Secretary's desk. His chief objections were that Caroline had been falsely accused of prostitution and wrongfully 'imprisoned'. Alongside these were numerous 'subsidiary allegations'.[79] In brief, these claimed that Caroline was:

> put upon 'tea diet' for six days; that to cover her illegal detention, an untrue statement was put on the diet sheet over her bed and that when having at length submitted to the examination, and being found 'not guilty' she was still imprisoned until the next day.[80]

Caroline also said that she had fallen from the 'donkey' or inspection table when she was examined on 5 February. It was alleged that afterwards, Miss Webb, the Lady Superintendent, or matron of the Lock Hospital offered Caroline inducements of food, clothing and money and promised her employment, to secure her silence.[81] It seems that the repealers wanted the CDA administrators embroiled in a public, protracted and messy investigation. The alternative was to capitulate, yet this route was also risky because the floodgates may have opened to other claimants with grievances to air. Repealers used a similar approach with great success in Southampton, Plymouth and Devonport during the early 1870s. Here, women accused of prostitution were encouraged to protest their innocence in the local law courts.[82] It will be remembered that this option was unavailable to Caroline, because her case was not heard by a magistrate. Further evidence of the NARCDA's competence can be seen from how it altered its response to CDA legislation over time. Speaking to the Select Committee on 6 July 1881, Shaen noted:

> In the early days we rather searched for cases in order to ascertain the workings of the Acts; of late years we have ceased to do that, and have only gone into cases that have been forced on our attention.[83]

Consequently, Shaen bypassed the usual bureaucratic avenues and appealed directly to the Home Secretary. Thus, he drew the corridors of Westminster into a high-stakes game of brinkmanship. The Hon. Adolphus Liddell replied to Shaen, on behalf of the Secretary of State for the Home Department, on 5 February (erroneously dated 5 January) 1876. His letter was brief and to the point, simply confirming that Shaen's allegations would be properly investigated. Liddell referred the matter to Assistant Chief Constable Captain William Harris. On 15 February 1876, Harris sent Liddell the constabulary and medical staff reports. In his accompanying letter, he reiterated that Caroline 'was the constant companion of prostitutes and soldiers [and] a frequenter of brothels'. At this early stage, it seems that Harris had already thrown his lot in with his officers. The documents were forwarded to Shaen on 22 February.[84] Given his connection with Wheeler through the repeal movement, it is probable that he was already familiar with their contents. Shaen waited until 20 April 1876, before responding. He renewed his outrage at Caroline's treatment and the administration of the CDA in general. He also detailed a number of inconsistencies between the various statements. For instance, according to Capon's testimony, Constable Clark was present when Caroline signed the 'submission form'. Yet this detail was absent from Clark's statement. Shane also identified conflicts within the different accounts of the examination that Caroline received prior to her discharge.[85] Summing up, he noted:

> In examining these reports and statements, it is important to bear in mind that they are not the result of anything like a judicial investigation, but that they are the prepared *ex parte* pleas of the persons charged with an abuse of official authority, that no precaution seems to have been taken to prevent the police and doctors presenting a concerted story.[86]

Given Harris' earlier comments, it is easy to appreciate why Shaen expected an independent investigation. For historians, the task of separating the facts from the rhetoric is aggravated by the passage of time and the availability of source documents. Catherine Lee experienced similar problems when trying to substantiate whether women were coerced into signing submission forms to avoid court appearances and imprisonment. She noted 'since these alleged incidents were on most occasions a matter of one person's word against another, it is difficult from the surviving evidence to evaluate the validity of the claims'.[87] Lee concluded that:

> the Kentish evidence suggests that for the most part the policing of the Acts was not carried out with excessive zeal or brutality, but by a small number of officers with heavy workloads who adhered to administrative procedure and worked in collaboration with local police forces.[88]

This explanation, however, is not entirely compatible with Caroline's experience with the CDA authorities. The key to this and similar incidents may be embedded in records, which thus far have not been discussed in great detail. The technique of record linkage can help to unlock their potential and explain why the CDA constabulary and medical staff showed such an interest in individuals like Caroline.

IV

In line with his colleagues, Constable Green wrote his declaration on 16 June 1876. He stated:

> I have known her for about three years, during which time I have frequently seen her in company with different soldiers, and she is the constant associate of prostitutes and a frequenter of brothels. I reported this woman's conduct to late Inspector Langstone, and he went to her residence to speak to her, but I am not certain whether he saw her or not.[89]

Several things are clear from the above. First, that Green raised concerns about Caroline's behaviour, without saying outright that she was a prostitute. Second, that he had previously referred her conduct to his immediate superior. Without collaborating evidence, it is difficult to ascertain whether this was true or intended to add gravitas to his statement. However, a report from 1874 highlights how 'one hundred and nineteen young girls … between the ages of 12 and 18, and 123 women between the ages of 18 and 30, and 12 above that age, who have been found in bad company and improper places, have been rescued'.[90] For illustrative purposes, the figures were supported with anecdotal evidence from CDA districts like Chatham:

> On the 2nd January 1874, Eliza … aged 19, of 11 … Street, Chatham, had left her home, and was subsequently found in the company of prostitutes and soldiers, by police constable (106) William Verrier. The constable pointed out the consequences of her remaining in such company, whereupon she consented to return to her home, and her mother expressed her thanks for having saved her child from ruin.[91]

Setting aside the report's melodramatic tone, two things are immediately clear. First, that the CDA authorities protected Eliza's true identity. Second, that Constable Verrier's intervention was intended to warn her about the risks of prostitution. There are strong similarities between this episode and Caroline's multiple experiences with the Metropolitan constables. Clearly, she did not heed any of the reprimands that she received. Records from 1871 suggest that Green had patrolled the town's streets for at least four years, prior to Caroline's detention. Therefore, he would have known that prostitutes often mixed with the more 'respectable' inhabitants who lived in the town's poorer districts.[92] Evidently, something else about Caroline's situation unsettled him. Perhaps, he knew from experience that young girls like her could easily descend into prostitution? Remember, he was first acquainted with Caroline when she was just fourteen or fifteen, which might explain his sense of ire towards her friends and associates. Although desperation was often a significant causal factor, many females were also lured into prostitution because it promised them a better life than they would otherwise have enjoyed.[93]

At this time, authority figures were increasingly concerned about juveniles who might be susceptible to grooming.[94] Inspector Silas Rendel Anniss was responsible for policing the CDA in Plymouth, Devonport and Dartmouth. He was questioned closely about this issue during the 1881 Select Committee sessions.[95] He observed that if:

> young girls are left alone, they are sure to induce others to do the same, so that the number would be speedily increased. A young girl becoming a prostitute under 15 or 16, or up to 17 years of age, if she is left alone, will be sure to get others to accompany her in her mode of life ... I have had to bring a girl on my books at 14 [4 April 1880], and she had been the cause of leading nearly a dozen into vice.[96]

Anniss described the girls as 'decoys'.[97] Catherine Lee suggested that Anniss had a long-standing reputation within the repeal movement for using 'cruel methods' to enforce the CDA, whilst Judith Walkowitz accused Anniss of outright misogyny.[98] In fairness, Walkowitz also admitted that he had a talent for 'espionage and surveillance work'. Moreover, she accepted that his career was never blighted by accusations of 'bribery or official corruption'.[99] Even so, Anniss appeared to be an informed and credible witness, who coped well with the pressures of the witness stand. His reputation is further reappraised by the testimony of the Rev. Prebendary Charles Thomas Wilkinson, DD, who also spoke to the 1881 Select Committee; Wilkinson was a senior clergyman at Exeter Cathedral and had also been Vicar of St. Andrew's Church Plymouth for twelve years. He knew Anniss well, both as a member of his congregation and through his work with reclamation and rescue societies. Wilkinson thought that Anniss' character combined 'kindness with firmness'. Wilkinson also served on the committee of a female penitentiary. In 1880, he helped to establish the 'Friendless Girls Association'. He played an active role in the latter, acting as the committee's vice-president and chairman.[100] Susan Mumm has noted that schemes like this were established in towns and cities across

Britain during the nineteenth century. Their purpose was to rehabilitate large numbers of 'fallen women'. Mumm argued that 'in 1840 there was space for 400 women in Church of England penitentiaries, but by 1893 more than 7,000 women could be accommodated each year, primarily in institutions run by Anglican nuns'.[101] Wilkinson described Anniss' work with his organization:

> He has brought girls under my observation. I am speaking of acts done within the last two or three years. More than that, he has come to me even so late as 10 o'clock at night to ask me to go and see dying girls, and within the last three months I have, as a clergyman, been visiting one of those girls whom Inspector Anniss brought under my notice.[102]

There was a small female refuge like this at Chatham, when Caroline was held at the Lock Hospital. It had room for twelve or thirteen girls and was supported by the local townsfolk through a subscription scheme. The aforementioned Adam Stigant, chairman of Chatham's Board of Guardians and Local Health Board, contributed to its upkeep. It was run separately from the CDA. Stigant was questioned by the 1881 Select Committee about the refuge and more widely about the town's reclamation scheme. He thought that one of the benefits of the CDA was that they brought prostitutes into contact with 'good men and women' who wanted to help them to rehabilitate.[103] When asked about these individuals, he replied:

> The matron of the Chatham Lock Hospital is a very good woman, and then there is the chaplain … the ladies of the garrison have exerted themselves; the wives of the commandant and others; they have visited these girls, and talked to them, and it is my conviction that that influence has been for good.[104]

Stigant was talking about Miss Mary Ann Webb, the matron of the Lock Hospital – the same woman who supposedly tried to bribe Caroline. Webb was a native of Chatham. Her career at the Lock Hospital began in 1870. Like the other officials, she made a statement about her contact with Caroline at the Lock Hospital on 16 June 1876. She also responded more directly to Caroline's allegations before the 1882 Select Committee. As before, there is insufficient space within the remainder of this chapter to discuss this evidence in great detail. However, several key points drawn from both testimonies shed further light on this case and also raise questions about Caroline's credibility as a witness. For instance, to counter suggestions that she was a prostitute, Caroline claimed that she worked in a crockery-ware shop in the Brook. Prudently, Miss Webb checked this story with the shop's owner, Miss Randall. It transpired that Caroline was actually employed 'to wash the doorstep, on account of her not being in a fit condition to enter the house' because she was 'infected with vermin'.[105] Caroline also said that she was made to wear 'prison clothes' at the Lock Hospital and that her discharge was delayed, even after it was established that she was not infected. Again, Miss Webb quashed both allegations with plausible explanations. In her 1876 statement, she said that Caroline was given hospital attire because 'her own clothing was so infected with vermin' it had to be placed in 'disinfecting fluid'.[106] Webb showed the 1882 Committee a sample of the hospital uniform to prove that it was not substandard. She agreed that Caroline had been discharged late from the hospital. However, she reasoned that this was because Caroline's clothes were still drying and because she waited for her mother to collect her.[107]

Miss Webb also unpicked the more serious allegations relating to the food and money bribes. Caroline was placed on a 'tea diet' by Dr Weld after she refused to be examined. Miss Webb was informed of this later in the day, when she was in 'sole charge' of the institution. In an evident act of kindness, she sent Caroline a portion of her own food, instructing the nurse to emphasize that she was not undermining the doctor's instructions. As a cautionary measure, she informed the doctor about her actions the following day. Miss Webb also did not dispute that both Caroline and Rachel received small sums of money. However, she denied that any impropriety was involved. Instead, she noted that Mrs Wybrow spoke to Mrs Adamson, the nurse in charge of No. 3 Ward, when she visited Caroline in hospital. Before she knew her identity, Mrs Adamson gave Rachel '6d. out of charity' after she complained that she was 'very poor' and that she had not eaten for three days. Furthermore, Caroline was also given 6d. in compensation for a scarf which was mysteriously missing from her possessions when she left the hospital.[108]

Miss Webb's meticulous responses to Caroline's accusations contrast sharply with the evidence provided by the constabulary. Her responses were sufficiently detailed to allow any interested parties to conduct further enquiries, suggesting that she had little to hide. In keeping with Stigant's comments, she seems to have been genuinely concerned about the well-being of those under her care. Additionally, she put Caroline in touch with Mrs Carr, the owner of a servants' registry office. Through this contact, Caroline secured domestic work after her discharge. Miss Webb paid Caroline 5s. to incentivize her to keep this position. She promised her another 5s. if she stayed for three months 'and if a twelvemonth, 10s. more'.[109] Sadly, Caroline was dismissed after a few days when her new employer complained about her character.[110] Suggestions that Miss Webb's altruism was linked to self-interest seem to be misguided. Her business arrangement with Carr predated her acquaintance with Caroline by several months.[111] Wheeler was clearly embarrassed when the 1882 Committee observed that the alleged 'hush money':

> was taken from a fund placed at Miss Webb's disposal by private charitable persons, by means of which she has for many years been able to assist numbers of young women to get into service.[112]

Discussing this reclamation scheme, Miss Webb noted that aside from the official cases, she dealt with 'a great many' more privately.[113] Again, this goes against Lee's suggestion that CDA administrators always strictly adhered to official policies.[114] Based on this dialogue, an abstract of the number of patients who were admitted to the

Table 3.1 Paper handed in by Miss Webb, 9 June 1882. Number of admissions of patients, reforms, &c., at the Lock Hospital, Chatham, from 1 January 1871 to 31 December 1880

	1871	1872	1873	1874	1875	1876	1877	1878	1879	1880
No. of cases admitted	570	710	663	504	408	436	572	483	476	526
No. of individuals	351	362	374	345	300	270	347	285	269	208
No. of reforms, viz										
To homes	39	11	21	17	16	15	10	16	17	30
To friends	27	38	55	30	20	30	27	35	56	47

Source: Data derived from Parliamentary Papers, *Report from the Select Committee on Contagious Diseases Acts*, Cmd. 340 (1882), 'Appendix, No. 25', p. 600.

Chatham Lock Hospital between 1 January 1871 and 31 December 1880 was included in the 1882 report (see Table 3.1).

This shows that around 16 per cent of women passed through the institution's official rescue scheme in 1874, the year before Caroline's detention, more than two-thirds of which were placed with friends. The remainder went into the sort of homes described by Susan Mumm. Miss Webb recognized that some of these placements were unsuccessful and that females sometimes returned to the streets several times afterwards.[115] Individuals with alcohol or other addictions were particularly vulnerable.[116] The number of rescued women dropped to around 12 per cent in 1875.[117] Whether this lull was in any way due to the repealers' investigation is questionable. However, the numbers either side of this period indicate that Caroline's experience was really not so unique. Certainly, she received warnings and assistance in equal measure. Both appear to have been part of a wider tapestry of official and unofficial mechanisms that the authorities used in CDA towns like Chatham to steer young girls away from prostitution.

The investigation into Caroline's alleged mistreatment was co-ordinated by Mr W.H. Sloggett, the inspector of Certified Hospitals. He sent his report to the Secretary of State for War on 21 June 1876. Sloggett accepted the police officer's claims that Caroline had 'for a considerable period of time' consorted with 'registered prostitutes and private soldiers in brothels and on the lines at Chatham'. Referring to the hospital records, he also pointed out that Caroline spent no longer than one day on the 'tea diet', rather than the six that she had alleged in her statement.[118] Miss Webb was also completely exonerated. In the process, Sloggett raised grave doubts about Caroline's truthfulness and by extension her character. The subtext of this decision was that the constabulary and Miss Webb should carry on as before.

However, Sloggett was unwilling to preside over a whitewash. The medical team was criticized over several procedural irregularities. First, that Caroline was wrongfully detained on Form L. Instead, Sloggett agreed with Shaen that she should 'have been summoned before the magistrates' the moment that she refused to undergo the inspection. He also emphasized that Dr Weld exceeded his authority when he placed

Caroline on the 'tea diet' for her misconduct towards him 'in the wards'. It was accepted that Dr Weld had probably done this to save her 'from the alternative and legal measure of getting her sent to gaol'.[119] Dr Weld and Dr Jardine were reminded of these policies in a letter that was posted from the War Office on 5 July 1876. Mr Sloggett also recommended that all 'visiting surgeons under the Acts' should be informed that the War Office should receive copies of all 'official communications in reference to their duties'.[120] Clearly, this measure was intended to close any administrative loopholes and prevent similar occurrences. At a stroke, the central authorities, on paper at least, exercised greater oversight over the administration of the CDA in the subjected districts. Yet Catherine Lee has observed that the vast majority of prosecutions for non-compliance in Kent occurred in the five years immediately after the introduction of the 1869 Act.[121] This suggests that this particular episode did not result in a drastic upturn in recalcitrant prostitutes refusing examinations or, for that matter, officials asserting their authority through the courts.

Thus, this brief but significant interlude in Caroline's life drew to a close. Within a year she married a soldier.[122] She moved frequently with her husband's regiment throughout southern England and Ireland. By 1881, she had returned to Chatham with her family. It settled back into the lodging house that she had previously shared with her mother in Seaton Court. The prostitutes Kate Simmonds, Elizabeth Coppin and Alice Gilbert, who first prompted the constabulary's interest in Caroline, still resided at the address. However, one final question mark hung over Caroline's character.[123] On 20 April 1883, the Judge Advocate General besmirched her reputation during a Parliamentary debate on the CDA. He noted: 'from what I have lately heard of the subsequent career of that girl, I am not disposed to place much reliance on her story'.[124]

V

This chapter placed the micro-history of Caroline Wybrow's detention in the Chatham Lock Hospital in the context of the wider literature on the administration of the CDA. It examined the case from three different perspectives. First, that Chatham was included in the initial wave of subjected districts to prevent the spread of venereal disease amongst the large numbers of servicemen who were stationed in the region. The town had a long-standing problem with vice. This was linked to the military and naval installations but was also aggravated by the region's burgeoning male-dominated industrial sector. In contrast, female employment opportunities were less secure and largely confined to poorly paid and often seasonal occupations like domestic service. Rachel and Caroline's experience typified the difficulties that many poor women in this region faced, particularly in households without a male breadwinner. The Wybrows lived in low-grade accommodation along with the debris of society. Additionally, their earnings were irregular and required topping up from other sources, including poor relief and charitable donations. For many women, as a result, prostitution offered respite from their desperate situation.

The second part of this study considered Caroline's brush with the authorities from the repealers' perspective. Initially, the incident attracted little public attention. The case only gained momentum once Shaen and Wheeler were on-board. Both were seasoned campaigners and formidable opponents of the CDA. Unlike Caroline, they were well connected and capable of mounting an extremely effective campaign in the face of considerable opposition. They identified and exploited inconsistencies in the application of the law. In contrast to Walkowitz's findings, they also managed to pitch the central authorities against the local CDA officials.

The final part of this survey used record linkage to build considerably on the work of Walkowitz, Joyce and Lee, particularly in relation to the role that reclamation schemes played in the administration of the CDA at Chatham and in other subjected districts. It highlighted how Caroline was counselled and warned by the constabulary and Lock Hospital staff over a period of several years about her contact with prostitutes. This guidance was part of an informal culture that sat alongside the more regular mechanisms of the CDA. Officials used these along with their local knowledge and professional expertise to warn young girls about the perils of prostitution and to assist vulnerable individuals. In most cases, they were not trying to persecute but rather were working within the confines of the law to save these girls from a life of further degradation. Even so, Caroline's experience, as well as the testimonies of Anniss, Webb and Dr Weld, indicate that their efforts met with mixed success. Yet, if they had not intervened, countless numbers of susceptible young females may have fallen more completely under the compass of the CDA much sooner.

Micro-histories like this are important because they survey the historical terrain from a novel standpoint. Caroline's experience encourages historians to regard the management of the CDA within a binary framework of formal and informal mechanisms. This is further illustrated by the aggregate of cases dealt with by Miss Webb and the Rev. Wilkinson, as well as the constabulary narratives in the Assistant Commissioner's Reports. Therefore, the present study goes far beyond crude suggestions that the Acts were blunt instruments, which had limited impact on how prostitution was controlled during the second half of the nineteenth century.

Finally, this chapter has also highlighted how record linkage and micro-histories can greatly improve what is known about the administration of the CDA at Chatham. Future studies could draw on such techniques and methodologies more comprehensively to compare and contrast the interplay between the formal and informal apparatus of the Acts across a greater number of subjected districts. In this respect, micro-histories like Caroline's have a significant role to play. Not least, because they help to explain the probable motives and causes behind the actions of particular individuals and/or events. In this respect, they provide the human dimension that is often missing from quantitative-based research. The last word belongs to Caroline. Undoubtedly, she was extremely spirited and in all likelihood provoked authority figures with her insolence and the company that she kept. She was also shown to be an unreliable witness. For this, she was partly responsible for setting in motion the events described above. Whether this is sufficient evidence to link her to prostitution in this instance is left to the reader to decide.

Notes

1. A.W. Ager (2014) *Crime and Poverty in Nineteenth Century England: The Economy of Makeshifts* (London: Bloomsbury), p. 19 and M. Hamilton (1978) 'Opposition to the Contagious Diseases Acts, 1865–86', *Albion: A Quarterly Journal Concerned with British Studies*, Vol. 10, No. 1, pp. 14–27.

2. The author would like to extend his thanks to K. McGivern and M. Harrall-Ager for reading an early draft of this chapter.

3. J.R. Walkowitz (1999) *Prostitution and Victorian Society: Women, Class, and the State* (Cambridge: Cambridge University Press), p. 2.

4. S.A. Slater (2010) 'Containment: Managing Street Prostitution in London, 1918–59', *Journal of British Studies*, Vol. 49, No. 2, pp. 332–57.

5. M. Luddy (2008) *Prostitution and Irish Society, 180–1940* (Cambridge: Cambridge University Press) and D. Minto (2014) 'Review of *Common Prostitutes and Ordinary Citizens: Commercial Sex in London, 1885–1960* by Julia Laite', *The Journal of the Historical Association*, Vol. 99, No. 335, pp. 347–9.

6. Hamilton, 'Opposition to the Contagious Diseases Acts', p. 19.

7. B. Joyce (1999) *The Chatham Scandal: A History of Medway's Prostitution in the Late Nineteenth Century* (Rochester: Baggins Book Bazaar/Bruce Aubry), *passim*.

8. C. Lee (2013) *Policing Prostitution* (London: Pickering & Chatto Publishers Ltd.).

9. Ibid., p. 134.

10. Ibid., p. 5.

11. Parliamentary Papers, *Annual Report of Assistant Commissioner of Police of Metropolis on Operation of Contagious Disease Acts*, Cmd. 351 (1881) p. 14. See also, Joyce, *The Chatham Scandal*, p. 79.

12. Ager, *Crime and Poverty*, p. 120.

13. Ibid., pp. 47 and 127.

14. Parliamentary Papers, *Report from the Select Committee on the Contagious Diseases Acts*, Cmd. 351 (1881), p. 301.

15. Ibid., p. 310.

16. Parliamentary Papers, *Report from the Select Committee on Contagious Diseases Acts* Cmd. 340 (1882), p. 101.

17. Walkowitz, *Prostitution and Victorian Society*, pp. 92–3.

18. Ibid., p. 2.

19. Parliamentary Papers, *Report from the Select Committee on Contagious Diseases Acts* (1882), p. 556.

20. Ibid., p. 556.

21. Ibid., p. 43 and Parliamentary Papers, *Annual Report of Assistant Commissioner of Police of Metropolis on Operation of Contagious Disease Acts*, p. 14.

22. Parliamentary Papers, *Report from the Select Committee on Contagious Diseases Acts* (1882), p. 43 and Parliamentary Papers, *Annual Report of Assistant Commissioner of Police of Metropolis on Operation of Contagious Disease Acts*, p. 14.

23. Walkowitz, *Prostitution and Victorian Society*, pp. 100–1 and *The Morning Post*, 21 August 1866, Issue 28921, p. 6.

24. Parliamentary Papers, *Report from the Select Committee on Contagious Diseases Acts* (1882), p. 556.

25. Parliamentary Papers, *Report of Royal Commission upon the Administration and Operation of the Contagious Diseases Acts. Vol. 1 – The Report*, Cmd. 408–10 (1871), p. 3.

26. F.B. Smith (1990) 'The Contagious Diseases Acts Reconsidered', *Social History of Medicine*, Vol. 3, No. 2, pp. 197–215, at p. 197.

27. Walkowitz, *Prostitution and Victorian Society*, p. 12.

28. Parliamentary Papers, *Report of Royal Commission upon the Administration and Operation of the Contagious Diseases Acts. Vol. 1 – The Report*, p. 4.

29. Ager, *Crime and Poverty*, p. 12.

30. Ibid., pp. 13–15.

31. Ibid. and Parliamentary Papers, *Report from the Select Committee on Contagious Diseases Acts* (1882), p. 52.

32. F.M.L. Thompson (1963) *English Landed Society in the Nineteenth Century* (London: Routledge & Kegan Paul Ltd.), p. 16.

33. Walkowitz, *Prostitution and Victorian Society*, pp. 21–2 and Ager, *Crime and Poverty*, pp. 80–1.

34. Joyce, *The Chatham Scandal*, p. 9.

35. Ibid.

36. Ager, *Crime and Poverty*, pp. 84 and 124.

37. Ibid., pp. 84 and 121–6.

38. Joyce, *The Chatham Scandal*, pp. 9 and 188.

39. Lee, *Policing Prostitution*, p. 136 and Walkowitz, *Prostitution and Victorian Society*, pp. 164 and 173.

40. Joyce, *The Chatham Scandal*, pp. 68–9.

41. Parliamentary Papers, *Report from the Select Committee on Contagious Diseases Acts* (1882), p. 561.

42. Ibid., p. 65.

43. Parliamentary Papers, *Report from the Select Committee on the Contagious Diseases Acts* (1881), p. 229.

44. Joyce, *The Chatham Scandal*, p. 8.

45. Parliamentary Papers, *Report from the Select Committee on Contagious Diseases Acts* (1882), pp. 46 and 48.

46. Parliamentary Papers, *Report from the Select Committee on the Contagious Diseases Acts* (1881), pp. 251 and 256.

47. Ibid., p. 251.

48. Parliamentary Papers, *Report from the Select Committee on Contagious Diseases Acts* (1882), pp. 7 and 17–18.

49. Lee, *Policing Prostitution*, p. 183.

50. J.R. Walkowitz and D.J. Walkowitz (1973) '"We Are Not Beasts of the Field": Prostitution and the Poor in Plymouth and Southampton under the Contagious Diseases Acts', *Feminist Studies*, Vol. 1, No. 3/4, pp. 73–106 at pp. 73–4. See also T. Crook (2008) 'Accommodating the Outcast: Common Lodging Houses and the Limits of Urban Governance in Victorian and Edwardian London', *Urban History*, Vol. 35, No. 3, pp. 414–36.

51. Walkowitz, *Prostitution and Victorian Society*, pp. 192–213.

52. Parliamentary Papers, *Report from the Select Committee on Contagious Diseases Acts* (1882), p. 560.

53. Ibid., p. 560.

54. Ibid.

55. Ibid.

56. Form H specified that the patient voluntarily agreed to 'periodic examinations' under the terms of the CDA – see ibid., p. 565.

57. Ibid., pp. 560–1.

58. Parliamentary Papers, *Report from the Select Committee on Contagious Diseases Acts* (1882), pp. 396–7 and Parliamentary Papers, *Report from the Select Committee on the Contagious Diseases Acts* (1881), p. 488.

59. Parliamentary Papers, *Report from the Select Committee on Contagious Diseases Acts* (1882), pp. 409–10.

60. Ibid., p. 556.

61. L.M. Agustín (2005) 'Helping Women Who Sell Sex: The Construction of Benevolent Identities', Rhizomes: Cultural Studies in Emerging Knowledge, Issue 10, available at http://www.rhizomes.net/issue10/index.html.

62. F.W. Lacey (1953) 'Vagrancy and Other Crimes of Personal Condition', Harvard Law Review, Vol. 66, No. 7, pp. 1203–26, at p. 1204.

63. Agustín, 'Helping Women Who Sell Sex', p. 17.

64. A.J. Engel (1979) '"Immoral Intentions": The University of Oxford and the Problem of Prostitution, 1827–1914', *Victorian Studies*, Vol. 23, No. 1, pp. 79–107, at p. 80.

65. Minto, 'Review of *Common Prostitutes*', p. 347.

66. S. Mumm (1996) '"Not Worse than Other Girls": The Convent-based Rehabilitation of Fallen Women in Victorian Britain', *Journal of Social History*, Vol. 29, No. 3, pp. 527–47, at p. 527.

67. Parliamentary Papers, *Report from the Select Committee on Contagious Diseases Acts* (1882), p. 52.

68. Ibid., p. 52.

69. Ibid., p. 53.

70. Walkowitz and Walkowitz, 'We Are Not Beasts of the Field', p. 74.

71. Parliamentary Papers, *Report from the Select Committee on the Contagious Diseases Acts* (1881), pp. 333–6.

72. Ibid., p. 337.

73. Parliamentary Papers, *Report from the Select Committee on Contagious Diseases Acts* (1882), pp. 560–1.

74. Ibid., p. 562.

75. Walkowitz, *Prostitution and Victorian Society*, pp. 92–3.

76. Parliamentary Papers, *Report from the Select Committee on Contagious Diseases Acts* (1882), p. 52; Parliamentary Papers, *Report from the Select Committee on the Contagious Diseases Acts* (1881), p. 302 and *The Shield*, 8 April 1876, Issue 255/46, p. 113.

77. Parliamentary Papers, *Report from the Select Committee on Contagious Diseases Acts* (1882), p. 65.

78. Ibid.

79. Ibid., p. 562.

80. Ibid.

81. Ibid., pp. 555–9.

82. Walkowitz and Walkowitz, 'We Are Not Beasts of the Field', *passim*.

83. Parliamentary Papers, *Report from the Select Committee on the Contagious Diseases Acts* (1881), p. 317.

84. Parliamentary Papers, *Report from the Select Committee on Contagious Diseases Acts* (1882), p. 556 and Walkowitz, *Prostitution and Victorian Society*, pp. 559–60.

85. Ibid., pp. 556 and 562 respectively.

86. Ibid., pp. 556 and 562–3 respectively.

87. Lee, *Policing Prostitution*, p. 151.

88. Ibid., p. 160.

89. Parliamentary Papers, *Report from the Select Committee on Contagious Diseases Acts* (1882), p. 560.

90. Parliamentary Papers, *Contagious Diseases Acts: Copy of Annual Report, for 1874, of Captain Harris, Assistant Commissioner of Police of the Metropolis, on the Operation of the Contagious Diseases Acts*, Cmd. 97 (1875), p. 2.

91. Ibid., pp. 2–3.

92. Parliamentary Papers, *Report of Royal Commission upon the Administration and Operation of the Contagious Diseases Acts. Vol. 1 – The Report*, p. 798.

93. Walkowitz and Walkowitz, 'We Are Not Beasts of the Field', pp. 81–3.

94. Anniss categorized juvenile prostitutes as being below the age of 21. However, evidence provided by Miss Mary Ann Webb to the 1882 Committee suggests that children as young as 'eight, nine, and ten years old' passed through reclamation organizations in London. Moreover, she highlighted how girls regularly pretended to be older than their actual age, thus casting doubt on the reliability of the statistics. See Parliamentary Papers, *Report from the Select Committee on the Contagious Diseases Acts* (1881), pp. 189–91 and Parliamentary Papers, *Report from the Select Committee on Contagious Diseases Acts* (1882), p. 413.

95. Parliamentary Papers, *Report from the Select Committee on the Contagious Diseases Acts* (1881), p. 189.

96. Ibid., p. 187.

97. Ibid., p. 159.

98. Lee, *Policing Prostitution*, p. 136.

99. Walkowitz, *Prostitution and Victorian Society*, pp. 81 and 163.

100. Parliamentary Papers, *Report from the Select Committee on the Contagious Diseases Acts* (1881), pp. 127–9.

101. Mumm, 'Not Worse than Other Girls', p. 528.

102. Parliamentary Papers, *Report from the Select Committee on the Contagious Diseases Acts* (1881), p. 229.

103. Ibid., p. 257.

104. Ibid., p. 258.

105. Parliamentary Papers, *Report from the Select Committee on Contagious Diseases Acts* (1882), pp. 408–9.

106. Ibid., p. 566.

107. Ibid., p. 410.

108. Ibid., pp. 128 and 566–7.

109. Ibid., pp. 566–7.

110. Ibid.

111. Ibid., pp. 409 and 566–7.

112. Ibid., p. 66.

113. Ibid., pp. 408–16.

114. Lee, *Policing Prostitution*, p. 160.

115. Parliamentary Papers, *Report from the Select Committee on Contagious Diseases Acts* (1882), p. 113.

116. Mumm, 'Not Worse than Other Girls', p. 534.

117. Parliamentary Papers, *Report from the Select Committee on Contagious Diseases Acts* (1882), p. 113.

118. Ibid., p. 568.

119. Ibid.

120. Ibid.

121. Lee, *Policing Prostitution*, p. 155.

122. Parliamentary Papers, *Report from the Select Committee on Contagious Diseases Acts* (1882), p. 54.

123. Lee, *Policing Prostitution*, p. 160.

124. House of Commons Debates, 20 April 1883, Vol. 278, cc735–859.

CHAPTER 4
THE BONNIE AND CLYDE OF THE BLACKOUT: THE SHORT CRIMINAL CAREERS OF GUSTAV HULTEN AND ELIZABETH JONES

Clifford Williamson

I

On 23 January 1945, a verdict of guilty was handed down at the Old Bailey in London to Karel Gustav Hulten and Elizabeth Marina (Maud) Jones for the murder of George Edward Heath in October 1944. Hulten and Jones had killed Heath in the pursuit of robbery. It was known at the time as 'the cleft chin murder' due to a physiological facial characteristic of Heath's. Both Hulten and Jones were figures in the *demi-monde* of wartime London; Hulten was an American deserter and Jones was a stripper. They had hooked up only shortly before and after a few previous, sometimes violent, acts of criminality, they had graduated to homicide.

The case was typical yet unusual. It was typical, as it seemed just another crime during wartime that exploited the characteristics of the blackout. But it was unusual first, in that the prosecution of Hulten was in the English courts of law rather than under the aegis of the Judge Advocate General (JAG) of the United States as was customary as a result of the 1942 *United States (Visiting Forces) Act* (VFA). It was also unusual in that after the verdict, and following an appeal for clemency to the Home Secretary, only Jones had her death sentence commuted to life.

The criminal career of both was brief but spectacular, and the case highlights a whole series of judicial, moral and diplomatic issues. First, it illuminates the sexual and gender politics of wartime; Jones was portrayed as both victim and culprit due to her sex, her age and her perceived vulnerability. The case also brought to the fore concerns about the role of deserters in criminality. However, it also highlighted aspects of the special relationship between Great Britain and the United States, as it was a unique example of the English criminal law being allowed to take precedence over the US military criminal code. We can also see in this case a foretaste of the emerging debate on the death penalty, alongside evidence of the discretionary role of the Home Secretary in appeals for clemency and its application.

Although Hulten and Jones's crime noir is in one sense a glaringly clichéd piece of pulp fiction turned fact, it is also an important and complex episode in the history of crime and punishment. As such this event really benefits from the micro-historical approach as by offering an 'intensive historical investigation' to use the words of Magnsson and

Szijártó, we can present the main advantages of this methodological approach to extract meaning from the past.[1]

First, we can discuss micro-history as a 'threefold unity of time, place and action'.[2] The period setting is the Second World War, a conflict where macro-level experience predominates in terms of human and economic cost, but where individual experience is equally valuable to examine the response of people to the unique demands of this epoch. The place is London and its suburbs – the city of the blitz, the blackout and the black market – where opportunities for crime and misbehaviour were legion. The criminal action itself is that of homicide and we are persuaded to ask precisely how are individual examples of murderous behaviour understood in an era where mass killing was commonplace?

The second aspect of micro-history addressed by this case is the 'search for answers to large questions in small places' as Joyner suggests.[3] The great historical question here is how do the circumstances of wartime shape behaviour? This is relevant since there is no doubt that the crimes of Hulten and Jones were influenced by the conflict. First, neither of them would have had the means, motive or opportunity without the special circumstances of wartime. Hulten would still have been in New England making house with his wife. Jones would arguably not have gravitated to the sleazy underworld of London's Soho, without there being the demand created by the massive number of young men in services descending on London with cash on the hip.

The third main feature identified by Magńsson and Szijártó in micro-histories is that of agency. They argued: 'For micro-historians, people who lived in the past are not merely puppets on the hands of great underlying forces of history, but they are regarded as active individuals, conscious actors.'[4] The crime perpetrated by Hulten and Jones was premeditated and this is acknowledged by the verdict at their trial that found them both guilty of murder in the first degree. For whatever reason, best known to themselves, they did what they did knowing that it was against the law. Yet they broke through the normal processes of empathy and fear of retribution to do it. It is not my intention here to offer a speculative psychological diagnosis of the motivations of both, but the issue of agency is clearly evident in this event.

Agency also becomes especially pertinent in another crucial aspect of this case and that is over the Prerogative of Mercy. Since the early nineteenth century, the Prerogative of Mercy has been a power vested in the post of the Home Secretary. Put simply, this minister has the power to decide which, if any, of the death sentences handed down by the courts in England and Wales should be enacted and which should be respited to a long-term prison sentence. It was a responsibility that was carried out purely at the discretion of the office holder; there were no official rules, no stated criteria and little guidance on the matter. It is therefore based largely on agency, and micro-history is arguably one of the best ways to illuminate the history of this prerogative and its use.

The main sources used in this chapter are derived from contemporary primary sources such as newspapers, government publications such as *Hansard* as well as a suite of secondary sources ranging from scholarly texts to popular true crime histories. A significant amount of information has been drawn from the 1953 *Royal*

Commission on Capital Punishment.[5] This reflected widely on the death penalty and, in particular, the use of the prerogative of mercy. Its sentiment and tone also fit into an era in the history of the death penalty where there was a general political consensus on retention, where voices for abolition though growing were still in the minority. Likewise, the report is primarily reflective of current practice around the operation of the death penalty at the time of the 'cleft chin murder'. It also adds personal insight to our arsenal of sources since it gathered evidence via interviews with, amongst others, senior Home Office civil servants – some retired others still in place – as well as senior politicians who had to administer the law. It therefore reflected the reality of application of the prerogative in this period. Lastly, the report has the most detailed statistical evidence that provides the basis for much of the analysis of the use of the prerogative in Section VIII.

II

In his 1945 essay 'The Decline of the English Murder' for the *Tribune* newspaper, George Orwell argued that 'it is difficult to believe that any recent English crime will be remembered so long and so intimately' as those murders and murderers 'whose reputations have stood the test of time'.[6] He was referring specifically to the 'cleft chin murder'; however, his slightly wistful nostalgia was misplaced. It has been a crime that has had considerable longevity and a dark appeal for denizens of true crime histories, the history of the home front in the Second World War and those who study all manner of aspects of criminality and deviance.

Ironically, it was Orwell himself who would rather inadvertently start the process off with his *Tribune* essay. The appeal of the murder as a late wartime *cause célèbre* would inevitably lead to others attempting to cash in. The first and in many respects the definitive account of the Hulten/Jones crime spree was by R. Alwyn Raymond, who wrote the unimaginatively titled *The Cleft Chin Murder* later on in 1945.[7] The author styled his work 'a gripping authentic account of the lives of two people, ordinary young people, brought together by chance'.[8] It is largely a narrative account written in the style of detective pulp fiction with most of the information drawn from the transcript of the trial. This format was followed by C.E. Bechofer Roberts in his edited volume *The Trial of Hulten and Jones* also from 1945.[9] After a hiatus of over forty years, interest in the case was piqued in 1989 when a motion picture appeared loosely based on the case called *Chicago Joe and the Showgirl*, but it would be in the early twenty-first century that it would be revived as both a popular and a scholarly focus of concern. Two works in 2003, Donald Thomas's *An Underworld at War* and Maureen Waller's *London 1945: Life in the Debris of War,*[10] would use the case to highlight, in the case of Thomas, aspects of criminality in wartime, and for Waller a 'prime example of a young woman being led astray and indulging in the sort of violent, immoral behaviour the war had fostered'.[11] In 2015, Edna Gammon published *A Fatal Pick Up* that is largely a verbatim transcript of the trial of Hulten and Jones.[12]

Aside from the popular histories of the murders, there have been two significant scholarly studies of the case, both published in 2013: the first by Matthew Grant in his chapter for *Moral Panics, Social Fears, and the Media: Historical Perspectives* edited by Nicolas and O'Malley and the second by Carol Dyhouse as part of her monograph *Girl Trouble*.[13] Grant characterized the importance of the case as revealing 'the process by which normative notions of family, national identity, and citizenship were established by exposing errant behaviour and juxtaposing it with established notions of "correct" conduct …'[14] He saw the case as having 'all the hallmarks of a moral panic' but that it did not escalate into one in the 'classic model' due, to the influence of the press in restraining the usual process of recrimination, since this could have undermined wartime unity by 'questioning the sexual morality and participation of a far larger number of women'.[15]

For Dyhouse the case was part of an evolving discourse about the nature of the types of deviance associated with adolescent females. The 'Good Time Girl', as she became known, was a prominent folk devil during wartime that was

'… no better than she ought to be.' She had probably had her head turned by watching too many Hollywood movies. She was likely to wear cosmetics and cheap perfume and to own a fur coat.[16]

The 'cleft chin murders', Dyhouse argued, 'brought into sharp focus' fears about young women in wartime that were to carry on into the post-war period.[17] These anxieties would culminate in a joint Magistrates Association and British Medical Association report *The Unstable Adolescent Girl* published in 1946.[18]

III

Karl Gustav Hulten was born in Stockholm, Sweden, in 1922. His mother and father separated the following year. Karl emigrated with his mother that same year to the United States, eventually settling in the less obvious location of Cambridge in Massachusetts rather than Worcester, where the bulk of New England's Swedish-Americans lived and worked.[19] This may have been due to the fact she was a single mother working as a domestic, unlike the Worcester-based diaspora recruited into the heavy manufacturing industries that dominated the city. There is no evidence of delinquency in the early life of Hulten; his mother claimed that he was not a bad boy, and he even worked for the Salvation Army.[20] He was a lorry driver by trade, married an undistinguished local girl, Rita Pero, and they had a child. Hulten was called into the armed forces in May 1942 and arrived in England in January 1944 as part of the 101 Airborne Division, which was based in Newbury in Berkshire where he served in the motor pool. Whilst in England he had occasional run-ins with the US Military Police mainly for going absent without leave.[21] In late September 1944, Hulten stole a military truck that had been parked outside Reading train station and drove off with it. Hulten eventually made his way to London where on 3 October he met, through a mutual friend, Elizabeth Maud Jones at the Black and White Café near Hampstead tube station.[22]

Of the two it has been Jones who has garnered the most scholarly and cultural attention, notably from Grant and Dyhouse. Whereas Hulten is often portrayed as a Walter Mittyesque, inept, gangster wannabe, the picture painted of Jones is very different. It is her participation in the 'cleft chin murder' that would elevate her to representing *sine qua non*, the 'good time girl' as folk devil. She was born Elizabeth Marina (later Maude) Baker in Neath, South Wales in 1926. She was an incorrigible adolescent, running away from home for the first time at the age of thirteen and subsequently sent to an approved school in Sale, Cheshire. Baker was amongst the disproportionate number of girls as compared to boys (50 per cent of females as opposed to only 10 per cent in 1936 alone) who were sent to approved schools as a result of the 'moral danger' clause of the 1933 Children and Young Persons Act.[23] This allowed for young persons to be sent to approved schools not as a result of criminal offences but for their protection as a result of moral concerns. Baker, however, on one occasion absconded from the school with another pupil to journey to London. At the age of sixteen she returned to Neath where she met and married Stanley Jones, a corporal in the Airborne Forces, a man ten years her senior. She claimed that he assaulted her on their wedding night and she promptly left him, though they were reconciled for a short time afterwards.[24]

A measure of how Baker has been portrayed in popular literature can be found in Gammon's description of her reason for marriage: 'in the cunning mind of Baker, Jones was going to be the means to get her away from the life she was leading …'[25] She is seen as manipulative, conniving and immoral. Donald Thomas also emphasized this by using her in his monograph which described her as a 'graceless blonde waif of little appeal or presence'.[26] She left permanently for London in January 1943, initially seeking out a career as a dancer, but ultimately gravitating towards the strip clubs of the capital. She was in George Orwell's words an 'unsuccessful stripper' only making one attempt at burlesque, before quitting after she was booed off the stage.[27] Jones thereafter worked as a party host and there is some suspicion as a prostitute as well, but her main income was the 32s. per week that she received as a marriage allowance from the army.[28] When she met Hulten, who now went by the name of Ricky Allen, Jones had similarly fashioned herself as 'Georgina Grayson'.

Between 4 and 9 of October 1944 'Allen' and 'Grayson' went on a haphazard but violent crime spree that would culminate in the murder of George Heath, between the late night of the 6th and the early hours of the morning of 7 October.[29] The first incident that they would be involved in was on the second night after they met, when Hulten knocked a female bicyclist off her bike and robbed her, leaving her dazed on a country road outside of Reading.[30] The next evening the couple would attempt to rob a taxi driver in south London, but were foiled due to the intervention of the passenger in the cab who was a US officer. After this, they turned their attention to another victim, a woman by the name of Violet May Hodge. This eighteen-year-old had been walking home alone and was offered a lift and, after a short journey into Berkshire, the car stopped and all three got out and Hodge was attacked with an iron bar, robbed, dumped in a ditch and left for dead. She managed to raise the alarm at a local farmhouse, got medical help and survived the ordeal.[31]

George Heath was a private hire cab driver hailed by Jones on the evening of 6 October and he agreed to take the couple to a location near Staines in the suburbs of London. On reaching their destination, Heath was shot, robbed, shoved out of the car and left fatally wounded.[32] The precise chain of events that led up to the shooting of Heath was the source of most of the dispute at the subsequent trial, as was Jones's role as co-conspirator. On Sunday the 8th their final attempt at robbery was foiled when Hulten tried to steal a fur coat from a woman outside the Berkeley Hotel in Piccadilly, but when a policeman turned up they drove off in Heath's vehicle. The next evening Hulten would be arrested as the result of an observant policeman noticing the stolen car, and the police cornered him as he was leaving the flat of another lady friend near where the car was parked.[33]

IV

The rules governing the prosecution of criminal acts committed by US military personnel whilst on active service in the United Kingdom were established with the passing of the *United States of America (Visiting Forces) Act* of 1942.[34] The Act came about ostensibly as a result of an exchange of letters between the British Foreign Secretary Anthony Eden and John G. Winant, the American Ambassador to Great Britain on 27 July 1942.[35] The Act was something of a departure for the United Kingdom as under the 1933 *The Visiting Forces British Commonwealth Act* it had sought to retain the right to prosecute Foreign Service personnel in British service courts who committed crimes that targeted civilians or civilian property.[36] However, the *Allied Forces Act* passed in 1940, which established the right of exile nations to create armed forces in Great Britain out of exiled troops, allowed for extra-territorial authority of these nations with personnel in the United Kingdom to be extended to their own military justice system, rather than be subject to the legal systems of the host nation. This was done via an Order in Council and was based on pre-existing treaty arrangements between 'H.M.G and the Allied Governments' in exile.[37] However, on a number of occasions, there were limitations to this extraterritoriality with the right to prosecute major crimes such as murder, manslaughter and rape retained by the UK authorities. To begin with this was the case with US service personnel.

The US and British authorities sought to reach a clearer understanding of the rules relating to sovereign rights and extraterritoriality. The need for the act was expressed by Herbert Morrison, the British Home Secretary, in opening the debate on 4 August 1942 when he said that 'the American members of the American Armed Forces are, of course, accustomed to their own procedure and the principles of their own law … they are more familiar in dealing with their own in their own customary way'.[38] Further to this, Morrison argued that by passing extraterritorial rights to the US JAG they would have 'a freer hand to see that the appropriate punishments are inflicted on their own violation'.[39] He also argued that the VFA was 'in the interests of good feelings between the two countries and particularly in the matter of good feelings between our own population and our own authorities and the American Forces'.[40] He concluded that '... we anticipate no friction' between the two authorities.[41] He justified this by saying so far 'the American Authorities have been exceedingly helpful and co-operative'.[42]

In the exchange of letters by Eden and Winant, it was made clear that any American serviceman accused of an offence against a British civilian would be heard in open court.[43] The issue of murder figured prominently in the debate on the VFA especially what would happen if the victim were a British civilian. Previously this power had been reserved to British courts but the VFA would surrender this right and place it under the JAG. There were concerns expressed that in doing so it would cause a degree of grievance and upset, expressed most notably by the MP for Southampton Dr Russell Thomas.[44] Morrison sought to reassure members over this matter by pointing to similarities in the law and also in terms of the punishment handed down for homicide in the US *Articles of War*.[45]

A further area where there was also some degree of concern expressed in Westminster was over offences that were not capital crimes under English and Scots Law, but that under the US *Articles of War* became such crimes, with the offence of rape being one such crime.[46] This issue was raised during the debate when Mr Garro Jones, MP for Aberdeen North, drew attention to the potential problems of differential punishment.[47] There was a mechanism under the Act for the resolution of such anomalies[48] and the Attorney General sought to allay fears on this by pointing out that death was not an exclusive form of punishment for rape, and that life imprisonment could also be imposed instead by a US military court martial.[49] This would be a source of real dispute and much scholarly debate, most notably in the case of Leroy Henry, an African American who in 1944 was accused of raping a woman from Combe Down near Bath. He was condemned to death by the military authorities, but a local outcry over the sentence resulted in the United States Supreme Commander Dwight D. Eisenhower not just commuting the sentence, but quashing the entire conviction, freeing Henry completely.[50] Six of the eighteen capital sentences handed down during the war would be exclusively for rape; all of the people executed were either African Americans (four) or Mexican Americans (two) and none were white.[51] However, two white Americans would be executed for crimes that involved both rape and murder.[52] Scholars Lilly and Thomson would latterly characterize the practice as 'sexual racism'.[53]

V

The decision to commit Hulten for trial alongside Jones under English Law and waiving the *VFA* was controversial. There is little in the way of extant documentary evidence as to the rationale behind the move. There is some evidence, asserted most notably by Gammon and others, that it was because the US government and President Roosevelt in particular were embarrassed that an American soldier had behaved in such a disgraceful way. Thus, in order to restore confidence, he should face British justice, and this should 'serve as a warning to English girls hobnobbing with flashy yanks'.[54] This is a problematic interpretation as up until the 'cleft chin murder' there had been no compulsion to try and execute thirteen American servicemen in military tribunals for murder and/or rape of British civilians. So why should this case be different?

Thomas has a different interpretation of the decision. He saw it as down to the possible legal implications of trying the two defendants separately. He said:

> At first, it was announced that Hulten's court martial would be postponed until the girl's trial was over. Unfortunately, this might have resulted in her being hanged before she could be called as a witness in the later case. In these circumstances, the United States asked the British Government to try both accused.[55]

This is a more substantial and potentially realistic interpretation as it was based on legal argument rather than sentiment. Two roughly simultaneous trials for the same crime by two defendants had a whole host of potential difficulties. What would have happened if Hulten had been acquitted of murder by the JAG but at the same time Jones had been also acquitted? Having both committed for trial would remove any such potential problems.

A final reason, not put forward by either Gammon or Thomas, is one that goes back to the exchange of letters between Winant and Eden and missed during the passing of the *VFA* in Parliament. At no time did anyone consider that there was going to be a criminal conspiracy that involved a civilian and a serviceman and it was completely overlooked in the discussions. It is almost always the case that defendants are tried together if they are indicted for the same offence. There may be separate verdicts but that was a matter for the jury to decide. In examples where servicemen from different national armed forces were indicted for involvement in a criminal conspiracy they would be court martialled separately. This was understood and expressed during the passing of the VFA and also accepted under the *British Commonwealth VFA* of 1933 and the *Allied Forces Act* of 1940. This unprecedented case came about due to the indictment of Elizabeth Jones, who was a civilian. As there was no provision in the VFA, or an agreed procedure, the only solution to this dilemma was to hand over Hulten to the English Courts.

Hulten was handed over to the US Provost Marshals and the JAG on 10 October. Whilst in custody he surrendered the name and address of Jones and she was arrested 11 October and appeared at Feltham Police Court on 14 October to be remanded in custody until 3 November.[56] In the meantime, the decision was made to try both together and the VFA subsequently was waived.[57] At a second hearing that took place at the Magistrates court in Feltham on 27 November both entered a plea of not guilty to the charge of murder.[58] They were both committed for trial at the Old Bailey on 3 December 1944 and the trial was set to begin on 16 January 1945.

The trial of Hulten and Jones was to last for six days from 16-23 January 1945. Every day crowds waited for many hours until the opening of the court to grab a place in the public galleries.[59] The first day saw the trial brought temporarily to a halt as the defence counsel for Hulten tried to have two statements signed by his client declared inadmissible, claiming that Hulten had not read them and that they were not his words but the words of the chief investigator for the JAG Lieutenant De Mott.[60] After careful consideration, the presiding Judge Mr Justice Charles decided to allow them to be submitted in evidence. This decision occurred not least because, despite claiming not to have read them, there were witnesses who said that Hulten had read them very carefully and even made corrections to the spelling.[61] The reason for the attempt to have the statements removed became clear as the trial progressed. In his statement to De Mott, Hulten had said that he had intended to intimidate Heath by firing through the door of the cab, but that just as he was about to do so, Heath had moved to his right and straight into the sights of Hulten's firearm as he fired it.[62] The defence wanted to push the argument that Hulten had discharged the weapon by accident when he attempted to free his hand from the armrest on the door of Heath's taxi, and had snagged it on a leather strap that protruded from the door. Not surprisingly, this change of evidence was to be a major focus of both the prosecution and defence.

The first of the defendants in the witness box was Jones. She admitted to having been with Hulten on the night of the murder and had observed the crime. Her only action, she said, during the murder of Heath was to hand Hulten a handkerchief, and she denied having helped to move Heath's body from the car or of rifling through his pockets. Jones claimed to have been constantly in fear of Hulten. On their first meeting she claimed he had 'showed her a gun' and said he 'would use it on her' if she told anyone about it. Immediately after the murder Hulten had, she alleged, brandished the firearm and said 'I'll do the same to you' if she did not co-operate.[63] When cross-examined by Hulten's KC she claimed that when she got into the taxi with Hulten she assumed that he was going to take her home.[64] She later modified the answer by claiming that she was suspicious about Hulten's intentions when he first told her to get a taxi.[65] The Judge when questioning Jones got her later to admit that when Hulten had said to get a taxi she knew he meant 'Let's go and rob a taxi …'[66] Within the first couple of days of the trial both defendants had seriously compromised their defence cases. Hulten had done this as a result of a botched attempt to have his earlier statements ruled inadmissible and by changing his story as to the course of the events. Jones's defence had slowly been undermined too by her inability to stick, to her story, as well gradually acknowledging the truth of incriminating evidence against her.

Hulten in the witness box also immediately started to revise his second version of the events that led up to the death of Heath, but also he sought to pass on the blame for the murder on to Jones. The first thing he attempted to do was to discredit Jones's defence that she was afraid of him. He denied having threatened her, or that he had lifted his hands to her, or that she was at all dominated by him. Instead he claimed that it had been Jones who had come up with the idea of robbing someone for cash.[67] He then sought to describe the shooting of Heath as an accident, but first added to previous statements by claiming that he did not know the gun was in fact loaded. When challenged on having changed his story he claimed that the original statement had been arrived at through De Mott asking a series of questions, and Hulten replying, but the Lieutenant putting his own answer to it on the statement and not Hulten's.[68]

The Judge addressed the jury on 23 October and summed up the case. He said, 'If the shot was fired during, and in the forwarding of, the commissioning of robbery, and this caused death that was murder.' He continued that even if it was fired during the felony 'in order to frighten. That still would be murder'.[69] As far as a plea of manslaughter was concerned, he told them that the jury would have to believe that Hulten did not know that the gun was loaded and that it had it was an 'accident unconnected with the intended robbery'. As for Jones, Justice Charles said that the jury could acquit her 'if they found that she entered into the matter against her will, as she would not be an accomplice in law'.[70]

VI

It took one and half hours for the jury to return a verdict of guilty on both Hulten and Jones on 23 January 1945.[71] In addition, the jury recommended mercy for Jones but not Hulten.[72] Mr Justice Charles had little to say to the two convicts beyond the passing of a sentence of death on both, though he did say that the recommendation to clemency would be passed on to the Home Secretary.[73] The only comments from the convicted came from Jones who was heard to shriek, 'Oh! Why didn't he tell the truth?' as she was taken down from the dock.[74]

Shortly after being convicted, both Jones and Hulten appealed the verdict.[75] In Massachusetts, Hulten was able to call upon the services of important state and federal figures. His family counsel was the state senator Charles Innes and he recruited both US senators for the State, Leverett Saltonstall and David L. Walsh, to lobby the Secretary of State Edward Stettinius.[76] Innes outlined that the basis of the appeal was with regard to Hulten's mental state. He argued that there was 'proof beyond doubt' that Hulten 'obviously was suffering from battle shock' as a result of his experiences as part of the D-day landings in Normandy.[77] He pointed out that no evaluation of Hulten's mental state was made prior to his trial and conviction.[78] If the appeal failed, Inness said that he would submit a detailed legal argument to the Home Secretary, on behalf of Hulten's wife and mother, supporting commuting the sentence of death to life imprisonment.[79]

The appeal against Hulten and Jones's conviction was heard at the Court of Appeal on 19 and 20 February 1945 with Justices' MacNaghten, Wrottersley and Croom-Johnston presiding. The KC for Hulten, John Maude, led off the proceedings and laid out four grounds for appeal.

(1) The Judge omitted to direct the jury adequately on the law related to manslaughter: (2) That he wrongly admitted in evidence two statements made by the appellant: (3) That he did not adequately assist the jury in his direction to them on law related to implied malice: and (4) That in summing up he did not put the defence adequately to the jury.[80]

On the first ground it was Hulten's counsel's argument that whilst in the dock, Hulten had stated that he had never intended to use the firearm but that he had 'unwittingly pulled the trigger'. This would, in his counsel's opinion, 'constitute manslaughter and not murder because the mind of the man was not behind the gun'.[81] On the second ground of the appeal, overwritten statements presented in the name of the appellant, Maude argued that although Hulten had voluntarily made statements, they had been 'elicited as the result of questions put to him … which was contrary to the rules laid down by the Judge'.[82] Similarly, the second written statement was arrived at via means similarly at odds with judicial rules, and therefore should have been ruled inadmissible.

The lead counsel for Jones, Mr Casswell, presented three grounds for her appeal:

(1) That the crime was manslaughter not murder; (2) That the Judge's direction on the subject on what constituted aiding and abetting was totally inadequate; and (3) That he went out of his way to attack Jones's character'.[83] He echoed Hulten's counsel's view that there was sufficient evidence for the death of Heath to be seen as manslaughter, and that the jury was 'entitled to be given proper direction on the subject'.[84] As far as aiding and abetting, Casswell claimed that it had not been established at all that Jones had assisted in any way in a 'common design' and therefore could not have been guilty of murder.[85] For Casswell, the crux of this aspect of the appeal was the issue of 'implied malice'.[86] If Hulten's statement that he had accidentally shot Heath was believed and it was therefore manslaughter, there can be no implied malice in his action, which is he did not consciously shoot the victim, and further no 'common design' that implicated Jones in the murder thus would exist. On the third count, Casswell decried comments from the bench, which impugned his client's reputation, and also that passages in Jones's original statement were not read in court that were of 'great materiality' to her defence.

Justice MacNaghten delivered the appeal verdict. He concentrated first on the admissibility of Hulten's written statements and was satisfied that the statements had been written in accordance with Home Office instructions.[87] On the question of manslaughter, MacNaghten said 'that there was no evidence on which the jury could properly have arrived' at the said verdict, especially as Hulten had offered two different accounts of what had happened to cause the firearm to discharge.[88] On the appeal by Jones, MacNaghten rejected it. As the chief Justice had already rejected manslaughter as a possible verdict, he concentrated on the issue of aiding and abetting. According to MacNaghten, Jones was fully aware that by joining Hulten in his plan she was therefore involved in a criminal conspiracy. If that 'common design' had resulted in murder, as the verdict from the jury suggested, she was therefore culpable. On the suppression of parts of her statement to police in which she claimed only to have participated as she was in fear of her life, the appeal court decided that 'there was nothing in support of that defence but her word, and her whole conduct before, during and after the event was inconsistent with it'.[89] She was therefore in MacNaghten's words a 'willing actor in the matter (and) having done these things was rightly convicted'.[90] On the third count, the

Justices said that 'they did not think that the interventions were open to the objections made against them'.[91] The only crumb of comfort for Jones was that appeal court justices offered the opinion that she was probably guilty of murder in the second degree.

Hulten and Jones planned a further appeal this time to the House of Lords. Oliver Locker-Lampson, the MP for Birmingham Handsworth, it was reported, was to ask the Attorney General on their behalf on 26 February 1945 to 'issue his fiat' so that the appeal could be heard by the law lords.[92] On 6 March, the Attorney General announced that he had refused to issue a certificate for the appeal to proceed and therefore the execution of both convicts would go ahead on 8 March.[93]

VII

The application of the Prerogative of Mercy illuminates the issue of agency, a key theme in micro-history. Here we see the role of individual actions and how they shape events. The Home Secretary had, up until the abolition of the death penalty in 1965, the responsibility to decide which persons convicted of a capital crime would be executed. On one of the walls in the office of the Home Secretary in Whitehall there was a board on which was written the names of all those who were currently condemned to death. It was a permanent and grisly reminder of one of the tasks that came with such high office. Roy Jenkins, who was Home Secretary from 1965 to 1967, described the room as a place of 'immense gloominess'.[94]

The 1949–53 *Royal Commission on Capital Punishment* set the context under which recommendations of mercy and the Royal Prerogative operated. In the first instance it is, as the royal commission pointed out, entirely on the juries 'own initiative' and that the 'judge never prompts them and does not even remind them to do so if they wish' to recommend mercy.[95] There is no obligation to offer a reason behind the decision, though in 426 out of 460 recommendations one was advanced.[96] The commission advanced the view that an appeal to enact the royal prerogative was 'occasionally added only in deference to the scruples of a juror opposed to capital punishment or as a compromise between a verdict of murder and one of manslaughter'.[97]

After the recommendation is forwarded to the Home Secretary, there is a further level of scrutiny before a decision is made. Although the exercise of the Royal Prerogative is in the hands of the Secretary of State, it is often the case that it is arrived at with the assistance of the head of the departmental civil service and this is further augmented through 'a broad-based body of doctrine' which was outlined in the 1949 *Royal Commissions on Capital Punishment.*[98] There were three categories of murder where a 'reprieve was a foregone conclusion'.[99] These were so-called mercy killings, survivors of genuine suicide pacts and women convicted of the murder of their child.[100] Aside from these there were other categories of murder that required 'special close scrutiny', in case of any 'extenuating circumstances'. Amongst these were murders 'committed by two or more people with different degrees of responsibility' – this proviso was especially relevant to the 'cleft chin murders'.[101]

Between 1900 and 1949, there were 460 instances where a jury made a recommendation of mercy.[102] Amongst the totals, 107 were on the grounds of pitiable circumstances, 71 due to the youth of the convicted person, 60 due to provocation and 51 due to jealousy.[103] Of those recommended for a reprieve 349 would gain respite, which is roughly 75 per cent of the total. This shows that the recommendation for mercy was scarcely an automatic process. There was latitude for the Home Secretary to decide. In addition, there could be mercy granted without a recommendation by a jury and, between 1900 and 1949, 207 individuals would have their sentence commuted without such a recommendation.[104] In total 46 per cent of all convictions were commuted; however, there was a huge disparity in terms of gender with 40 per cent of men and 91 per cent of women gaining a reprieve.[105] The Royal Commission expressed the opinion that there was a 'natural reluctance' to carry out the death penalty on a woman. Beyond that there was little in the way of explanation of why gender would be such a determinant in the exercise of the Royal Prerogative.[106] It is in this light that the decisions over Hulten and Jones should be considered.

The decision over whether to apply the Prerogative of Mercy fell to Herbert Morrison as Home Secretary. Morrison was one of the key Labour Party figures in the wartime coalition government. We have a better idea as to the decision-making process over the application of the prerogative, and specifically over Hulten and Jones, from Morrison than from most of his predecessors as he described it in his autobiography. His biographers have also found further sources that revealed his thinking at the time. More substantially, the telegram that he sent to Hulten's mother, and also his wife, outlining his reasoning was reproduced in full in the *Boston Globe*.[107] However, Morrison maintained, during his time in the Home Office, the tradition of purdah so when Locker-Lampson MP asked him about clemency for Jones on 8 March 1945, he said nothing.[108]

His biographers summed up Morrison's attitude to the death penalty at the time suggesting that: 'his personal instincts were tough and punitive … he definitely believed in an "eye for an eye"'.[109] On the quasi-judicial decisions, such as the prerogative, they wrote that Morrison acted with 'detachment' looking 'closely at extenuating circumstances which might justify a pardon'.[110] His autobiography added some significant detail on his approach and revealed the widespread high-level discussion on the Hulten and Jones case. He described the overall responsibility over capital punishment as a 'heavy one for any Home Secretary'.[111] 'I was,' he wrote, 'glad to be able to approve a reprieve in a number of cases'.[112]

On 6 March 1945, Morrison communicated his decision on reprieves for Jones and Hulten. Jones was to be spared the gallows but for Hulten, as *The Times* reported, it was decided 'that there are not sufficient grounds to justify … in recommending any interference in the due course of the law'.[113] Morrison was to say later that the decision was 'infinitely more difficult to decide' than many that had come before him.[114] A telegram was dispatched to Hulten's family via Charles H. Innes, detailing more fully the Home Secretary's decision.[115] Morrison had sought guidance as to Hulten's mental state to see if there were any grounds that could see the MacNaghten rules on insanity applied, but had concluded 'that there were no medical grounds for a reprieve'.[116] In addition, Morrison was clear that the prosecution had proved intent on the part of Hulten and that the verdict of guilty was therefore safe and he 'found no grounds to dissent from this view'.[117] The sentence therefore was to be carried out the following day on 8 March 1945 at Pentonville Prison in London.

In New England, the Hulten family was reportedly 'bitter' at the news of the reprieve for Jones, saying 'that they both did wrong, and if they gave the girl clemency, he should have it too'.[118] The American Ambassador expressed similar sentiments when he visited Morrison on the day of the announcement of the reprieve.[119] Winant said to him 'you cannot hang my soldier if your British Girl gets off. Both are Guilty'.[120] Morrison replied:

> Yes I agree … but there is only one reason for the decision; the girl was only eighteen at the time of the crime. Under British law we cannot hang under eighteen and the girl is only just over.[121]

This is what we can call the unofficial 'Maxwell rule' after Morrison's chief civil servant who was most associated with the practice that came to set an age bar.[122] Section 53 of the 1933 *Children and Young Persons Act* had raised the age under which an execution could take place from sixteen to eighteen years of age.[123] The last eighteen-year-old to be executed before 1945 was in 1925, though the last to be executed before abolition was Francis Forsyth in 1960.[124] During his time in the Home Office, Morrison would reprieve all of those aged eighteen at the time of their conviction, but he would nonetheless allow three men aged nineteen to go to the gallows.[125] Age was, as previously mentioned, the second most often advanced plea in recommendations for mercy.[126] Another factor would almost certainly have been gender. Since 1900, the number of people executed who were under the age of twenty-one at the time was 28, none of whom were female.[127] There were seven women who were initially condemned but all were reprieved by the Home Secretary.[128] The 1949–53 Royal Commission recorded gender as a factor in thirteen clemency recommendations.[129]

The US ambassador had, according to Morrison, 'fought hard for his man' but left the hour-long meeting 'more miserable than I had never known him'.[130] Later, Winant would acknowledge that Morrison had been fair in his decision and equally patient in listening to him.[131] Morrison could have found himself in the midst of a major diplomatic constitutional and political crisis. Ernest Bevin had, even before the announcement of a reprieve for Jones, intervened on her behalf.[132] Morrison described this as a 'little naughty' on the part of the Minister for Labour.[133] Winston Churchill meanwhilst told Morrison that he had been wrong to reprieve Jones.[134] Churchill had amassed some experience of the pressures over the prerogative during his own short time in the Home Office between 1910 and 1911, when there were twenty-five uses of the prerogative of which only one was for a female convicted of murder.[135] Morrison in his autobiography also mentioned that he had discussed the case with King George VI.[136]

In South Wales there was some evidence of hostility to the respiting of the execution with graffiti of a gallows appearing on a wall in Jones's hometown of Neath.[137] After her conviction, Jones poured out her anger in letters: 'I would rather die than serve a prison sentence. God – what a jury! How I hate the London people. Hate them like poison.'[138]

These were scarcely the words of someone grateful for a recommendation of mercy. When Jones was told of the reprieve from the Governor of Holloway Prison, she assumed according to one account of the event that she was about to be released.[139] She asked for a pen and paper to write a letter to her mother asking her to bring her best clothes and organize a homecoming party.[140] The Governor then abruptly told her that she was not being released and that she was facing ten to twelve years in jail, prompting her to fall into hysterics and be placed in the prison hospital.[141] Elizabeth Maud Jones would serve nine years, initially in a borstal in Aylesbury, before being released on licence in 1954.

Hulten was executed on 8 March 1945. His last act prior to his death, according to the *Boston Globe*, was to convert was to Catholicism, the religion of his wife.[142] Outside the gates of the prison, Mrs Elsie Van der Elst, a noted campaigner for the abolition of capital punishment, was overheard to have repeatedly cried 'You let the girl off, but you hang the man! It is a damned shame!'[143] She and another campaigner, Charles Francis Smith, were carted off to Clerkenwell police station and charged with 'being concerned in causing grievous bodily harm to a policeman.'[144] Following an investigation, all charges were dropped against Mrs Van der Elst, but Smith was fined £3, ordered to pay 10 guineas costs and had his driving licence endorsed.[145]

Hulten was one of nineteen US servicemen executed in the United Kingdom during the Second World War.[146] He was not to be the last however, as four others would go to the gallows after him. The final execution was of Aniceto Martinez on 15 June 1945 for the rape of Agnes Cope, one of four men to get the death penalty for this offence under the US *Articles of War*. All but Hulten were tried, convicted and the sentence carried out under the auspices of the JAG. This was as a consequence of the agreement reached between the British and US governments and written into law in the 1942 *United States VFA*. Hulten was the only US serviceman to be tried, sentenced and executed under English law in a civilian court and prison.

VIII

The 'cleft chin murder' provides the threefold unity of time, place and action that is at the core of micro-history. With regard to time it allows for a discussion, in detail, of the unique context and circumstances of wartime, in this case the Second World War. Total war especially on the home front is a transformative phenomenon. It sees the interruption of normal patterns of life and behaviour, subversion of normative cultural and societal relations and the overthrow of entire patterns of living; sometimes only temporarily and sometimes forever.

The London Blitz and the endurance of the terror bombing of the Luftwaffe by its population created a new personality for the city, as it was now the people's city at the heart of the people's war. In many ways, it mixed time and place into a species of unique character and moment. Like Stalingrad, or even Berlin, it was a vision of the impact of war on urban life. It had always been the most attractive location for those seeking the bright lights, even before the war. However, the Second World War would further heighten the exotic character of the city. Elizabeth Jones had imagined a glamorous London, as a stark alternative to provincial Wales, and moreover an opportunity especially in its burgeoning *demi-monde* to metamorphose into Georgina Grayson. Hulten also had a vision of the British capital. Like many of the thousands of deserters of all nationalities it was the place to gravitate towards, as it was vast enough and the blackout opaque enough to conceal him within. It too offered opportunity: for crime, for sex and (like Jones) a chance to reinvent himself. In this he became something larger than a conscript private in the motor pool – instead he was Ricky Allen, an officer and former Chicago mob gunman.

The actions of the two were extraordinary as they were such an extreme departure from acknowledged previous behaviour. There had been some indicators of deviance and delinquency in both prior to the spree. Jones had displayed it for the longest period first as an adolescent and latterly as an adult. Hulten's delinquency only manifested itself whilst on military service, but it quickly snowballed into murderous violence. The actions of theft, armed robbery, attempted murder, then murder are astonishing for their increasing seriousness but also for the rapidity of their escalation.

The most important element of micro-history displayed by this chapter is that of agency. It is impossible for a historian to truly get to the heart of the motivations of both Hulten and Jones during their short-lived crime spree, as it requires a deeper psychological knowledge of which most are not qualified to provide. Likewise we do not have substantial enough primary sources to seriously offer even tentative assessments. The decision-making process for both of the main protagonists is thus illusive, but the fact that this occurred when it did is interesting as it offers a collision of time, place and action. In the midst of war, in a city transformed by conflict and presented with opportunity they did what they did.

The crime spree of Hulten and Jones pushed the boundaries of *demi-monde* deviance beyond its traditional urban stomping ground and into the suburbs and the fringes of rural England, in this case Staines, at that time a sleepy Epsom suburb. However, this was not Agatha Christie's St Mary Mead where poisoners carried out crimes amid manicured lawns, or where little men such as Dr Crippen were the quintessential bourgeois sociopaths of the sort much lamented by Orwell in 'The Decline of the English Murder'. The blitzed cities were a perfect location for criminality concealed by wartime restrictions, but as the 'cleft chin murder' demonstrated, it also allowed for opportunities to extend into London's Metroland.

The process of agency is more transparent when we look at the operation of the Prerogative of Mercy. Although it is meant to be a secret decision, we have, in this case at least, far greater insight into the motivations and behaviour of the person at the heart of the process: the Home Secretary Herbert Morrison, than we do in any other case. In this respect, separated from the more immediate 'cleft chin murder' context, we have the chance to examine and see more prerogative in operation. We see agency in the interplay between personal attitudes towards capital punishment, established (if unwritten) procedure, diplomatic, legal and moral questions and pressures. We can discern in Morrison's decision subtleties over the question of defendant maturity. Jones was eighteen years old and so it was permissible to execute her as had happened before and after to convicted persons of that age. However, the key aspect that allowed for the reprieve to be granted was that she had only just turned eighteen prior to involvement in the murder of George Heath. We can see deeply into the operation of the prerogative due to this case and therefore have another angle in which to view the whole debate around the death penalty.

This chapter has also sought to reclaim the 'cleft chin murder' from the sensationalist school of true crime history and instead to integrate it into the main body of serious scholarly study of deviance through the prism of micro-history. It links to other chapters in this collection in two ways, first by offering a single example of criminality as a vehicle to see larger questions around delinquency and misbehaviour, but also alongside the chapters by Kilday and Watson to see how much of a factor gender is in the operation of the justice system and the treatment of offenders. It was George Orwell who was to help keep, rather inadvertently, the Hulten/Jones crime in the public eye, but now it can be seen as a crucial academic case study in the interplay between war and criminality.

Notes

1. S.G. Magńsson and I.M. Szijártó (2013) *What Is Micro-history? Theory and Practice* (London: Routledge), p. 4.

2. Ibid., p. 5.

3. Ibid., p. 5.

4. Ibid., p. 7.

5. Parliamentary Papers, *Royal Commission on Capital Punishment, 1949–1953 – Report*, Cmd 8932 (1953).

6. G. Orwell (2009) *The Decline of the English Murder* (London: Penguin), p. 16.

7. R. Alwyn (1945) *The Cleft Chin Murder* (London: Claude Morris).

8. Ibid., p. 1.

9. C.E. Bechofer Roberts (1945) *The Trial of Hulten and Jones* (London: Jarrolds).

10. D. Thomas (2003) *An Underworld at War* (London: John Murray) and M. Waller (2003 Kindle Edition) *London 1945: Life in the Debris of War* (London: Studio), p. 28.

11. Waller, *London 1945*, Loc 3989.

12. E.E. Gammon (2015 Kindle Edition) *A Fatal Pick Up* (London: Mereo Books).

13. M. Grant (2013) 'Citizenship, Sexual Anxiety and Womanhood in Second World War Britain: The Case of the Man with the Cleft Chin', in S. Nicolas and T. O'Malley (eds) *Moral Panics, Social Fears, and the Media: Historical Perspectives* (London: Routledge), pp. 177–90 and C. Dyhouse (2013 Kindle Edition) *Girl Trouble, Panic and Progress in the History of Young Women* (London: Zed Books).

14. Grant, 'Citizenship, Sexual Anxiety and Womanhood', p. 178.

15. Ibid., p. 180.

16. Dyhouse, *Girl Trouble*, Loc 1677.

17. Ibid.

18. 'The Unstable Adolescent Girl', *British Medical Journal*, 16 December 1946, pp. 909–12.

19. See E.J. Salomonsson (2015) *Swedish Heritage of Greater Worcester* [American Heritage] (Clemson: History Press).

20. *Boston Globe*, 3 February 1945, p. 1.

21. Gammon, *A Fatal Pick Up*, Loc 116.

22. Thomas, *An Underworld at War*, p. 243.

23. S. D'Cruze and L.A. Jackson (2009) *Women, Crime and Justice in England since 1660* [Gender and History] (London: Palgrave Macmillan), p. 152.

24. Gammon, *A Fatal Pick Up*, Loc 69.

25. Ibid., Loc 69.

26. Thomas, *An Underworld at War*, p. 243.

27. Orwell, *The Decline of the English Murder*, p. 16.

28. Thomas, *An Underworld at War*, p. 243.

29. Ibid., p. 245.

30. Gammon, *A Fatal Pick Up*, Loc 69.

31. Ibid.

32. Thomas, *An Underworld at War*, p. 244.

33. Ibid., p. 245.

34. *United States of America (Visiting Forces) Act*, 5 & 6 Geo. 6. (1942), chap. 31. This is a much-neglected aspect of law and the Second World War and is crying out to be reassessed.

35. Ibid., pp. 4–7.

36. N. Bentwich (1942) 'The U.S.A Visiting Forces Act, 1942', *The Modern Law Review*, Vol. 6, No. 1/2, pp. 68–72, 69.

37. Hansard, *House of Commons Debates*, 382, 4 August 1942: 877.

38. Ibid., col. 876.

39. Ibid.

40. Ibid., cols 877–8.

41. Ibid., col. 878.

42. Ibid.

43. *United States of America (Visiting Forces) Act*, p. 5.

44. Hansard, *House of Commons Debates*, 382, 4 August 1942: 898.

45. Ibid., col. 876.

46. United States of America War Office (1920) *The Articles of War* (Washington: Government Printing Office), Article 92.

47. Hansard, *House of Commons Debates*, 382, 4 August 1942: 886.

48. *United States of America (Visiting Forces) Act*, p. 5.

49. Hansard, *House of Commons Debates*, 382, 4 August 1942: 921.

50. See G. Smith (1987) *When John Bull Met Jim Crow* (London: I.B. Tauris), pp. 185–6.

51. J.R. Lilly and J.M. Thomson (1997) 'Executing US Soldiers in England, World War II', *British Journal of Criminology*, Vol. 57, No. 2, pp. 262–88, at p. 268.

52. Ibid., p. 268.
53. Ibid., p. 262.
54. Gammon, *A Fatal Pick Up*, Loc 3697 and *New York Times*, 3 September 1989.
55. Thomas, *An Underworld at War*, p. 246.
56. *The Times*, 16 October 1944, p. 2.
57. Ibid., 28 November 1944, p. 2.
58. Ibid.
59. Waller, *London 1945*, Loc 3967.
60. *The Times*, 17 January 1945, p. 2.
61. Ibid., 20 January 1945, p. 2 and 24 January 1945, p. 2.
62. Ibid., 18 January 1945, p. 2.
63. Ibid., 20 January 1945, p. 2.
64. Ibid., 21 January 1945, p. 2.
65. Ibid.
66. Ibid.
67. Ibid., 20 January 1945, p. 2.
68. Ibid.
69. Ibid.
70. Ibid.
71. Ibid., 24 January 1945, p. 2.
72. Ibid.
73. Ibid.
74. Ibid.
75. Ibid., 26 January 1945, p. 2.
76. *Boston Globe*, 24 February 1945, p. 7.
77. Ibid.
78. Ibid.
79. Ibid.
80. *The Times*, 20 February 1945, p. 2.
81. Ibid.
82. Ibid.
83. Ibid.
84. Ibid.
85. Ibid.
86. Ibid., 21 February 1945, p. 2.
87. Ibid.
88. Ibid.
89. Ibid.
90. Ibid.
91. Ibid.

92. Ibid., 26 February 1945, p. 2.

93. Ibid., 6 March 1945, p. 2.

94. R. Jenkins (1991) *A Life at the Centre* (London: Macmillan), p. 179.

95. Parliamentary Papers, *Royal Commission on Capital Punishment*, pp. 8–9.

96. Ibid., p. 313.

97. Ibid., p. 9.

98. Ibid., p. 12.

99. Ibid., p. 11.

100. Ibid., p. 11.

101. Ibid., p. 12.

102. Ibid., p. 313.

103. Ibid.

104. Ibid., p. 9.

105. Ibid., p. 13.

106. Ibid., p. 12.

107. *Boston Globe*, 8 March 1945, p. 22.

108. Hansard, *House of Commons Debates*, 408, 8 March 1945: 2207.

109. B. Donoghue and G. Jones (2001) *Herbert Morrison Portrait of a Politician* (London: Phoenix), p. 309.

110. Ibid.

111. Lord Morrison of Lambeth (1960) *Herbert Morrison – An Autobiography* (London: Odhams), p. 227.

112. Ibid.

113. *The Times*, 7 March 1945, p. 4.

114. Lambeth, *Herbert Morrison*, p. 227.

115. *Boston Globe*, 8 March 1945, p. 22.

116. Ibid.

117. Ibid.

118. Ibid.

119. Donoghue and Jones, *Herbert Morrison*, p. 310.

120. Lambeth, *Herbert Morrison*, p. 228.

121. Ibid.

122. Donoghue and Jones, *Herbert Morrison*, p. 310.

123. *Children and Young Persons Act*, 23 Geo. 5 (1933), chap. 12, Section 53.

124. Parliamentary Papers, *Royal Commission on Capital Punishment*, p. 308.

125. Ibid.

126. Ibid., p. 313.

127. Hansard, *House of Commons Debates*, 408, 8 March 1945: 2207.

128. Parliamentary Papers, *Royal Commission on Capital Punishment*, p. 316.

129. Ibid.

130. Lambeth, *Herbert Morrison*, p. 228. Tragically Winant would take his own life in 1947 shortly after his return to the United States from the United Kingdom.

131. Ibid., p. 228.

132. *Boston Globe*, 24 February 1945, p. 7.

133. Lambeth, *Herbert Morrison*, p. 228.

134. Ibid.

135. Parliamentary Papers, *Royal Commission on Capital Punishment*, p. 316.

136. Lambeth, *Herbert Morrison*, p. 228.

137. Dyhouse, *Girl Trouble*, Loc 1736.

138. Waller, *London 1945*, Loc 4007.

139. Gammon, *A Fatal Pick Up*, Loc 3626.

140. Ibid.

141. Ibid.

142. *Boston Globe*, 8 March 1945, p. 22.

143. Ibid., 9 March 1945, p. 2.

144. *The Times*, 9 March 1945, p. 2.

145. Ibid., 4 May 1945, p. 2.

146. R. Clerk (2009) *Capital Punishment in Britain* (Hersham: Ian Allen), p. 316.

SECTION II
VIOLENCE AND THE VIOLENT

CHAPTER 5
LOVE, VENGEANCE AND VITRIOL: AN EDWARDIAN TRUE-CRIME DRAMA
Katherine D. Watson

I

In December 1906, readers of the *Evening Express* learned that 'All the elements of a sensational melodrama were contained in the story told at the Guildhall during the examination of Emilie Foucault, a Frenchwoman, who was charged with throwing vitriol on M. André Delombre, a young Frenchman.'[1] But this was just a foretaste of things to come. At her four-day trial in April 1907, the frank accounts given by both Foucault and her victim captured the public imagination: all the couple had to do was tell the truth about their erstwhile romance and how it had gone horribly wrong. In so doing, they exposed issues that illuminate important aspects of Edwardian criminal justice and crime reporting.[2] As a young, attractive woman driven to distraction by a callous lover, there was more empathy for Foucault than for Delombre, who never managed to gain the sympathy of the court or the public, even though he had been blinded and scarred so 'as would make him for the rest of his life an object somewhat repulsive.'[3] But it was this experience of physical ruination that makes his story important, for it was in many ways typical of the English heyday of a cruel crime: the use of oil of vitriol (concentrated sulphuric acid) to disfigure falsehearted lovers, unfaithful spouses or obstructive love rivals.[4] Furthermore, as middle-class foreigners, Foucault and Delombre reinforced gendered stereotypes about crimes of passion, which were typically associated with France.[5] Finally, the case was structured according to the conventions of Victorian melodrama, at a time when the art form was waning but its key characteristics were still easily recognizable.[6] First and foremost, therefore, this became the tale of an honourable woman wronged by a villainous man; although Delombre was made to pay a terrible price, the newspapers reversed the roles of victim and perpetrator almost from the outset. Foucault's acquittal was thus plainly signposted by the press coverage, which reflected the growing distinction between the tabloids' stress on sensationalist human interest and the broadsheets' focus on legally informed crime reportage.[7] By turns tragic, graphic, poignant and even amusing, their narrative highlighted popular responses to love, betrayal and revenge.

This chapter uses the doomed love affair between Foucault and Delombre to investigate two linked themes: attitudes to interpersonal violence;[8] and the nature of personal relationships and the emotions that underpin them, studied so far mostly in cases of male aggression towards women.[9] Given that both parties had a story to tell, assault prosecutions offer a valuable means of accessing the lived experiences of the past from the opposing perspectives of victim and perpetrator, and therefore reveal a great deal about the intimate relationships that underlie crime statistics.[10] Love and sex usually stood at the heart of the infrequent, but distinctive, form of assault known as vitriol throwing, which peaked in England between 1840 and 1940. This intentionally disfiguring offence is here examined as a manifestation of popular conceptions of passion and retribution centred on the shame and despair of the perpetrator in reaction to the victim's emotional cruelty, amounting to what was in essence English acceptance of the French concept of a *crime passionnel*, albeit under the designation of 'provocation'.[11] Given the importance of first-person justification of the actions taken in such emotion-centred crimes, the timing is significant: defendants had only been permitted to give evidence on their own behalf since the Criminal Evidence Act 1898 irrevocably altered trial procedure. Thereafter, defendants who wished to offer an alternative interpretation of the evidence against them had to do it from the witness box, opening themselves to the perils of cross-examination.[12] Foucault navigated this hurdle with poise and dignity, so that her self-portrayal as a desperate woman who had acted from pure motives served as an effective counterbalance to her concurrent identity as a divorced, adulterous unwed mother.[13] Despite the fact that her actions cost Delombre an eye, Foucault's performance in court ultimately trumped his.

II

The incident at the centre of this story occurred at Tranter's Hotel in London on 18 November 1906. It was the culmination of an almost decade-long relationship between Emilie Victorine Foucault, then 28, and André Jacques Delombre; it was the eve of his 26th birthday. The acid burnt Delombre on the left side of his face, and he was taken to St Bartholomew's Hospital, remaining there for eighteen days before being released to a nursing home, which he left on Christmas Eve.[14] He therefore remained unknown to the public until he appeared at the Mansion House police court on 13 December to give evidence at his attacker's committal hearing. Victorian and Edwardian police courts were frequented by journalists looking for a good story: as magistrates tried cases summarily and committed others for trial in the higher courts, the testimony they heard was sifted, packaged and presented to readers.[15] Despite presenting a pitiable figure, Delombre never got the chance to benefit from press attention for he had already been upstaged by Foucault, who possessed attributes guaranteed to garner sympathy: she was female, attractive, middle class – and pregnant.

After the attack Foucault was remanded to Holloway Prison, so the first the public learned of this 'dramatic' case focussed on her: 'WOMAN'S PLEA FOR CHILD/Does Not Want it Born in Prison.'[16] Initial reports were largely supportive, firmly placing her within a privileged but foreign class as 'a well-connected and highly-educated Frenchwoman' who could afford to pay 'substantial bail'. Although her plea for bail was described as 'somewhat pathetic', the sense was not pejorative but rather sympathetic. Her solicitor noted she was 'intensely anxious that her child should not be born within prison walls', adding that when Delombre had been cross-examined 'a very different aspect would be put on the case'.[17] The magistrate was unconvinced and Foucault was again remanded in custody, but the press coverage had already identified her as a suitable object of popular and legal consideration because the incident had occurred following 'a last appeal [to Delombre] in vain to save the good name of her child'.[18] From the outset, therefore, Foucault was portrayed as a casualty of male seduction, betrayal and abandonment who had been forced into action by honourable intentions.

The *Evening Express* reported her committal hearing under the headline 'Marriage or Death', in two identical articles that cited the wrong date (18 October) but otherwise accurately summarized the case,[19] though without much of the detail that later emerged at the trial. Delombre, who was 'very highly connected in Paris' – his father was a former government minister – had met Emilie Berger, the daughter of a small tradesman, in 1898 when he was a seventeen-year-old agriculture student. They developed an 'intimacy' that continued after her marriage (to Eugène Foucault) in 1899, her subsequent widowhood, remarriage in 1903 and swift divorce.[20] When Delombre's parents learned of the relationship they urged him to end it, but Foucault threatened to shoot not only him but his father and brother too.[21] In an effort to avoid her he came to England in October 1906. But she tracked him down and insisted on speaking with him in private. They went to Tranter's Hotel, where she hired a room. Foucault 'ordered coffee, and whilst they were drinking it she said:– "What I have to say is this. Either you shall marry me or you shall kill yourself, if you are not a coward, or else I shall kill you."' He refused and as he turned to leave she hurled the contents of a cup into his face. 'He screamed with pain, and tried to escape from the room, but found the door locked. Finally, it was broken open by a policeman.'[22] She was taken to a police station, where a loaded revolver was found in her possession. On this evidence, she was committed for trial at the Central Criminal Court.

The *Times* reported the hearing dispassionately but in considerably more detail, revealing facts that could be construed as negative reflections on Foucault's character but favourable to her defence. Thus, the newspaper revealed the exchange between Foucault and Delombre *after* she demanded marriage: 'Marry you! Certainly not. Why should I? You do not love me – indeed, you hate me, and neither do I love you.' To which she replied, 'Don't be uneasy. I shall not be troublesome, we need not live together. I only want my child to bear your name.' Upon his continued refusal she 'took up the coffee cup and violently threw the contents in his face', with the result being that 'Delombre's left eye was almost completely destroyed, and he was permanently disfigured'.[23] Unlike the *Evening Express*, however, *The Times* reported what happened next. Acting-Sergeant Hodges told the court what Foucault said to him at the police station following her arrest: she had 'raised the cup to her own lips, intending to commit suicide in Delombre's presence, but a remark of his caused her to lose control of herself, and without knowing what she was doing she flung the contents in his face'. Moreover, she 'appeared to be very distressed at the injury she had inflicted'. Evidence of suicidal intent in the form of her will redated at Paris on 17 November 1906 was found in her purse.[24] The newspaper's thorough reportage thus provided a less sensational and less overtly sympathetic narrative, yet still managed to give readers a largely positive impression of a woman driven by desperation to a deed she had not intended.

The *Daily Mirror* took yet a different approach in its succinct account of the committal hearing. It adopted a neutral attitude to Foucault, 'a young French widow who followed student for revenge', despite the fact that Delombre's face was 'terribly disfigured'. Unlike the *Evening Express* and *The Times*, however, *The Daily Mirror* stressed the foreignness of the events, describing them as 'a typical French vitriol drama'.[25] In doing so it opened up an additional facet of the narrative, and one that readers would have been well aware of. For, by the late Victorian period, vitriol had entered popular culture as a weapon associated with a stereotypical perpetrator: a woman who acted from motives of jealousy and revenge. This expectation was well entrenched by the 1880s and was played out numerous times in the melodramas, short stories and novels of the next forty years;[26] it was even repeated as late as 1936 when a textbook of forensic medicine stated that chemical burns 'may be caused by attempts by jealous women to disfigure their rivals, as in vitriol-throwing'.[27]

Furthermore, the Victorians and Edwardians assumed that vitriol throwing was far more common in France than in England.[28] Historians such as Joëlle Guillais, Ruth Harris, Mary Hartman and Ann-Louise Shapiro have shown that a so-called crime wave among bourgeois and upper-class women developed in France during the 1870s, characterized by the use of revolvers and vitriol throwing, so that a new verb came in to use: *vitrioler*, to burn with acid. The French concept of the crime of passion allowed greater judicial leniency for violent women in circumstances normally associated with sexual disappointment caused by men's abuse and betrayal and, consequently, the *vitrioleuse* was often acquitted.[29] The class bias associated with the crime has also been noted by Lucy Bending, who has shown that early criminologists allowed the violence of the deed to be occluded by social status. In Lombroso and Ferrero's *The Female Offender* (1895), violence distinguished the instinctive working-class criminal, for whom vitriol throwing was not a crime of passion but an expression of an 'innate desire to inflict pain'. For those of elevated social position, however, it was the sign of 'a sufferer pushed beyond endurance into action'.[30] Emilie Foucault was immediately located firmly within this latter category.

However, the assumption that French crimes of passion were committed largely by bourgeois women is incorrect: in murder cases most perpetrators had a working-class background and, during the 1870s, 82 per cent were male.[31] Eliza Ferguson's work on Parisian crimes of passion found that men outnumbered women three to one as defendants, with very few middle- and upper-class cases. But acquittal rates for women were disproportionately high, a fact attributable to a tacit acceptance of the notion that in certain circumstances, intimate violence was understandable, excusable or even legitimate.[32] In Victorian England, by contrast, violence by women was neither understandable nor acceptable: 'physically violent women of any class were widely condemned as abnormal', and women who resorted to violence even in the face of male provocation were likely to lose public and legal sympathy.[33] Meanwhile, the defence of provocation was increasingly withdrawn from men who killed their intimate partners, as a result of social pacification and changing standards of masculinity. Self-control and non-violent dispute resolution became the expected responses to bad behaviour. Violence by men towards women was increasingly vilified, and assault was gradually designated as wounding, prosecuted more vigorously and punished more severely.[34]

However, once English law had criminalized vitriol throwing, cases could present exceptions to these principles. The Offences Against the Person Act 1861 made it a felony to burn, maim or disfigure anyone with a corrosive fluid; the maximum punishment was life in prison.[35] But there was a legal loophole: no offence was committed if there was no intent to injure. So despite the premeditated nature of the crime – perpetrators had to buy the acid, put it in a cup or vessel and get within close range of the victim – defendants who could claim principled motives or that the acid had spilled accidentally were likely to be acquitted.[36] Victorian criminal statistics do not provide exact figures for the proportion of serious assaults that involved vitriol throwing,[37] but the records of the Old Bailey, London's Central Criminal Court, are indicative of its infrequency: only sixty-one cases were tried between 1837 and 1913, out of a total of more than 5,000 trials for wounding. Just over a third (36%) of those accused were male, and most were working class. Table 5.1 shows the distribution of verdicts by gender. An unknown number of less serious incidents were dealt with as aggravated assaults and tried summarily in London's fifteen police courts.[38]

Records of these trials confirm that English juries were willing to show the same lenience to vitriol throwers that French juries did, either by acquitting defendants[39] or recommending those convicted to mercy on the grounds of provocation.[40] Judges usually accepted this and gave lighter sentences of a few months or years in prison, sometimes with hard labour. If a victim had been blinded, terms of five to ten years seem to have been typical in the late Victorian and Edwardian eras.[41] The harshest penalties, prison terms of ten years or more, were reserved for defendants who had no legitimate claim to provocation. This included cases of revenge for matters unrelated to a broken

Table 5.1 Trials at the Old Bailey, London, for throwing a corrosive fluid 1837–1913

	Gender of Defendant and Verdict			
Substance	Male – guilty	Female – guilty	Male – not guilty	Female – not guilty
Vitriol	14	30[a]	8[b]	9
Nitric acid	3	3	1	1
Unspecified	5	10[c]	0	7[c]
Hydrochloric acid	1	6	2	2
Other corrosive fluid	4	0	3	1
Total	27	49	14	20

Source: http://www.oldbaileyonline.org.
[a] Includes one woman found guilty but insane, 1897.
[b] Includes two men tried twice for the same offence and acquitted each time, 1868 and 1888.
[c] Includes one woman tried twice for the same offence, acquitted and then convicted, 1886.

relationship, and people who had a history of violence. The harshest sentence, twenty years' penal servitude, was handed down in 1866 to a man who had blinded two people.[42] The same tacit acceptance identified by Ferguson in Parisian trials seems to have existed in London also: crimes of passion in which a person was provoked to violence by the hurtful actions of a loved one, especially a lover or spouse, were not punished as harshly as the law permitted, especially if the accused expressed remorse. In the words of a magistrate in 1847, 'when seduction was the beginning, mischief was almost sure to overtake the seducer in the end'.[43] This notion pertained all the more strongly to women and continued to influence judicial attitudes in the interwar period, as for example in 1924 when a judge remarked that 'there was no passion which was so likely to drive a woman to desperate methods as the passion which was caused by jealousy'.[44]

The story of Emilie Foucault and André Delombre was therefore familiar to an English audience, as a melodrama in which both played their roles to perfection: she came to England with both vitriol and a revolver to demand that he, the faithless lover, make an honest woman of her. He refused, so she followed a recognized course of action. But the story did not end there, as Foucault still had to stand trial and both had to tell their stories in open court. Of course she was much the better known of the two by the time the trial began. While Delombre, perhaps understandably, stayed out of public view, she captured headlines again when her son was born, an event that caused her trial to be postponed twice. The first adjournment was noted in February 1907 when *The Cambrian* reported briefly on the 'BABE BORN IN PRISON/FRENCH WOMAN'S TRAGEDY IN LONDON'.[45] The following month she was again medically unfit to stand trial but appeared briefly in court wearing white kid gloves. No doubt correctly interpreted as a visible sign of respectability, they suggested the perfect headline: KID GLOVE PRISONER.[46]

Foucault was one of eighty-four defendants listed for trial at the April Sessions of the Old Bailey.[47] Several of her fellow prisoners were also foreign-born, a fact that the grand jury saw as a problem: 'We are impressed with the number of cases in which aliens appear, and we are unanimously of opinion that the exclusion of undesirable aliens and the deportation of others should be more rigidly enforced.'[48] In the wake of the Aliens Act of 1905, which targeted Eastern European Jewish refugees,[49] it is by no means certain that Foucault was one of the intended targets of this barbed comment, particularly as she was the only woman among the five foreigners tried, at least three of whom were Jewish.[50] But clearly she needed to present herself in the best possible fashion.

III

Foucault's trial began on Tuesday 23 April 1907, before Mr Justice Jelf (1837–1917).[51] The fearsome rhetorician Sir Charles Mathews (1850–1920) led for the prosecution,[52] with Walter Frampton (1871–1939) as junior counsel. Foucault was defended by George Elliott KC (1860–1916) and Basil Watson (*c.* 1878–1941) and seems to have made a good first impression: '... there was a flutter of interest in the crowded court when the prisoner made her appearance. She is a brunette of pre-possessing appearance, and was tastefully attired in a black velvet dress and bodice. Foucault does not speak English, and the evidence had to be interpreted to her.'[53]

Nonetheless, initial press reports adopted an air of cautious neutrality. At the end of the first day the *Evening Express* juxtaposed positive and negative headlines: '"ABANDONED." /LOVE AND REVENGE/VITRIOL-THROWING OUTRAGE/Pretty French Woman in the Dock/YOUNG MAN FOLLOWED FROM PARIS TO LONDON'.[54] This was perhaps because of the careful way in which Mathews framed the case in his detailed opening statement, which stressed the fact that Foucault had never requested marriage, yet began to issue threats to kill followed by what seemed rather like blackmail: she would have birth cards printed and send them to Cabinet Ministers and friends of the family. Furthermore, she had clearly planned the attack.[55] Delombre's testimony supported this version of events: Foucault told him she was pregnant in June 1906 but did not seem upset when he said he would not acknowledge the child. By autumn she had still not mentioned marriage, and at Tranter's Hotel they had an amicable lunch together; she 'chatted unconcernedly about everything and about English customs generally'. It was only once they had gone up to her room that she demanded marriage and threw acid in his face when he refused.[56] But Mathews had been prescient in noting at the outset that 'In this country accusations of this kind were, happily, rare, but on the Continent in many instances a vast amount of sympathy was given to accused in such cases, and not to the person who had been injured.'[57]

Under cross-examination, Delombre was encouraged to reveal more details of his relationship with Foucault, since defending counsel obviously thought that he might damage his own credibility – not as an eyewitness to the events in question, but as the innocent victim of an unprovoked assault. Reported the next morning under the subheadline 'HOW IT ALL BEGAN',[58] Elliott used extracts from some 400 love letters written by Delombre to Foucault as a basis for cross-examining the former. The judge was not at first amenable to this tactic, a fact that the trial transcript does not explain but which press reports describe thus:

IMPORTING AMERICAN METHODS/His Lordship asked if the letters were being put before him as a matter of mitigation in case prisoner was found guilty, or, if not, what bearing did they have on the case? Mr Elliot [*sic*] said he was going to show that from 1898 to 1906 Delombre had the woman entirely under control. His Lordship hoped that by going into the relations which existed between the parties before this occurrence counsel was not taking a precedent from the other side of the Atlantic – a precedent which he hoped would never be introduced into this country. Mr Elliot said he would have to read eleven of the letters.[59]

Although clearly concerned by the potential invasion of yet more foreign ways into England – the tendency of American defence lawyers to obfuscate important legal points by introducing irrelevant facts to make their clients appear more favourable to jurors,[60] the judge nonetheless agreed to the letters. Elliott had set a trap and now guided Delombre into it.

While the actual questions that Elliott posed to his witness are not included in the trial transcript, it is clear that the extracts he selected and asked Delombre to read aloud showed the young man in a poor light. He had made promises that he signally failed to keep; had sex with the defendant within a day of her first marriage; regularly expressed his desire to be with her; referred to a possible child of her second marriage as his 'adopted son'; and advised her to lie during the divorce proceedings instituted by her second husband.[61] One letter proved especially damning:

> Mr Elliot [sic], resuming his cross-examination, asked if witness wrote to prisoner as follows just before her marriage [to Foucault]: ... 'I weep to think that you will be the wife of this clodhopper. The chattel of this dullard. You who are so fine, so delicate; but I know well I shall not have to be jealous of him. To serve you, to help you, I will play the cat to your bear. Such will be my role and my part in public, but below the surface, in the land of the Arabian nights, I shall serve you, help you always, love you always, and make you happy.' His Lordship: I would not have asked you not to read these letters if I had known such a letter as that was forthcoming. Witness, further cross-examined, said he went to prisoner's wedding, and the very next day had improper relations with her.[62]

As they were intended to do, such revelations raised questions about Delombre's character that, given the judge's reaction,[63] must have been obvious to all present in court. For her part, according to *The Cardiff Times*, 'the lady throughout was absolutely calm and showed no excitement if she felt any ... Madame Foucault, who is a fairly good-looking young woman ..., followed the evidence very closely and smiled frequently as the prosecutor's evidence was translated to her.'[64] Even greater sensation ensued when Elliott resumed his cross-examination the following morning. A letter of April 1906 revealed that Delombre knew then that Foucault might be pregnant and gave her money for an abortion. He tried to deny this, and that they had ever quarrelled about having a child,[65] seeking to divert the court's focus from himself back to Foucault's alleged violent tendencies. In doing so, however, he inadvertently caused a moment of courtroom drama, the details and impact of which can only be fully understood when a single narrative is stitched from the strands contained in several first-hand accounts.

It began when George Elliott asked Delombre about a revolver that Foucault used to threaten him. 'Did you take a revolver from her? – Yes. Did she say she intended to kill herself? – No, she wanted to kill me. Did she say she would take poison? – Yes, that was in 1904'[66] – after which he resumed 'relations' with her. Delombre then added that he had taken the loaded revolver from Foucault and had it with him, 'pointing to his pocket at the same time with a dramatic gesture.'[67] One can only imagine the alarm that this caused,[68] which is not reflected in the official transcript;[69] but no one panicked and alarm seems to have turned to amusement:

> Mr Justice Jelf: I had no idea that a witness would come into court with a loaded revolver in a case of this kind. M. Delombre removed the revolver, which was

wrapped in tissue paper, from his breeches pocket, and, at the judge's direction, handed it to Mr Frampton amid a profound sensation in court. Mr Justice Jelf (addressing Delombre): I do not think you ought to come into court with a loaded revolver in your pocket. M. Delombre: I did not know the custom here. I thought I would bring it as I took it. Mr Justice Jelf: You might have brought it in a locked box, with a key. Do not do it again. Mr Elliot [sic]: I do not think M. Delombre had any improper motives in bringing the revolver here. Sir Charles Mathews: I think the revolver had better be given to the police. Mr Justice Jelf: Yes. The police had better take it outside and withdraw the charge. The weapon was accordingly handed over … amid a titter of merriment, which his lordship sternly rebuked.[70]

Readers should be struck by what this incident tells us about how Edwardian courts functioned. The Old Bailey had just been rebuilt and was opened by King Edward VII on 27 February 1907,[71] but there were evidently no systems in place for ensuring that witnesses (and presumably others) did not enter with weapons. Although courtroom architecture lies outside the scope of this chapter,[72] this is just one area of criminal justice history that true-crime narratives can help to isolate from the mass of official statistics and sensational reportage.

But the main focus of this chapter is the emotions that underlie interpersonal violence, and popular responses to them. In this case, honour proved to be crucial. At the end of his cross-examination, Delombre denied that Foucault had told him his family were men without honour, claiming that 'It is because I have honour that I am here.'[73] Mathews' re-examination of his chief witness again focussed on Foucault's violence, then suggested that she had stolen some of the letters that Elliott had referred to. Then the prosecution turned to its other witnesses: a hotel porter (who understood French and whom the press reported as testifying that Foucault told him that 'she wanted a name for her child, and wanted her honour back');[74] two police constables; two surgeons; Eugène Sueur (with whom Delombre lived in London); and Acting-Sergeant Hodges, a bilingual officer in the City of London Police to whom Foucault had poured out her story (adding that if she'd wanted to kill Delombre she could have shot him). The judge commended Hodges and the City police for their professionalism and 'kindly regard to the accused'.[75]

On the following morning the accused woman took the stand to tell the story of her life and love following an impassioned address by George Elliott, who told the jury that this was a story that should have ended in marriage and that although Foucault was not faultless, having 'shamed her womanhood, and … fallen very low', she was 'more sinned against than sinning'. As the man who had dragged her down, Delombre should be the last person to accuse her. In a direct allusion to a point made by Mathews in his opening address, Elliott urged the jury to offer Foucault the same justice that she would receive in France or America. Then she walked to the stand. Journalists noted that her skirt brushed Delombre but he did not look at her; eventually, however, he turned to face her as she testified through an interpreter.[76]

Her extensive testimony was reported in much less detail than Delombre's because it served only to confirm what everyone already knew: she had loved him since she was twenty; twice attempted suicide because he would not marry her and had urged abortion; and had planned to commit suicide at Tranter's Hotel. The acid struck Delombre by accident when she threw it *away* from herself upon feeling the child moving within her.[77] The newspapers again reveal an interesting point not noted in the trial transcript:[78] with the aid of a prison wardress, Foucault reconstructed the scene as it took place in the hotel room; then the court adjourned briefly whilst, on the advice of the prison medical officer, Dr George Griffith, she was given a cup of tea![79] On the whole she presented a figure of 'pitiable despair' in the dock.[80]

When Foucault was cross-examined, Sir Charles Mathews did his best to prove that she had blinded Delombre deliberately. But this tactic provoked the judge's ire:

> He did not see what would be gained by blackening the character of either party. Such matters had nothing to do with the main issue … It was perfectly common ground … that the prisoner came to England with a great grievance … that M. Delombre, who had lived with her under circumstances more discreditable than he … had really had to investigate before, should, when the critical time of the child being born arrived, refuse to marry her or in any way recognise the child.[81]

Upon Mathews' insistence that he needed to present the facts, Jelf retorted, 'I shall treat irrelevant facts as being a thousand miles off. The jury have to say whether the mixture was thrown intentionally or not.'[82] And this of course was the crux of the matter. The further evidence given, including a spirited defence by Dr Griffith (evident only from press reports)[83] and some pointed questions to Foucault by Jelf about what she knew of the effects of vitriol, were minor features of the drama's dénouement. Elliott's summing up, reported in *The Times* alone, referred to Foucault's excitable French temperament and reminded the jury that as men of heart and conscience they could restore her to freedom; Mathews' reply was noted but not recorded.[84] Jelf's summing up was reported selectively in the press: *The Times* included his critique of the ease with which vitriol could be purchased, the *Evening Express* noted the introduction of evidence that had very little bearing on the actual indictment and several newspapers reported his direct criticism of Delombre, whose actions had displayed a 'callous cruelty' to Foucault's husbands.[85] Having been instructed to decide whether the prosecution had satisfied them beyond reasonable doubt that what the prisoner did was done intentionally to do grievous bodily harm, the jury retired to consider their verdict.[86]

The court was crowded when they returned after a mere quarter hour. Foucault, 'who throughout the trial had, strangely enough, not displayed any marked emotion, was seen to be greatly agitated'. When the foreman announced 'We find the prisoner not guilty', she 'collapsed into the arms of the wardress standing near, and then recovering herself, shouted something in French to her counsel and solicitors, with whom she heartily shook hands'.[87]

In an interview given the day after her acquittal, Foucault commended the English jurymen, many of whom had apparently congratulated her after the verdict. Though she had never doubted the result, she had feared Mathews' eloquence: 'He is such a powerful pleader, but feeling I had power, too, I stared into his eyes and remained calm and brave.' Her honour vindicated, her performance was not yet concluded, for Foucault took a final opportunity to highlight the melodrama she had created: she would keep Delombre's 400 letters for her son, so he would know 'all that I have suffered and gone through'. Remarking on the coincidence that the boy had a birthmark on his right temple, 'the very spot where the acid fell on M. Delombre' (actually, it was the left side), she vowed to bring her child up on English lines, as she was fond of the English people and English methods.[88]

And so the 'vitriol drama' concluded, even as others began. *The Daily Mirror* followed its final article on Foucault with a brief notice of a housemaid who threw acid on her fiancé after he took up with another woman.[89] In early May, a young woman threw hydrochloric acid over a man whom she had sued for breach of promise: counsel for the prosecution said she seemed to have been following the Foucault case and 'declared she had the acid for the purpose of suicide'.[90] But this woman's appeal to the court failed to play to the stock assumptions created by melodrama-inspired thinking: even though Lilian Woodcock, a shop manager, had twice attempted suicide she was found 'guilty, under great provocation' and sentenced to twelve months' hard labour.[91]

IV

During the Edwardian period there was approximately one case of vitriol throwing per month,[92] and in 1916 the British Board of Film Classification included its effects among the forty-three grounds for deletion laid down for the guidance of film censors.[93] It was a recognized phenomenon: a stereotypical yet unequivocal act with an exaggeratedly visual dimension that demonstrated high emotional states and their dramatic resolution. It encapsulated a conclusion to a narrative of sin and slighting repaid justly by fate; it foregrounded and displayed both dishonour and betrayed honour. In short, vitriol throwing in the Edwardian period comprised many of the standard tropes of Victorian melodrama, none more so than the case of Emilie Foucault and André Delombre. Both fit easily into familiar roles (a demure young woman exploited by a villainous aristocrat), and in the end evil was thwarted and virtue triumphed.[94] Whether or not Foucault referred explicitly to her lost honour, it is clear that this is how the press, and ultimately the jury, interpreted her story. As Eliza Ferguson has noted of 1880s Paris, 'jurors were no more immune to powerful emotions than the defendant',[95] and so Foucault's narrative was central to the way the trial unfolded. So was Delombre's, for at every turn it revealed him to be a man without honour.

The Foucault–Delombre micro-history has thus opened to analysis the emotions that lurked under the surface of a well-documented crime and public responses to that crime, thereby suggesting avenues for further research on the role of emotion in interpersonal offences and their subsequent impact in court. The nature of the crime itself and the reasons for its relative infrequency are perhaps all the more important given that vitriol throwing was well known to the Victorians and Edwardians yet has been little studied by historians. Today, however, it seems to be experiencing something of resurgence.[96] Furthermore, the narrative highlights a separate issue: the use of true-crime stories to shed light on how lawyers navigated the courtroom environment and so shaped the development of the criminal trial. The period under study lends itself particularly well to such an aim because the press was well developed and hungry for crime news, but methodological problems abound: it may always be easiest to do this sort of analysis for London because of the *Proceedings of the Old Bailey*, incomplete as they may be.[97]

The exclusion of barristers' opening and closing statements, some verbatim testimony and the judge's summing up, together with the failure to note court recesses and re-enactments poses methodological problems for criminal justice historians who wish to use the *Proceedings* to shed light on the evolution of trial procedure. Newspaper reportage clearly offers an additional layer of important detail, but holds its own weaknesses: selective and possibly inaccurate reporting. Andrew Hobbs has warned against assuming that *The Times* represents the best source of nineteenth-century news,[98] and a focus on trials held at the Old Bailey could skew the historiography of crime and criminal justice towards a London-centred understanding of jury behaviour, or an incomplete interpretation of how London trials proceeded – unless future work more closely examines what actually happened in court.

Finally, the varying emphases and interpretations placed on evidence and performance by legal and journalistic sources require careful consideration. Although criminal justice historians have often been more interested in criminals than victims, this chapter shows the importance of the latter in gaining a full understanding of how the criminal justice system worked. True-crime narratives enable historians to discover more about crime, emotion and criminal justice, to move beyond statistics to the lived experiences of the people on whom they rest.

Notes

1. *Evening Express*, 15 December 1906, p. 2. This conservative English-language daily newspaper circulated in the district of Cardiff but provided the fullest coverage of the case.

2. D.J.R. Grey (2015) '"Agonised Weeping": Representing Femininity, Emotion and Infanticide in Edwardian Newspapers', *Media History*, Vol. 21, No. 4, pp. 468–80. On Edwardian provincial press sensationalism, see J. Benson (2009) 'Calculation, Celebrity and Scandal: The Provincial Press in Edwardian England', *Journalism Studies*, Vol. 10, pp. 837–50.

3. *Evening Express*, 23 April 1907, p. 3.

4. K.D. Watson (2009) 'Is a Burn a Wound? Vitriol-Throwing in Medico-Legal Context, 1800–1900', in I. Goold and C. Kelly (eds) *Lawyers' Medicine: The Legislature, the Courts and Medical Practice, 1760–2000* (Oxford: Hart Publishing), pp. 61–78.

5. J.F. McMillan (2000) *France and Women, 1789–1914: Gender, Society and Politics* (London and New York: Routledge), pp. 103–5; E.E. Ferguson (2006) 'Judicial Authority and Popular Justice: Crimes of Passion in Fin-De-Siècle Paris', *Journal of Social History*, Vol. 40, pp. 293–315. The association of crimes of passion with France persisted for decades; see for example 'Crimes of Passion', *The Times*, 20 October 1956, p. 7.

6. R. McWilliam (2000) 'Melodrama and the Historians', *Radical History Review*, Vol. 78, pp. 57–84.

7. J. Rowbotham, K. Stevenson and S. Pegg (2013) *Crime News in Modern Britain: Press Reporting and Responsibility, 1820–2010* (Basingstoke: Palgrave), pp. 84–113. See also J. Carter Wood and P. Knepper (2014) 'Crime Stories: Criminality, Policing and the Press in Inter-war European and Transatlantic Perspectives', *Media History*, Vol. 20, No. 4, pp. 345–51.

8. For assault, see P. King (1996) 'Punishing Assault: The Transformation of Attitudes in the English Courts', *Journal of Interdisciplinary History*, Vol. 27, pp. 43–74 and P. Handler (2007) 'The Law of Felonious Assault in England, 1803–61', *Journal of Legal History*, Vol. 28, pp. 183–206. For changing nineteenth-century attitudes to violence, see J. Carter Wood (2004) *Violence and Crime in Nineteenth-Century England: The Shadow of Our Refinement* (London: Routledge).

9. A. Clark (1987) *Women's Silence, Men's Violence: Sexual Assault in England 1770–1845* (London and New York: Pandora Press); S. D'Cruze (1998) *Crimes of Outrage: Sex, Violence and Victorian Working Women* (London: Routledge); E. Foyster (2005) *Marital Violence: An English Family History, 1660–1857* (Cambridge: Cambridge University Press); and J. Bailey (2006) '"I dye [sic] by Inches": Locating Wife Beating in the Concept of a Privatization of Marriage and Violence in Eighteenth-Century England', *Social History*, Vol. 31, pp. 273–94.

10. Historians of crime have long had a fascination with statistics, either those they generate themselves from archival sources or those compiled by the government. For an introduction to some of the historiographical issues raised, see R.M. Morris (2001) '"Lies, Damned Lies and Criminal Statistics": Reinterpreting the Criminal Statistics in England and Wales', *Crime, History & Societies*, Vol. 5, pp. 111–27.

11. English common law acknowledged provocation as an excuse for crime, see for instance J. Horder (2007) *Excusing Crime* (Oxford: Oxford University Press), pp. 43–98 and B.J. Brown (1963) 'The Demise of Chance Medley and the Recognition of Provocation as a Defence to Murder in English Law', *The American Journal of Legal History*, Vol. 7, pp. 310–18. The defence of provocation reduced murder to manslaughter, and historians accordingly discuss cases that might be considered crimes of passion under this rubric; see for example M. Wiener (1999) 'The Sad Story of George Hall: Adultery, Murder and the Politics of Mercy in Mid-Victorian England', *Social History*, Vol. 24, pp. 174–95.

12. 61 and 62 Vict c. 36. See also D. Bentley (1998) *English Criminal Justice in the Nineteenth Century* (London: Hambledon Press), pp. 198–204.

13. Judith Knelman (1998) *Twisting in the Wind: The Murderess and the English Press* (Toronto: University of Toronto Press), pp. 233–48 has shown that by the end of the nineteenth century accused murderesses could be viewed with compassion when they presented themselves as 'more sinned against than sinning' (p. 236). This is precisely the impression that Foucault made on journalists (see note 76).

14. The trial was published in *Central Criminal Court Sessions Paper*, Seventh Session, v. 147, April 1907 (London, 1907), pp. 49–71 (hereafter *Sessions Paper*); it is online at *The Proceedings of the Old Bailey, 1674–1913*, www.oldbaileyonline.org,ref.t19070422-43. All references are to the original print version. Information about Delombre's injuries is on pp. 52 and 59–60.

15. Rowbotham, Stevenson and Pegg, *Crime News in Modern Britain*, p. 9.

16. *Evening Express*, 5 December 1906, p. 4.

17. Ibid.

18. Ibid.

19. *Evening Express*, 14 December 1906, p. 3 and 15 December 1906, p. 2.

20. Ibid.

21. Ibid.

22. Ibid.

23. *The Times*, 14 December 1906, p. 4.

24. Ibid.

25. *The Daily Mirror*, 14 December 1906, p. 5.

26. S. Baring Gould (1880) *Mehalah: A Story of the Salt Marshes* (London: John Murray), chap. 24 and 25; G. Gissing (1889) *The Nether World* (London: Dent), chap. 23; A. Conan Doyle (1892) 'The Adventure of the Blue Carbuncle' in his *The Adventures of Sherlock Holmes* (London: George Newness), pp. 73–85 and 'The Illustrious Client', *Collier's Weekly*, 8 November 1924; J. Buchan (1924) *The Three Hostages* (London: Hodder and Stoughton), chap. 19 (a threat only) and G. Casserly (1926) *The Desert Lovers* (London: Blackledge), reviewed in *The Scotsman*, 1 April 1926, p. 2.

27. D. Kerr (1936 edition) *Forensic Medicine* (London: Black), p. 110.

28. P. Spierenburg (2008) *A History of Murder: Personal Violence in Europe from the Middle Ages to the Present* (Cambridge: Polity Press), pp. 188–92. See also *The Times*, 4 November 1881, p. 9.

29. See J. Guillais [trans. Jane Dunnett] (1990) *Crimes of Passion: Dramas of Private Life in Nineteenth-Century France* (New York: Routledge), pp. 148–9; R. Harris (1988) 'Melodrama, Hysteria and Feminine Crimes of Passion in the Fin-de-Siècle', *History Workshop*, Vol. 25, pp. 31–63; R. Harris (1989) *Murders and Madness: Medicine, Law, and Society in the Fin-de-Siècle* (Oxford: Oxford University Press), pp. 238–39; M.S. Hartman (1985) *Victorian Murderesses* (New York: Schocken Books), pp. 239–40 and A.-L. Shapiro (1996) *Breaking the Codes: Female Criminality in Fin-de-Siècle Paris* (Stanford, CL: Stanford University Press), pp. 76–80.

30. L. Bending (2000) *The Representation of Bodily Pain in Late Nineteenth-Century English Culture* (Oxford: Oxford University Press), pp. 233–4. Lombroso's views were embedded in his belief that women were inferior to men and thus less criminal than men, but that criminal women were primitive and masculine in comparison to their law-abiding, feminine and civilized sisters. In further distinguishing between the 'born criminal' and the 'criminal by passion', Lombroso created a clear class distinction that could be easily applied to vitriol throwers. See C. Lombroso and G. Ferrero [trans. Nicole Hahn Rafter and Mary Gibson] (2004 edition) *Criminal Woman, the Prostitute, and the Normal Woman*, (Durham, NC: Duke University Press), pp. 3–11.

31. Spierenburg, *A History of Murder*, p. 188. For a contemporary perspective, see R. Ferrari (1918) 'The "Crime Passionnel" in French Courts', *California Law Review*, Vol. 6, pp. 331–41.

32. E.E. Ferguson (2010) *Gender and Justice: Violence, Intimacy, and Community in Fin-de-Siècle Paris* (Baltimore: John Hopkins University Press), pp. 1–17. For a case study of honour and emotion that resulted in acquittal, see E.E. Ferguson (2014) 'Emotion, Gender and Honour in a Fin-de-siècle Crime of Passion: The Case of Marie Bière', in C. Strange, R. Cribb and C.E. Forth (eds) *Honour, Violence and Emotions in History* (London: Bloomsbury), pp. 145–61.

33. J. Rowbotham (2000) '"Only When Drunk": The Stereotyping of Violence in England, c.1850–1900', in S. D'Cruze (ed.) *Everyday Violence in Britain, 1850–1950: Gender and Class* (Harlow: Longman), pp. 155–69, at pp. 163 and 167.

34. M.J. Wiener (2004) *Men of Blood: Violence, Manliness, and Criminal Justice in Victorian England* (Cambridge: Cambridge University Press), pp. 9–39.

35. 24 and 25 Vict c. 100, s. 29. Vitriol throwing became a capital offence in Scotland in 1825, see Watson, 'Is a Burn a Wound?' *passim.*

36. Bending, *The Representation of Bodily Pain*, p. 234. See for example *The Times*, 10 July 1865 and the 4 and 11 August 1881, as well as the trials of Louis Wheeler, 1885 (t18850302-369) and Susan Sophia Grant, 1886 (t18860913-977) available at http://www.oldbaileyonline.org.

37. Judicial statistics for 1907 reveal that in London and Middlesex there were, respectively, 39 and 1 trials for felonious wounding, and 229 and 20 trials for malicious wounding (misdemeanour) in the higher courts (the Old Bailey and quarter sessions); see Parliamentary Papers, *Judicial Statistics, England and Wales, 1907. Part I – Criminal Statistics* (4544), Vol. CIV (1909), p. 59.

38. For a contemporary list of London police courts, see Parliamentary Papers, *Return of Summary Convictions for Street Betting in the Metropolitan Police District during the years 1903, 1904, and 1905* (179), Vol. XCIX (1906), p. 747.

39. For example, the trials of Elizabeth Hodges, 1853 (t18530404-511); Annie Vinten, 1862 (t18620106-199); Thomas Bryant, 1873 (t18730922-578); Eleanor Myers, 1881 (t18810228-308); Freeman Ellingham, 1897 (t18970524-415); and John Lawrence, 1909 (t19090622-54) all available at http://www.oldbaileyonline.org.

40. For example, the trials of Jane Haynes, 1860 (t18601217-78); John Metze, 1863 (t18630302-489); Ann Mills, 1879 (t18791020-950); Ellen Giles, 1892 (t18920111-178); Helen Nemetsclek, 1900 (t19000625-446); and William Lilley, 1906 (t19060521-31) all available at http://www.oldbaileyonline.org.

41. For example, John Metze and Ann Mills (see note 40) as well as Margaret O'Brien, 1871 (t18710403-342) and Maria Abbott, 1900 (t19001210-74) were all sentenced to five years after blinding their victims. Frederick Parker, 1906 (t19060625-15) got five years even though the victim (his sister) was not badly injured, almost certainly because he was a habitual drunkard with a long record of summary convictions. Available at http://www.oldbaileyonline.org.

42. See the trial of John Wainwright, 1866 (t18660409-378) available at http://www.oldbaileyonline.org.

43. *The Times*, 1 December 1847, p. 7.

44. *The Times*, 18 September 1924, p. 9. This comment reiterated the Victorian assumption that violent women must either be evil or effectively insane: Rowbotham, 'Only When Drunk', p. 163.

45. *The Cambrian*, 1 February 1907, p. 3.

46. *Evening Express*, 22 March 1907, p. 2.

47. *The Times*, 23 April 1907, p. 9.

48. *Evening Express*, 24 April 1907, p. 2.

49. J. Pellew (1989) 'The Home Office and the Aliens Act, 1905', *The Historical Journal*, Vol. 32, pp. 369–85.

50. See the 1907 trials of Charles Laroche for fraud (t19070422-38), Louis Gold and Harry Cohen for procuring (t19070422) and Isaac Eidinow for fraud (t19070422) all available at http://www.oldbaileyonline.org. Gold and Cohen were certified for expulsion under the Aliens Act.

51. For a short biography, see *The Times*, 25 July 1917, p. 9.

52. The son of actors, Mathews tended to adopt a melodramatic rhetoric in order to turn sympathy away from the defendant; but like melodrama itself, this style was becoming unfashionable by the turn of the century. See A. Lentin (2004) 'Mathews, Sir Charles Willie, Baronet (1850–1920)', *Oxford Dictionary of National Biography Online* (Oxford: Oxford University Press), available at http://www.oxforddnb.com/ (accessed 10 August 2015).

53. *Evening Express*, 23 April 1907, p. 3.

54. Ibid.

55. Ibid. The formal record of the trial does not record Mathews' opening statement, but the *Evening Express* summarized it.

56. *Sessions Paper*, pp. 50–1.

57. *Evening Express*, 23 April 1907, p. 3.

58. *Evening Express*, 24 April 1907, p. 3; much of this article was reproduced in the *Weekly Mail*, 27 April 1907, p. 7.

59. Ibid.

60. H.B. Taft (1905) 'The Administration of Criminal Law', *Yale Law Journal*, Vol. 15, pp. 1–17 at p. 12 and L.M. Friedman (1993) *Crime and Punishment in American History* (New York: Basic Books), pp. 252–5.

61. *Sessions Paper*, pp. 53–4.

62. *Weekly Mail*, 27 April 1907, p. 7 and *Evening Express*, 24 April 1907, p. 3.

63. The *Evening Express* used the subheading 'His Lordship Amazed'.

64. *The Cardiff Times*, 27 April 1907, p. 8.

65. *Sessions Paper*, p. 55.

66. *The Cardiff Times*, 27 April 1907, p. 8.

67. *Weekly Mail*, 27 April 1907, p. 7.

68. This was the only part of the day's proceedings reported in *The Manchester Guardian*, 25 April 1907, p. 3 and *The Daily Mirror*, 25 April 1907, p. 5. *The Times* did not report it at all. *The Cambrian* reported it briefly with details of the attempted abortion, 26 April 1907, p. 8. *The Cardiff Times*, which reported the entire trial in some detail, used the subheading 'Court Alarmed'.

69. *Sessions Paper*, p. 56.

70. *Weekly Mail*, 27 April 1907, p. 7.

71. http://www.oldbaileyonline.org/static/The-old-bailey.jsp#a1907 (accessed 16 September 2015).

72. L. Mulcahy (2011) *Legal Architecture: Justice, Due Process and the Place of Law* (Abingdon: Routledge).

73. *Sessions Paper*, p. 58. The notion of honour seems to have crept up on Delombre who, presumably wanting justice for his ruined face, decided to prosecute knowing that his sexual relationship with a married woman would be raked over. What he may not have expected was the extraordinary detail that Foucault was willing to reveal.

74. *Weekly Mail*, 27 April 1907, p. 7. It should be noted that the trial transcript (p. 59) does not record this.

75. *Sessions Paper*, p. 62.

76. *Weekly Mail*, 27 April 1907, p. 7 and *The Daily Mirror*, 26 April 1907, p. 4. The phrase 'more sinned against than sinning' appeared as a subheadline.

77. *The Daily Mirror*, 26 April 1907, p. 4 and *Evening Express*, 26 April 1907, p. 3.

78. *Sessions Paper*, pp. 62–7.

79. *The Daily Mirror*, 26 April 1907, p. 4.

80. *The Daily Mirror*, 27 April 1907, p. 13.

81. *Evening Express*, 27 April 1907, p. 3.

82. Ibid.

83. *Sessions Paper*, p. 70 and *Evening Express*, 27 April 1907, p. 3.

84. *The Times*, 27 April 1907, p. 6.

85. Ibid.; *Evening Express*, 27 April 1907, p. 3; *The Manchester Guardian*, 27 April 1907, p. 5 and *The Daily Mirror*, 27 April 1907, p. 13.

86. Ibid.

87. *Evening Express*, 27 April 1907, p. 3.

88. *Evening Express*, 29 April 1907, p. 2 and *The Daily Mirror*, 29 April 1907, p. 5.

89. *The Daily Mirror*, 29 April 1907, p. 5.

90. *Weekly Mail*, 4 May 1907, p. 1 and *The Cardiff Times*, 4 May 1907, p. 7.

91. See the trial of Lilian Sarah Woodcock, 1907 (ref. t19070528-46) available at http://www.oldbaileyonline.org.

92. F.J. Smith (ed.) (1910 edition) *Taylor's Principles and Practice of Medical Jurisprudence* (London: J.A. Churchill) Vol. 1, p. 605.

93. British Board of Film Classification History 1912–1949, available at http://www.bbfc.co.uk/education-resources/student-guide/bbfc-history/1912-1949 (accessed 16 September 2015).

94. McWilliam, 'Melodrama and the Historians', p. 61.

95. Ferguson, 'Emotion, Gender and Honour', p. 152.

96. 'Acid Attacks on the Rise in UK, According to Victim Report', *The Guardian*, 10 April 2014, available at http://www.theguardian.com/uk-news/2014/apr/10/acid-attacks-uk-rise-gangs (accessed 22 September 2015).

97. 'The Value of the Proceedings as a Historical Source', available at http://www.oldbaileyonline.org/static/Value.jsp#legal.

98. A. Hobbs (2013) 'The Deleterious Dominance of *The Times* in Nineteenth-Century Scholarship', *Journal of Victorian Culture*, Vol. 18, 472–97.

CHAPTER 6
CONSTRUCTING THE CULT OF THE CRIMINAL: KATE WEBSTER – VICTORIAN MURDERESS AND MEDIA SENSATION
Anne-Marie Kilday

I

It is difficult to account for the differences in the amount of interest displayed with regard to murders. The body of a murdered person is found one day stabbed to the heart, and all England is convulsed by the intelligence, 'latest particulars' are given by the papers, and eagerly devoured by the public, a large reward is offered by Government for the discovery of the murderer, and all Scotland-yard is on the alert. The body of another murdered person is found the next day with the skull fractured, and little or no notice is taken of the circumstance. The evidence given at the inquest appears in an obscure corner of the daily journals, under the head of 'Death under suspicious circumstances', the jury return an open verdict, no reward is offered by Government, the body is, perhaps, never identified, but is buried in a nameless grave, and there is the end of the matter.[1]

It is evident, not least from the other chapters in this volume, that micro-histories regularly tell us much about criminals, the crimes they perpetrate and their context. Yet micro-histories can also shed light on both authoritative reactions to illegality and more popular or customary attitudes to its committal. This chapter explores the latter perspective, whilst concerned with the origins of the intense and widespread fascination with homicide. This has seemingly widened its reach to such an extent (and at such alarming speed) that present-day social commentators have been at pains to point out the threat that it poses to modern, civilized society. Scholars have firmly situated the enduring zenith of this unhealthy obsession in the modern era, suggesting the last three decades of the twentieth century established what we could call 'the cult of the criminal'. Certainly the paroxysm and proliferation of multiple murderers (latterly defined as serial killers) stimulated the media's attention from that time onwards. Yet there is now evidence to suggest that the origins of this 'cult of the criminal' emerge earlier than the 1970s. Indeed our preoccupation with murder had already assumed powerful proportions long before some of the infamous (official) first-wave serial killers (such as Ted Bundy, Edmund Kemper, Peter Sutcliffe and Dennis Nilsen) were even born. For instance, historians such as Judith Flanders, Rosalind Crone and Lucy Worsley have compellingly argued that the Victorian popular fascination for murder was just as pervasive as in contemporary times.[2] Indeed, the only real difference between the two eras lies in the development of new media technologies from the late twentieth century onwards, which have enabled this fascination to reach a wider, global audience more rapidly than in earlier periods.

Whilst we can acknowledge the importance of the Victorian era in establishing the 'cult of the criminal' what is even more interesting for the purposes of this chapter is that our obsession with murder and fatal interpersonal violence has been somewhat selective. Evidently throughout history, some murders have fascinated more than others. Certainly, the opening quote to this chapter, from 1871, suggests this same selectivity was at play during the Victorian era. Indeed according to the author of these same editorial notes, some murders were deemed 'fashionable' and others 'unfashionable', but why was this the case? Scholars of modern criminality have tried to identify the triggers or elements of homicide cases that make them especially interesting to popular audiences in the present day. But can these prompts also apply to Victorian predilections and to what extent can micro-histories help us to uncover the subjectivity of the 'cult of the criminal' and its subsequent evolution?

This chapter uses a detailed micro-history of the notorious case of Katherine (Kate) Webster, an Irishwoman living in the London borough of Richmond indicted for the murder of her mistress, Mrs Julia Martha Thomas, at the Old Bailey in 1879. Through analysing media reactions to the courtroom evidence and the portrayal of Webster in the extensive press coverage that ensued, this chapter displays the aspects of this case that fascinated the Victorian populace and assesses why this particular homicide attracted so much attention for so long. According to one scholar, the Webster case achieved 'a dark immortality'[3] in the annals of crime, but were the reasons for its prolonged infamy the same as those suggested by scholars for the more modern era? In addition, what does this micro-history tell us about female homicidal activity and how it was regarded during the Victorian period – an era where prevailing gender ideologies encouraged the populace to instinctively recoil from female violence?

II

Historians, criminologists and sociologists have recognized the existence of a cultural obsession with violence and with homicide in particular, during the modern era. The United States of America has seemingly led the way with this, but other developed societies display an evident preoccupation with violence and the violent too, including Great Britain.[4] Mark Seltzer explains the allure of fatal violence as being symptomatic of a 'wound culture' which is a 'public fascination with torn and open bodies and torn and open persons, a collective gathering around shock, trauma and the wound'.[5] Society is thus attracted to 'the atrocity exhibition' where individuals 'wear their damage like badges of identity, or fashion accessories'.[6] The media's overblown attention to the crimes of multiple murderers since the 1970s has broadened and accelerated reverence for this 'wound culture' so that murderers routinely become celebrities and evidence of their crimes becomes memorabilia for collection.[7] Arguably then, a 'market for murder' was

Jack the Ripper

cultivated by popular interest in some of the most vicious, brutal and repugnant episodes to have occurred in criminal history.[8] Indeed, one derivative of this is the phenomenon of 'dark tourism' with individuals and groups touring places associated with death and suffering, including murder sites and locations associated with famous killers.[9]

Although modern society's fascination with the 'cult of the criminal' seems unrelentingly ubiquitous, closer analysis reveals our obsession is more qualified and discerning. Not all murders are deemed newsworthy, nor all murderers infamous. Indeed, analysing a compendium of micro-histories and case-studies led criminologists such as Yvonne Jewkes and David Wilson to argue for twelve criteria by which we can gauge the potential for public interest generated by a given true crime story. These are:

(1) **Threshold** (the perceived importance of the event in a global, national or local context);

(2) **Predictability** (the more novel or unusual a crime, the more interesting it seems);

(3) **Simplification** (the need for criminal episodes to be relatively comprehensible);

(4) **Individualism** (the need for crime stories to have human interest elements so that can be readily identified with);

(5) **Risk** (interest is seemingly greater in a crime if the offender is unknown or is at large);

(6) **Sex** (crime stories involving sex and violence generate more interest than those without such elements);

(7) **Celebrity** (even if a crime is mundane in content it generates interest if a well-known person is connected to the events);

(8) **Proximity** (a crime story will generate interest if it has spatially and cultural relevance to its audience);

(9) **Violence** (the most important trigger for the newsworthiness of a criminal episode is whether violence is evident or not);

(10) **Visual Spectacle** (in the twentieth and twenty-first centuries, graphic imagery is crucial for a crime story to be memorable and attain longevity of interest);

(11) **Children** (crime stories are effectively guaranteed extensive media exposure if they feature children as victims or offenders); and

(12) **Conservative Ideology and Political Diversion** (criminal episodes which transgress social norms and challenge conservative attitudes are typically newsworthy).[10]

Whilst David Wilson applauds Jewkes' attempts to offer a theoretical foundation for the study of popular fascination with particular offences and offenders, he argues that her criteria are not comprehensive, nor are they unproblematic. First, he argues that a crescendo of publicity is often associated with a criminal in the run up to their prosecution enabling their notoriety. Second and arguably linked to this preliminary

J. the - Rifle

point, if an offender is assigned a nickname by the media, their criminal exploits more readily achieve prominent news coverage. Third, Wilson suggests that crimes committed in the north of Britain are not as widely reported on as crimes committed in the south, regardless of the levels of brutality involved. Moreover, if the crime scenes are perceivably linked to lower social class, they will not attain as much publicity as incidents elsewhere. Wilson also argues that seemingly motiveless crimes are harder for the public to engage with than those where cause is more evident. Finally, he argues that criminal cases with extensive and varied witness testimony are far likely to achieve notoriety than instances where the public voice is absent, even if the crime itself was brutal, bloody or baffling.[11]

Arguably, Jewkes and Wilson are not that far apart in identifying the triggers which determine whether a given crime or criminal will grab the headlines in modern Britain. Yet their scholarship also reveals that what generates popular interest is not fixed or stable. Rather, our fascination with the 'cult of crime' depends on the specific circumstances of a given case and its context. Our predilections in this respect evidently change over time as that context evolves and is reshaped by social, cultural, economic and political events. But can this fascination with crime (and with murderous violence in particular) be traced back to earlier periods and does the contemporary fascination with murderous violence apply to popular audiences prior to 1900?

III

Certainly, an interest in death and suffering had been evident in Britain since the eighteenth century, when huge crowds gathered to witness public executions and individuals purchased the penitent confessions of condemned felons.[12] Yet, by the nineteenth century, the popular appetite for stories of murder had seemingly become voracious. Richard D. Altick argues that 'It was in, or just before, the early Victorian era that homicide first became institutionalised as a popular entertainment, a spectator sport.'[13] Moreover, this passion for murder and the macabre was projected like a 'crimson thread that [ran] through the fabric of Victorian society' as it was a passion shared by all individuals regardless of social class.[14] The emergence of 'the New Journalism' coupled with a glut of sensational murder cases in the mid Victorian era both focussed the critical spotlight of social and moral commentators on deviance and illegality for political effect. Collectively, all of these factors cemented a fascination for homicide in the Victorian consciousness.[15]

Michel Foucault has suggested that a new category of 'dangerous individual' emerged to thrill and threaten Victorian society in equal measure.[16] This shift is evident in newspaper reportage from the period as journalists provided detailed information regarding offenders *and* their offences.[17] Arguably, the addition of this personal dimension to the retelling of Victorian murders, alongside the broad circulation of considerable detail regarding specific murderous episodes, enabled Victorian audiences to be more readily enthralled by fatal violence than their forebears. Arguably then, the nineteenth century marks the real *origins* of the long-standing obsession with 'the cult of the criminal' in Great Britain and may even mark the early *zenith* of this preoccupation.

Although the homicide rate was in substantial decline during the nineteenth century, Victorians found murder endlessly fascinating nonetheless.[18] For instance, a typical homicide trial during the Victorian period could result in around 500,000 copies of the trial proceedings being produced by London printers alone. Particular episodes could generate much greater circulation figures, with one mid-century murder case necessitating the production of over 1,650,000 broadside pamphlets.[19] The 'market for murder' during this period was also evident in the number of plays, peep shows, puppet shows, waxwork exhibitions, ballads and novels inspired by contemporary homicide cases and available for consumers to buy or view at reasonable prices.[20] Moreover, early 'dark tourism' in the shape of 'murder-sightseeing' became a popular pastime long before the 1970s and the artefacts and evidence associated with famous criminal trials (now known as 'murderbilia') were regularly auctioned before substantial baying crowds oblivious to high Victorian morals and sensibilities.[21] This profitable and extensive fascination with murder and murderers continued into the modern era and extended its reach and significance with the advent of mass media and new communication technologies.[22]

Scholars of the obsession with the 'cult of crime' arguably underestimate the full extent of its power and hold over the populace during earlier periods. Moreover, their acknowledgement of the importance of the nineteenth century to 'the cult of the criminal' relates to male offenders alone and to serial killers (such as Jack the Ripper or H.H. Holmes) more specifically.[23] This ignores the significance of the Victorian moral panic over female killers and its impact upon the escalating obsession with fatal violence. The Victorian fascination with female killers is evident from comparing the media interest aroused by two micro-histories of homicide from 1879. The first, from March of that year, saw Thomas Perryman indicted at the Old Bailey for the murder of his mother Frances after an alcohol-fuelled skirmish in the family home in Kentish Town (London).[24] Thomas was accused of killing his mother by hanging her on an iron peg found on the back of a cupboard door in her bedroom before strangling her with a handkerchief, claiming that she had committed suicide.[25] Previous episodes of domestic abuse committed by Thomas against Frances incriminated him when the case came to court.[26] This, alongside his widely witnessed semi-permanent state of inebriation, the 'forensic' evidence presented in the case and the tragic suicide of his brother William, overcome with guilt at being unable to protect his beloved mother from the ravages of his violent elder brother, resulted in Thomas Perryman being capitally convicted of matricide.[27] The sensational Perryman case generated ninety-two separate newspaper reports in both London and regional English newspapers. By comparison, however, the case study which forms the focus for this chapter, the murder of Mrs Julia Martha Thomas by her servant Kate Webster (also in 1879), generated an astounding 597 separate newspaper articles. As we will see in Section IV, interest in this particular murder micro-history was far more extensive and enduring than many other true-crime histories from either the Victorian era or beyond. Likewise, much of the fascination aroused by the Webster case related to the central protagonist being a violent female.

The murderess fascinated Victorian society because she encapsulated the antithesis of accepted gendered behaviour.[28] Just as their forbears, Victorian women were expected to be paragons of virtue, gentility and femininity and were encouraged to perform their role as moral guardians (within the domestic sphere) whilst displaying the innate maternal instincts and ethical principles to nurture future generations. Yet a spate of sensational poisoning trials during the nineteenth century exposed the potential for female deviousness of predominantly middle-class women's performance of their domestic duties as they had poisoned their victims at home, during the course of food preparation. For Victorians then, female killers had not only committed a despicable offence, but had also stepped outside of the boundaries of 'expected' behaviour for their sex.[29] The dual threat that some women seemingly posed to Victorian society resulted in a pre-modern example of moral panic with social commentators crusading to reinstate traditional gender ideologies seemingly crucial for social stability. Concerns about female cunning became combined with fears of female violence in attempts to reinforce the ideological orthodoxy. During the second half of the nineteenth century the prevailing moral panic, coupled with the relative *rarity* of female killers in reality, made episodes of fatal female violence unduly prominent.[30] Female killers particularly interested a society already obsessed with murder and the macabre.[31] Moreover, just as our interest in 'the cult of the criminal' has intensified over time, our preoccupation with murderous women has arguably become more amplified too.[32]

IV

The case brought against Kate Webster at the Old Bailey in 1879 undoubtedly exemplified the fascination for murderous women in the Victorian era. Rather than providing a simple micro-history, this section concentrates on the elements of the case which exemplifies the modern era's 'cult of the criminal'. A detailed analysis of court records and the case's extensive newspaper coverage makes it possible to identify six factors arguably crucial to establishing the infamy of this true-crime history. These were (1) interesting back-story; (2) crime as mystery; (3) ultra-violent methodology; (4) criminal characteristics; (5) compelling endgame; and, (6) storyline stamina. Section V analyses these factors and compares them with the public interest triggers evident for crime stories in more modern periods. This underlines why British society has had such an enduring obsession with homicide and engages with reactions and attitudes to violent female criminality.

Interesting back-story

If Kate Webster's final testimony is to be believed, she had lived an interesting life even before she came to work in the London Borough of Richmond, the scene of her infamous crime. She was an Irish Catholic, born in Killane, County Wexford, in 1849. She had been married to a sea captain called John W. Webster whilst still a teenager, bearing him four children. Tragically, however, her husband and all four of their children perished in uncertain circumstances.[33] Widowed and destitute, Webster turned to theft but was soon convicted of larceny and sentenced to a short spell of imprisonment. These events occurred prior to her emigration to England and all transpired before she had reached twenty years of age.[34]

On arrival in Liverpool, sometime in the early 1860s, Webster turned petty thief once more, but she was not evidently a skilled criminal as she was apprehended again in 1867 and sentenced to four years penal servitude. Granted a ticket of leave in the third year of this sentence, Webster moved to London, where she lodged with a man called Strong. They had a bastard child together but Strong abandoned her and his son soon after his birth in 1874. Impoverished, alone and with a young baby to care for, Webster was convicted of larceny for a third time in May 1875 at the Surrey sessions, despite her best efforts to be peripatetic and to hide her identity through the use of aliases (such as Webb, Shannon, Gibbs, Gibbons, Lawler and somewhat ironically, Lawless).[35] Webster was well known to the police, however, and there is evidence to suggest that they had her under surveillance, suspecting her involvement in criminal gangs engaged in long firm swindles. This time, her criminal ventures (numbering thirty-six separate offences) earned her an eighteen-month prison sentence at Wandsworth Gaol. After her release, Webster was in trouble once again and in February 1877, she was indicted for a further felony and sentenced to twelve months imprisonment.[36]

In January 1879, Webster became a domestic servant in the house of wealthy eccentric Mrs Julia Martha Thomas, who lived in the London Borough of Richmond. Even by this point in her micro-history, Kate Webster had developed something of a reputation for recidivism and bold (or desperate) criminality in the face of both police and judicial authorities, who scarcely doubted her character and potential to cause trouble. Indeed, she was variously described by them at this time as 'a thorough jail-bird', 'an habitual rogue' and possessing 'an automatic inclination towards evil'.[37] The back-story of Kate Webster made for compelling reading amongst the Victorian public as her behaviour undermined her capacity for personal morality at a time when threatening female deviancy was firmly in the spotlight. Even before the fatal events of spring 1879 then, Kate Webster had already gained a degree of notoriety.

Crime as mystery

Public fascination with the Kate Webster case became established not long after the murder of Mrs Thomas. This was because newspapers widely reported that on 5 March 1879 a box containing 'a mass of flesh' and portions of a human body were found floating below Barnes Bridge in Richmond by local man Henry Wheatley.[38] At first the authorities dismissed the find as a vulgar prank carried out by university medical students.[39] But upon further detailed medical examination by the coroner Dr Thomas Bond, it became evident that dismemberment had not been discharged with anatomical skill and instead, that something more sinister had occurred, although the identity of the victim concerned remained unknown.[40] Contemporary newspapers thus dubbed the crime 'The Barnes Mystery' or 'The Thames Mystery' and speculation abounded over who was in the box and what had happened to them.[41] The find was of particular interest since it mirrored the mysterious discovery of body parts in a box under Waterloo Bridge in 1857. In this case the victim was never identified and the incident remained unexplained.[42]

With the 1879 case, poisoning and later dismemberment were initially considered as methodologies, but were eventually ruled out by the coroner.[43] As we will see, a far more gruesome fate had befallen the inhabitant of the recovered box, much to the excitement of a Victorian public who poured over press reports of ghastly murders in ever-increasing numbers. Moreover, the incomplete nature of the dismembered body (as parts of the lower torso, the feet, hands, arms and the head of the victim were missing[44]) intensified interest in the case, encouraging some individuals to rummage through foul-smelling detritus in local refuse sites in search of the remaining anatomical evidence. However, aside from the victim's foot which was indeed discovered on a dungheap as part of this macabre 'treasure-hunt', the unearthed material was dismissed by the authorities as either non-human or not linked to the case. Nevertheless, through incessantly reporting on all the clues and false leads stemming from public engagement in the case, as well theories developed from more formal police enquiries, the press had inflamed a great deal of interest in this apparent murder mystery, even in the initial phase of its discovery. Not long after the discovery of the infamous box was reported, a Mr Batterbee, who had become increasingly concerned for the welfare of his sister, Mrs Julia Martha Thomas, visited the Richmond police and suggested that he entertained 'a moral certainty, but no legal proof' that the remains were that of his beloved sibling.[45] Mr Batterbee was right in his assertions, but vindication of his suspicions was a long time in coming, as we will see.

Ultra-violent methodology

It was evident from witness testimony at the murder trial of Kate Webster, initiated on 30 June 1879, that the relationship between Webster and her mistress was routinely ill-tempered.[46] Although initial newspaper reports portrayed Mrs Thomas as a 'pure' and innocent victim, trial testimony challenged this to portray Mrs Thomas as a difficult, confrontational woman.[47] Relations between the two women were clearly strained and indeed, Mrs Thomas had asked Webster to leave her duties just one week after her arrival, but Webster had managed to persuade her employer to relent.[48] Despite this reconciliation, subsequent heated arguments about the quality and timeliness of Webster's work were revealed in court.[49] The altercation that resulted in the death of Mrs Thomas was of particular interest to the courtroom as it indicated motive and the question of premeditation. Yet it was the methodology used to commit the murder that piqued Victorian curiosity and established an enduring fascination for this case. Webster had employed such savage violence and brutality in killing her victim that her actions genuinely shocked a public already immersed in details of cruelty, gore and death to such an extent that could presume them to have been desensitized to accounts of murderous deeds.

After throwing Mrs Thomas down a flight of stairs, an intoxicated Webster then used rope to strangle her. On seeing her victim dead, Webster then tried to cover up her crime. She dismembered Mrs Thomas on the kitchen table using a razor, a meat saw and a carving knife and then proceeded to use a water-filled copper to boil her remains in the hope that they would disintegrate leaving no trace. This process was time-consuming however and also resulted in a foul smell potentially noticeable to neighbours, so Webster adopted an alternative strategy. She packaged up the body parts of her victim in various crates, boxes and bags and enlisted the help of Henry Porter and his son Robert (long-standing friends of Webster but oblivious that by aiding her they had become complicit in a homicide) to carry the packages to various locations where Webster surreptitiously disposed of them.[50]

The ferocious but cunning manner by which Kate Webster murdered and disposed Mrs Thomas stunned Victorians and press reports of the court proceedings reflected the atrocity describing Webster as 'an awful butcher', 'singularly fiendish', 'primarily a savage' and 'a perfect virago and tyrant'.[51] It was not just the barbarous methodology deployed that captivated the nineteenth-century populace, but also the fact that Webster was a woman who had seemingly committed the crime by herself for her own reasons. During a period noted for moral panics about female killers, Webster's murderous actions represented brazen brutality which was difficult to rationalize, understand or ultimately excuse. Indeed, many contemporary commentators both in and out of the courtroom suggested, albeit erroneously, that Webster obviously had an accomplice and could not possibly have committed this crime alone.[52]

Criminal characteristics

By the time of Kate Webster's trial, British society had begun to try to better understand female killers by regularly linking their exploits to episodic mental instability, caused by their distinctive biological and emotional composition. This medico-legal defence strategy enabled the actions of autonomous criminal women to be separated out from mainstream behaviours and to be considered as exceptional and anomalous. Such explanations invited traditional gendered stereotypes of female behaviour to remain unspoilt. Yet a defence of temporary mental incapacity was not attempted in the Webster case, probably because of her proven and extensive criminal past. Instead, disaffiliating her from other women occurred through her portrayal in the Victorian press. For instance, her physical appearance was deemed somewhat unattractive: 'aged about thirty-two; five feet five or six inches high; complexion sallow; slightly freckled; teeth rather good but prominent; stout, strongly-made and usually clothed in dark dress'.[53] She was said to be 'exceedingly firm in her demeanour', typically 'presenting an unmoved and self-possessed appearance' and 'a sharp, fixed gaze' as is partly evident from the image in Figure 1.[54] As we can see from this, Webster's features were coarsened or 'masculinised' and elsewhere she is variously described as 'an individual with very low and very brutal instincts' with 'a physique and demeanour which indicated much muscular power'.[55]

Figure 1 The prisoner Kate Webster.
Source: Illustrated Police News, 3 May 1879, Issue 794.

Aside from offering deconstructed versions of Webster's femininity, press portrayals focussed on her embodiment of particular characteristics seen to be typical amongst the Victorian criminal fraternity. These traits were, of course, wholly distinct from the attributes and virtues more commonly associated with the 'fairer sex'. Likewise, Webster's distinctive ethnicity counted against her during a period when anti-Irish sentiment remained a blatant feature of nineteenth-century society.[56] Her native origins were said to largely explain her unvarying duplicity and her predilection for alcohol.[57] In addition, press reports emphasized the aggressive nature of Webster's character (as evident from the images in Figures 2 and 3) describing her as 'atrocious and cold-blooded', 'bold', 'defiant' and someone who would 'not brook opposition being offered to her'.[58]

Figure 2 Kate Webster in the House of Detention.
Source: Illustrated Police News, 26 April 1879, Issue 793.

The press also fixated on the numerous lies that Kate Webster told in court. Initially, Webster claimed that a man called John Church was in fact the cold-hearted killer in this case. Webster argued that Church had murdered Mrs Thomas to rob the victim of her possessions and generate enough money from their resale to leave his wife and elope with Webster.[59] When this suggestion was thoroughly discounted by Church's cast-iron alibi for the night of the murder, she then tried to implicate her friend Henry Porter in the killing. This accusation was also disproved. Although both Church and Porter had been involved in the purchase of Mrs Thomas's stolen goods, they had done so in good faith, misled by Webster.[60] Next, Webster suggested that the father of her illegitimate son, John Strong, had been complicit and active in the murder of Mrs Thomas. However, there was no evidence to support this contention either.[61] Clearly, Webster was harnessing the contemporary belief discussed above that women were not autonomous actors in violent criminality. Indeed, the cornerstone of her defence was to persuade the court that at the behest of male protagonists invoking contemporary gender stereotypes and she suggested that her role in the 'Richmond Murder' had been relatively minor.[62]

Webster's shifting testimony resulted in her being described as 'an inveterate liar'.[63] Her innate capacity for mendaciousness appeared blatant and deliberate to onlookers, as if Webster actively revelled in the public attention brought by her flagrant dishonesty.[64] Moreover, as the defendant's character was so key to Victorian criminal trials (and those brought against women in particular), Webster's deceitfulness was inherently problematic

Figure 3 Kate Webster denouncing Church.
Source: Illustrated Police News, 10 May 1879, Issue 795.

and self-destructive. Her lies destroyed her reputation and rendered it almost impossible for her to avoid the hangman's noose. Such views were reinforced by accounts which detailed Webster's assumption of the identity of her victim (wearing the dead woman's clothes and jewellery) to fake ownership of her erstwhilst mistress' possessions and 'credibly' sell them off to unsuspecting vendors at substantial profits.[65] On the eve of her execution, when Webster did in fact tell an arguably closer version of the truth, implicating herself alone in the murder, no one knew whether to believe this particular version of events or not, ensuring that certain elements of the case remained mysterious.[66]

Alongside this catalogue of duplicity, Kate Webster was also portrayed as a woman with highly suspect 'personal' morals. Beyond being a drunkard, various contemporary newspaper articles suggested that Webster was 'wanton' or highly promiscuous and 'familiar' with a range of male associates.[67] Although Webster tried to manipulate this image to re-establish her femininity and portray herself as a victim of male exploitation (just as Emilie Foucault did in the previous chapter), this floundered due to her countless lies and her proven deceit.[68] Clearly Victorian press depictions of Kate Webster served to set her apart from the rest of her sex. Her 'masculinised' appearance, her 'Irish' ethnicity, her capacity for deception and her alleged immorality all distinguished Kate Webster from 'normal' Victorian women. But such portrayals also made her an intriguing criminal specimen for a Victorian public fascinated with the unfamiliar and the maleficent.

Compelling endgame

Press depictions of Kate Webster's criminal characteristics certainly contributed to the notoriety of her case, but elements of her arrest, her subsequent trial and its eventual outcome also made this true crime history a *cause célèbre* in late Victorian England. For instance, press attention regarding Kate Webster was stimulated when in March of 1879, the police formally named her as a suspect in the Richmond Murder but explaining she had evaded capture and was tantalizing still at large. Reports pounced on this detail describing Webster as a 'wanted criminal', a 'dangerous woman on the run'.[69] Webster had fled back to Ireland when she realized her impersonations had been discovered. These exploits enthralled the Victorian populace and, although she was soon arrested and brought back to London to stand trial, an entire nation was now fixated on the accusations against her.

The details of Webster's crime did indeed fascinate Victorian society, especially when she was indisputably revealed to be a bare-faced liar who 'ceased to be worthy of belief' and who enjoyed being the centre of attention.[70] Webster's attempts to implicate others in what transpired were ultimately in vain however, as were the attempts of her defence counsel to portray her as a misunderstood and victimized loving mother incapable of murder. The defence also claimed that the remains found were not that of Mrs Thomas and argued that even if they were that the victim might have died through natural causes.[71] This futile defence was inherently flawed and evidentially weak. It flew in the face of detailed and incontrovertible medical testimony, but it also contradicted evidence from Webster herself since she had attested on oath that Mrs Thomas had indeed been murdered, but by someone other than her.

Another piece of evidence given in court effectively sealed Webster's fate and gave Victorians more reasons to be fascinated by this case's central protagonist. Mary Durden testified that on 25 February 1879 (five days before the Richmond Murder) Webster boasted of her intention to sell various goods that had come into her possession as a result of an inheritance.[72] The merchandise described unequivocally matched that sold by Webster in the aftermath of Mrs Thomas's murder. Sensationally therefore, the testimony of Mary Durden described premeditation in this case. These were not the actions of a misunderstood miscreant acting rashly in hot blood and out of desperation. Instead, Victorian London had a cold-blooded killer in its midst, and a woman at that. Reports of these details produced shock and awe in equal measure.[73]

With the evidence now stacked against her, the outcome of Kate Webster's trial was almost inevitable. After a quick deliberation, the jury found her guilty and the judge sentenced her to death by hanging.[74] However, even this outcome did not diminish

Webster's audacity. To the court's amazement, Webster 'pled the belly', claiming to be pregnant in order to exact a stay on her execution, a highly unusual ploy by the middle of the nineteenth century.[75] After examination however, Webster's claim was proven to be a further ruse and she was taken away, a condemned woman.[76]

Webster still courted press attention whilst awaiting her death sentence for, as we have seen, she submitted further 'confessions' and pleas for clemency in attempts to acquire a pardon. But her prolonged and repeated mendacities eventually caught up with her. Somewhat unusually for a female felon in the Victorian era, no application for remission was ever made on her behalf and no family or friends visited her whilst incarcerated, much to her disappointment and consternation.[77] Kate Webster was executed in private at Wandsworth Gaol on 29 July 1879 by the hangman William Marwood as depicted in Figure 4.[78]

Figure 4 The execution of Kate Webster.
Source: Illustrated Police News, 2 August 1879, Issue 807. It should be noted that the picture inaccurately depicts Webster being visited in prison by her friends.

According to one newspaper report of her execution:

> The public must feel greatly relieved at the world being rid of so atrocious a criminal – a criminal who scrupled not to endeavour to incriminate innocent men to shield herself from the consequences of a monstrous crime.[79]

Unlike the vast audiences packing the courtroom to hear the details of her trial, only a handful of spectators waited outside the gaol to hear of her demise.[80] Nevertheless, somewhat shockingly, it was reported in a couple of accounts that her hanging had been botched and that she had to be hung twice.[81] This contention is dubious since William Marwood, the executioner, made no mention of any problems when referring to the case in his memoirs.[82] The suggestion of a botched execution may have been promulgated by contemporary campaigners against capital punishment, or by media men intent on milking every last drop of sensationalism from this gripping Victorian murder story.

Storyline stamina

As we have seen, the Webster case contained myriad elements which aroused public curiosity, rendering it an early example of the 'cult of the criminal' normally associated with more modern periods.[83] The Webster case was infamous in 1879 where crowds of people thronged to the Old Bailey to catch a glimpse of the defendant and, as we have already seen, the press coverage of the case was vast and extensive.[84] The story achieved further longevity through the widespread publication of a souvenir special issue of the *Illustrated Police News* containing images generated from the court proceedings.[85] This gripped Victorian readers keen on graphic and ghoulish pictorial keepsakes. In the aftermath of Webster's execution several newspapers reported that juvenile witnesses had detailed how she had sold them quantities of 'beef' dripping in the Spring of 1879 and that they now feared, in the wake of evidence presented at the trial, that the gloopy substance purchased had been rendered from the boiled cadaver of Mrs Thomas, rather than a butchered animal.[86] As one later commentator pointed out, however,

> there is no acceptable evidence that such a repulsive sale was ever made, and it is more than possible that the episode belongs rightfully with the rest of the vast collection of apocryphal stories that has accumulated, not unnaturally, about the persons and deeds of famous criminals.[87]

In addition to tales of purported involuntary cannibalism, the case survived in the Victorian consciousness through various public auctions of paraphernalia from the case[88] and through various waxwork exhibits of Kate Webster, including one shown at Madame Tussaud's from July 1879 until the middle of the next century.[89] According to Judith Knelman, the length of a criminal's 'stay' in the Chamber of Horrors at Madame Tussaud's is an indication of his or her prominence in the public mind, and Kate Webster's exhibit of more than six decades is further testimony to her undoubted notoriety.[90] The opinions of commentators and historians on the case since the last decades of the nineteenth century have also kept the case in the minds of many. Modern crime aficionados became all too aware of the Webster case in October 2010 when a skull was discovered during excavations in the Richmond garden of the renowned naturist Sir David Attenborough. After forensic examination and archival 'cold case' police research, the coroner Alison Thompson concluded in July 2011 that the remains found were those of Mrs Julia Martha Thomas. The hearing concluded that Mrs Thomas had been unlawfully killed via 'asphyxia by strangulation and a head injury'.[91] Some 133 years after her initial notoriety, Kate Webster once again made headline news as a cold-blooded killer. Her criminal history, retold to new generations, was as shocking and enthralling to modern audiences as it had been to Victorians. Thus Kate Webster's infamy outlived and surpassed that of many other criminal men and women from British history and her notoriety remained unbowed despite the passage of time.

V

It is clear from Kate Webster's micro-history that she became infamous as a result of her criminal misdeeds, but to what extent did the reasons for her notoriety coincide with the more modern ones outlined in Section II? Criminologists Yvonne Jewkes and David Wilson argue that criminal histories become either famous or forgettable in the twentieth-century context on the basis of certain criteria,[92] but can these factors be applied to the Webster case from the Victorian era? The case certainly had what Jewkes refers to as 'threshold' due to the rarity of Victorian homicides and the concerns aroused by episodes of fatal violence.[93] The Richmond Murder also defied 'predictability' and 'challenged conservatism' because of the violent methodology used and the fact that the protagonist was a woman.[94] The case centred upon an 'individual' giving a human interest angle to the story, around both Kate Webster and, to a lesser extent her victim, Mrs Thomas. There was also an 'evident motive', whilst the story contained both 'risk' and a crescendo of 'press interest' approaching the trial due to the initial mystery surrounding the dismembered remains found, the chief suspect being at large, and the ongoing uncertainty of whether Kate Webster had acted alone or with an accomplice. The 'violence' in the case was certainly graphic and offered an imagined 'visual spectacle' to the Victorian populace at a time when journalists maximized sensationalist news stories. The 'proximity' of the murder to the 'sanctuary' of the domestic sphere in a fairly respectable environ of the nation's capital was also crucial in capturing press attention.[95] Finally, a 'substantial volume of testimony and evidence' facilitated the wide circulation of case's details ensuring that this particular true crime history endured in the minds of the public.

However, some aspects of the case evade the criteria for 'dark immortality' established between Jewkes and Wilson. For instance, the micro-history was complex rather than 'simple' and Victorians seemed enthralled by it regardless. There was no sex involved.

No celebrities or children were directly concerned in the murder and the offender had no 'nickname' or moniker. Instead, there were other additional factors – essentially unique to this particular case – which gave it such prominence in the annals of crime history. The continual lies that Kate Webster told, alongside the bravado of her barefaced deception in assuming her victim's identity, propagated fascination with this case throughout the relevant judicial procedures and beyond. The fact that Webster had acted autonomously and with excessive violence in this crime warranted explanation by the media, by contemporary commentators and latterly by scholars as her actions so obviously transgressed norms of feminine behaviour.[96] Kate Webster's crime exemplified the dangers associated with the 'unwoman' – of what could happen if society ignored patriarchal conventions.[97] Indeed, it was arguably Webster' status as a social outsider that made the most significant contribution to her enduring notoriety.

Kate Webster was not simply a gendered outsider. Her ethnicity invoked the prevailing Victorian anti-Irish sentiment to suggest that Webster's criminality was almost inevitable due to her 'base' heritage and ancestry.[98] Furthermore, Webster's status as a domestic servant further contributed to notions of her social exclusion. By killing her employer and better, Kate Webster had both transgressed accepted gender boundaries and violated accepted social hierarchies.[99] Thus, Webster (and the type of 'unwoman' she represented) could be dangerous to society on many levels and in many different ways. Her infamy might have been complex, but it was assured, as the social relevance and appeal of this micro-history was extensive and multifarious.

VI

The case of Kate Webster clearly demonstrates that the 'cult of the criminal' and our fascination with individuals who kill are historic phenomenon and not simply constructs of the modern era. The case also shows that our obsession with fatal criminal violence was not solely restricted to the actions of male offenders as many modern scholars have suggested. Yet, as we have seen, our preoccupation with murder has been neither uniform nor homogenous. Not all crimes hit the headlines and not all criminals attain notoriety. Although some factors appear to be more important than others in determining whether or not a crime becomes infamous it is fair to say nonetheless, that in large part, infamy is subjective and case specific.[100] In the same way that the reasons for criminality are individualistic and based on specific circumstances, so the reasons for interest in particular criminal micro-histories are idiosyncratic and related to the context in which they occur, reoccur or are retold to new audiences.

Yet we should not think of Kate Webster as a mysterious 'other' woman for too long. Certainly, as a proven autonomous actor in a homicide, her character and her actions could not be conveniently or easily explained away by Victorian society (unlike the Foucault case in the previous chapter) and this undoubtedly further cemented her infamy in the minds of contemporary society. However, her ongoing notoriety should not be used to segregate her out as some sort of leviathan in the annals of criminal history. Our preoccupation with women's perpetration of fatal violence then and now has undoubtedly sustained the notion that female killers should be considered aberrant in comparison with their male counterparts. Yet, as this micro-history has detailed, Kate Webster was, at root, a violent murderess. Such micro-histories show that women's violence needs to be normalized, rather than sensationalized: She committed a crime autonomously using the violence men used and she did so for the same reasons. Kate Webster was different from other *women* in the Victorian era but was she necessarily different from other *criminals*? As well as helping us to better understand criminals and their activities, public reactions to criminal episodes, their fame or infamy, micro-histories can also help us to put crime in perspective. By analysing a crime in its context, micro-histories help us to better understand offending and offenders in the past as well as the present and can suggest new interpretative avenues for the analysis of future criminal behaviour.

Notes

1. *Pall Mall Gazette*, 28 September 1871, Issue 2067.
2. See J. Flanders (2011) *The Invention of Murder: How the Victorians Revelled in Death and Detection and Created Modern Crime* (London: Harper Press), R. Crone (2012) *Violent Victorians: Popular Entertainment in Nineteenth Century London* (Manchester: Manchester University Press) and L. Worsley (2013) *A Very British Murder: The Story of a National Obsession* (London: BBC Books).
3. L. Gribble (1957) *Famous Judges and Their Trials: A Century of Justice* (London: John Long), p. 65.
4. For further discussion of this cultural phenomenon in the United States, see ibid., pp. 13–16, 24–8, 84–6 as well as D. Schmid (2005) *Natural Born Celebrities: Serial Killers in American Culture* (Chicago: University of Chicago Press). For further discussion of the British experience of this, see S. D'Cruze, S. Walklate and S. Pegg (2011 edition) *Murder* (Abingdon: Routledge), chap. 2 and B. Morrissey (2003) *When Women Kill: Question of Agency and Subjectivity* (London: Routledge), chap. 1.
5. M. Seltzer (1998) *Serial Killers: Death and Life in America's Wound Culture* (New York: Routledge), p. 2. See also M. Seltzer (1997) 'Wound Culture: Trauma in the Pathological Public Sphere', *October*, Vol. 80, pp. 3–26.
6. Seltzer, *Serial Killers*, p. 3.
7. For further discussion, see Y. Kass-Gergi (2012) 'Killer Personalities: Serial Killers as Celebrities in Contemporary American Culture' (Unpublished BA Dissertation (American Studies), Wesleyan University, Connecticut), pp. 8–9, 13–16, 24–8; J.A. Fox and J. Levin (2005) *Extreme Killing: Understand Serial and Mass Murder* (Thousand Oaks, CA: Sage Publications), chaps. 1 and 3; Schmid, *Natural Born Celebrities*, Part Two and E. Leyton (1986 edition) *Hunting Humans: The Rise of the Modern Multiple Murderer* (Ontario: McClelland and Stewart), chap. 1.
8. B. King (1997) *Lustmord: The Writings and Artefacts of Murderers* (Burbank, CA: Bloat Books).
9. See T. Amirtha (2015) 'Why Dark Tourism Is Thriving', *Motherboard*, 29 October 2015, http://motherboard.vice.com/en_uk/read/sightseeing-in-hell (accessed 1 November 2015).

The phenomenon of 'dark tourism' has only recently received academic attention, although the University of Central Lancashire (UCLAN) has an established Institute for Dark Tourism Research – see http://www.uclan.ac.uk/research/explore/ groups/institute _for_dark_tourism_research.php. For more on this topic, see the publications listed at the UCLAN web site as well as J.J. Lennon and M. Foley (2010) *Dark Tourism: The Attraction of Death and Disaster* (Andover: Cengage Publishing); M.S. Bowman and P.C. Pezzullo (2009) 'What's So "Dark" about "Dark Tourism"? Death, Tours and Performance', *Tourism Studies*, Vol. 9, No. 3, pp. 187–202; but especially R. Sharpley and P. Stone (2009) (eds) *The Darker Side of Travel: The Theory and Practice of Dark Tourism* (Bristol: Channel View Publications).

10. For further discussion, see Y. Jewkes (2011 edition) *Media and Crime* (Los Angeles and London: Sage), pp. 45–64.

11. For further discussion, see D. Wilson (2011) *Looking for Laura: Public Criminology and Hot News* (Sherfield-on-Loddon (Hampshire): Waterside Press), chap. 5.

12. For further discussion, see V.A.C. Gatrell (1994) *The Hanging Tree: Execution and the English People 1770–1868* (Oxford: Oxford University Press).

13. R.D. Altick (1970) *Victorian Studies in Scarlet: Murders and Manners in the Age of Victoria* (New York: W.W. Norton and Co.), pp. 9 and 302.

14. See ibid., p. 10 as well as Crone, *Violent Victorians*, p. 80 and B. Walsh (2014) *Domestic Murder in Nineteenth-century England: Literary and Cultural Representations* (Farnham: Ashgate), pp. 16–17.

15. Altick, *Victorian Studies in Scarlet*, p. 17.

16. For further discussion, see M. Foucault (1978) 'About the Concept of the "Dangerous Individual" in Nineteenth-century Legal Psychiatry', *International Journal of Law and Psychiatry*, Vol. 1, No. 1, pp. 1–18.

17. For further discussion, see L. Perry Curtis (2001) *Jack the Ripper and the London Press* (New Haven and London: Yale University Press), chaps. 3, 4 and 5.

18. See V.A.C. Gatrell (1980) 'The Decline of Theft and Violence in Victorian and Edwardian England', in V.A.C. Gatrell, Bruce Lenman and Geoffrey Parker (eds), *Crime and the Law: The Social History of Crime in Western Europe Since 1500* (London: Europa Publications), pp. 238–370 and Worsley, *A Very British Murder*, pp. 127–8.

19. Altick, *Victorian Studies in Scarlet*, pp. 46–7. See also Perry Curtis, *Jack the Ripper and the London Press*, chap. 3.

20. See, for instance, Worsley, *A Very British Murder*, pp. 53–77, 79–106; Crone, *Violent Victorians*, pp. 80–116; Flanders, *The Invention of Murder*, pp. 4–68, 172–3 and J. Knelman (1998) *Twisting in the Wind: The Murderess and the English Press* (London and Toronto: University of Toronto Press), chap. 2.

21. See, for instance, Crone, *Violent Victorians*, p. 91 and Flanders, *The Invention of Murder*, pp. 3–4, 35.

22. See Worsley, *A Very British Murder*, p. 294.

23. See Kass-Gergi, 'Killer Personalities', pp. 22–7 and Schmid, *Natural Born Celebrities*, chap. 1. Both of these works focus entirely on the crimes of Jack the Ripper (unknown assailant who killed at least five prostitutes in Whitechapel, London, in 1888) and H.H. Holmes (murderer, bigamist and con artist who confessed to killing twenty-seven young women at his hotel in Chicago, IL, and at other locations in North America, during the 1890s) in relation to the nineteenth century's contribution to our fascination with fatal violence.

24. The Proceedings of the Old Bailey Online, The Trial of Thomas Perryman (1879), Ref. t18790331-395.

25. See ibid. as well as *Daily News*, 13 February 1879, Issue 10240 and *Reynolds' Newspaper*, 6 April 1879, Issue 1495.

26. See *Daily News*, 13 February 1879, Issue 10240 and *Reynolds' Newspaper*, 6 April 1879, Issue 1495.

27. See *Illustrated Police News*, 1 March 1879, Issue 785 and *The Bury and Norwich Post and Suffolk Herald*, 8 April 1879, Issue 5050.

28. See, for instance, Worsley, *A Very British Murder*, p. 139.

29. See A. Lloyd (1995) *Doubly Deviant, Doubly Damned: Society's Treatment of Violent* Women (Harmondsworth: Penguin); Walsh, *Domestic Murder*, pp. 13–14 and Knelman, *Twisting in the Wind*, p. 230. For further discussion of these cases and their prevailing impact on Victorian notions of female criminality, see M.S. Hartman (1977) *Victorian Murderesses: A True History of Thirteen Respectable French and English Women Accused of Unspeakable Crimes* (London: Robson Books); P. Wilson (1971) *Murderess: A Study of Women Executed in Britain since 1843* (London: Michael Joseph) and Knelman, *Twisting in the Wind*, Part Two.

30. For more on the rarity of female homicide, see M.B.W. Emmerichs (1993) 'Trials of Women for Homicide in Nineteenth-century England', *Women and Criminal Justice*, Vol. 5, No. 1, pp. 99–109 and M.M. Feeley and D.L. Little (1991) 'The Vanishing Female: The Decline of Women in the Criminal Process, 1687–1912', *Law and Society Review*, Vol. 25, No. 4, pp. 719–57.

31. See Knelman, *Twisting in the Wind*, p. 4 and Jewkes, *Media and Crime*, pp. 148–9.

32. For further discussion of more modern interest in female killers see D'Cruze, Walklate and Pegg, *Murder*, chap. 3; Wilson, *Looking for Laura*, pp. 109–10 and Jewkes, *Media and Crime*, pp. 122–3.

33. *The Times*, 2 April 1879, Issue 29531.

34. E. O'Donnell (1925) *Trial of Kate Webster in the Central Criminal Court, London, July, 1879, for the Murder of Mrs. Julia Martha Thomas* (Edinburgh: W. Hodge), p. 5. (Yale Law School Library, Ref. ID CTRG98-B3022).

35. For evidence of Webster's use of aliases, see *The Times*, 28 and 29 March 1879, Issues 29527 and 29528, respectively; *Reynolds' Newspaper*, 30 March 1879, Issue 1494 and *Bristol Mercury and Daily Post*, 31 March 1879 and 1 April 1879, Issues 9632 and 9633, respectively. See also K. Clarke (2013) *Bad Companions: Six London Murderesses Who Shocked the World* (Stroud: The History Press), p. 187.

36. O'Donnell, *Trial of Kate Webster*, pp. 6–9. For Webster's offences prior to 1879, see newspaper reports in the *Liverpool Mercury*, 25 May 1866, Issue 5716; *Birmingham Daily Post*, 29 March 1879, Issue 6466; *The Times*, 29 March 1879, Issue 29528 and *Bristol Mercury and Daily Post*, 1 April 1879, Issue 9633. See also N. Morland (1955) *Background to Murder* (London: Werner Laurie), pp. 171–4 and Clarke, *Bad Companions*, p. 187.

37. O'Donnell, *Trial of Kate Webster*, p. 15 and Morland, *Background to Murder*, p. 171.

38. O'Donnell, *Trial of Kate Webster*, pp. 2–3.

39. *Reynolds' Newspaper*, 30 March 1879, Issue 1494.

40. See *The Morning Post*, 19 March 1879, Issue 33299.

41. See, for instance, *Belfast News-Letter* and *Daily News*, 29 March 1879, Issues 19832 and 10278, respectively.

42. See O'Donnell, *Trial of Kate Webster*, p. 3 and Clarke, *Bad Companions*, p. 192.

43. See *Birmingham Daily Post*, 29 March 1879, Issue 6466.

44. *Reynolds' Newspaper*, 30 March 1879, Issue 1494.

45. Ibid. See also *Leeds Mercury*, 29 March 1879, Issue 12782.

46. See The Proceedings of the Old Bailey Online, The Trial of Catherine Webster (1879), Ref. t18790630-653.

47. For varying descriptions of Mrs Thomas, see *Daily Gazette*, 29 March 1879, Issue 3675; *Lloyds Weekly Newspaper*, 30 March 1879 and *Bristol Mercury and Daily Post*, 1 April 1879, Issue 9633.

48. See *The Bristol Mercury and Daily Post*, 1 April 1879, Issue 9633.

49. Ibid.

50. Ibid. See also *The York Herald* and the *Dundee Courier and Argus*, 1 August 1879, Issues 7009 and 8122, respectively and *The Sheffield and Rotherham and Independent*, 2 August 1879, Issue 7760.

51. See, Gribble, *Famous Judges and Their Trials*, p. 68 and O'Donnell, *Trial of Kate Webster*, pp. vii, 27 and 42.

52. See, for instance, *Daily Gazette*, 29 March 1879 and 8 July 1879, Issues 3675 and 3760, respectively and *Reynolds' Newspaper*, 13 July 1879, Issue 1509.

53. *Reynolds' Newspaper*, 30 March 1879, Issue 1494.

54. See *The Times*, 3 April 1879, Issue 29532 and *The Daily News*, 10 April 1879, Issue 10288.

55. See respectively *Illustrated Police News*, 9 August 1879, Issue 808 and *The Lancaster Gazette*, 16 July 1879, Issue 4946. For further discussion of the masculinized nature of press depictions of Victorian female killers in the press, see K.A. Tucker (2013) '"Abominations of the Female Sex": Five Case Studies of Late Nineteenth Century Criminal Women' (Unpublished MA (By Research) Dissertation, University of Central Lancashire), pp. 6–7.

56. See, for instance, D.M. MacRaild (2010 edition) *The Irish Diaspora in Britain, 1750–1939* (Basingstoke: Palgrave McMillan), chap. 7.

57. See, for instance, Knelman, *Twisting in the Wind*, p. 197; Morland, *Background to Murder*, pp. 171 and 173 and Tucker, 'Abominations of the Female Sex', p. 81.

58. See respectively *Illustrated Police News*, 19 July 1879, Issue 805; *The Bristol Mercury and Daily Post*, 1 April 1789, Issue 9633 and *Lloyds Weekly Newspaper*, 30 March 1879, Issue 1897.

59. See *The Bristol Mercury and Daily Post*, 1 April 1789, Issue 9633 and *John Bull*, 5 April 1879, Issue 3043.

60. See *The Sheffield and Rotherham Independent*, 15 April 1879, Issue 7668 and *John Bull*, 19 April 1879, Issue 3045 as well as the trial testimony referenced in the works cited at notes 40 and 52. It has been estimated that Webster would have made a profit of approximately two or three years' salary from the sale of her victim's possessions – see D'Cruze, Walklate and Pegg, *Murder*, p. 56.

61. See *Daily Gazette*, 10 July 1879, Issue 3762; *The Penny Illustrated Paper and Illustrated Times*, 19 July 1879, Issue 938 and *The Sheffield and Rotherham Independent*, 23 July 1879, Issue 7751.

62. For reports of Kate Webster's defence, see *Daily News*, 4 July 1879, Issue 10361; *The Morning Post*, 8 July 1879, Issue 33394 and *Lloyds Weekly Newspaper*, 13 July 1879, Issue 1912 as well as the trial testimony referenced at in the works cited in notes 40 and 52.

63. Morland, *Background to Murder*, p. 171.

64. See, for instance, *The Times*, 3 Aril 1879, Issue 29532; *The Graphic*, 19 July 1879, Issue 503 and *Illustrated Police News*, 9 August 1879, Issue 808 and accounts of Webster's dramatic but deceitful outburst in court reported in *Birmingham Daily Post*, 30 April 1879, Issue 6493.

65. See the trial testimony referenced at in the works cited in notes 40 and 52 as well as Wilson, *Murderess*, p. 195 and D'Cruze, Walklate and Pegg, *Murder*, p. 55. It has been estimated that Kate Webster stood to make the equivalent of two or three years wages from the sale of Mrs Thomas's furniture alone: see D'Cruze, Walklate and Pegg, *Murder*, p. 56.

66. See, for instance, *The York Herald*, 1 August 1879, Issue 8122.

67. See, for instance, *The Times*, 2 April 1879, Issue 29531; *The Huddersfield Chronicle*, 4 April 1879, Issue 3639 and *Lloyds Weekly Newspaper*, 10 April 1879, Issue 1899.

68. See, for instance, *The Sheffield and Rotherham Independent*, 10 July 1879, Issue 7740; *Aberdeen Weekly Journal*, 15 July 1879, Issue 7615 and *The Newcastle Courant*, 18 July 1879, Issue 10672 as well as the trial testimony referenced at in the works cited in notes 40 and 52. For further discussion of attempts to assume the role of victim in this case, see D'Cruze, Walklate and Pegg, *Murder*, p. 53, and for similar attempts in other murder cases brought against women at this time, see Hartman, *Victorian Murderesses*, p. 261; A. Ballinger (2000) *Dead Women Walking: Executed Women in England and Wales 1900–1955* (Aldershot: Ashgate), pp. 3 and 135–6 and Morrissey, *When Women Kill*, p. 17.

69. See, for instance, the report in *Reynolds' Newspaper*, 30 March 1879, Issue 1494.

70. *The York Herald*, 15 July 1879, Issue 6994. For additional accounts labelling Webster a liar, see *The Times*, 3 April 1879, Issue 29532; *Western Mail*, 4 April 1879, Issue 3091; *The Huddersfield Chronicle*, 5 April 1789, Issue 3640; *The Penny Illustrated Paper and Illustrated Times*, 12 July 1879, Issue 937; *Y Genedl Gymreig (The Welsh Nation)*, 17 July 1879, Issue 128 (I am grateful to Mrs Rhian Perridge for providing a translation of this account) and *Illustrated Police News*, 9 August 1879, Issue 808.

71. See the trial testimony referenced in the works cited at notes 40 and 52 as well as *The Graphic*, 24 May 1879, Issue 495; *Daily Gazette*, 8 July 1879, Issues 3760 and *Reynolds' Newspaper*, 13 July 1879, Issue 1509.

72. See the trial testimony referenced in the works cited at notes 40 and 52 as well as *Manchester Times*, 10 May 1879, Issue 1117 and *Leeds Mercury*, 8 July 1879, Issue 12868.

73. For further discussion of the reaction to proven premeditation in murders committed by women, see Ballinger, *Dead Women Walking*, p. 129.

74. See O'Donnell, *Trial of Kate Webster*, pp. 211–13; *John Bull*, 12 July 1879, Issue 446 and *The Penny Illustrated Paper and Illustrated Times*, 12 July 1879, Issue 937.

75. For more on the historic use of this plea, see J.C. Oldham (1985) 'On Pleading the Belly: A History of the Jury of Matrons', *Criminal Justice History*, Vol. 6, pp. 1–64.

76. See O'Donnell, *Trial of Kate Webster*, pp. 211–13; *The Cheshire Observer*, 12 July 1879, Issue 1405 and *The Blackburn Standard*, 12 July 1879, Issue 2282.

77. See *The York Herald*, 15 July 1879, Issue 6994 and *The Times*, 29 July 1879, Issue 29632.

78. For detailed descriptions of her execution, see (1879) *Trial, Sentence and Execution of Kate Webster for the Murder of Mrs Thomas at Richmond*, Bodleian Library, John Johnson Collection, Broadsides: Murder and Execution, 11 (18).

79. *The Penny Illustrated Paper and Illustrated Times*, 2 August 1879, Issue 940.

80. See *The York Herald*, 30 July 1879, Issue 7007 and *The Times*, 30 July 1879, Issue 29633.

81. See, for instance, *Freeman's Journal and Daily Commercial Advertiser*, 4 August 1879 and *The York Herald*, 28 August 1879, Issue 7032.

82. See D. Matthews (2010) *William Marwood: The Gentleman Executioner* (Peterborough: Fastprint Publishing), pp. 152–63.

83. For a corroborative opinion, see Altick, *Victorian Studies in Scarlet*, p. 225.

84. For contemporary commentary on the widespread frenetic interest in the Webster case, see *Y Genedl Gymreig* (*The Welsh Nation*), 3 April 1879, Issue 113; *The Huddersfield Chronicle*, 5 April 1879, Issue 3640; *Aberdeen Weekly Journal*, 9 April 1879, Issue 7531 which stated that the case was 'the most exciting of modern times'; *The Daily News*, 10 April 1879, Issue 10288 and *Baner ac Amserau Cymru* (*The Banner and Times of Wales*), 16 July, Issue 1168 (I am grateful to Mrs Rhian Perridge for providing a translation of the two Welsh accounts referenced at this note). See also W. Wood (1916) (ed.) *Survivors' Tales of Famous Crimes* (London: Cassell and Company), p. 96.

85. In addition to this special issue – 19 July 1879 Issue 805 – and the images already shown in this chapter, illustrations related to the Webster case can be seen in *Illustrated Police News*, 12 April 1879 Issue 791, 19 April 1879, Issue 792, 17 May 1879, Issue 796, 24 May 1879, Issue 797, 12 July 1879, Issue 804, 26 July 1879, Issue 806, 2 August 1879, Issue 807, and 9 August 1879, Issue 808 (represented on the front cover of this volume); *The Penny Illustrated Paper and Illustrated Times*, 5 July 1879, Issue 936, 12 July 1879, Issue 937 and *Lloyds Weekly Newspaper*, 4 May 1879, Issue 1902.

86. See, for instance, Gribble, *Famous Judges and Their Trials*, p. 69 and Altick, *Victorian Studies in Scarlet*, p. 226.

87. Gribble, *Famous Judges and Their Trials*, p. 69.

88. For reports of these auctions, see *Dundee Courier and Argus*, 18 July 1879, Issue 8110 and *Belfast News-Letter*, 31 July 1879, Issue 20018. It is interesting to note that one of the suspected accomplices in the Richmond Murder, John Church, purchased several items of memorabilia related to the case including a carving knife suspected to be used in the dismemberment of the victim's corpse.

89. For newspaper advertisements of these exhibits see , *The Morning Post*, 31 July 1879, Issue 33414 and *Liverpool Mercury*, 1 August 1879, Issue 9844. For commentary which describes such events as 'horrible and nauseous', see *Freeman's Journal and Daily Commercial Advertiser*, 4 August 1879.

90. According to Knelman, Webster's exhibit lasted until 1945 – see Knelman, *Twisting in the Wind*, pp. 23 and 198 and note 55 on that page.

91. See *The Telegraph*, 5 July 2011; *Daily Mail*, 6 July 2011 and *Daily Express*, 9 July 2011.

92. See the references at notes 13 and 14.

93. See C. Emsley (2005 edition) *Crime and Society in England, 1750–1900* (Harlow: Longman), p. 41–2 and M.J. Wiener (2004) *Men of Blood: Violence, Manliness and Criminal Justice in Victorian England* (Cambridge: Cambridge University Press), p. 13.

94. For evidence of the notoriety of violence in this case, see *The Hull Packet and East Riding Times*, 18 July 1879, Issue 4900 which reported that a female criminal was imprisoned for sharpening a knife in front of her husband and vowing that 'she would do to him as Kate Webster did to Mrs Thomas – cut his head off, and boil it in the wash-pot'. For further discussion of the importance of gender in this case, see D'Cruze, Walklate and Pegg, *Murder*, p. 56; Knelman, *Twisting in the Wind*, p. 15 and C.A. Conley (2007) *Certain Other Countries: Homicide, Gender, and National Identity in Late Nineteenth-century England, Ireland, Scotland and Wales* (Columbus: Ohio State University Press), p. 84.

95. For further discussion of the importance of location in this case and others like it in the Victorian era, see Walsh, *Domestic Murder*, pp. 3 and 13–14 and Knelman, *Twisting in the Wind*, p. 37.

96. For further discussion of the importance of this factor, see L. Zedner (1991) *Women, Crime and Custody in Victorian England* (Oxford: Clarendon Press), p. 28; Emsley, *Crime and Society*, p. 107; Ballinger, *Dead Women Walking*, p. 130 and Tucker, 'Abominations of the Female Sex', pp. 30, 79 and 88.

97. For further discussion of the threat posed by unruly women in the Victorian era, see Zedner, *Women, Crime and Custody*, pp. 5–6.

98. For further discussion of the association between the Irish and criminality during the Victorian era, see Conley, *Certain Other Countries*, pp. 3–4, 41–3, 51–2 and Emsley, *Crime and Society*, p. 99. For more on the importance of ethnicity in this particular case, see Tucker, 'Abominations of the Female Sex', pp. 81 and 87 and D'Cruze, Walklate and Pegg, *Murder*, pp. 56–7.

99. For further discussion of the notoriety brought about by the violence of domestic servants against their masters/mistresses in the Victorian era, see Knelman, *Twisting in the Wind*, chap. 7; Altick, *Victorian Studies in Scarlet*, chap. 12; Flanders, *The Invention of Murder*, p. 187; Emsley, *Crime and Society*, p. 99; D'Cruze, Walklate and Pegg, *Murder*, p. 53 and Morrissey, *When Women Kill*, p. 18. In the wake of the Webster case, see the commentary on this issue provided in *Illustrated Police News*, 19 July 1879, Issue 805.

100. For further discussion, see Morrissey, *When Women Kill*, p. 18.

SECTION III
POLICE AND POLICING

CHAPTER 7
'HAND IN GLOVE WITH THE PENNY-A-LINERS': THE BOW STREET 'RUNNERS' IN FACTUAL AND FICTIONAL NARRATIVE
David J. Cox

I

> We are not by any means devout believers in the Old Bow Street Police. To say the truth, we think there was a vast amount of humbug about those worthies. Apart from many of them being men of very indifferent character, and far too much in the habit of consorting with thieves and the like, they never lost a public occasion of jobbing and trading in mystery and making the most of themselves. Continually puffed besides by incompetent magistrates anxious to conceal their own deficiencies, and hand-in-glove with the penny-a-liners of that time, they became a sort of superstition. Although as a Preventive Police they were utterly ineffective, and as a Detective Police were very loose and uncertain in their operations, they remain with some people a superstition to the present day.[1]

In today's media-driven world, most of us are familiar with the workings and function of modern police and detectives, from 'fly-on-the-wall' reality programmes to 'police procedurals'. In an overwhelmingly literate society we can also read about the work of the police in newspapers or simply log on to discover detailed information about the daily lives, deeds and misdeeds of our law-enforcement officials. However, this was not the case in the mid-eighteenth century, when the 'Runners' were founded. The introductory quote is taken from one of several factual and fictional narratives concerning the 'Runners' that are compared and contrasted in this chapter, which explores the numerous ways in which the 'Runners' – Britain's earliest professional detective force – have been portrayed in literary texts including autobiographies, newspaper trial reports, novels, plays and poems. From their creation in 1748/9, the exciting, daring and often dangerous activities of this small group of men have aroused the attention and interest of writers in a multiplicity of literary forms, leading to numerous and often contrasting portrayals.

Despite being the first professional detective force in British history (predating the creation of the Metropolitan Police's Detective Department by almost a century), little serious academic research had been carried out into their activities until relatively recently.[2] No 'official' account of the Bow Street Office was commissioned during its existence, and the first attempt at an account of its history was not published until 1888.[3] Apart from occasional (often disparaging) mentions in wider histories of policing, it was not until 1932 that Gilbert Armitage wrote his highly derivative 'biography' of the Office.[4] In the mid-1950s, Patrick Pringle produced a couple of ground-breaking studies on the subject, whilst in the 1970s other authors concentrated on particular aspects of their history.[5] However, it has only been in the past few years that John Beattie and David Cox respectively have carried out intensive research into both the metropolitan and provincial activities of the Bow Street personnel, which has gone some way to rescuing the 'Runners' from historical obscurity.[6] Despite this research, much remains to be discovered about the 'Runners' at a micro-historical level, and it is hoped that this chapter, by focussing on one particular aspect of their history – namely their appearance in both factual and fictional narratives – goes at least some way to further illuminating their often complex relationship with the general public during the period of their existence.

Today the 'Runners' are remembered as little more than a hazy folk memory, comprising of a vague (and incorrect) notion that they were something to do with Robert Peel and his London 'Bobbies'. Their name lives on in various unconnected and often surprising forms: a 1970s American psychedelic rock group, a competition for black-powder firearms, a guest house on the south coast of England, a public house in Staffordshire and several computer games. However, throughout their existence, their exploits (both real and invented) were reported in newspapers and other print media, with their reputation often discussed and much disputed. It is this particular aspect of their story that is the subject of this chapter, which aims to discuss two main questions concerning the relationship between the 'Runners' and the general public. First, to what extent has there been either implicit or explicit blurring of fact and fiction in order to mould the 'Runners' and their activities into a coherent narrative that suited the aims and objectives of the various writers and commentators? Second, to what degree has this contributed to the often confused and contradictory ways in which the 'Runners' have been presented by writers both during the period of their existence and after their demise?

This chapter therefore looks at how various narratives have contributed to the public's wider (mis)understanding of the character and work of this influential band of men, both during and after their period of existence.[7] The historical background to the formation and functioning of the 'Runners' is first outlined in Section II below in order to contextualize the later sections concerning their appearance in both factual and fictional narratives.

II

The 'Runners' were formed in the winter of 1748/9 by Henry Fielding, novelist and newly appointed Chief Magistrate of Bow Street Court in Westminster.[8] Six ex-parish constables of Westminster (together with a servant of Saunders Welch, High Constable of Holborn) comprised the original force, which Fielding intended as a countermeasure to the perceived increase in serious crime (especially violent robberies) then occurring in the capital.[9] The 'Runners' received limited Governmental funding from late 1753 and

Henry's half-brother, Sir John Fielding (who succeeded as Chief Magistrate following Henry's death in 1754), continued to develop and expand the force to include various uniformed patrols throughout his period in office (1754–80).[10]

By the early nineteenth century, the force comprised a small number (between six and eight men) of plain-clothes detective officers (who much preferred to be distinguished from the less senior Bow Street ranks by the term Principal or Senior Officer – the nickname 'Runner' being viewed by them as demeaning). There was also a system of both mounted patrols which operated in the outskirts of London including the turnpiked roads that ringed the capital and, a large body of uniformed constables (kitted out in scarlet waistcoats, giving rise to their contemporaneous nickname of 'Robin Redbreasts'), who followed regular beats within the Metropolis.[11] The total complement of Bow Street personnel at any one time in the first decades of the nineteenth century numbered around 250. The Principal Officers themselves never operated in uniform, their sole badge of office being a tipstaff surmounted with a three-dimensional representation of the Royal crown.[12]

The Principal Officers were not restricted to the capital with regard to their activities, and for much of the period of their existence, they were attested as constables with power of arrest within the four counties surrounding the Metropolis. They also regularly investigated crimes that originated in the provinces and were often involved in complex cases that could last weeks if not months, and which took them to Scotland, Wales and the Continent.[13] Whilst the uniformed foot patrol was disbanded in 1829 following the creation of the Metropolitan Police, the horse patrol continued until August 1836, when it was subsumed into Peel's new force.[14] The Principal Officers continued to operate under the control of the Bow Street magistrates in uneasy tandem with the Metropolitan Police (which had no official detective element before the creation of the Detective Department in 1842) until their demise in 1839.[15] Sir Frederick Roe, Chief Magistrate of Bow Street 1832–7, seems to have taken a dim view of the newly created Metropolitan Police, having very little regard for their potential detective capabilities, and fighting an ultimately unsuccessful rear-guard action to maintain his force of detectives. He is reported to have caustically commented that 'the police force is like gas-light; it is a very useful outdoor force, but it is not fit for the detection of thieves'.[16]

III

With regard to the Bow Street 'Runners' appearance in factual narratives, both Fieldings were acutely aware of the power of the printed word to influence both the general public and those in positions of authority. Henry Fielding, as the author of best-selling picaresque novels such as *Tom Jones* (1749), was particularly familiar with the use of literature in order to get his point across. In his career as a playwright and novelist he had unceasingly satirized Sir Robert Walpole's government, leading indirectly to the passing of the Theatre Licensing Act 1737, which introduced political censorship of theatrical productions.[17] From as early as 1751, when he published an extended treatise into the causes of crime and the ways in which it should be dealt with, Henry Fielding was at pains to justify his creation of the 'Runners'.[18] He answered considerable criticism that the members of his force were just another type of glorified 'thieftakers' (private bounty hunters who received rewards for successful prosecution of offenders and who were widely regarded as corrupt in the extreme) in the form of a series of rhetorical questions:

I will venture to say, that if to do Good to Society be laudable, so is the Office of a Thief-catcher; and if to do this Good at the extreme Hazard of your Life be honourable, then is this Office honourable. True, it may be said; but he doth this with a View to a Reward. And doth not the Soldier and the Sailor venture his Life with the same View? [...]. If to bring Thieves to Justice be a scandalous Office, what becomes of all those who are conven'd in this Business, some of whom are rightly thought to be among the most honourable Officers in Government? If on the contrary they be, as it surely is, why should the Post of Danger in this Warfare alone be excluded from all Share of Honour?[19]

Similarly, Sir John Fielding, in his *Plan for Preventing Robberies within Twenty Miles of London, With an Account of the Rise and Establishment of the Real Thieftakers*, published in 1755, was equally at pains to correct any public misconceptions as to the honesty and trustworthiness of what he referred to as his 'set of brave fellows'.[20] Unlike private thieftakers, the 'Runners' could not operate independently; they had always to first obtain official sanction from the magistrates before accepting any case.

Both Fieldings were quick to take advantage of the rapid and continuing growth in popular literature by creating their own newspapers, which ceaselessly promoted the system of policing at Bow Street. Henry began the process with the short-lived *Covent Garden Journal* (1752–6), whilst John continued with the publication of the *Public Advertiser* from late 1754, followed by the *Quarterly* and *Weekly Pursuits* in 1772.[21] On 3 December 1773, John published the first edition of *Fielding's General Preventive Plan or Public Hue & Cry*.[22] This claimed that:

The front page of this newspaper is stuck up in the Market Place of every Corporate Town from Cornwall to Edinburgh, by order of the mayors and chief officers of such corporations and also in some conspicuous place of the Public Road, by the Magistrates of the counties at large to which it is sent.[23]

The publication was often flagrant in the self-promotion of the Bow Street system of policing. For example, in 1809 *Hue & Cry* carried details of the robbery of the Whitehaven Bank, in which some £15,000 was stolen, remarking that the particular nature of the case 'renders it extremely difficult for any other than the Bow Street police to discover, explore and trace'.[24] The other constituents of the Bow Street police were also often praised for their effectiveness. In 1816, for instance, *Hue & Cry* referred to a case involving the Horse Patrol, 'whom scarcely any robber can escape', whilst in 1822 it similarly reported that 'the Day Patrol lately established at Bow Street has already been of great service in clearing the streets of pick-pockets; the most experienced men of the Night Patrol having been appointed to this service'.[25]

However, *Hue & Cry* was a specialist publication, designed as Bow Street's official 'mouthpiece', to be distributed to magistrates throughout the country. Despite the avowed intention that it be placed on public display in market squares, it was not conceived to be of interest to the contemporaneous literate public. A lawyer stated in 1825 that:

> The *Hue & Cry* is not sold like other newspapers. It is sent by order of the Home Office or Chief Police Office [...] – to the men of law in town or country it was scarcely known more than by name.[26]

In 1829 the social reformer Edwin Chadwick similarly dismissed the effectiveness of the publication, stating that 'it is never seen by the public, nor can we learn that it is ever regularly seen by the officers of the several police establishments'.[27] Section IV below therefore discusses from whence the contemporary general public gained much of its knowledge and perception of the work and functioning of the Bow Street Office.

IV

The contemporaneous general public were largely forced to rely on newspaper trial reports, the published *Proceedings* of the Old Bailey or in some cases partial transcripts of the various *Parliamentary Select Committee Reports* in which the 'Runners' appeared, as no official account of their work was available during their existence. Therefore, the public's perception of the 'Runners' with regard to their probity, their effectiveness and their usefulness was often guided by the respective attitude of newspaper editors to the Bow Street system of policing. This could range from approbation to opprobrium and it is therefore not surprising that this range of opinion appears to have been replicated amongst the public (and indeed by those who came into contact with them). For example, in 1811, during an appearance on a charge of pickpocketing at the Royal Opera House, defendant Thomas Northem appealed to the trial judge, stating:

> I believe there will be enough witnesses called, whose words will go further than a Bow Street Officer's. I believe my Lord, you know that Bow Street Officers is [*sic*] not very nice in what they say.[28]

This view is in stark contrast to that of the radical agitator and writer, Samuel Bamford, who was briefly detained at Bow Street Office:

> The demeanour of the Bow Street officers was, without exception, such as might be expected from men who knew their duty, and had the full power to perform it. It presented a striking contrast to the conduct which was at that time generally practised by men of the same station at Manchester.[29]

That the Bow Street Officers were relatively well known by reputation throughout the country as a whole is suggested in the following two accounts. Firstly, in a request sent to the Bow Street Magistrates for Principal Officers to travel north in order to quell prospective rioting by the wonderfully named 'Northamptonshire Nutters', the Warden of New College, Oxford, stated that:

> One or two officers from Bow Street would be quite sufficient: it is not the number but the name; the circumstances of an officer from Bow Street being on the spot will inspire the rioters with terror.[30]

Secondly, Mr E. Brown, a surgeon charged with conspiring to engrave false bank notes in Birmingham, was arrested by Samuel Taunton, who told him that 'You must come with me. I am a Bow Street Officer.' The suspect is reported to have replied somewhat melodramatically, 'Then I am a dead man.'[31]

V

In the late eighteenth and early nineteenth centuries, newspapers devoted a considerable amount of column inches to the reporting of felonies – then as now, crime helps to sell copy. Metropolitan newspapers regularly reported on the proceedings of the Old Bailey and the other courts within the capital, whilst provincial papers often devoted several columns in each issue to important national or local trials. Although newspapers remained comparatively expensive until the repeal of Stamp Duty in 1855, by the end of the eighteenth century, newspapers were becoming increasingly popular amongst the newly emergent middle class. The *Staffordshire Advertiser* of 18 April 1795 gives some indication of the number of publications involved:

> There are at this time one hundred and fifty-eight newspapers published in Great Britain and Ireland viz. 38 in London, 72 in the county towns of England; 14 published daily in London, 10 three times a week, 2 twice a week and 12 weekly.[32]

The lower classes, often illiterate or semi-literate, were not necessarily barred from gaining access to such newspapers. Rather, it was fairly common practice for articles or reports to be read aloud either in public venues or the increasingly popular coffee houses.[33] During the period of the 'Runners', literacy rates increased considerably and the price of newspapers also fell. A survey, reported in the *Manchester Guardian* of 25 April 1838 for instance, suggested that some two-thirds of the population were literate to a varying degree. Stamp Duty had been reduced from 4d. to 1d. just two years before this, thereby making newspapers much more affordable.[34]

The 'Runners' featured prominently in many such newspaper reports of trials (both metropolitan and provincial). In my previous research into the provincial activities of the 'Runners' between 1792 and 1839, based on an analysis of *The Times* (established

1785), the *Manchester Guardian* (established 1821) and the *Staffordshire Advertiser* (established 1795), individual 'Runners' are mentioned by name in over 450 reports, with anonymous reports adding almost another 100 to the total number.[35] Consequently, several of the individual 'Runners' became known by name and reputation to a wider public. For example, in 1818, following the successful prosecution of a violent burglary and robbery suspect in Middleton, Northamptonshire, *The Times* reported that 'the county magistrates, in admiration of the zeal, intelligence, and courage of Lavender, have resolved to give him a very handsome reward', after he arrested five people 'with extraordinary celerity and resolution'.[36] Some two years earlier the same publication had been keen to separate the Principal Officers from the less senior Bow Street personnel during the 'Blood-Money Scandal' of 1816, in which four patrol members were found guilty of compounding felonies and illegally profiting from their employment. *The Times* stated categorically that the accused 'must not be confused with the Bow Street Officers, who are respectable persons; their names are Townsend, Sayer, Pearkes, Lavender, Vickery, Adkins, Taunton and Bishop'.[37]

It was not just from the higher courts that the public learned of the activities of the 'Runners'. Several of the Bow Street Chief Magistrates were more than happy to allow newspaper reporters into their court. This occasionally got the Chief Magistrate into trouble. In 1811, for example, James Reid (Chief Magistrate 1806–13) was censured by Judge Archibald McDonald for letting the editor of *Hue & Cry* hear and subsequently print details of prejudicial information against a defendant in a fraudulent arson trial:

> I am extremely sorry that, when this officer made a report of what he had heard and seen of this business to Justice Reid, that any editor of a newspaper should have been present, and have taken notes of what was stated by Adkins to the magistrate at Bow Street, and that partial statements should have been inserted in the public newspapers, in order to inflame the public mind.[38]

However, this incident did not deter the Chief Magistrates from allowing reporters into Bow Street, and in 1824 Sir Richard Birnie must have felt vindicated in his decision to continue the practice, when the *Manchester Guardian* reported that:

> Sir Richard [Chief Magistrate 1821–32], we perceive has been sneeringly echoing – in a case where the publication of a police report has just led to the detention of a thief – the solemn twaddle of Mr Justice Park, about the mischief of publishing police reports. What a mortification it must be to the knight of the common pleas, to be so snubbed by his Bow Street brother![39]

However, not all newspaper coverage was unerringly favourable to the 'Runners'. In 1825 a damning letter purporting to be from a suspected burglar, John Ingram, was published in *The Times*, referring to the alleged corrupt nature of Daniel Bishop, one of the most well known of the 'Runners'. It stated that 'Mr Bishop of Bow Street, is very learnt, and if you don't understand this, he will explain. He takes a fee for his opinion, like all others connected with the law.'[40] The use and employment of the 'Runners' by the Royal family and aristocracy also came in for some criticism. In a highly sarcastic article, *The Times* remarked that 'the Knights of the Order of Bow Street are become such necessary appendages of the *haut ton*, that no grand Fête can go off with *éclat* without them'.[41] Consequently, Principal Officers were often asked for by name when their services were required by this élite group of people and their friends. In his evidence to the 1822 Select Committee for example, Sir Richard Birnie stated that applications were often received for particular Officers.[42] That newspapers provided the main source of information about the work of the 'Runners' is perhaps unsurprising; with a paucity of other forms of media, the public relied heavily on Fleet Street and its provincial equivalents for its news and information.[43]

However, there was another source of information available to the literate public in the form of the *Proceedings* of the Old Bailey (now the Central Criminal Court). From 1678, the Old Bailey Session Papers (also known as the *Old Bailey Proceedings*) were published on a regular basis (usually eight times per year). A century later, the City of London oversaw the publication of the papers, insisting that the *Proceedings* should provide a 'true, fair, and perfect narrative' of each and every trial heard.[44] This had an unforeseen side effect in that the length of the *Proceedings* greatly increased, making them less commercial, so the interested public increasingly turned to newspapers and other publications as the source of their information. One of these sources (at least with regard to major London-based trials) was the highly selective *Newgate Calendars*, also known as the *Malefactors' Bloody Register*, first published in 1773, but these contained only limited information about the 'Runners' and their operation, concentrating instead on sensational trials from the past.

With specific regard to the 'Runners' appearances in the Old Bailey *Proceedings*, previous research has shown that they featured in almost 300 metropolitan cases between 1792 and 1839.[45] This figure does not of course include any provincial cases in which the 'Runners' were involved (and elsewhere it has been shown that they spent much if not the majority of their time on provincial investigations).[46] Neither does it include any mention of the less senior Bow Street personnel, who appeared in almost 1,300 metropolitan trials held at the Old Bailey. The cases differ considerably in length and detail, with some only taking up a few lines, whilst others consist of many pages. Consequently the amount of information concerning the 'Runners' is highly variable, but in some of the trials, the 'Runners' are well represented in terms of how they operated.

There were also occasional brief biographical accounts of at least some of the Bow Street Officers in contemporary narratives. Captain Rees Howell Gronow, a famous Regency dandy who published a series of *Memoirs* during his adventurous lifetime, gave a short and mildly humorous series of anecdotes concerning the life and work of one of the most famous 'Runners', John Townsend:

> On one occasion the Duke of Clarence [the future King William IV] recommended Townsend to publish his memoirs, which he thought would be very interesting. Townsend, who had become somewhat deaf, seemed rather surprised but said he would obey H.R.H.'s commands. A few weeks afterwards, Townsend was on duty

at Carlton House, when the duke asked him if he had fulfilled his promise. His answer was: 'Oh, sir, you've got me into a devil of a scrape! I had begun to write my amours, as you desired, when Mrs Townsend caught me in the act of writing them and swore she'd be avenged: for you know, your Royal Highness, I was obliged to divulge many secrets about women, for which she'll never forgive me.'[47]

In more serious mode, Gronow also stated that Townsend 'was said, *in propriâ personâ*, to have taken more thieves than all the other Bow Street officers put together.'[48] Henry Angelo, fencing master to King George III, also mentions Townsend in his *Reminiscences*, when he spotted him at the Pantheon Masquerades in 1795: 'His portly figure soon discovered him to me – my old and very pleasant *slang* friend, Townsend, of Bow Street memory.'[49]

Some of the Principal Officers appear to have been acutely conscious of their putative place within history, with a few compiling various forms of autobiographical accounts of their respective life and work.[50] This suggests that they thought their activities worthy of record, and this was fairly unusual amongst the non-élite of early-nineteenth-century society. However no autobiographical account by a Principal Officer was published during his working lifetime. In 1852, some thirteen years after his retirement, ex-Principal Officer Samuel Hercules Taunton published a brief anonymous account of some of the more interesting cases in which he had been involved.[51]

The only known surviving autobiography of a Principal Officer is that of Henry Goddard, who served at Bow Street from 1834 to 1839, after previously being employed at Marlborough Street since 1824. This detailed four-volume account of his life as a detective was compiled between 1875 and 1879 but was not published during his lifetime, being intended rather as a memorial for his surviving family. It was not until 1956 that an edited and annotated version of Goddard's *Memoirs* was actually published.[52] Other autobiographical snippets of information can be found within various Parliamentary Select Committee reports in which several Principal Officers were called to give evidence, and their words recorded for posterity. Although these were published, they were not readily available to the public, being prohibitively expensive to purchase.[53] Contemporary access by the general public to 'factual' narratives of the work of the 'Runners' was therefore confined to two main sources through newspapers and through their testimony as witnesses at the Old Bailey.[54]

The above discussion has focussed on 'factual' sources of information concerning the activities of the 'Runners', but this was not the only type of literature by which the public gained knowledge of such detectives. Section VI therefore turns to a discussion of the 'Runners' appearances in fictional writings.

VI

Fiction often played an important role both in the portrayal of the 'Runners' and their role within the contemporary criminal justice system. Such fictional representations were not always favourable to either the 'Runners' or their superiors. In 1773 John Fielding unsuccessfully tried to prevent a performance by David Garrick at the Drury Lane Theatre of John Gay's *Beggar's Opera*, on the grounds that previous productions of the scandalous play had always resulted in an increase of immoral and criminal behaviour within the city.[55] In the same year and as a backlash against Sir John's campaign, a deeply satirical anonymously penned play, entitled *The Bow Street Opera in Three Acts. Written on the Plan of the Beggar's Opera*, was staged in the capital.[56]

Described both as 'a burlesque of a burlesque' and 'a trenchant satire of the London Magistrates' Court', the play was a scathing attack on both contemporary politics and justice.[57] It features a character based on the radical John Wilkes (who replaces the Macheath character in Gay's original), together with a caricature of John Fielding (very thinly disguised as 'Justice Blindman' – Sir John had been blinded as the result of an accident at the age of nineteen). It is not clear whether or not this was a direct response to Fielding's actions regarding Garrick, but the play is very critical of the perceived arbitrary nature and chaos of court proceedings at Bow Street. Other characters include Justice Wolf, Justice Clumsey, Justice Wrong and Justice Cunning, and the magistrates were referred to collectively and pejoratively as 'the Old Ladies'.

In Act II, entitled 'Blind Justice', Bess Bunter, a prostitute who is up before the Bench, sings the following satirical air to Justice Blindman:

In the days of your youth you could bill like a dove
And your surgeon can witness how fervent our love
The life of a justice in kissing should pass
You have oft kissed my face – you may now kiss my arse![58]

The Brown Bear (a public house near Bow Street Office used as an unofficial lock-up) is also mentioned in the play, and in Act II Scene I the stage directions state 'The Old Ladies seated, Officers, Constables, Thieftakers, Clerks and Runners, attending'. It would seem that the 'Runners' referred to in the directions here are court messengers rather than Principal Officers, as the latter are mentioned separately and disparagingly as 'Thieftakers'. In any case, in this instance it is the Bow Street magistrates rather than the 'Runners' who are the principal subjects of the play, presumably much to Sir John's chagrin.

One of the first definite printed references to Bow Street Officers as 'Runners' is in a poem by Reverend Henry Bate, printed 5 March 1785 in the *Morning Herald*, in which he penned the following lines after the artist Nathaniel Hone accused Sir Joshua Reynolds of plagiarism:

What's Raphael, Guido and the rest?
Poor dogs, Sir Joshua, at the best!
If no idea bright
They lose – without Hone's demi-devil
Like Bow Street runner – most uncivil
Bringing the theft to light.[59]

Throughout the remainder of the eighteenth century the 'Runners' made remarkably few appearances in various forms of fictional literature. They are briefly alluded to in Byron's 1824 *Don Juan*, after the eponymous hero has shot and killed the footpad Tom:

> Who in a row like Tom could lead the van,
> Booze in the ken, or at the spellken hustle?
> Who queer a flat? Who (spite of Bow Street's ban)
> On the high toby-spice so flash the muzzle?
> Who on a lark, with black-eyed Sal (his blowing),
> So prime, so swell, so nutty, and so knowing?[60]

They also appear to dubious humorous effect in *The Handsome Wife*, a 'comic' ballad with racist overtones printed around 1845, in which a husband is cuckolded, and his wife discovered in an adulterous relationship with a black servant:

> I thought when I had married her,
> That I was surley bless'd for life;
> For every gent said to me, 'sir,
> You've got a very handsome wife,'
> I thought so too, until I found
> That she used to paint and then
> It was well known to all around
> That she kept two fancy men.
> [...]
> My wife got in a certain way,
> And took strange fancies in her head,
> Nothing was right that I could say,
> Until, at last, she went to bed.
> The nurse came knocking at my door,
> She said, 'Your happiness begins,
> Your lady, sir, is in the straw,
> And got two lovely colour'd twins.'
> Next day, while labouring with the gout,
> A Bow-street Officer called on me,
> Said he, 'Old chap, I've found her out.
> I charge her, sir, with bigamy'.
> So they took away my handsome wife,
> And I got lectured by the mayor
> For the future I'll lead a single life,
> For of beauty I have had my share.[61]

In the first decades of the nineteenth century a particular type of fiction emerged in which the 'Runners' began to feature much more prominently – the detective novel.

The origins of the detective novel remain a subject of fierce debate amongst literary historians, with several citing *Things as They Are* (aka *The Adventures of Caleb Williams*) written by William Godwin in 1794 as the first English example of the genre. However, it is clear that Godwin himself viewed his work as a 'narrative of fictional adventure', and no plain-clothes police officer or private 'detective' is featured in the novel.[62] It is not until the second quarter of the nineteenth century that two serious contenders for the accolade of the first true English detective novel emerge: *Richmond: Scenes from the life of a Bow Street Runner*, published anonymously, and (much more convincingly) *Delaware or The Ruined Family*, written by George Payne Rainsford James.[63]

The 1976 reprinted and edited version of *Richmond* is subtitled by its editor, E. L. Bleiler, as 'the first collection of detective stories in English'.[64] The book purports to be written by a real-life Principal Officer (and this view is supported by Bleiler), although the internal evidence of the publication is extremely contradictory on this point. 'Richmond' states that on joining the Bow Street Police, 'My only objection was the scarlet waistcoat; which, although not quite so bad and low as a livery, was still a badge I could have gladly dispensed with', strongly suggesting that he was a uniformed Patrol Constable or Conductor of Patrol rather than a more senior plain-clothes 'Runner'.[65] Bleiler posits the fact that 'Richmond' features himself operating outside London, in several of the cases described in the book, as a decisive indication that 'Richmond' was a Principal Officer. However, research has shown that Principal Officers were occasionally accompanied on their provincial investigations by less senior colleagues (probably in order to gain experience with an eye to possible promotion), thereby negating this argument.[66]

Several well-known contemporary 'hack' writers, including Thomas Surr and Thomas Gaspey, have been promoted as the possible creators of *Richmond*, but its definitive authorship remains unknown.[67] Turning to the contents of the book, *Richmond* recounts the author's early life in considerable detail; it is not until the eighty-seventh page that he is employed by Bow Street. There follows a series of five cases in which the eponymous hero is involved, including a kidnapping, capture of resurrectionists, horse-swindling, forgery and false pretences. The stories are of limited literary merit, being somewhat pedestrian in style, but the book is of considerable historical interest, with some knowledge of both the procedure of the Bow Street Office and the provincial activities of the Principal Officers being exhibited within the recounting of the cases.[68] *Richmond* is certainly the first novel to introduce the 'Runners' to a wider literary audience in a format other than newspaper or trial reports.

The other contender for the first true 'detective' novel to feature Bow Street Officers is G.P.R. James' *Delware or The Ruined Family*, published only six years after *Richmond*. Although now little known and relatively forgotten, James enjoyed a phenomenally successful and prolific literary career, publishing almost one hundred novels during his lifetime (peaking at a rate of over three a year), together with numerous poems and factual historical studies. He became the best-selling novelist in America in the early 1850s.[69] He was also British Consul in Virginia and more latterly Venice, achieving all this within a relatively short lifespan, dying at the age of fifty-nine in 1860.[70]

The novel was written in 1830–1 and published in 1833. It was a slight departure from James' usual more overtly romantic subject material. It was republished with minor alterations in 1848 under the title *Thirty Years Since: or The Ruined Family*, this time with James as the acknowledged author.[71] *Delaware* is a tortuous though engaging story of honour, murder and middle-class treachery and in other respects resembles much of the rest of James' oeuvre. However, it is unique in the annals of literature, being the first novel to feature Principal Officers (both fictional and real) in its cast of characters. The complex and labyrinthine plot is too involved to go into detail, suffice to say that Captain William Delaware RN, an upright and honest young man, is maliciously framed for robbery and murder. He is arrested but escapes from custody in order to clear his name, with his friends and family employing the services of Bow Street in order to help uncover the truth and unmask the real culprits.

James invents a Principal Officer, 'Mr Cousins', who plays a leading part in the detection of the offender but also gives a 'cameo' appearance to a real Principal Officer, George Thomas Joseph Ruthven.[72] Ruthven (1792/3–1844) was one of the most well known 'Runners', becoming famous for his part in foiling the Cato Street Conspiracy of 1820. He is also one of the very few 'Runners' whose likeness is known, being both immortalized in an engraving of the Cato Street Conspiracy by George Cruickshank and also having sat for an anonymous full-length painting depicting him outside Bow Street Office at around the same time.[73] In *Delaware* Ruthven is sent over to France in order to liaise with the French authorities and is even given dialogue in the novel.[74] Throughout the work, James exhibits a considerable knowledge of the work of the Principal Officers. Several of the Principal Officers did indeed travel throughout Europe during the course of their investigations; for example, in real life Ruthven was occasionally detailed for investigative work on the Continent, as he could speak French and was apparently familiar with 'Gallic ways'.[75]

Similarly James' fictional creation, Cousins, is depicted as making an admirably thorough forensic investigation of the crime scene (thus predating his far more famous counterpart, Sherlock Holmes, by over half a century), including the examination of footprints, quickly leading him to establish that:

'As far as I could make out, it must have been done by two men [...] for I got the tread of one very near whole – that is to say, the round of his boot heel, and more than three inches of the toe from the tip, backwards – so that one of them had a remarkably long foot. There is the measure and shape of it, as far as I could get it – more than twelve inches, you see, sir.'

'And the other!' said Dr Wilton – 'the other man's foot – what was the length of it?' 'Ah, sir, that I could not get at!' replied the officer. 'There was nothing but about five inches of the fore-part of the sole; but that I got twice, and it is as different a foot, you see, from the other as one would wish to find – twice as broad, and square toed. And then I got the mark of a hand, too, which must have been at the poor old devil's throat when they were cutting it, for it was all blood. It had rested on the cornice of the dado; and the fellow, whoever he was, wanted part of the third finger of his left hand.'[76]

It is perhaps not too fanciful to imagine that a young Arthur Conan Doyle had read *Delaware*, as James remained a popular author throughout the nineteenth century. The dialogue in the above passage certainly would not appear out of place in a Sherlockian adventure, and furthermore 'Dr Wilton' is not far removed from 'Dr Watson' in both name and characterization.

The application of basic forensics to crime scenes such as that carried out by the fictional Cousins was integral to the real-life investigations of the Principal Officers. Whilst many forensic tests, such as the ability to discern human from animal blood (not possible until 1895), or fingerprinting (not utilized effectively in England until the second decade of the twentieth century), were not available to the officers, they did often make detailed examinations of both the crime scene and associated artefacts.[77] In 1813, during his and colleague Samuel Taunton's investigation into the murder of a gentleman farmer in Staffordshire, Principal Officer Harry Adkins carried out the earliest documented ballistics forensic examination in the world. He matched the pistol lead shot recovered from the murder victim to that of a bullet mould found secreted near the scene of the crime, thereby establishing that the bullet had been fired from a particular pistol found in the possession of the suspect.[78]

James was also obviously aware of the Bow Street Officers' almost legendary knowledge of contemporary criminals and their whereabouts. Cousins' knowledge of the criminal fraternity proves invaluable in establishing the true perpetrators of the robbery and murder:

> 'Harding! Harding!' said Cousins thoughtfully; 'I wonder if that could be the Harding who was a sort of valet and secretary to ———– the banker, and who pocketed a good deal of his cash when he failed. He had well nigh been hanged, or at least taken a swim across the pond – but the lawyer let him off for some disclosure he made, and got him a new place too, they say!'[79]

Cousins' and Ruthven's dogged determination prove successful and *Delaware* reaches a satisfyingly moral conclusion, with Captain Delaware being absolved of all blame, happily reunited with his true love (who of course had never wavered in her belief in his absolute integrity), and the real culprits receiving their 'just deserts'.

VII

Although *Delaware* proved to be yet another successful publication for G.P.R. James, with its first print run selling out, 'Runners' do not appear to have featured so prominently again in any other novel during the period of their existence. They were not to appear in leading roles in fictional detective stories for almost another century and a half, despite the increasing popularity of the detective novel throughout the remainder of the nineteenth century. Possible reasons for this lack of contemporaneous fictional fame include the rise of the Metropolitan Police and the concomitant creation of the Detective

Department in 1842. This development also led indirectly to the increasing appearances of fictional detectives – for example Dickens' Inspector Bucket in *Bleak House*, who made his first appearance in 1852.[80] It is also perhaps significant that Dickens was, as indicated at the beginning of this chapter, no believer in the efficacy of the Bow Street system. He was however fascinated and impressed by the work of the Detective Department, whom he (mistakenly) believed were far more professional and scientific in their approach than the 'Runners' had ever been. The contrast between his portrayal of the 'Runners' as bumbling inepts and James' efficient and observant Cousins is striking.

The increasing interest in police detectives in turn stimulated public familiarity with the private or 'consulting' detective as portrayed by the most famous of them all, Sherlock Holmes, who made his first appearance in *A Study in Scarlet*, serialized in *Beaton's Christmas Annual* in 1887.[81] An increasingly literate Victorian public seem to have required their detectives to be contemporary and recognizably modern men or, from the 1860s onwards, women, rather than relics from the Hanoverian age – Sherlock Holmes for example frequently embraced new technologies and scientific techniques.[82] The rise of various forms of mass transport also enabled the Victorian detective a far greater degree of narrative mobility and opportunities for plot twists than their Georgian equivalents, who were constrained to often agonisingly slow progress by horse, stagecoach or post-chaise, thereby denying the opportunity for fast-paced narrative development. By the early decades of the twentieth century, although there was a proliferation of fictional detectives such as Lord Peter Wimsey and Simon Templar, the 'Runners' seem to have been almost forgotten.[83]

During the interwar period, the 'Runners' do make the occasional appearance in detective or adventure fiction, but usually as figures of fun. For example, a fictional 'Runner', Jerry Hunt (incorrectly portrayed wearing a scarlet waistcoat) is made a scapegoat of ineptitude and pomposity in *The Further Adventures of Dr Syn*.[84] In this, the fourth of the seven rip-roaring '*Boys' Own*'-style adventure stories written by actor and author Russell Thorndike, Hunt is given the comprehensive runaround by the eponymous anti-hero Dr Syn, incumbent of Dymchurch vicarage, Kent, who led a double life as a notorious master smuggler and fearless adventurer known as 'The Scarecrow' of Romney Marsh. Hunt is humiliated and eventually bound and gagged before being released unharmed, 'not caring to boast of his misfortunes on Romney Marsh'.[85]

Since the 1970s, the 'Runners' have undergone something of a revival with regard to their fictional depictions. 'Runner' Edmund 'Beau' Blackstone features in a series of six historical 'whodunnits' penned by Derek Lambert under the *nom-de-plume* Richard Falkirk, whilst Bruce Alexander wrote the *Sir John Fielding Mysteries*, a series of eleven historical novels featuring the exploits of the 'Blind Beak' of Bow Street, published between 1994 and 2005.[86] Other authors, including Georgette Heyer and Lisa Kleypas, have used fictionalized 'Runners' as the love interest in several of their historical romances. Most recently, the baton of depicting fictionalized Bow Street Runners has been ably taken up by Karen Charlton, in her *Detective Lavender* series, based on real-life Principal Officer Stephen Lavender (who became Deputy Constable of Manchester's police force in 1821).[87] Charlton's books arose from the discovery that one of her husband's ancestors, Jamie Charlton, had been arrested by Stephen Lavender in 1810. She is the first modern-day author of historical fiction to utilize recent academic research in her portrayal of the 'Runners'.[88]

The 'Runners' have recently enjoyed a similar resurgence in interest in other forms of narrative fiction. They featured briefly in a 2007 film version of *Sweeney Todd*; in a major though disappointing 2008 Channel 4 television series, *City of Vice*; and most recently in an entertaining 2013 four-part Radio 4 Extra series, *London Particulars*. In one episode (entitled 'The Last of the Bow Street Runners'), former Bow Street Officer Pip Shepherd joins forces with a Metropolitan police officer to thwart the attempts of various criminals in early-Victorian London, although it is not made clear what position the hero held at Bow Street.

VIII

That the 'Runners' were not portrayed more frequently in fictional contemporaneous narratives is at first sight somewhat perplexing; after all they were for several decades the only detective police force in the United Kingdom and certainly became well known in London and its environs. However, when one bears in mind the relatively low literacy levels of the eighteenth and early nineteenth century, together with the fact that their existence almost exactly parallels the development of the English novel (especially with regard to the detective genre), it is perhaps less surprising that they were not widely represented in fictional narratives during their respective lifetimes.

In conclusion, it is clear from the above brief survey of the various factual and fictional forms used to portray the 'Runners' from the time of their inception until the present day that no one single or cohesive narrative as to their life and work has been employed. Instead, numerous varied and often conflicting depictions have left us with a muddled and confused picture as to the activities, effectiveness and history of the 'Runners'. Their existence often was, and continues to be, hijacked by writers keen to promote their individual viewpoints as to the qualities or otherwise of the Fieldings' 'set of brave fellows'. However, it is hoped that this chapter, by employing a micro-historical approach to the 'Runners' depiction in factual and fictional narratives, has demonstrated that such an approach can prove fruitful in illuminating both a specific aspect of their often complex and convoluted development, as well as helping to contextualize their place within the wider field of police history.

Notes

1. C. Dickens (1850) 'A Detective Police-Party' in *Household Words*, Vol. 1, No. 18 (Saturday 27 July 1850), pp. 409–14 at p. 411. 'Penny-a-liners' were hack journalists who were paid a penny for every line that was printed – see J. Grant (1837) *The Great Metropolis* (Two Volumes) (London: Saunders & Otley), Vol. 2, pp. 282–324.

2. The Metropolitan Detective Department was not even the second professional detective force in Britain; Glasgow had employed plain-clothes detectives from 1821; see A. Dinsmor (2000) 'Glasgow Police Pioneers', *Journal of the Police History Society*, Vol. 15, pp. 9–11 at p. 11.

3. P. Fitzgerald (1972 reprint of 1888 edition) *Chronicle of Bow Street Police Office: With an Account of the Magistrates, 'Runners' and Police* (Two Volumes) (Montclair, NJ: Patterson Smith).

4. G. Armitage (1932) *The History of the Bow Street Runners 1729–1829* (London: Wishart & Co.), *passim*.

5. P. Pringle (1956) *Hue & Cry: The Birth of the British Police* (London: Museum Press); P. Pringle (1958) *The Thief Takers* (London: Museum Press); A. Babington (1999 edition) *A House in Bow Street: Crime and the Magistracy, London 1740–1881* (London: Macdonald) and J. Lock (1982) *Tales from Bow Street* (London: Hale).

6. D.J. Cox (2012) *'A Certain Share of Low Cunning': A History of the Bow Street Runners 1792–1839* (London: Routledge) and J.M. Beattie (2012) *The First English Detectives: The Bow Street Runners and the Policing of London 1750–1840* (Oxford: Oxford University Press).

7. The most notable study of literature and crime in the eighteenth and nineteenth centuries remains I.A. Bell (1991) *Literature and Crime in Augustan England* (London: Routledge). Other recent studies include A. Maunder and G. Moore (eds) (2004) *Victorian Crime, Madness and Sensation* (Aldershot: Ashgate) and A.G. Srebnick and René Levy (eds) (2005) *Crime and Culture: An Historical Perspective* (Aldershot: Ashgate).

8. Cox, *'A Certain Share of Low Cunning'*, p. 28.

9. Ibid., p. 28.

10. Ibid., pp. 30–1.

11. Ibid., pp. 36–7.

12. Throughout this chapter the term 'Runners' refers solely to the Principal Officers. For accounts of the activities and constituency of the Bow Street police establishment, see D.J. Cox, *'A Certain Share of Low Cunning'* and Beattie, *The First English Detectives*.

13. Cox, *'A Certain Share of Low Cunning'*, pp. 144–5 and 172.

14. Armitage, *The History of the Bow Street Runners*, p. 129.

15. The other London Police Offices which were created in 1792 also had their own Principal Officers who appear to have operated in a similar way to those of Bow Street, albeit seemingly on a more geographically restricted basis.

16. Parliamentary Papers, *Parliamentary Report on the Metropolis Police Offices 1837/8* (578), Vol. XV, p. 191.

17. D.J. Cox, K. Stevenson, C. Harris and J. Rowbotham (2015) *Public Indecency in England 1857–1960* (London: Routledge), p. 105.

18. H. Fielding (1988 reprint of 1751 edition) *An Enquiry into the Causes of the Late Increase of Robbers and Related Writings* (Edited by Malvin R. Zirker) (Oxford: Clarendon Press).

19. Fielding (1988 edition) *An Enquiry*, pp. 153–4. For an account of the activities of thieftakers, including the notorious Jonathan Wild, self-proclaimed 'Thieftaker-General', see D.J. Cox (2013) *Crime in England 1688–1815* (London: Routledge), pp. 70–4, and J.M. Beattie (1986) *Crime and the Courts in England 1660–1800* (Oxford: Oxford University Press), pp. 55–8.

20. J. Fielding (1755) *A Plan for Preventing Robberies within Twenty Miles of London, With an Account of the Rise and Establishment of the Real Thieftakers* (London: A. Millar).

21. The *Covent Garden Journal* was first published in January 1752 and ran until Henry's death. In October 1754 the *Public Advertiser* was introduced, continuing in various guises until 1794. The *Quarterly* and *Weekly Pursuits* were sent free to magistrates on request.

22. This publication eventually became the *Hue & Cry and Police Gazette* and continued (with several changes in name) long after the demise of both the Fieldings and the Bow Street policing system.

23. *Hue & Cry*, 3 December 1773.

24. *Hue & Cry*, 1 April 1809.

25. *Hue & Cry*, 14 December 1816 and 16 November 1822.

26. *The Times*, 17 December 1825, Issue No. 12840.

27. Quoted in L. Radzinowicz (1956) *A History of English Criminal Law and Its Administration from 1750*, Vol. 2 (London: Stevens & Sons), p. 461 and see also E. Chadwick (1829) 'Preventive Police', *London Review*, Vol. 1, pp. 252–308, at p. 276 and p. 280.

28. *Old Bailey Proceedings*, The Trial of Thomas Northem, 29 May 1811, Ref. t18110529-42.

29. S. Bamford (1964) *Passages in the Life of a Radical* (Oxford: Oxford University Press), p. 81.

30. *Jackson's Oxford Journal*, 9 September 1826, Issue No. 3828. Disappointingly prosaic in origin, the 'Northamptonshire Nutters' was the collective phrase for a group of itinerant workers employed to gather in the annual harvest of hazelnuts in Oxfordshire.

31. *Manchester Guardian*, 5 January 1828.

32. Stamp Duty grossly inflated the price of newspapers to 6d. or 7d. per issue – about £3.50 in modern-day prices.

33. J. Black (2001) *The English Press 1621–1861* (Stroud: Sutton), p. 62.

34. The role of newspapers in reporting crime is discussed further in Cox, 'A Certain Share of Low Cunning', pp. 6–9 and Cox, *Crime in England 1688–1815*, pp. 148–50. See also Black, *The English Press*, pp. 54–7.

35. D.J. Cox, '"A Certain Share of Low Cunning": The Provincial Activities of the Bow Street Runners 1792–1839' (Unpublished PhD thesis, Lancaster University).

36. *The Times*, 27 October 1818, Issue No. 10498. See also the *Morning Post*, 27 October 1818, Issue No. 14905.

37. *The Times*, 11 July 1816, Issue No. 9884.

38. Anon. (1811) *The Trial of the Reverend Robert Bingham, Taken in Shorthand by Mr Adams, by Order of the Directors of The Union Fire Office, London* (London: J.M. Richardson), p. 226.

39. Justice Park was the Chief Magistrate at the Court of Common Pleas, one of the superior courts of civil law.

40. *The Times*, 7 April 1825, Issue No. 12621.

41. *The Times*, 4 April 1800, Issue No. 4760. The *haut ton* – literally 'high tone' – was a contemporary expression referring to the most fashionable members of polite society in London.

42. Parliamentary Papers, *Parliamentary Report from the Committee on the State of Police of the Metropolis 1822* (440) Vol. IV, p. 15.

43. Fleet Street has always been closely associated with the Press since it was the headquarters of the first daily newspaper, the *Daily Courant*, first published in 1702. The area also housed numerous coffee houses and taverns, providing further means by which news was imparted throughout London.

44. www.oldbaileyonline.org/static/Publishinghistory.jsp.

45. Cox, 'A Certain Share of Low Cunning', pp. 125–30.

46. See ibid., for more details of their provincial activities.

47. C. Summerville (2006) Regency Recollections: Captain Gronow's Guide to Life in London and Paris (Welwyn Garden City: Ravenhall), p. 193.

48. Ibid., p. 192.

49. H. Angelo (1830) Reminiscences of Henry Angelo (Two Volumes) (London: Henry Colburn and Richard Bentley), Vol. 2, pp. 332–3.

50. For an overview of detectives' autobiographies in Britain, see H. Shpayer-Makov (2006) 'Explaining the Rise and Success of Detective Memoirs in Britain', in C. Emsley and H. Shpayer-Makov (eds) Police Detectives in History, 1750–1950 (Aldershot: Ashgate), pp. 103–33.

51. Anon (S.H. Taunton) (1852) 'A Reminiscence of a Bow Street Officer', Harper's New Monthly Magazine, Vol. 5, No. 28, pp. 483–94.

52. H. Goddard (1956) (with an introduction by Patrick Pringle) Memoirs of a Bow Street Runner (London: Museum Press).

53. See, for example, Parliamentary Papers, Report from the Committee on the state of Police of the Metropolis 1816 (510) Vol. V; Parliamentary Papers, Third Report from the Committee on the State of Police of the Metropolis 1818 (423) Vol. VIII; Parliamentary Papers, Report from the Committee on the State of Police of the Metropolis 1822 (440) Vol. IV and Parliamentary Papers, Report from the Select Committee on the Police of the Metropolis 1828 (533) Vol. VI.

54. J.M. Beattie (2006) 'Early Detection: The Bow Street Runners in Late Eighteenth-century London', in C. Emsley and H. Shpayer-Makov (eds) Police Detectives in History, 1750–1950 (Aldershot: Ashgate), pp. 15–33 at p. 24.

55. Gay's Beggar's Opera predated this performance by almost half a century, being first published in 1728, when it was an immediate success.

56. (1773) The Bow Street Opera. In Three Acts. Written on the plan of the Beggar's Opera. All the Most Celebrated Songs of Which Are Parodied and the Whole Piece Adapted to Modern Times, Manners and Characters (London: Marriner).

57. (1774) The Monthly Review, Vol. 49, p. 346. See also F. Englemann (1773) 'A Late-Eighteenth Century Ballad Opera and John Wilkes: The Bow Street Opera', in U Böker, I. Detmers and A. Giovanpolous (eds.) John Gay's The Beggar's Opera 1728–2004 Adaptations and Re-writings (Amsterdam: Rodopi) pp. 169–92 at p. 169.

58. (1773) The Bow Street Opera, 13th Air, Act II. 'Your surgeon can witness …' is an implicit reference to syphilis, which was treated by mercury preparations obtained from surgeons or apothecaries.

59. The Reverend Henry Bate was nicknamed the 'Fighting Parson' and was also a poet, playwright and the part-proprietor and editor of two influential London newspapers: the Morning Post and the Morning Herald.

60. Baron G.G. Byron (1824) Don Juan (London: J. & H.L. Hunt), Canto 11, Verse 19. Byron exhibits an impressive knowledge of thieves' 'cant' (specialist language) in this verse: 'ken' refers to a 'flash-house' or haunt of thieves; 'spellken' was a theatre or playhouse; to 'queer a flat' was to perpetrate a criminal act on an naïve victim; whilst to 'flash a muzzle' on the 'high toby spice' was to produce a pistol whilst committing a highway robbery – Byron is here referring to Bow Street's (often successful) efforts to thwart and arrest highwaymen.

61. Anon. (c. 1845) *The Handsome Wife* (London: Ryle & Co). The 'Runners' had by this time been disbanded but were obviously still well known enough to be utilized in comic verse.

62. William Godwin's own account of *Caleb Williams*, 20 November 1832, is available online at www.dwardmac.pitzer.edu/ANARCHIST_ARCHIVES/godwin/caleb/caleb1.html (accessed 25 March 2016). For detailed accounts of the development of the detective novel from the early nineteenth century through to the twentieth century, see H. Worthington (2005) *The Rise of the Detective in Early Nineteenth-Century Popular Fiction* (Basingstoke: Palgrave Macmillan); L. Lad Panek (2011) *Before Sherlock Holmes: How Magazines and Newspapers Invented the Detective Novel* (Jefferson, NC: McFarland & Co.) and H. Shpayer-Makov (2011) *The Ascent of the Detective: Police Sleuths in Victorian and Edwardian England* (Oxford: Oxford University Press).

63. Anon. (1827) *Richmond: Scenes from the Life of a Bow Street Runner* (London: Henry Colbourn) and see also G.P.R. James (1833) *Delaware or The Ruined Family* (Three Volumes) (London: Cadell).

64. E.F. Bleiler (1976 reprint of 1827 edition) (ed.) *Richmond – Scenes from the Life of a Bow Street Runner* (New York: Dover Publications).

65. Ibid., p. 87. The author also refers to operating 'without waiting for the return of the chief officer' (p. 100), further suggesting that the eponymous hero occupied a less senior post.

66. See Cox, 'A Certain Share of Low Cunning', pp. 36–7.

67. Thomas Skinner Surr (c.1770–1847) was a novelist who wrote a popular novel, *Winter in London* (1806). Thomas Gaspey (1788–1871) was a novelist and parliamentary reporter for many years with the *Morning Post*.

68. Some of the cases and events mentioned in the book appear loosely based on actual events, probably gleaned from contemporary newspaper reports.

69. S.M. Ellis (1927) *The Solitary Horseman* (London: The Cayme Press), p. 134.

70. Ibid., p. 249.

71. G.P.R. James (1848) *Thirty Years Since: or The Ruined Family* (London: Simpkin Marshall & Co). The new title probably deliberately echoes Alexander Dumas' less well-known sequel to *The Three Musketeers*, published in 1845 under the title of *Twenty Years After*.

72. For biographical details of Ruthven's life and work, see D.J. Cox (2010) 'Ruthven, George Thomas Joseph (1792/3–1844), Police Officer', *Oxford Dictionary of National Biography Online* (Oxford: Oxford University Press). See also the brief account by his great-great-great-granddaughter Frances Bevan: F. Bevan (2006) 'Criminals and Conspirators', *Ancestors*, 51, pp. 33–5.

73. Currently privately owned by one of Ruthven's direct descendants.

74. James (1833) *Delaware*, Vol. III, pp. 165–6.

75. *Manchester Guardian*, 24 May 1822.

76. James, *Thirty Years Since*, pp. 221–2.

77. S.H. Palmer (1992) *Police and Protest in England and Ireland 1780–1850* (London: Longman), p. 533.

78. See Cox, 'A Certain Share of Low Cunning', pp. 181–3 for further examples of basic forensics carried out by the Bow Street 'Runners'.

79. James, *Thirty Years Since*, p. 224.

80. C. Dickens (1852) *Bleak House* (Four Volumes) (Leipzig: Bernhard Tauschnitz).

81. A. Conan Doyle (1887) 'A Study in Scarlet', *Beaton's Christmas Annual*, Vol. 28, pp. 1–95.

82. See for example A. Forrester (2012 reprint of 1864 edition) *The Female Detective* (London: British Library).

83. The fictional detective Lord Peter Wimsey first appeared in D.L. Sayers (1923) *Whose Body?* (New York: Boni & Liveright) and the first appearance of Simon Templar can be found in L. Charteris (1928) *Meet the Tiger* (London: Ward Lock).

84. R. Thorndike (1927) *The Further Adventures of Dr Syn* (London: Rich & Cowan).

85. Ibid., p. 135.

86. See as examples of the respective series: R. Falkirk (1974) *Beau Blackstone* (New York: Stein & Day) and A. Bruce (1995) *Blind Justice* (New York: Berkeley).

87. K. Stockton (2012) *The Missing Heiress* (London: Knox Robinson).

88. Stockton recently stated that '*A Certain Share of Low Cunning: A History of the Bow Street Runners 1792–1839* written by David J. Cox became the main source of my research' – www.shotsmag.co.uk/feature_view.aspx?FEATURE_ID=213.

CHAPTER 8
CITIZENS' COMPLAINTS AND POLICE (UN)ACCOUNTABILITY: THE CAREER OF A PARISIAN *COMMISSAIRE DE POLICE* OF THE *BELLE ÉPOQUE*

Anja Johansen

I

Citizens' complaints provide fascinating insights into deviant behaviour amongst police personnel and how police managers deal with allegations of police malpractice. They also highlight the permeable boundaries between legality and illegality surrounding the actions of police personnel. Persistent allegations and evidence of police wrongdoing suggest that police often benefit from impunity when violating citizens' rights and breaching legal boundaries. Deviant police officers present police chiefs with the managerial dilemma of either disciplining the erring officer – and thereby implicitly or explicitly admitting fault on the part of the police organization – or justifying or denying the acts of the policeman with the risk of alienating the complainant, and perhaps the wider community.

This chapter investigates these ambiguities through a micro-study of the dubious professional record of one particularly deviant Parisian *Commisssaire de Police*, Léon Alexandre Kien, who was the object of persistent complaints and numerous disciplinary investigations between 1897 and 1918. Kien's well-documented career provides rare insights into citizens' grievances against police malpractice, as well as the functioning of disciplinary procedures within Paris' police and the handling of problem officers by successive police prefects. This micro-history serves as prism to reflect much broader aspects of police–public relations, which are otherwise difficult to study and contextualize due to limited documentation.

Improving the relationship with the public first emerged as a concern within the Paris police by the late nineteenth century, when Police Prefect Lépine sought to raise professional standards and increase the prestige of the force amongst the population. However, no formalized complaints procedures were developed, as this would inevitably commit the police chiefs to engage with the criticism from citizens. So whilst complaints procedures became part of the legitimizing police rhetoric in other European countries – no matter how remote from the actual reality – the Paris police remained seemingly impenetrable to citizens' grievances about police malpractice.

The Paris police force of the Third Republic has had a very mixed press: voices from the left-liberal and socialist camp scorned the Paris police in the 1870s and 1880s for poor professional standards, for not respecting citizens' rights and for allowing personnel with anti-Republican Bonapartist sympathies to run riot against political activists on the republican and socialist left.[1] From the 1890s, voices appeared from the far right, who complained about police corruption and politically motivated police attacks on their supporters.[2] Allegations as well as major scandals showing brutal or illegal policing practices continued to affect the reputation of the Paris police force through the interwar years and the Nazi occupation into the 1960s, with bloody crackdowns on Algerians and student protesters.[3] These episodes of police malpractice added to what Berlière and Lévy recently described as 'the weight of history', by further feeding a 'black legend' of conspiracy theories and allegations of systematic police violence and corruption.[4]

The main narrative by French historians has vacillated between highly critical assessments of policing in times of conflict, and sympathetic, sometimes apologetic, justifications of successive Republican governments, who repeatedly closed their eyes to malpractice and justified a system whereby police forces had almost no direct accountability towards citizens. This is often explained by the Third Republic's need to ensure loyalty from police, the *gendarmerie* and the army. Successive interior ministers therefore carefully avoided conflicts with the Paris police, responsible as it was for the security of all key republican institutions.[5] As a result, dubious policing practices were tolerated and police managers were allowed to exercise internal organizational discipline without much interference from government and judiciary.

It was only from the 1990s, when police scholars and historians began to look closely at the Paris police force, that the basis was created for a better understanding of the practices of the police prefecture in a wider context. The research by Jean-Marc Berlière as well as a younger generation of police scholars has done much to counter the 'black legend' of French – and notably Parisian – policing of the nineteenth and twentieth centuries.[6] Berlière in particular has insisted on the gradual improvement of policing standards (better education, professionalization and discipline) during the twenty-year period from 1893 to 1913, when Lépine headed the Paris police prefecture. That the Paris police force got more professional and disciplined is undoubtedly true. However, Lépine was caught between his managerial concerns for professionalism and discipline on the one hand and, on the other, his insistence on never publicly admitting fault on the part of the police.

The micro-study of *Commissaire* Kien's professional conduct – at the edge and sometimes beyond the law – reflects important aspects around crime and deviance amongst police personnel. It highlights that it was not just Kien's unacceptable behaviour, but also the official police denial, that alienated and frustrated Parisians, even stout republicans and natural supporters of law and order. Modern research on police deviance provides a useful framework by which to assess and contextualize Kien's professional conduct and the reluctance of Lépine to seriously discipline his persistent malpractice. Gottschalk distinguishes between three types of transgressive behaviour.[7] At the most serious end is actual criminal activity (corruption for personal gain, theft from a crime scene, involvement in organized crime, homicide or violent assault where the policeman's profession is incidental to the act). These should be distinguished from what he terms 'functional misconduct', that is, breaches of the articles in the penal code which are specifically related to the professional functions and powers of the policeman (abuse of authority, excessive violence against prisoners or members of the public, evidence manipulation and perjury, and unauthorized disclosure of information).[8] Because these breaches are often – although not always – committed in order to achieve efficient law enforcement and crime fighting, such behaviour is the least likely to be sanctioned by police managers as they are often justified with reference to 'effective policing'. At the least serious end of the spectrum, Gottschalk identifies what could be termed police 'occupational deviance' (sleeping, drinking or absenteeism), which are breaches of disciplinary rules, but only occasionally criminal.[9] The allegations against Kien fall within all three categories, although only the 'functional misconduct' and the 'occupational deviance' were substantiated by the disciplinary investigations. It is also worth noting that none of his transgressive behaviour promoted effective crime fighting or order maintenance.

Kien's case illustrates two important features of police non-accountability of the early twentieth century. In the first place, it shows how a persistent offender against procedures, legal boundaries, professionalism and good policing practice was allowed to occupy the position as police stationmaster despite a lengthy trail of complaints and disciplinary investigations. The other feature is how in France, concerns from members of the public were left in a procedural limbo a long time after other European countries, like Britain or Prussia, had established formal procedures for the handling of citizens' complaints.

The micro-history of Kien's catalogue of malpractice allows unique insights into how citizens' complaints were handled within the Paris police prefecture. The following analysis looks at the complaints raised against Kien (Section II), the problems arising from inadequate complaints procedures (Section III), the handling of complaints against Kien by the internal disciplinary body (Section IV), and the culture of patronage within the police which may have emboldened Kien in his persistent misbehaviour (Section V).

II

A recent study into offending police officers in the London Metropolitan Police of the twenty-first century makes two observations which are relevant to contextualizing Kien as a deviant police officer: that a small proportion of individuals account for the major proportion of deviant behaviour and that, most often, police managers are aware of who the 'problem officers' are.[10] The features that characterize 'problem officers' are (i) early onset of offending behaviour; (ii) late desistance, that is, at what stage the officer ceases to cause a disciplinary problems; (iii) frequency of offending behaviour; and (iv) length of career.[11] In all respects, Kien's disciplinary record identifies him as a 'problem officer'. Yet, despite being the object of numerous complaints and allegations of serious misconduct, he was consistently promoted and ended his career as *commissaire classe exceptionnelle* and retired with full pension. Moreover, it is clear that Police Prefect Lépine was aware of Kien's disciplinary problems as early as 1897, if not before.

From his personnel file, which is kept in the Archives of the Paris Police Prefecture, we can follow Kien's background and professional progress.[12] He was born in 1863, the son of an *ex-brigadier* and a mother who had been a domestic servant.[13] Kien's educational attainment of a *baccalauréat* (secondary school diploma) identifies him as (lower) middle class and allowed him to join the Paris police at clerical level as *secrétaire suppléant* (assistant clerk).[14] Kien therefore never occupied the lower ranks as street police, nor did he have any background in the army beyond the compulsory military service, unlike most of the men recruited for the lower ranks. Instead, the position as *secrétaire suppléant* (assistant clerk) functioned as practical training for men who would proceed to managerial posts at the middle or upper ranks of the police hierarchy.[15] Kien joined the police in 1888,[16] five years before Lépine became police prefect of Paris. His recruitment was therefore not subjected to the same stringent scrutiny as later candidates,[17] but all his promotions happened under Lépine. Over the following seven years he fulfilled secretarial functions at six Parisian police stations, before being promoted from 1895 to *commissaire* in several municipal forces just outside Paris. These posts functioned as a springboard for his applications to three successive posts as *commissaire* at police stations under the Paris police prefecture between 1901 and 1918.[18]

As *commissaire*, Kien was the head of one of the eighty Parisian police stations[19] with managerial responsibility for a staff typically including one clerk, a *secrétaire suppléant* (assistant clerk), as well as a number of *inspecteurs* and *gardiens de la paix* (police constables).[20] In addition to his managerial role, his core functions were judicial, as he fulfilled many of the traditional functions of a *juge de paix* (roughly equivalent to a justice of peace) alongside administrative responsibilities for record-keeping and accountancy within the police station.[21] The post gave him status as *fonctionnaire* (civil servant) which, amongst other advantages, gave him a particularly protected position against legal challenges from members of the public. Within the Republican hierarchy, the post was considered sufficiently senior for his name to appear in the *Almanach national*, which listed all the occupants of leading official positions in the French Republic. We can see from Kien's activities that as *commissaire* he was involved in crime fighting and law enforcement according to his own discretion. The complaints against him were not related to him appearing at the home of suspected criminals alongside detectives or his involvement in fist fights with anarchists, as this was perfectly within his remit. Yet, whilst Kien was in a position to largely define which police functions he would take active part in, he showed great ignorance or contempt for legal boundaries and procedures during such interventions.

Early evidence of serious problems surrounding Kien dates from 1897, with a letter of complaint from a group of middle-class citizens of Asnière, alleging that Kien had criminal connections.[22] We have no way of knowing whether this was the beginning of his professional misconduct, or whether previously allegations of dubious connections and disrespect of legal boundaries had simply been ignored by his superiors and tolerated as 'normal'. However, by the turn of the century his professional conduct looked increasingly deviant: it was obviously considered unacceptable by members of the public and his superiors began to take notice. Between 1897 and his retirement in 1918, he managed to clock up at least seventeen disciplinary investigations – although because of the inconsistent recording of such cases, it is possible that there were more.

Kien comes across as the stereotypical ill-behaved Parisian *commissaire*, almost to the level of caricature, as described by Yves Guyot[23] and later by Ernest Raynaud[24] for the 1880s: a rough, often semi-illiterate, former soldier of low social origins and professionally socialized into his police function under the Second Empire. Such characters were supposed to have been weeded out by Lépine's introduction of higher professional standards, stricter disciplinary procedures and more rigorous recruitment criteria. The raising of standards amongst the rank and file as well as amongst stationmasters was a managerial priority not only for Lépine but amongst police chiefs across France. Thus, *Commissiare* Pelantant from Grenoble most specifically emphasized high expectations to moral and professional conduct from police managers as role models for their subordinates.[25] Contemporary observers as well as historians agree that, by the first decade of the twentieth century, standards had improved considerably in all ranks.[26] Berlière also cites the decline in the annual number of dismissals and resignations between the 1870s and the 1890s as evidence of real improvement in quality of personnel.[27]

The disciplinary record of *Commissaire* Kien throws some doubts both over the actual achievements, as well as over the root causes of ill-behaved police officers. Whilst many of the behavioural problems of rudeness and brutality were presumed to stem from low levels of formal education and low social origins,[28] no such excuse could be made for Kien. Unlike the caricature of the *commissaire* of the 1880s, Kien did not lack education. Rather, with his *baccalauréat* diploma, he was considered 'educated'. Nor can the multiple complaints about his vulgar and often violent behaviour towards members of the public be explained as caused by growing up amongst the rough and ignorant. Instead we can suggest that a combination of his personality, the extensive powers he enjoyed as head of a police station, as well as the lack of any meaningful consequences emerging from the multiple disciplinary investigations against him gave little incentive for him to change his professional style. Despite Kien's professional and personal shortcomings being well known to Lépine, this old disciplinarian vehemently defended his man against any outside criticism, and it was only after Lépine's retirement in 1913 that Kien began to face serious consequences for his professional conduct. We will address the probable reasons for this staunch protectionist stance in Section V.

III

Another question emerging from Kien's dubious professional record is why it proved almost impossible for complainants to obtain any form of redress or acknowledgement of fault against the Parisian police. Kien's behaviour may have been grudgingly tolerated in the 1880s. However, by the turn of the century, with rising popular expectations to police professionalism, Kien's behaviour was increasingly perceived as intolerable, not only by the public but increasingly also amongst his superiors.

The collection of complaints and investigations against Kien are key to our understanding of the power relations between an ill-behaved police *commissaire* and frustrated members of the public, as it gives us unique insights into how complaints against the Paris police force were handled within the organization. The documentation about citizens' complaints against the Paris police is limited, and the complaints and investigations against Kien constitute by far the best documented against any individual police officer. The majority of complaints cases appear in personnel files, whilst an additional 180 cases are filed in two dossiers covering the years 1896–1911.[29] It is not clear why these cases have been filed separately, and we have no way of knowing how representative these cases are. The first dossier, starting in 1896, contains only complaints against the *commissiares* in Parisian police stations. The dossier starting in 1907 on the other hand includes complaints against all personnel at Parisian police stations. This suggests that whilst managerial control of the lower ranks had previously been left to the *commissaire* at local police stations, from 1907, there was a move towards closer scrutiny from the chiefs within the police prefecture.

Seen from the perspective of ordinary Parisians, complaining against the police was a tortuous process, with limited prospect of any tangible outcome, and with the added risk that a complaint against a local police employee might create a lot of trouble for the complainant. The fact that many of the allegations were made anonymously reflect the fear of consequences that complainants might legitimately have experienced. Nevertheless, the documents relating to Kien and citizens' complaints against other officers also reveal that Parisians from all creeds and casts voiced their dissatisfaction. Well-connected members of the social and political elites as well as ordinary people with no connections or protection complained about the police.[30]

The complaint narratives cover a range of allegations. There are some expressing concerns about disciplinary failings (non-intervention against criminals, policemen being drunk on duty or absent from duty and/or sloppiness in professional standards). The vast majority of complaints though refer to behaviour that was perceived to be 'unacceptable' by both the complainant and often the wider public, if one is to believe the reporting of individual cases in the press. Although not strictly in breach of formal rules, the complaints against Kien of rough and impolite police behaviour were typical. Such police behaviour violated the ever rising popular expectations that policemen should be forthcoming and respectful, whilst rigorously observing procedures and legal boundaries, particularly where the rights of citizens were at stake. Finally, a substantial number of complaints contain allegations of breaches of the paragraphs in the penal code which placed restriction on police behaviour in relation to members of the public (excessive violence, breach of legal boundaries, illegal arrests, perjury, corruption or allegations of involvement in criminality). The complaints against Kien are thereby typical of complaints in general, but the seriousness of Kien's behaviour and the persistence of complaints across two decades mark him out as unusual. What is particularly noticeable is the disconnect between what members of the public saw as 'problematic' and what police chiefs seemed to perceive as 'problematic' police behaviour. As complainants had few means to force police chiefs to act upon complaints, or even register them formally, there was very limited space for meaningful conversation between aggrieved citizens and police authorities.

By the turn of the twentieth century, a new player appeared on the scene in the form of the *Ligue des droits de l'homme* (the League of Human Rights, hereafter LDH). This civil rights organization was formed in 1898 on the basis of networks built up over the previous years in support of Captain Alfred Dreyfus.[31] Within the first two years of its existence, the LDH grew to become a mass organization with considerable financial muscle enabling it to engage in individual complaints against any public authority. The LDH provided an extremely influential, informed and well-connected ally for aggrieved citizens, and quite a few of the high-profile complaints cases from after 1903 were supported by the LDH. These included at least two cases against Kien, as we shall see below. This gave complainants access not only to first-class legal advice, but also to publicity for their case, both in LDH's bimonthly newsletter for members and also in the wider public media, because major Parisian newspapers such as *L'Aurore, Le Temps, Le Siècle, La Lanterne* and *L'Humanité* had close links to leading members of the LDH. Yet, even with its considerable resources and leading members amongst the political, judicial and media elites, the LDH had difficulties getting very far with actual complaints cases against Paris police personnel.[32]

One key problem in this respect was the absence of any concept of 'citizens' complaints' against the police in French law or procedural practice. In legal terms then, it was only possible for members of the public to challenge the police with two very specific types of complaints. A case could be presented before the administrative courts if an individual could establish a legal claim that questioned or overrode a specific police decision or act. Such cases typically concerned requests for individuals being exempted from general rules, or compensation claims for loss or damages caused by police actions or non-actions. The other type of complaint from the public that was recognized in law was alleged breaches of the penal code, specifically the paragraphs concerning illegal arrest, abuse of power or perjury. Such complaints could – in principle at least – be raised with the public prosecutor and, if substantiated, be tried at the criminal tribunals. In practice, however, it was almost impossible to bring a criminal prosecution against police personnel for such offences, as we will see. In addition to administrative challenges and criminal allegation, members of the public could also notify the police authorities about police personnel failing in relation to disciplinary matters.

The consequence of the structuring of complaints against the police exclusively around administrative claims, and allegations of breaches of criminal and disciplinary codes, was that any complaint which did not fit into these three categories fell into a legal-procedural void. There were no rules or procedural framework around 'behavioural complaints'. For instance, it was not stated that citizens had the right to complain, nor did any rules or procedures exist for how the authorities were supposed to process 'behavioural complaints'. By the late nineteenth century, this institutional deficiency distinguished the French system from other European countries. The London Metropolitan police pioneered the first formal citizens' complaints scheme for the handling of 'behavioural complaints' by 1831.[33] Similar procedures were later extended to country and borough police across Britain.[34] In Prussia, the 1883 legislation on regional administration established formal complaints procedures relating to police behaviour alongside procedures for complaints against other public authorities.[35]

In nineteenth-century France, some elements of a 'police complaints system' did exist in the sense that members of the public could not be prevented from expressing their grievances. People complained verbally at the local police station or sent letters of complaint to local police chiefs, to the Paris police prefect, to the interior minister or to any person with some influence within the establishment who might bring the complaint to the attention of the relevant police authority. According to Guyot, the Parisians of the 1880s complained all the time, but the police just took no notice.[36] The micro-history of Kien's career reveals that by the turn of the century, at least the Paris police prefecture began to do just that.

In the absence of a formalized complaints procedure, historians rely on the micro-study of individuals as these provide a rare window into how the police handled complaints from members of the public. The micro-study of cases against Kien and other senior police personnel reveals that the internal police disciplinary body, the *contrôle général*, came to play a central role in investigations and decision-making. Indeed, many of the complaints dossiers include investigative reports from the *contrôle général*. We can see that some complaints were addressed either directly to the police prefect whilst many were forwarded to the police prefect from other recipients. Most importantly, these cases reveal that allegations about criminal acts which complainants sent directly to *le procureur de la république* (the public prosecutor), and which should have been investigated by the prosecution authorities, were often forwarded without prior investigation to the police prefect to be investigated by the *contrôle général*. This transfer of criminal allegations for arbitrary arrest, misuse of power, excessive violence and perjury committed by police personnel from the *procureur* to the *contrôle général* meant that such allegations were handled as disciplinary matters rather than criminal acts. This helps to explain why French courts only played a very minor role in keeping Parisian policemen to account. It was far more difficult in the French system to bring a civil or criminal prosecution against serving police officers than in Prussia or Britain, although in neither of these jurisdictions was prosecution of police personnel by any means an easy process.[37] In Paris, investigations of all types (criminal acts, disciplinary issues and behavioural complaints) all ended up with the *contrôle général*. This was not correct procedure according to the Code of Criminal Procedure, but complainants had no way of knowing that this was how the system worked in reality.

Nevertheless, within these limitations, the *contrôle général* functioned highly professionally and effectively as a disciplinary investigation body, with the production of reports which were mostly characterized by rigorous investigations of events. Unfortunately, as we can see again and again in the reports produced on Kien, the conclusions drawn by the *contrôle général* do not always seem logical in relation to the actual findings. This discrepancy can be explained by the dual function of these reports. On the one hand, their main purpose was to serve as a managerial tool to provide the police prefect with accurate and detailed insights into the performance and possible failings of his personnel. On the other hand, the reports needed to reach conclusions justifying why the police prefect should not take further action beyond possibly suggesting some sort of internal disciplinary sanction.

This again helps to explain some of the fundamental tensions within the Paris police force under Lépine. Undoubtedly, under his leadership, the Paris police had become a far more disciplined and professional corps, with younger generations having benefitted from compulsory school education, combined with the development of professional training after 1883.[38] Although problems of impoliteness, rudeness, violence and alcoholism continued to be major causes of disciplinary action throughout the pre-First World War era,[39] the increasingly tight discipline did much to improve standards of policing, particularly amongst lower-ranking police personnel.[40] However, it is clear that the investigations and reports from the *contrôle général* were not geared towards public relations and did not reflect popular understandings of what constituted unacceptable and transgressive acts by policemen. The micro-study of the investigations against Kien show that the reports from the *contrôle général* only very partially and inadequately addressed behavioural issues as perceived by members of the public, despite the recognition amongst police managers of the need to improve relations with the public. By treating all types of complaints as managerial issues of discipline, the police authorities missed an opportunity to engage with citizens' concerns. The cases against Kien confirm what frustrated citizens had long complained about, namely facing something of a brick wall when complaining about unacceptable police behaviour. With no formal right to complain and no formal procedures to follow, aggrieved citizens had no way of knowing how their complaints were being processed – if at all – and police authorities were under no obligation to inform them about the handling or outcome of the associated investigations.

IV

Amongst the many cases found in the special 'complaints dossiers', *Commissaire* Kien has the dubious honour of being the only police officer who became the object of several complaints – five in all – in addition to another twelve which were kept in his personnel file.[41] The micro-study of Kien provides a rare opportunity to place his deviant behaviour in context with other senior police officers. Together the many unrelated complaints provide a detailed picture of a man with extremely unpleasant manners, complete disrespect for legal boundaries and due procedures, as well as serious problems of anger management.

What is more significant, the micro-study reveals that his multiple professional failings were known and recognized by the *contrôle général* as early as 1897. These include lax professional standards, disregard for correct procedures and legal boundaries; evidence of sloppy book-keeping and frequent absenteeism; rude and sometimes violent approaches to members of the public. Added to this, came multiple allegations about drunkenness, gambling, socializing with known criminals as well as local pimps and madams. These problems were repeated in other complaints during his later years as head of the police stations at Enfants-Rouges, Porte de Saint Denis and Ternes. This should have identified him early on as unsuited to a managerial post such as head of a police station, but it is only by 1916 that a note to that effect was entered on his professional record. Over two consecutive years in 1916 and 1917, an entry about professional qualities reveals the unambiguous assessments of Kien's leadership qualities. On the question 'Does he have the ability to lead an important department', the answer is categorically 'No'. This is followed by the character assessment: 'Intelligent, but insufficient moral authority' (1916) and 'Intelligent, but lacking in character and not outstanding' (1917).[42]

Problems were evident from early on in Kien's role as stationmaster in Asnière, a northern suburb of Paris. The first complaint received in 1897 concerned his heavy-handed intervention in a civil dispute between a lady and her wet nurse over a sum of 46 francs owed by the wet nurse to her employer. The report from the *contrôle général* relates in detail how Kien overstepped his authority by going to the private address of the wet nurse's sister to seize cash in drawers and purses to meet the required sum of money.[43] The report concludes that there was no need for the police to forcibly seize the money, and the employer had only asked for *Commissaire* Kien to act as a neutral deal-broker. In a letter from Lépine to Kien, the police prefect does not mince his words. He stated:

> I have read with regret the findings of the inquiry by the *contrôle général* … You have committed an arbitrary act, for which I cannot condemn you strongly enough [*je ne saurais trop sévèrement vous blâmer*] … I invite you to return, as quickly as possible, the sum of money to Mademoiselle Hué which she has been forced to hand over in unacceptable circumstances [*dans des conditions inadmissibles*].[44]

Two additional complaints were filed that year: one was addressed to the police prefect by a M. Schwartz about Kien's rude and illegal handling of a dispute between him and a couple of former employees.[45] This resulted in a very long report from the *contrôle général*, which ultimately exonerated Kien. Yet, whilst this investigation was being conducted by the *contrôle général*, an article appeared in *Le Journal* which complained about Kien spending most of his time at the racing courses at Compiègne whilst Asnière was plagued by a wave of burglaries and violent attacks.[46] This led to yet another investigation by the *contrôle général*. Over three months, Kien was the subject of a so-called discrete enquiry which means that inspectors from the *contrôle général* were observing his comings and goings around the clock but without his knowledge. This was only the first of a series of similar undercover investigations that Kien was subjected to during his career. The final report of November 1898, although largely exonerating Kien for allegations of spending too much time at the racecourses at Compiègne, reveals a rather unsettling picture of his lifestyle and professional conduct.[47] Local residents, who had been interviewed by the investigators, described Kien as showing little interest in the issues they reported to the police. They found him *grossier* (rude) and lacking in a sense of duty, and seven named middle-class residents complained about being treated without due politeness. More specifically, the report mentions that Kien frequently visited the *Café du Théâtre* and *Café Concert Colin*, but no evidence that he '*eut des relations avec des femmes*' (was having relationships with 'women') could be found, indicating nonetheless that allegations of his engaging with prostitutes had been made. This is followed by a sentence which seems to imply that his previous conduct was not exactly irreproachable either: 'He has just got married, and over the past month he appears to have moderated his lifestyle' (*avoir modifié son genre d'existence*). The report concludes that the allegations about Kien's lifestyle were 'exaggerated', although it does not contradict the substance of the allegations. It concludes that 'Kien lacks a bit of manners and discipline; he is often absent and as a result neglects his duties [*négligeant par suite son service*], but one may hope that being married will have a moderating effect on his habits.'[48]

It did not. When Kien became *commissiare* at the police stations first at Enfants Rouges, then at St Denis, he managed to acquire at least three more complaints, with at least one leading to disciplinary investigation.[49] He then moved to the police station in Ternes in late 1905, where he remained until retirement in December 1918.[50] These professional moves were the result of Kien applying for more attractive and prestigious posts, and not the result of managerial decisions that could be regarded as demotion.

The micro-study of Kien as a 'problem officer' also allows investigations into whether there was a wider public story to the individual complaints against him. Because of his unusual surname it is possible to track him in the press, and such press reports sometimes offer important clues about the wider context and the public reputation of individual police officers, despite the accounts often being flawed by errors and political bias. In the case of Kien, we do find that he acquired a certain public reputation in the course of his career. In the late 1890s, whilst *commissaire* in Asnière, at least two long newspaper articles appeared, both concerned with his sloppy professional conduct. As mentioned above, one article appeared in *Le Journal* which led to the first undercover investigation against him. Two years later Clemenceau's Parisian daily *L'Aurore*[51] published similar claims of sloppy professional conduct and unacceptable behaviour towards members of the public. Despite these articles, Kien does not appear as a 'known' entity beyond his local area, and over the following decade his name is only mentioned very occasionally. It was only by 1908–9 that the Parisian press began to notice him as a 'problem officer', when he was linked to a string of badly handled personal interventions.

In July 1908 for example, Kien and two police officers entered a restaurant of dubious reputation with great fanfare to arrest some of the regular customers whom Kien suspected of anarchist activities. He also sought to seize a red banner which Kien found politically offensive.[52] Unfortunately, however, he had underestimated the readiness of these men to put up a fight, and Kien himself got a very bad beating before being eventually rescued by the two policemen under his command.[53] This subsequently led to the arrest of two cab-drivers, Maurice Girard and another – variably referred to as 'Jacques' or 'Jacquart' – both accused of the attack on Kien. In the court case against the two cab-drivers running over January and February 1909, Girard and Jacquart were supported by the LDH, who maintained that the two were innocent.[54] The defence claimed that the two cab-drivers had been arrested solely on the basis of testimony by the two police officers present, despite plenty of evidence that both Girard and Jacquart were far from the restaurant in question at the time of the attack.[55] The case against Girard and Jacquart was eventually abandoned. However, Kien had become noticed by the Paris press nonetheless.

Only a few months after this event, Kien's unfortunate public image was further established by the mishandling of an investigation against a Mademoiselle Pellet (or Pelet), which became a *cause célèbre* of police incompetence and malpractice.[56] The Pellet case even led Prime Minister Clemenceau to contact Lépine to complain about Kien. Clemenceau had become aware of the case through the LDH and extensive press reporting.[57] Kien had transgressed his mandate by illegally interrogating a young girl because a jealous wife suspected that her husband was having an affair with the teenager. Clemenceau requested Lépine to discipline Kien,[58] but Lépine stood by his man, categorically denying that Kien was guilty of any error. According to Lépine, the mishandling of the Pellet case was all the fault of the examining magistrate.[59] Nevertheless, the letter that Lépine addressed to Kien employs a very different tone and shows the discrepancies between his unwillingness to admit errors to anyone outside the police, such as Clemenceau, and the tone he used internally towards his subordinates:

> The way you proceeded in this case was absolutely contrary to the powers accorded to you by law, and I ask you to take notice of the observations that I put to you concerning this cases, so that in the future your professional conduct adhere strictly to these principles.[60]

The micro-history of Kien's career also allows us to follow the changing tides at the top management within the Paris police prefecture, which preceded his resignation in late 1918. Patience with Kien seems to have finally run out by June or July 1913. The changed attitude towards Kien from his superiors within the police was most likely a consequence of Lépine having retired earlier in 1913. The new man heading the Paris police, Célestin Hénnion, came in with an agenda of further tightening recruitment policy and internal discipline.[61] Compared to the complaints previously raised against Kien, the 1913 case seemed rather banal. The director of a funeral parlour complained that Kien favoured his competitor by giving him all the business of burying the bodies of unidentified suicide cases.[62] The allegations smacked of corruption and kickbacks, but the *contrôle général* placed most of the blame on Kien's subordinate *Inspecteur* Chopineau. Kien nevertheless got a *blâme sévère* (serious red mark), and although he had received a *blâme sévère* by Lépine on two previous occasions, this was the first time that the *blâme sévère* was registered in his personnel record.

Although Kien remained in post, there seemed to be increased focus on his performance over the following years. The micro-history of the end of his career thereby provides some important insights into where the limits were drawn of acceptable professional conduct after Lépine's retirement. It also indicates how Kien's new superiors went about undermining his position. In the course of 1915 he was again the subject of a secret investigation by the *contrôle général* sparked by a complaint by a municipal councillor, M. Jousselin. The allegations were similar to those raised in 1898: that *Commissaire* Kien had neglected his duties at the police station whilst spending most of his time in cafes and restaurants of dubious reputation, often in company with characters known for their links to local criminals. As in 1898, the *contrôle général* describes the original allegations as exaggerated, although the report does not refute the claims that Kien spent much time in cafes and restaurants to the detriment of his duties at the police station. The report also insinuates that Kien was frequently drunk on duty, although no disciplinary action seemed to follow.[63]

A final note from the police prefecture dated April 1918 implies that Kien had been the object of yet another investigation, although no report from the *contrôle général* has been included in the dossier. On this occasion, the allegations claimed that money was disappearing from the police station, and this time the CID (*police judiciaire*) became involved. Despite the severity of these allegations, a note from Police Prefect Raux to the *police judiciaire* briefly states that Kien's police station overall functioned in a satisfactory manner, although the record-keeping was found to be in disarray. Raux further notices that Kien only checked the records two or three times a week (these were supposed to be updated every day), that financial accounts were not properly kept and that the handling of 'found objects' was unsafe and chaotic.[64] These are the last documents in Kien's personnel file. As soon as the First World War came to an end, Kien retired at the age of fifty-five – or was he asked to leave?

V

What makes the micro-history of Kien stand out is not only the frequency of complaints made against him, but also the relatively supportive reactions from within the police organization, despite the chiefs being in full knowledge of the serious problems that had undoubtedly occurred. How was Kien allowed to continue his career despite these incessant complaints and investigations into professional misconduct across more than two decades? One aspect of this probably lies in the importance of patronage and personal support within the Paris police. Since the beginning of the Republican era, police critics and the popular press, as well as memoirs from retired police officers, were teeming with rumours about how corrupt or problematic policemen got off scot-free because of their connections to people high up in the police hierarchy or to influential politicians. The extent to which rumours of personal connections between individual policemen and influential individuals shaped the functioning of the police is difficult to say. However, patronage *did* play a significant role in the recruitment and promotions within the police. Personal recommendation was a practice institutionalized to such an extent that the pre-printed form detailing the professional background and progress of all police personnel contained a special column for 'Recommendations', which ran through the entire form, so that one could see who had supported the police officer at different stages in his career.

The importance of recommendations is perhaps not surprising in the context of the nervousness of the early Third Republic, when the young republican regime was keen to fill the ranks of the Paris police with politically reliable personnel. Applicants for middle and higher posts in the police had to be recommended by someone within the higher police hierarchy or with known republican credentials. Towards the turn of the century, as the Paris police force had become increasingly professionalized and promotions increasingly rested on professional merit, multiple attempts were made to do away with the recommendation system.[65]

In the case of Kien, it is difficult to overlook patronage as a significant factor in his apparent invulnerability to complaints and disciplinary investigations, as he was going off the rails over a twenty-one-year period. In Kien's career summary there is only one person indicated as providing him with recommendations, but it is an important individual nonetheless: Lucien-Célestin Mouquin, *sous-directeur de la police municipale*, and from 1903 director of the criminal investigation department of the Paris police.[66] Mouquin was closely associated with Lépine and, as it happens, he was also Kien's half-brother: Mouquin's mother married ex-brigadier Kien when he was eight years old,[67] and his brother Léon Alexandre was born eleven years his junior. By the time Mouquin recommended his half-brother to the police in 1888, he already held the position as *commissaire* and was well embarked on his very successful career within the police. Like Kien, Mouquin also appears to be helped along by close family relations. An internal police investigation into Mouquin's political sympathies and activities during the Paris *Commune* makes thinly veiled references to an 'influential' father, whose identity seems to be known to the police.[68] So despite being the illegitimate son of a domestic servant, Mouquin had received an education well beyond what could be expected for a young man of his particular social background. According to two internal investigations from the 1870s, Mouquin also had impeccable republican credentials, and even got away with testifying against the police prefecture in the famous 1879 process against the republican newspaper *La Lanterne*.[69] Because of their different surnames, the close family connection between Kien and Mouquin may not have been obvious to the wider public. Nevertheless, at least one anonymous complaint from 1909 not only mentions this connection, but claims that Kien frequently boasted about being untouchable because he was the *frère de lait* (having the same mother) as Mouquin.[70] If this anonymous denunciator knew about the connection between Kien and Mouquin, there are reasons to believe that Kien did not make any secret of it. Whether the connection to Mouquin was the key factor that sheltered Kien from serious disciplinary consequences from his professional failings is difficult to know, but it suggests that Kien himself believed it did. Mouquin retired in 1911, and with Lépine's retirement in 1913, Kien's position within the police became noticeably more difficult, eventually untenable.

VI

The career of Kien, as illuminated by this micro-history, gives a unique insight into police–public relations of the *Belle Époque* by providing evidence of the ambiguous attitude by police authorities towards the public. Police Prefect Lépine was keen on improving the public image of the police, but as this micro-study reveals he showed little interest in any meaningful engagement with the specific concerns expressed by members of the public. Whilst the reports by the *contrôle général* provided him with detailed knowledge of poor behaviour and sloppy professional conduct, Lépine systematically denied any wrongdoing in communications with critics from outside the police. This allowed a 'problem officers' like Kien to continue his career despite multiple disciplinary investigations and the occasional *blâme sévère*.

Police critics often complained that Parisian police officers were beyond accountability to the public and to the law, but such concerns were brushed off by successive interior ministers. The micro-history of Kien provides evidence that the suspicions by police critics were not completely unjustified.

Despite these frustrations, we see increasing assertiveness from aggrieved individuals and from civil liberties groups such as the LDH or socialist organizations and trade unions. Although this pressure from complainants increasingly placed police chiefs on the back foot, complainants and their supporters very rarely managed to break though the organizational defence of the police prefecture.

The lack of transparency and repeated denial of wrongdoing, particularly in the face of overwhelming evidence to the contrary, seriously undermined public trust and police legitimacy. It also fanned the 'black legend' of the Paris police, and French police forces more generally. It gave some credibility to wild conspiracy theories claiming deep corruption and dark practices within French police forces, well beyond the mundane reality of everyday policing. This was the long-term legacy of Lépine's cover-up of deviant police officers like Kien.

Notes

1. Y. Guyot (1879) *La Préfecture de Police par un Vieux Petit Employé* (Paris: La Lanterne); Y. Guyot (1884) *La Police* (Paris: Charpentier) and Q. Deluermoz (2012) *Policiers dans la Ville: La Construction d'un Ordre Public à Paris, 1854–1914* (Paris: Sorbonne), pp. 172–5.

2. J-M. Berlière (2008) 'La Carrière Exceptionnelle d'un Commissaire Special', in D. Kalifa and P. Karila-Cohen (eds) *Le Commissaire de Police au XIXe Siècle* (Paris: Sorbonne), pp. 173–91, at pp. 178–9. See also L. Daudet (1934) *La Police Politique, Ses Moyens et Ses Crimes* (Paris: Denoël).

3. J-M. Berlière and R. Lévy (2011) *Histoire des Polices en France de l'Ancien Régime à nos Jours* (Paris: Nouveau Monde), pp. 463–5.

4. Ibid., p. 461.

5. M. Agulhon (1990) *La République 1880–1932* (Paris: Hachette); S. Bernstein and G. Bernstein (1987) *La IIIe République* (Paris: Seuil); P. Bruneteaux (1996) *Maintenir l'Ordre* (Paris: FNSP); G. Carrot (1984) 'Le Maintien de L'ordre: France de la fin de l'Ancien Régime jusqu'à 1968' (Unpublished Thesis, Université Nice); J-M. Mayeur (1973) *Les Débuts de la IIIe République 1871–1898* (Paris: Seuil) and M. Rebérioux (1975) *La République Radicale 1898–1914* (Paris: Seuil). For a critical perspective, see J-P. Machelon (1976) *La République contre les Libertés* (Paris: FNSP).

6. J-M. Berlière (1993) *Le Préfet Lépine: Vers la Naissance de la Police Moderne* (Paris: Denoël); J-M. Berlière (1996) *Le Monde des Polices en France* (Paris: Complexes); Berlière and Lévy, *Histoire*; Deluermoz, *Policiers*; and L. López (2014) *La Guerre des Polices n'a pas eu Lieu: Gendarmes et Policiers, Co-acteurs de la Sécurité Publique sous la Troisième République (1870–1914)* (Paris: Sorbonne).

7. P. Gottschalk (2009) *Knowledge Management in Police Oversight* (Boca Raton, FLO: Brown Walker Press), pp. 16–17 and P. Gottschalk (2010) *Police Management – Professional Integrity in Policing: Criminal Justice, Corrections and Law Enforcement* (New York: Nova Science), p. xii. These are based on categories defined in UNODC (2006) *The Integrity and Accountability of the Police: Criminal Justice Assessment Toolkit* (New York: United Nations), pp. 17–19.

8. Gottschalk, *Knowledge Management*, pp. 16–17,

9. Ibid., pp. 16–17.

10. C.J. Harris (2012) 'The Residual Career Patterns of Police Misconduct', *Journal of Criminal Justice*, Vol. 40, pp. 323–32.

11. Ibid., p. 324.

12. Archives of the Police Prefecture (hereafter APP), KA 63, *Dossier du Personnel – Kien*.

13. APP, KA 90, *Dossier du Personnel – Mouquin*: Report of 26 March 1874.

14. APP, KA 63, *Dossier du Personnel – Kien*: Career Summary No. 59.919.

15. See analysis of the careers of Ernest Raynault (entry 1885) and Gaston Faralicq (entry ca. 1895) in J-M. Berlière (1991) 'Professionalization of the Police under the Third Republic in France 1875–1940', in C. Emsley and B. Weinberger (eds) *Policing in Western Europe: Politics, Professionalism and Public Order, 1850–1940* (New York: Greenwood Press), pp. 36–54, at pp. 39–40.

16. APP, KA 63, *Dossier du Personnel – Kien*: Career Summary No. 59.919.

17. Berlière, 'Professionalization', p. 40.

18. APP, KA 63, *Dossier du Personnel – Kien*: Career Summary No. 59.919.

19. In France, the position of *commissaire de police* refers to many different posts and the functions of French *commissaires* underwent significant alterations in the course of the nineteenth century. For further discussion, see D. Kalifa and P. Karila-Cohen (2008) 'L'homme de L'entre-deux: L'identité Brouillé du Commissaire de Police au XIXe siècle', in Kalifa and Karila-Cohen (eds) *Le Commissaire de Police*, pp. 7–26, at pp. 7–12.

20. See (1880) 'Notes sur la Préfecture de Police' (internal police instructions). See also Guyot, *La Police*, pp. 98–9.

21. Guyot, *La Police*, p. 92.

22. APP, KA 63, *Dossier du Personnel – Kien*: Letter included in the report by Contrôle Général of 23 December 1897.

23. Guyot, *La Police*, p. 144.

24. E. Raynaud (1926) *La Vie Intime des Commissariats: Souvenirs de Police* (Paris: Payot), pp. 11–12. See also M. Anderson (2011) *In Thrall to Political Change: Police and Gendarmerie in France* (Oxford: Oxford University Press), p. 31.

25. Commissaire L. Pelantant (1906) *Rapport sur le Service de la Police* (Grenoble: Imprimérie Générale), pp. 26–31.

26. Ibid., pp. 12–15 and A. Gigot (1903) 'Des Garanties de la Libereté Individuelle', *Revue Pénitentiaire: Bulletin de la Société Général des Prisons*, Vol. 27, pp. 1070–82, at p. 1082. See also Berlière, *Le Préfet Lépine*, p. 8.

27. Berliere, 'Professionalization', note 25.

28. Ibid., p. 42.

29. See APP, BA 1554, 'Plaintes Contre les Commissaries 1896–1906' and APP, BA 899, 'Plaintes Contre les Commissaries de Police et le Personnel des Commissariats 1907–1911'.

30. Deluermoz makes a similar observation of greater social diversity amongst complainants from the 1890s in a limited number of complaints against police constables. See Deluermoz, *Policiers*, pp. 261–4.

31. W. Irvine (2007) *Between Justice and Politics: The Ligue des Droits de L'Homme, 1898–1945* (Stanford: Stanford University Press), pp. 5–6 and E. Naquet (2014) *Pour L'Humanité: La Ligue des Droits de L'Homme de L'Affaire Dreyfus à la Défaite de 1940* (Rennes: Presses Universitaires de Rennes), pp. 43–5 and pp. 70–7.

32. A. Johansen (2013) 'Defending the Individual: The Personal Rights Association and the Ligue des Droits de l'homme, 1871–1916', *European Review of History*, Vol. 20, No. 4, pp. 559–79.

33. D. Taylor (1997) *The New Police in Nineteenth-century England: Crime, Conflict and Control* (Manchester: Manchester University Press), pp. 77–8. The Police Offices (London) Act, 1833, Section 10 established procedures whereby police constables, if convicted by two magistrates of disobedience to orders, neglect of duty or misconduct, could be fined up to £10 or three months' imprisonment.

34. *Parliamentary Papers*, A Return of all General Orders, Issued by the Magistrates Appointed under the Act of 1829, Since the Formation of the New Police: Instructions Part I, Police Constables, Cmnd. 505, Vol. XXIII (1830), Section 10. For detailed descriptions of rules and procedures in England and Wales, see H. Vincent (1912 edition) *A Police Code and General Manual of the Criminal Law* (London: Butterworth and Co.), pp. 13 and 38.

35. Prussian *Landesverwaltungsgesetz* of 1883.

36. Guyot, *La Police*, p. 257.

37. A. Johansen (forthcoming) 'Beyond the Reach of the Law? The Role of Parisian Courts in Prosecuting Police Malpractice during the Belle Époque' (work in progress).

38. Berlière, *Le Monde*, p. 73.

39. Berlière, *Le Préfet Lépine*, p. 119.

40. Archives Nationales (Paris), F7/13043 'Organisation de la Police, 1906–1936' contains a lot of material on early police unionism 1909–13, including complaints about levels of disciplining. See also R. Fosdick (1969 edition) *European Police Systems* (Montclair, NJ: Patterson Smith), p. 266.

41. APP, KA 63, *Dossier du Personnel – Kien*.

42. APP, KA 63, *Dossier du Personnel – Kein*: 'Notice de Renseignement', 14 January 1916 and 17 January 1917.

43. APP, KA 63, *Dossier du Personnel – Kien*: Report by *Contrôle Général*, 23 December 1897.

44. APP, KA 63, *Dossier du Personnel – Kien*: Letter from Police Prefect Lépine to Kien, 7 January 1898.

45. APP, KA 63, *Dossier du Personnel – Kien*: Complaint from M. Schwartz included in the report by *Contrôle Général*, 23 August 1898.

46. 'Nombreux vols à Asnière', *Le Journal*, 15 August 1898.

47. APP, KA 63, *Dossier du Personnel – Kien*: Report by *Contrôle Général*, 4 November 1898.

48. Ibid.

49. APP, KA 63, *Dossier du Personnel – Kien*: Report from Contrôle Général, 12 January 1904 and Letter from Kien to Police Prefect Lépine, 18 November 1905 in response to a complaint by Mme Gosset; Complaint letter from Oscar Buttner, 14 November 1905.

50. APP, KA 63, *Dossier du Personnel – Kien*: Career Summary No. 59.919.

51. 'Arrêté Volontairement', *L'Aurore*, 2 July 1899, p. 3.

52. *L'Aurore*, 8 July 1908.

53. Ibid.

54. 'La Cour de Cassation Rejette les Pourvois de Maurice Girard et de Jacques', *L'Aurore*, 7 February 1909, p. 2.

55. 'Le Chauffeur Girard en Correctionnelle', *L'Aurore*, 4 and 5 February 1909, p. 3 and 'La Cour de Cassation Rejette les Pourvois de Maurice Girard et de Jacques', p. 2.

56. Apart from a long article in *L'Humanité*, 17 May 1909, the case is first mentioned the same day in *Le Siècle* and *L'Aurore* and thereafter extensive coverage followed.

57. APP, KA 63, *Dossier du Personnel – Kien*: Letter from Clemenceau to Police Prefect Lépine, 1 June 1909.

58. Ibid.

59. APP, KA 63, *Dossier du Personnel – Kien*: Letter from Police Prefect Lépine to Clemenceau, 29 June 1909.

60. APP, KA 63, *Dossier du Personnel – Kien*: Letter from Police Prefect Lépine to Kien, 20 June 1909.

61. For instance, Hennion forcing the retirement of M. Tonry, directeur de la police municipale, in June 1913.

62. APP, KA 63, *Dossier du Personnel – Kien*: Report by *Contrôle Général*, 30 June 1913 [No. 59919].

63. APP, KA 63, *Dossier du Personnel – Kien*: Report by *Contrôle Général*, 13 December 1915.

64. APP, KA 63, *Dossier du Personnel – Kien*: Letter by Police Prefect Fernand Raux to the Director of the Criminal Investigation Department (*Police Judiciaire*), 18 April 1918.

65. Berlière, 'Professionalization', p. 40, note 16.

66. APP, KA 90, *Dossier du Personnel – Mouquin*: Career Summary No. 54.941.

67. APP, KA 90, *Dossier du Personnel – Mouquin*: Report of 26 March 1874.

68. Ibid.

69. *La Lanterne*, 7 October 1879, pp. 2–3.

70. APP, KA 63, *Dossier du Personnel – Kien*: Anonymous complaints letter of February 1909.

CHAPTER 9
BOBBIES, BOOZE AND BAGATELLE: POLICING VICE IN EARLY VICTORIAN LONDON
Rachael Griffin

I

Just before noon on Sunday 17 September 1843, two travellers entered the Bricklayer's Arms complaining to the publican, Joseph Weaver, of their thirst and exhaustion after a long walk into London from the country. Weaver served them each gin and water and was promptly arrested. The two travellers, it transpired, were undercover policemen on duty to detect violators of Sabbatarian legislation.[1] Weaver contested his arrest two days later before the magistrate at Marlborough Street police court because the legislation in question allowed publicans to provide 'Refreshment for Travellers' at any time of day or night.[2] The police knew that travellers were exempt from Sabbatarian rules and their disguise as countrymen suggests that they tried to use this loophole against Weaver. The publican's counsel was adamant that his client 'had been entrapped by the police in a manner which he hoped neither magistrates nor Police Commissioners would sanction'.[3] The prosecution insisted that the officers were not disguised but merely dressed 'so as not to be known for policemen' and that other patrons were drinking at the time. Weaver's defence maintained that the two undercover officers were the only men served and that they had, indeed, posed as travellers. Witness George Milton told the magistrate, 'The first person who was admitted said he was a countryman, and had walked a long way that day. The man's appearance was that of a weary traveller, and his dress was like that of a person from the country.'[4] Mr Maltby, the presiding justice, had the difficult task of deciding between the two accounts when 'each swore positively to circumstances which were diametrically opposed to each other'. Maltby, not able to believe that the police conspired against Weaver and then wilfully perjured themselves before him, sided with the prosecution and fined Weaver forty shillings and costs.[5]

This case is one of many involving undercover police in Victorian London. The Metropolitan Police regularly used plain-clothes officers to maintain public order and enforce the law, even though this was not initially an official police duty.[6] Undercover policemen were negatively associated with despotism and spying, an opinion formed during the French Revolution when news of Joseph Fouché's (Napoleon's Minister of Police) liberal use of government espionage reached English newspapers.[7] Fears that Metropolitan Police officers might be used as spies were inflamed when Sergeant

Popay was accused of acting as an *agent provocateur*. Popay's membership in the National Political Union, a moderate reforming body formed by Francis Place in 1831, and the accusation that he incited violence, sparked a select committee investigation that publicly censured his behaviour and embarrassed the police.[8] The problem – then as now – was how to ensure the accountability of undercover officers. The police commissioners, chastened by the Popay incident, answered this question by attempting to restrict the use of plain-clothes men in the metropolis. Home Office correspondence and Metropolitan Police records indicate, however, that the commissioners had trouble limiting the number of plain-clothes men on duty. Superintendents often ignored the rules and placed men in plain clothes at their own discretion. An exasperated Commissioner Charles Rowan, one of the two police commissioners, reminded his superintendents in 1845, 'there shall be no particular men in the Division called Plain Clothes men'.[9] In spite of these exhortations, undercover constables were constantly on duty throughout the metropolis, with or without official approval. Sergeant Goff testified in an 1845 trial that he was 'often in plain clothes … I go in plain clothes by order of the inspector sometimes, and sometimes by order of the superintendent … sometimes two men, sometimes four men are employed to go about in plain clothes'.[10]

Undercover officers were especially useful for infiltrating pubs and gaming houses to detect illegal activity. Drinking and gambling were popular leisure activities in nineteenth-century London. These vices, enjoyed at all social levels, were hardly new, but one of the mandates of the Metropolitan Police – established in 1829 – was to tackle public disorder in London and to enforce Sabbatarian and anti-gaming legislation. It was difficult for officers in uniform to catch violators red-handed because no publican would illegally serve alcohol in view of a known policeman and the mere sight of a bobby would clear a gaming house within seconds. Before making arrests, the police needed officers inside to prove illegal activity and identify suspects for prosecution. Undercover sting operations required authorities and the public to place absolute trust in the police. Cases like Weaver's indicate, though, that overzealous officers could and did misuse this authority, thus putting undercover vice policing at the intersection of debates about police legitimacy, government power and individual rights.

This chapter uses several cases of police enforcement of Sabbatarian and anti-gaming legislation in London to frame a discussion of the limits of police power in Victorian London. By looking at the way the Metropolitan Police detected vice crimes, this chapter demonstrates the benefits of a micro-historical approach to criminal justice by looking at how policemen and those they arrested negotiated the world of vice crimes. Whilst proscriptive sources such as legislation and police regulations suggest that undercover tactics were prohibited, daily police orders and newspaper evidence from London's police courts indicate that local officers frequently doffed their uniforms to detect illegal drinking and gaming. Examining how police used (and misused) authority in this context reveals conflicting attitudes towards undercover policing held by the public, the police and London's magistrates. Only through a micro-history that examines how individual cases were policed and prosecuted can we unearth the realities of vice policing in the Victorian capital and the varied experiences of police and policed.

II

The public house was significant to the cultural life of the English working class.[11] In an era where homes were crowded and cold, the pub was one of the few places outside of Church for social congregation open to workers.[12] From mining communities in the north of England, to crowded tenements in London, the pub offered labourers warmth, food, light and sociability.[13] Alcoholic drinks, especially ales, were popular substitutes for clean drinking water. Intoxicants were a 'thirst-quencher' in an era when consuming water and milk could be perilous and, port, ale and gin were either cheaper than coffee and tea or the same price. It is more than likely that a tired labourer would rather down a few pints of refreshing ale after work than a cup of coffee or tea.[14]

Britain's high per capita number of drinking establishments concerned urban MPs, who voted in favour of establishing a select committee to investigate drunkenness in 1834.[15] The chair of the Select Committee on Inquiry into Drunkenness, novice MP for Sheffield James Silk Buckingham (who drank no wine or spirits himself), believed that alcohol was a danger to Britain given the existence of 'distinctive British attitudes and institutions [that] fostered an unusual level of drunkenness'.[16] The committee's *Report* concluded that drunkenness amongst the working classes was on the rise and this epidemic would be the social, economic, political and moral downfall of the British State. Estimating the existence of one pub per twenty families in England, Scotland and Wales, the *Report* claimed that labouring men were unable to resist cheap and easy access to alcohol.[17]

Public drunkenness and disorder were a headache for the police whose job it was to keep streets clear of idlers, drunks and prostitutes. In his testimony before the 1834 committee, Rowan argued that public houses should close earlier, especially on Sundays when 11 am closing let many intoxicated people into the streets just as Church services began.[18] He had offered similar advice several years earlier to the Committee on the Observance of the Sabbath Day in 1831. Then too, he lamented that public houses were often used to pay workers' wages late Saturday, so that by Sunday morning earnings had all but been drunk away. Sunday closing would protect family incomes and public order by leaving little time between wage distribution and closing.[19] Rowan was greatly concerned by rampant public intoxication caused by Sunday drinking and told the committee that the police regularly dealt with the effects of ill-timed closing hours by 'taking up those who are guilty of drunkenness and disorders in the streets'.[20] The focus of police activity was overwhelmingly on working-class drinking because it was most likely to lead to excessive public drunkenness and disturbances.[21]

Several regulatory measures governed drinking establishments in the nineteenth century. The first was the 1830 Beer Act, which limited pub and beer house hours to 4 am–10 pm on weekdays and required them to close during morning and afternoon services on Sunday (10 am–1 pm and 3–5 pm).[22] This act was amended in August 1834 after the publication of the select committee's *Report*, restricting beer houses to selling beer and cider for off-premises consumption unless granted a specific certificate.[23] Against Rowan's advice, closing times were not altered. The 1840 Beerhouse Act replaced the 1830 and 1834 Acts and contained stricter rules for selling alcohol: only householders rated at £15 could apply for a licence to retail beer; excise officers could drop in without notice; beer houses could only open between 5 am and midnight on weekdays; and, to protect pious churchgoers from the detritus of a hard night's drinking, had to close between midnight Saturday and one o'clock on Sunday afternoon.[24] It was not until 1854 that exclusively Sabbatarian legislation was passed; the *Act for Further Regulating the Sale of Beer and other Liquors on the Lord's Day* required all alcohol purveyors to close between 2.30 pm and 6 pm on Sundays and at 10 pm on Sunday evening, on penalty of a £5 fine for every illicit sale made during prohibited hours.[25] The 1854 Act also allowed police constables to enter 'any House or Place of public Resort for the Sale of Beer, Wine, Spirits, or other fermented or distilled Liquor or Liquors' at any time.[26] The 1872 Licensing Act finally streamlined the hours at which drinking establishments could be open: weekdays from 5 am until 11 pm and Sundays between 1 pm and 3 pm, and again from 6 pm until 11 pm.[27] Also clarified were exemptions to these provisions: only 'an inmate, servant, or a lodger on such premises, or a *bona fide* traveller' would be allowed on the premises during closed hours. Any individual who could not prove they fell with these categories could be arrested without warrant and the publican fined.[28]

Notwithstanding the volume of legislation prohibiting the sale of alcohol on Sundays, publicans routinely flouted the rules. The police frequently received tips about illegal Sunday drinking from local victuallers irritated that lawbreakers profited whilst those who obeyed the law suffered. Police Commissioner Richard Mayne preferred the police to arrest Sabbath breakers on tips of this kind, because it did not require police officers to enter pubs.[29] Officers had the right to enter any licenced establishment if they believed a crime was in progress. Yet a uniformed officer could hardly enter a pub during restricted hours on Sunday and expect to see illegal activity.[30] Without tips from the public, the most effective way to catch illegal alcohol sales was to send officers in undercover and superintendents routinely placed men in plain clothes to gather their own evidence. The police exploited the legal loophole – as men like Weaver discovered – that allowed publicans to serve alcohol to lodgers and travellers during restricted hours. Plainclothesmen seem to have happily disguised themselves as tired travellers, ordered drinks and promptly arrested proprietors for violating the terms of their licences.[31]

This behaviour trod the thin line between detecting a crime and inciting one. If there were no other patrons drinking illegally when officers disguised as travellers ordered drinks, this was entrapment. The commissioners of police repeatedly urged their men not to ensnare publicans in this way, but there was widespread disregard for these rules.[32] Regardless of the efficiency of subterfuge to root out violations, the commissioners were against such sneakiness because it smacked of misconduct and courted scandal. In midsummer 1840, Rowan verbally reminded his superintendents not to use plain-clothes officers to detect breaches of liquor laws.[33] Mayne issued a similar reminder in 1844, arguing that officers in disguise were 'likely to … induce parties to commit the offence'.[34]

Regardless of the commissioners' displeasure with the practice, undercover policemen continued to enter pubs and spirit shops on Sundays to detect liquor law violators. In the mid-1850s, Mayne gave another verbal warning to his superintendents against this practice. Officers in plain clothes, he complained,

> go with a bias on their minds calculated to make them think they ought to prove a case against the party, they should be assured that if they prevent the Commission of the offence, they will be considered to have performed their duty equally well if the offence is prevented by his observations.[35]

Although the police were allowed to enter any public house under the 1855 Intoxicating Liquors Act, the commissioners prohibited officers from doing so 'unless the Police have reasonable grounds for believing that a violation of the law is at the time going on within the house or place'.[36] Even so, Mayne outlined firm rules in 1863:

> no Serjeant [sic] or Constable when so employed is to go into a Public-house or Beer-shop, unless in the immediate pursuit of a Felon who he knows is then in the house. In every other case where it may appear desirable to go into a Public-house or Beer-shop, he is to wait until he can obtain the co-operation of a Constable or superior Officer in Uniform.[37]

There is ample evidence to show that superintendents hardly ever followed this rule because undercover tactics were the easiest way to detect illegal drinking. Police regulations indicate that though official rules forbade disguised officers from entering pubs and other drinking establishments, superintendents and individual officers felt that successful arrests and prosecutions justified their use of disguises. Micro-history, encouraging the detailed study of everyday life, helps identify the discrepancy between regulations and lived experience in Victorian vice policing. Police policy reveals official views about police practice, whilst police orders and newspaper crime reports indicate the realities of daily law enforcement.

Newspaper evidence offers additional details about Sabbath-breaking cases in crime reports, which describe cases charged in magistrates' courts. Plain-clothes officers were routinely on duty to detect Sabbath breakers, especially in the 1840s and 1850s, when many cases appear in London newspapers about publicans brought before magistrates by zealous police officers. London's police court magistrates adjudicated Sabbath breaking summarily.[38] Magisterial comments about undercover police investigations into violations of the liquor laws indicate that, barring any severe misconduct, they gave police officers ample leeway to ensnare malefactors. London's magistrates were more concerned with cracking down on flagrant disregard for the law, than debating with defence counsel about the limits of government power.

The press, however, felt otherwise. Police use of undercover officers to detect liquor law violations was often the subject of criticism in the press. An article in *Lloyd's Weekly London Newspaper* in October 1851 for instance, entitled 'Misuse of Plain Clothes by the Police' concerned another publican, this time the landlord of the White Horse. Two plain-clothes constables attempted to enter the establishment just before one o'clock on a Sunday afternoon and were barred by the owner, J.W. Booth. The officers claimed that they knew people were drinking at the White Horse and tried to enter. Booth claimed that the policemen came inside, asked to be served and had been refused. The constables denied Booth's accusation. In Booth's version the officers entrapped him, whilst the officers' story was that Booth refused them entry. It is not possible to say which version of events is true, but the magistrate sided with the police and fined Booth. The newspaper, however, believed that the police had misused their power by attempting to entrap the publican.[39]

In a similar instance, two plain-clothes constables went to the Coachmaker's Arms in Paddington at around eleven o'clock on the morning of Sunday 4 October 1856. The officers testified that they saw two men served with beer before they themselves ordered ale. After being served they arrested the proprietor, James King. When King was presented at Marylebone police court, witnesses for the defence categorically rejected the policemen's story. D. Chapman, a plumber who had been in the pub when the constables entered, testified that the charge was completely unsubstantiated because the ale pump was broken: 'The pipes of the engine were out of order, and no ale could be served by them.' Chapman was at the Coachmaker's Arms that day to fix them, where he saw the two undercover officers whom, according to his statement, King refused to serve. Another witness, one of King's lodgers, also testified that no one had been served that morning. In the face of 'so much doubt', magistrate Mr Long dismissed the case. *The Morning Chronicle* had fewer doubts, describing the case as a 'Conspiracy Against a Beershop-Keeper' with 'Doubtful Police Evidence.'[40] There is certainly evidence of police misconduct here. It may have been that the police knew King to be a routine Sabbath breaker and, unable to catch him in the act, chose to call his bluff on the wrong day. A more sinister interpretation is that the officers abused their power and falsely accused King to impress superior officers or simply because they could.

Unless, as in King's case, there was severe doubt about the prosecution's case, magistrates usually sided with the police in Sabbath-breaking cases. Weaver and Booth's cases indicate that magistrates were more likely to believe police officers whose only official interest should have been to enforce the law, rather than publicans who had a financial interest in flouting liquor legislation. Publicans, their counsel and the press vigorously opposed the police in these cases, often characterizing police tactics as entrapment, or worse, spying. Magistrates, however, consistently defended the right of constables to use undercover tactics to detect breaches of the liquor laws. Mr Broughton at Marlborough Street police court told a defendant in October 1852, for example, that:

He did not approve of the police being in the position of spies; but … it was a very legitimate purpose to apply the police to, sending a constable in plain clothes where spirituous liquors were sold, in order to obtain evidence sufficient to ensure a conviction.[41]

At Thames police court, Mr Yardley echoed this feeling: 'There is no harm in the means adopted to detect the defendant. No trap was laid … There is nothing illegitimate in the mode of finding out what was going on.'[42] In King's case, however, there clearly was some harm in the methods used by the police, although the magistrate seems not to have investigated the matter further.[43] London's police magistrates, then, sometimes placed a higher premium on detecting illegal drinking than on the method of detection.[44]

A micro-historical approach to Victorian Sabbatarian legislation indicates that vice policing was a far more complicated business than statutes or official police procedure reveals. Everyday practice was informed by the realities of law enforcement. Examining government documents and newspapers that reflect daily police practice exposes tensions within the police and between police and publicans. Police Commissioners Mayne and Rowan prohibited undercover policemen infiltrating drinking establishments, whilst their superintendents chose to disobey orders they felt were inefficient. Newspaper reports from the police courts indicate that publicans and their customers resented police incursion into their businesses and leisure time, a frustration at times shared by a press ever-watchful for incidents of police misconduct.

III

Anti-gambling investigations reveal different tensions between the press, magistrates and the police. Whilst magistrates and the press supported undercover operations against gaming houses, the commissioners of police and their officers were hesitant, fearing the public would accuse them of violating householders' rights.[45] Although public gaming and low gaming houses, like Sunday drinking, were considered immoral 'nuisances' – threatening public order, public morals and family security – the location of secret gaming caused problems for the police.[46] Victorian legislation attacked lower-class gambling, which most often took place in the street, drinking establishments or in secret gambling dens.[47] Whilst public areas and pubs were already under surveillance, private gaming clubs were located in private residences. Police officials worried that, unless they could prove gambling had occurred at the time of a raid, raids on private establishments were illegal entries. The press, surprisingly, seemed unworried by the distinction and supported undercover police action against gamblers in no uncertain terms, as did London's Magistrates, who continued to hear police evidence gathered in undercover operations.

Commissioner Mayne and Superintendent Thomas Baker of St. James' Division testified before an 1844 Select Committee on Gaming that the police were exceedingly cautious about proceeding against private gaming houses. Officers were wary of entering an alleged gaming house, even with a warrant, because they feared that cases of trespass might be brought if they could not prove that gambling took place *at the time* they entered the premises. Concern for the reputation of the police force and the safety of its officers meant that warrants often took months to execute.[48] Mayne feared that police 'conduct might be called arbitrary and unconstitutional, in breaking into a house, where no conviction took place', whilst Baker worried that if he executed a warrant and found no evidence of gaming he would have acted 'almost as a common felon'.[49]

Whilst the police remained wary about their legal rights to enter private residences, London's magistrates disagreed. Former Marlborough Street magistrate George Long told the 1844 select committee that if police provided evidence of gaming implements on the premises, that was sufficient proof for him.[50] Thomas J. Hall, chief magistrate at Bow Street, also defended the police against liability for trespass, saying:

> As soon as the superintendent reports there are good grounds for believing that a house is a common gambling-house, and the oath is made by two householders, he is safe, whatever the result may be.[51]

The necessity of depositions from two householders to obtain a warrant against a gaming house also caused delay, because the police, even when they had solid grounds of suspicion, often had difficulty finding individuals to testify. Mayne and Baker reported to the select committee that it was nearly impossible to get locals to report on oath against local gambling dens.[52] In St. James' Division, Baker routinely received complaints from the public about gaming houses, usually from wives whose husbands moved to gambling dens after pubs closed at midnight on Saturday or from individuals who had been 'fleeced'.[53] Yet, many complainants refused to provide a formal deposition because 'some of them said their trade would be affected, and it was an unneighbourly thing'.[54] So, whilst locals unofficially reported illegal gambling to the police, officers were unable to proceed without formal complaints. As a result, very few cases were effectively prosecuted. Only seven private gaming dens were raided between 1839, when the Police Act authorized raids on the oath of two local householders, and 1844.[55] When the police did act, however, they did so with the tacit support of the city's magistracy.

St. James' was a popular neighbourhood for gambling and contained both 'high' and 'low' gaming houses.[56] Superintendent Baker and his officers were too familiar in the district to properly investigate many illegal gaming establishments so, he told the 1844 committee, 'I have been obliged to have inspectors and men in the greatest disguise, from other parts of the metropolitan district, and even then they have been known.'[57] Prosecutions against gaming house keepers in St. James' were funded by the parish, which enthusiastically supported the 1839 Police Act and the officers who enforced it.[58] At one of the early prosecutions under the Act, St. James' vestry clerk, Mr Buzzard, encouraged the magistrate not to show leniency to a first-time offender because 'the magistrate's decision would be mainly instrumental in determining whether gamblers would be allowed to violate the law with impunity in his parish'.[59] Buzzard wanted to see the reputation of his St. James' improved. He was not alone: 'The public has no sympathy with the keepers and frequenters of these common Gaming-houses,' reported the 1844 committee, 'and a display of activity on the part of the Police in carrying into effect the Law for the suppression of such houses must always, Your Committee are convinced, meet with general approbation.'[60]

One of the first cases brought under the 1839 Police Act was the prosecution of an illegal gaming housekeeper named Thomas Jackson, who ran a secret den called the

'Cottage Club' from 60 Jermyn Street.[61] Notwithstanding magisterial support for police action, officers remained careful and frequently sent undercover officers to a suspected establishment before a raid to ensure they would catch gambling in progress. Two officers went undercover at The Cottage to find evidence of illegal gambling, but once they reached the gaming room, Jackson threw them out. The inspectors returned shortly after with Superintendent Baker and raided the premises. Like most illegal gaming dens, there were a series of doors guarding the entrance. 'When I broke into the House,' recounted Baker, 'I had four doors to contend with … There was the front door, a green door just at the foot of the stairs, and at the top another very heavy door, and then the room door.'[62] The raiding party seized eight rakes and ninety-six dice for prosecution evidence. Jackson's counsel, Mr Adolphus, cried foul and criticized 'the tyrannical and arbitrary power' wielded by the police to enter his client's house undercover.[63] 'The police', fumed Adolphus, 'had gone to the extremity of the Act of Parliament; they had broken open doors, and had carried off all the property they could find'. Although Adolphus questioned the constitutionality of the raid, neither the press reporter nor the magistrate, Mr Long, agreed. The police had confiscated the contents of the house because physical evidence of gambling was necessary for the prosecution case. Adolphus' histrionics had little effect on Long, who defended the police and the legislature. '[I]t was the duty of a magistrate', he said, 'to put that law in force with impartiality and to the best of his ability'. The police had complied exactly with legislation and, on that basis, he fined Jackson £50. The newspaper report, although it recounted Adolphus' tirade, did not join in the barrister's criticism of the police.[64]

Even when two householders made a complaint and the police commissioners issued a warrant, superintendents still wanted to ensure that, when their men entered, all of the necessary proof was in plain view. Raiding an empty gaming house was not an option because evidence of gaming (such as dice, boards, cards, rakes, etc.) was important to prove the charge in court. In February 1843, Baker raided another gambling den, this time in St. James' Street. He sent Inspector Beresford in undercover beforehand to ensure that the suspects and evidence were in place. Magistrate Mr Hardwick was pleased with the prosecution and felt 'that the proper steps required by law have been taken to enable the police to act'. He further defended the undercover operation, stating unequivocally in open court, 'The police have done nothing but their duty; they have complied with all the requisitions of the law, and the law must be enforced in order to put down the nuisance of such houses.'[65]

There was very little criticism – except from defence counsel – about the methods used by police to detect illegal gambling. Immediately after the 1839 Act was passed, Mr Greenwood, magistrate at Hatton-Garden police court, lamented during a gaming examination that the police did not act quickly enough:

'I can only say', that the police now have most extensive powers under the new act, and it is a matter of surprise to me that they [gaming houses] are suffered to exist. The police ought to exercise their power. It is a farce to have a police at all, if such things are allowed.[66]

Mr Long at Marlborough Street supported fining the landlords of gaming houses heavily as a deterrent to others.[67] Before fining several proprietors of a gambling den in August 1842, Mr Hardwick, magistrate at Marlborough Street, threw his support behind the police: 'He considered that a gaming-house of the low character of the one maintained by the defendants was one of the worst pests of society, and he should, as far as was in his power, help to suppress them by putting the law in force against all convicted.'[68] Mr Beadon, magistrate at Marlborough Street police court in 1859, expressed his view that undercover police work was necessary to bring gambling cases to light: 'Very often cases could not be brought clear against persons but from doing this in the plain clothes detective system, and the judges have laid it down as the only way of getting at proof.'[69]

Prosecutions of Sunday drinking violators were routine and regularly reported, yet, as we have seen, gambling prosecutions were infrequent. The press noticed this discrepancy and criticized the police for not aggressively enforcing the law. The Standard had been excited at the passage of the Police Act, reporting 'that the Commissioners of Police intend to declare a general war against all such places'.[70] Yet, when the expected war on gambling did not materialize, The Times lamented that the French police strictly enforced laws against gaming houses whilst English officials did not. The English police claimed the article, 'appear to be satisfied with the occasional conviction'.[71] When prosecutions did occur, the police were praised in the press, even when the charge was made on the basis of undercover operations. After the police raided a large gaming establishment in March 1844, for example, The Times praised the police for 'The manner in which the capture was planned and executed' commenting that it 'reflect[ed] great credit on those concerned in it'.[72]

Newspaper evidence reveals that the press approached illegal drinking and illegal gambling differently. Local newspapers were quick to isolate possible misconduct when police went undercover to entrap publicans, yet at the same time criticized the police for not showing more initiative against illegal gaming houses. In Sabbatarian cases, publicans were portrayed as legitimate businessmen under attack from overzealous police officers. In gaming cases, by contrast, proprietors of private gaming dens were described as thieves. The Observer reported in December 1839 that during a recent prosecution the police seized misnumbered and loaded dice as well as a fixed roulette table. The paper publicized this information 'in order that every man entering a gaming-house may be assured that he is not merely indulging in the ruinous excitement of play, but that he is wilfully handing himself over to a gang of professional robbers'.[73] Whilst the press might portray policemen entrapping publicans, officers were, by contrast, helping clean up the city when they used similar tactics against gambling den proprietors. Newspaper reports indicate how legislation was enforced on the ground and the opinions of the various stakeholders. When it came to gambling, both the press and London's magistrates stood behind the Metropolitan Police when they used covert strategies. The police, by contrast, were more reticent to raid suspected gambling dens because they feared counter-suits for false entry.

IV

This micro-history of policing vice in Victorian London demonstrates that the police commissioners, individual officers, London's magistrates and the press sometimes disagreed about the best way to detect vice crimes. For much of the period under consideration, the commissioners of police fought against the use of plain-clothes officers to detect crimes because the issue was politically explosive. To maintain public confidence in the accountability of Metropolitan Police officers, Mayne and Rowan eschewed undercover policing in favour of the benign uniformed bobby on the street. The reality, however, was quite different and plain-clothes constables could be found across London at all times because police superintendents flouted the rules and deployed undercover officers to detect illegal drinking and gaming.

The officers in the cases examined by this study energetically – at times too enthusiastically – undertook their detective assignments and were happy to use a bit of guile to catch malefactors. The press was alert to any suggestion that the police abused power but press responses to undercover vice policing were hardly consistent; whilst there was criticism of police tactics to discover Sabbath breaking, no comment was made when officers used similar ruses against illegal gaming houses. Press criticism of the police was, thus, issue specific and London's newspapers were in agreement that entrapping legitimate business owners, whether or not they broke the law, was a misuse of police power, whilst entrapping the proprietors of illegal gaming establishments was acceptable. Once cases arrived in court, defence counsel questioned police motives, often using the colourful language of tyranny and espionage to protest police activity. Yet, London's magistrates threw their support behind undercover strategies that brought otherwise undetectable infractions to light; unless there was significant doubt surrounding police investigations, magistrates gave police the benefit of the doubt and almost always sided with the prosecution. These varied responses to covert police operations indicate that public concern about the legitimacy of police activity depended upon the target. Proprietors of legitimate businesses, like pubs, were considered more worthy of protection than those who ran illegal gaming dens. Even when publicans disobeyed Sabbatarian legislation, the police commissioners and the press stepped in to protect their rights as business owners. Men who promoted illegal gambling enjoyed no such rights according to the press and magistrates, even though police officials worried about the repercussions of storming private residences.

The incidents in this chapter reveal an ongoing discussion in early Victorian society about the enforcement of moral legislation and the limits of police power. Through intensive research that has pieced together both authoritative and societal opinions regarding the policing of early Victorian London, this chapter has revealed and illuminated nuances in the historical record that generalized studies fail to identify. The micro-historical approach indicates that the police, London's magistracy and the press approached undercover vice policing in different and, at times, conflicting ways. Drinking and gambling were contentious moral issues as was the behaviour of London's new Metropolitan Police.

The cases examined here are about law and policing, yet legislation and police regulations suggest what legislators and senior police officials thought good policy and practice, were not how the law was enforced by individual officers or how the public and press reacted to police activity. No one questioned that the laws against Sunday drinking and illegal gambling should be enforced; the debate concerned the most appropriate *way* to enforce them. The press was willing to tolerate aggressive undercover operations to prosecute illegal gambling, but steadfastly protected the rights of publicans when the police employed similar tactics against Sabbath breakers. Clandestine police methods were not, then, universally reviled, but their reception depended on who they were directed against, suggesting that the London press had, with some caveats, accepted the new police and their plain-clothes units as part of the criminal justice fabric of the city. These cases emphasize the importance of a micro-historical approach to identifying historical issues obscured by broader approaches. Only by acknowledging the contribution of micro- and macro-historical approaches can we hope to achieve historical enquiry that balances the intentions of lawmakers with the realities of policing lawbreakers.

Notes

1. Sabbatarian legislation prohibited the sale of alcohol during the hours of divine service on Sundays. In 1843, it was illegal to serve alcohol before one o'clock on Sunday afternoons.
2. 2 and 3 Vict., c. 47, s. 42 (1839).
3. *The Times*, 20 September 1843.
4. *The Standard*, 20 September 1843.
5. *The Times*, 20 September 1843.
6. R. Griffin (2015) 'Detective Policing and the State in Nineteenth-century England: The Detective Department of the London Metropolitan Police, 1842–1878', Ph.D. Thesis, The University of Western Ontario. When Metropolitan Police constables first trod their beats in September 1829 there were no official detectives in their ranks. Detective policing was considered too controversial in a police establishment sold to parliament and the people as a preventive force. Both the 1829 and 1863 instruction books for police officers emphasized, 'the principal object to be attained is "*the Prevention of Crime*"'. See for instance National Archives, *General Instructions* (1829) Records of the Metropolitan Police Office (MEPO) 8/1, p. 1 and Metropolitan Police (1862) *General Regulations, Instructions, and Orders, For the Government and Guidance of the Metropolitan Police* (London: HMSO), p. iii [Emphasis original]. Home Secretary Sir Robert Peel and the two Metropolitan Police Commissioners also assumed that Bow Street's officers would continue to detect crime in the metropolis, which they did until their disbandment in 1839. National Archives, Home Office Registered Papers (HO) 45/292, 14 June 1842. For a history of the Bow Street officers, see J.M. Beattie (2012) *The First English Detectives: The Bow Street Runners and the Policing of London, 1750–1840* (Oxford: Oxford University Press) and D.J. Cox (2012) *A Certain Share of Low Cunning: A History of the Bow Street Runners, 1792–1839* (Cullompton: Willan Publishing).
7. See, for example, *The Morning Chronicle*, 4 January 1802; *Cobbett's Annual Register*, 3 April 1802 and *The Times*, 11 July 1815 and 27 July 1815.

8. H. Shpayer-Makov (2011) *The Ascent of the Detective: Police Sleuths in Victorian and Edwardian England* (Oxford: Oxford University Press), p. 31 and Parliamentary Papers, *Report from the Select Committee on the Petition of Frederick Young and Others*, Cmd. 627, XIII (1833).

9. National Archives, MEPO 7/11, 10 December 1845.

10. *Old Bailey Proceedings Online*, The Trial of George Sanders and Elizabeth Sanders, 5 January 1846, Ref. t18460105-469.

11. J. Carter Wood (2014) 'Drinking, Fighting and Working-Class Sociability in Nineteenth-century Britain', in S. Schmid and B. Schmidt-Haberkamp (eds.) *Drink in the Eighteenth and Nineteenth Centuries* (London: Pickering and Chatto), pp. 71–80 and J. Carter Wood (2004) *Violence and Crime in Nineteenth-century England: The Shadow of Our Refinement* (New York: Routledge), pp. 75–6.

12. B. Harrison (1971) *Drink and the Victorians: The Temperance Question in England, 1815–1872* (London: Faber & Faber), p. 55.

13. P. Bailey (1978) *Leisure and Class in Victorian England: Rational Recreation and the Contest for Control, 1830–1885* (London: Routledge & Kegan Paul and Toronto: University of Toronto Press), pp. 9–10; A. Metcalfe (2006) *Leisure and Recreation in a Victorian Mining Community: The Social Economy of Leisure in North-East England, 1820–1914* (London and New York: Routledge), p. 15 and p. 34 and Harrison, *Drink and the Victorians*, p. 47.

14. Harrison, *Drink and the Victorians*, pp. 37–9.

15. B. Harrison (1968) 'Two Roads to Social Reform: Francis Place and the "Drunken Committee" of 1834', *Historical Journal*, Vol. 11, No. 2, pp. 272–300, at p. 277.

16. Ibid., p. 276.

17. Parliamentary Papers, *Report from the Select Committee on Inquiry into Drunkenness*, Cmd. 559 (1834), pp. iii–vi.

18. Ibid., p. 26.

19. Parliamentary Papers, *Report from the Select Committee on the Observance of the Sabbath Day*, Cmd. VIII (1831), p. 4.

20. Ibid., pp. 55–6.

21. Carter Wood, *Violence and Crime in Nineteenth-century England*, pp. 75–6. London was hardly the only place where Sunday drinking was rampant. Robert Storch's study of the new police in northern England indicates that police crackdowns on illegal Sunday drinking (in addition to other working-class entertainments) were as hated as in London. See R. Storch (1976) 'The Policeman as Domestic Missionary: Urban Discipline and Popular Culture in Northern England, 1850–1880', *Journal of Social History*, Vol. 9, No. 4, pp. 481–509.

22. 11 Geo. IV and 1 Gul. IV, c. 64 s. 14 (1830). The penalty for breaking the law was 40s. per offence.

23. In order to obtain a licence, applicants had to provide a certificate of character signed by six rated men of the parish – see 4 and 5 W. IV, c. 85, s. 2 (1834).

24. 3 and 4 Vict., c. 61, s. 15 (1840). The 1839 Metropolitan Police Act had also prohibited the sale of alcohol before 1 pm on Sundays – see 2 and 3 Vict., c. 47, s. 42 (1839). Licensed victuallers (publicans) were different from beer housekeepers because they received their licences during annual licensing sessions heard by local magistrates.

25. 17 and 18 Vict., c. 79, s. 1 (1854). The one exemption from this rule was 'Refreshment for Travellers.'

26. 17 and 18 Vict., c. 79. s. 3 (1854). It seems that some constables interpreted this section of Act somewhat liberally, using it as an opportunity to tipple whilst on duty. Subsequent legislation imposed a £1 fine on any publican who 'harbours or entertains … any Constable during any Part of the Time appointed for his being on Duty' – see 23 Vict., c. 27, s. 39 (1860). Drunkenness amongst police constables was a serious concern during the early years of the force. A look at the police orders in the 1830s, 1840s and 1850s reveals numerous censures and dismissals for being drunk on duty. For example, see National Archives, MEPO 7/6, 11 February and 9 May 1830. After Christmas 1858, Commissioner Mayne inserted a note into the police orders indicating his satisfaction that 'the offence of drunkenness during the late Christmas holidays has been much less than last year' – see MEPO 7/20, 6th January 1859.

27. 35 and 36 Vict., c. 94, s. 24 (1872).

28. 35 and 36 Vict., c. 94, s. 25 and 35 (1872).

29. From 1829 until 1850, Rowan and Mayne were joint commissioners. Colonel Rowan retired in 1850 and was replaced by Captain William Hay. Hay and Mayne had a troubled working relationship and after Hay's death in 1855 Mayne remained the sole commissioner aided by two new assistant commissioners. For further discussion, see P. Thurmond Smith (1985) *Policing Victorian London: Political Policing, Public Order, and the London Metropolitan Police* (Westport: Greenwood Press), p. 36.

30. Constables had full rights to enter public houses whilst in uniform if they suspected that a crime was being committed inside. See 17 and 18 Vict., c. 79, s. 3 (1854); 23 Vict., c. 27, s. 39 (1860); 32 and 33 Vict., c. 27, s. 12 (1869); and, 35 and 36 Vict., c. 94, s. 35 (1872).

31. The Metropolitan Police were not the only police force to use these tactics. In October 1859 the issue was raised at a meeting of the Manchester and Salford Licensed Victuallers after several members felt that 'the police in plain clothes … endeavour[ed] to entrap them into violations of the law during prohibited hours, and represent[ed] themselves to be travellers'. See *The Era*, 9 October 1859.

32. National Archives, MEPO 7/6, 1 July 1840; MEPO 7/9, 19 June 1844; and, MEPO 7/16, 21 February 1855.

33. National Archives, MEPO 7/6, 1 July 1840.

34. National Archives, MEPO 7/9, 19 June 1844.

35. National Archives, MEPO 7/16, 21 February 1855.

36. Metropolitan Police, *General Regulations*, p. 193 and 18 & 19 Vict., c. 118, s. 4 (1855).

37. Any time an officer in plainclothes entered a beer shop or pub was to be reported in the Special Report the following morning. See National Archives, MEPO 7/24, 25 May 1863.

38. Transgressions of Sabbatarian and gambling legislation were tried summarily by magistrates and punishable by fine or imprisonment.

39. *Lloyd's Weekly London Newspaper*, 14 December 1851.

40. *The Morning Chronicle*, 6 October 1856.

41. Ibid., 25 October 1852.

42. Ibid., 8 November 1858.

43. An Edinburgh police officer and his wife were found guilty of perjury in an attempt to get a conviction against a publican under the Scottish Public House Act. See *The Daily News*, 13 October 1857.

44. Magistrates' motivations are difficult to unveil. Class ideology may have influenced their decisions. From 1839, magistrates had to be barristers with seven years' experience and

were paid up to £1,200, placing them firmly in the middle or upper middle class, whilst the publicans who appeared before them usually ran establishments for lower- or lower-middle-class patrons. 2 and 3 Vict., c. 71, s. 3 and 9. Magistrates also often dealt with cases of public nuisance or public drunkenness and may have seen Sabbatarian prosecutions as a way to stem the flow of public order infractions.

45. Legislative attempts to restrict gambling before the new police in the eighteenth century fell on the shoulders of parish constables, though they could often only gather information about such establishments. For further discussion, see D.T. Andrew (2013) *Aristocratic Vice: The Attack on Duelling, Suicide, Adultery, and Gambling in Eighteenth-century England* (New Haven and London: Yale University Press), p. 181.

46. Parliamentary Papers, *Report from the Select Committee on Gaming* (1844), Cmd. 297, p. vi. Although Victorian legislation focussed on working-class gaming by targeting, many raids turned up 'respectable tradesmen' in low gaming houses, see the report just noted, p. 33 and also D. Miers (2004) *Regulating Commercial Gambling: Past, Present, and Future* (Oxford: Oxford University Press), pp. 43–6.

47. As Superintendent Thomas Baker of St. James' Division testified before the 1844 select committee on gaming, respectable gaming houses were not a public nuisance and popular members' clubs such as White's, Brooks', Boodles and Crockford's were untouched by government interference. Baker also suggested that raids against respectable gambling houses were more difficult 'Because of the expense of getting people of that description to go in by treachery.' Baker had to pay a club member to vouch for two of his undercover officers in order to get them inside. It was also more problematic to find local householders to complain because the more respectable establishments were far less of a public nuisance. See Parliamentary Papers, *Report from the Select Committee on Gaming*, pp. 38–9. An editorial in *The Times* in December 1842 lamented that the police focussed so heavily on low gaming houses and left the wealthy alone – see *The Times*, 8 December 1842. See also Miers, *Regulating Commercial Gambling*, pp. 61–3.

48. Parliamentary Papers, *Report from the Select Committee on Gaming*, p. 30.

49. Ibid., pp. 9–10 and p. 13 (Mayne) and also pp. 30–1 (Baker).

50. Ibid., pp. 26 and 28.

51. Ibid., p. 20.

52. Ibid., p. 11 (Mayne) and p. 30 (Baker).

53. Ibid., pp. 35–6.

54. Ibid., p. 11.

55. Parliamentary Papers, *The Three Reports from the Select Committee of the House of Lords Appointed to Require into the Laws Respecting Gaming* (1844), Cmd. VII, p. 64. The Act allowed the police to enter premises on affidavits from two local householders and with the support of the local superintendent. The police were also allowed to use force to enter – see 2 and 3 Vict., c. 47, s. 48 (1839).

56. When asked how he would distinguish a respectable gaming house from a low gaming house, Baker responded, 'The distinction is this: for instance, the Berkeley club would not let a Jew into it, nor a common fellow that has hardly a shoe to his foot.' See Parliamentary Papers, *Report from the Select Committee on Gaming*, p. 39.

57. Ibid., p. 38.

58. The parish went so far as to place placards with the relevant clauses of the 1839 Act around the parish 'intimating their intention rigidly to enforce the Act'. See *The Standard*, 7 September 1839.

59. *The Morning Post*, 21 November 1839.

60. Parliamentary Papers, *Report from the Select Committee on Gaming*, p. vii.

61. *The Times*, 10 December 1839.

62. Parliamentary Papers, *Report from the Select Committee on Gaming*, p. 32.

63. *The Times*, 10 December 1839.

64. *The Morning Post*, 10 December 1839.

65. *The Times*, 24 February 1843.

66. Ibid., 18 October 1839.

67. Ibid., 25 December 1839.

68. *The Morning Chronicle*, 4 August 1842.

69. *The Daily News*, 6 April 1859. Before 1839 the police had to prove that illegal gambling was for money. An illegal gaming case against a publican was dropped in March 1839 because the police could not prove that games of bagatelle at the Mercers' Arms were played for profit – see *The Era*, 17 March 1839. The passage of the Police Act six months later removed this requirement – see 2 and 3 Vict., c. 47, s. 49 (1839).

70. *The Standard*, 27 August 1839.

71. *The Times*, 26 September 1843.

72. Ibid., 27 March 1844.

73. Quoted in *The Morning Chronicle*, 2 December 1839.

SECTION IV
STORIES OF CONFINEMENT

CHAPTER 10

'I AM AFRAID SHE IS PERFECTLY RESPONSIBLE FOR HER ACTIONS AND IS SIMPLY WICKED': RECONSTRUCTING THE CRIMINAL CAREER OF JULIA HYLAND

Helen Johnston, Barry Godfrey and Jo Turner

I

A micro-historical approach to the reconstruction of criminal careers and lives provides the historian with a unique insight into everyday lives of people; in our case, as crime historians, the everyday lives we are concerned with in particular relate to convicts who experienced the nineteenth-century criminal justice system.[1] Micro-history offers us the opportunity not only to reconstruct the everyday life of these long-term prisoners, but also enables us to ground their experiences within the reality of nineteenth-century penal policy and as much as possible, their lives outside of this system. From such analysis, we can draw out the 'general' experience and also contribute to a historical approach which is often regarded as of great interest to the public.[2] In this chapter, we will examine the life of one female convict, Julia Hyland, reconstructing her life inside and outside of the criminal justice system. Initially, however, we shall examine the methods by which we created these micro-histories and the sources on which they are based.

II

When penal transportation to Australia began to decline from the 1850s and then ended in 1868, a system of licensing that had encouraged the resettlement of convicts released in Australia was transferred for use in England and Wales. The licensing or 'ticket of leave' system became part of the newly created convict prison system. The convict prisons, administered and controlled by the government (and not by local authorities as was the case with local prisons), was where prisoners sentenced to long periods of incarceration, known as 'penal servitude', would serve their sentences.[3] A sentence of penal servitude gradually and then completely replaced the sentence of transportation, as the system evolved in the middle decades of the nineteenth century. Penal servitude was made up of three parts. The first was separate confinement (up to twelve months' relative isolation in prison, where prisoners only left their cells for chapel and exercise and where all communication between inmates was prohibited). The second was labour on the 'public works' (working for the government or in the interest of the prison. Male convicts for example laboured at constructing dockyards and roads or undertook excavations, whilst female convicts worked in the laundry for their own prison and others, as well as sewing for the whole convict system). The final part of the sentence was release on licence or a 'ticket of leave'.[4] In serving a five-year sentence of penal servitude, the offender might serve up to twelve months in separate confinement before being moved to the public works. They could then spend a maximum of four years on public works but the system operated to release all but the most recalcitrant prisoners early. The overwhelming majority of convicts did not serve their whole sentence and were released from prison, with up to 30 or 40 per cent of their sentence unserved. On average, 1,300 prisoners were released on licence per year between 1854 and 1919, which was roughly a quarter of the sentenced convict prison population.[5] On licence they were subject to certain terms and conditions: they had to report to the police after release and thereafter on a monthly basis; they had not to commit any further offences; and more generally, they were encouraged to gain employment and lead an honest life. Those who failed to report themselves, who committed further offences, or who were suspected of leading a dishonest life had their licence revoked and were returned to the convict system to serve out the rest of their sentence. Those who committed crimes serious enough to warrant a further sentence of penal servitude would have to serve out their previous sentence in addition to the new one imposed.[6]

Despite media and public disquiet about serious offenders being released from prison in England and Wales and committing further offences, the system worked to a fairly regularized and mechanical structure by the 1870s.[7] As criminologists and historians, the records of the prison system offer us a window into the everyday prison life of those who experienced penal servitude and enable us to reconstruct the micro-histories of hundreds of male and female convicts' experiences. Many of these life histories would otherwise be invisible or lost within the machinery of nineteenth-century criminal justice. Using a methodology previously employed by Godfrey et al., we created 'lifegrids' of 650 male and female convicts who were released on licence from convict prisons between 1853 and 1887.[8] The penal records and licensing papers of those convicts are held in the National Archives, classified as Prison Commission 3 and 4 (PCOM 3 & 4). There are some 45,000 in total and a proportion of these have been digitized by www .ancestry.co.uk (currently only female licences). The licensing papers and penal record of the individual convicts provide a wealth of information on the personal details and prison experiences of each inmate. The penal record details the names and known aliases of the prisoner, the sentence they received, where they were convicted and to which prisons they were sent. They also include details of any previous convictions and the penalties received. Other personal details include their age, marital status and number of children, previous occupation, whether or not they could read or write and their religious preference. The record may also contain a photograph of the convict. With regard to the internal workings of the convict prison system and the prisoner's experience of prison, the penal record also contains all of the details of the date of every prison they have been committed to and the work or employment undertaken there, as well as information on their progress at school and a commentary on their behaviour. In addition, we can observe the letters that convicts sent out and received (when permitted); whether they made any special requests (such as a special letter to find out about their children or to enquire about preparations being made due to a death in family); if they had any visitors; and, whether or not they broke any of the rules and regulations of the prison, and if so, how they were punished.

These penal records and licensing papers formed the central spine or foundation of our research narrative and building on this, we then searched to find every record we could about each individual thus reconstructing as much as possible about their life outside as well as inside the convict system. We then spanned out from the prison record, to their criminal histories through the use of the Old Bailey Proceedings Online, subsequent appearances at the Central Criminal Court; Home Office Criminal Registers (HO26 and HO27) that give details of offenders from 1805 to 1892; Metropolitan Police Habitual Criminal Registers (MEPO 6) covering 1881–1940; and, other Prison Commission records such as Prison Registers (PCOM 6), which contain details of all prisoners held at various English prisons from 1856 onwards. Beyond the reach of the criminal justice system, we also searched their personal, family and employment histories, through a continued process of record linkage or prosopography. We used a wide range of extant sources including Census returns from 1841 to 1911 inclusive (which detailed residence, family status and occupation at an individual level); birth, marriage and death indices (detailing if and when an offender married, if they had children and why they died); military records; British Library Nineteenth Century Newspapers Online, *The Times* Digital Archive and the *Guardian* Digital Archive (which provided trial reports as well as potential reports on other family members). The now considerable data we had collected on individuals were then organized into a 'lifegrid': a micro-history of one individual's life and life events. We then used this information to analyse their social and personal circumstances alongside their offending and incarceration.

The micro-histories of individual offenders are important in revealing everyday prison experiences, but they can also contribute to larger questions about the power and operation of nineteenth-century penal policy and criminal justice. In addition, this approach has a considerable amount to contribute to 'history from below'. Whilst most marginalized populations have left few traces of their lives, this detailed and eclectic methodology, drawing on hugely detailed sources about a disadvantaged population, has the potential to help us answer the larger questions about crime, criminal careers and imprisonment in the nineteenth century. In addition, the case study chosen, the life of Julia Hyland, allows us to explore more documentation about her life such as her request to change religion whilst in prison. This was not an uncommon request and provides us with some insight into the place of religion within the lives of those experiencing imprisonment.

III

Wigan-born Julia Hyland was first before the courts in 1868. Aged just fourteen years old, she was prosecuted for being drunk and riotous in Manchester and sentenced to a fine of ten shillings by the magistrates.[9] As a fourteen-year-old this was a fairly large sum, and in default she may have been imprisoned for fourteen days. The records do not state whether this was Julia's first experience of prison life. In other ways, the records would also reveal inaccuracies (her surname was recorded as 'Hiland' in some documents whilst in others it was recorded as 'Highland') and the information therein should be treated with a degree of caution until verified by other sources. For example, Hyland is recorded as having had a child by the age of fourteen, which seems unlikely. Yet as this information is repeated consistently in the prison records and in the census, it is actually likely to be true. The records also state that Julia had several summary convictions for drunkenness in her teens. However, it was property offending that would help to determine the course of Julia's life. On 27 March 1871, she was back before the same court in Manchester for stealing two sheets and she was immediately imprisoned for two months.[9]

The lessons the magistrates intended Julia to learn had not hit home, and later that year she was sentenced to three months in Manchester for stealing another sheet.[10] Sheets, and all kinds of cloth and linen, were easily disposed of. Rag-gatherers and market-stall holders bought cheap and stolen cloth regularly, and as it was difficult to identify as stolen, the risks were fairly low. She might also, of course, have stolen the sheets for her own home, which was now filled with new husband, John Hardman, and a child (which may or may not have also been John's child).[11]

In October 1872, aged eighteen, Julia was prosecuted for stealing clothes, but, because she had previously been convicted of indictable crimes, her punishment this time would be considerable. She was sentenced to twelve months in custody, but also a further seven years' police supervision under the 1871 Prevention of Crime Act.[12] Since the 1860s, there were attempts to keep a watchful eye over released convicts, at least for the period they were released on licence. The 1869 Habitual Offender Act and the Prevention of Crime Act of 1871 extended this power by giving the sentencing Judge the power to order a set period of police supervision for persistent offenders. On release from prison, supervisees were required to report to the police and inform them every fortnight of where they were residing. If any person under supervision reoffended, consorted with thieves and prostitutes, or could not prove they were making an honest living, they could be imprisoned for up to a year. Julia served the full year to which she was sentenced and was then released from Manchester City Prison on 23 October 1873.[13]

The following spring, Julia Hyland was arrested for being drunk and riotous again in Manchester, but she only received a small fine.[14] As a factory worker (probably in the cotton mills) she was able to clear the debt, avoiding seven more days in gaol. However, the legacy of her last theft was still hanging over her, and she breached her liabilities under the Prevention of Crime Act in July 1874. In a contemporary newspaper report she is recorded as stating that 'she had reported herself, but she had been in the workhouse several times, owing to her husband not supporting her'.[15] Her failure to report to the police on a fortnightly basis earned her a further six months in custody.[16] Julia was released back to the marital home (which now contained two children as well as her husband) at Greys Mill, Pollard Street, Ancoats, in January 1875. In July of the same year, however, she was convicted of the larceny of oilcloth and the courts felt that this time the full weight of the Prevention of Crimes Act should be imposed. They sentenced Julia at

Manchester Quarter Sessions to seven years' penal servitude and, following release from prison, a further seven years' police supervision, a standard sentence at the time, for a recidivist offender.[17]

Julia was first received at Millbank to carry out the mandatory part of every penal servitude sentence, a period when she was kept separated from other prisoners. When the training part of her sentence commenced, 'Prisoner B. J. 184' was then put to work in the prison in the sewing and knitting rooms. Julia was allowed to attend chapel along with the other prisoners, but on 19 December 1875 she was charged with 'refractory conduct on way back from chapel and destroying prison property'.[18] Under the progressive marks system, Julia had been accumulating remission marks and earning a better diet and a quicker release on licence. However, as a result of her prison 'offence', she was deprived of fifty-six remission marks, and further punished with Penal Class diet (bread and water) for twenty-eight days and she was not allowed to have any books (Julia could both read and write). She would also have to pay compensation for the damage she had caused.[19] Julia must have been quite ill in the spring of 1876 because she was removed to the Fulham Infirmary. Although no further details are given in her prison record, prisoners were rarely hospitalized outside of their own prisons unless the condition was chronic or serious (for sick female convicts, Woking Prison was usually the place they were sent). She remained in Fulham Prison, which was a training prison where female prisoners were educated, and where they carried out work in the laundries, kitchens and sewing/knitting rooms, for some three years.

Julia seemed to have entered a turbulent phase of her confinement. In July 1876, she was punished for destroying prison property, using threatening language towards another prisoner, and violently striking another prisoner on the head and face with her shoe and dragging her along the ward by her hair, apparently without provocation.[20] She then received punishment for resisting prison warders, and for tearing out pages from her spelling and library books.[21] She assaulted two other prisoners in October (including her previous victim, with whom she seemed to be developing a feud).[22] Then, on Christmas Eve, she assaulted prisoner Ellen Smith in the exercise yard and was locked in her cell for the whole of Christmas Day as a punishment.[23]

Julia's physical description in the prison records reflects the toll that her fights, and the prison regime, were both taking. She was described as being 4 feet 11 inches tall, with cuts and scars on her eyebrows, forehead, cheeks, nose and shoulders. She was slightly marked with smallpox, with extensive burns on her back.[24] She probably gained or gave more physical scars during her next fights with prisoners (some of whom she had tangled with in the past), but she was provided with an opportunity to leave past feuds and conflicts behind when she was transferred back to Millbank.

During her sentence she had often asked for permission to write additional letters to her children. Prisoners were allowed to write every six months, but Julia asked repeatedly to send out more letters, and in September 1878, she requested a portrait of her youngest child. However, all of her requests were refused. After every refusal, Julia engaged in acts of rebellion and disturbance, but, in truth, she was committing acts of disobedience or violence fairly regularly by this stage. In October for instance, she was punished for leaving her place in the chapel line, rushing at prisoner Mary Young and throwing her down, striking her and pulling her hair, breaking the window in the penal cell, throwing slops over the floor, shouting, screaming, using bad language, threatening to take the life of Matron, and using threatening language to the Lady Superintendent. She then violently resisted the male officer when being removed from the surgery to the penal ward, kicking him and other wardens, shouting, screaming and using more obscene language.[25] She lost remission for all of these prison offences and was also reduced to Penal Class again.[26] The same month she was punished for destroying her clothing and her cell pan, by being forced to wear a heavy and uncomfortable canvas dress, and she was physically restrained in a straitjacket whenever she was let out of her cell.[27] Whilst it was relatively common for female prisoners to commit minor offences, it was less common for them to be placed in a canvas dress or straitjacket.

Although the canvas dress was removed after one month, the physical restraints must have been applied for a very long time, because the records state that Julia was punished for removing them in January 1878. As a punishment for that infraction, she was made to wear the canvas dress again, this time for three months.[28] Later that same year, more offences followed, and on many occasions the records note that she was excitable when she got in trouble and that she was violent and abusive towards prison staff (including the medical officers, the lady superintendent, the wardens, etc.).[29] For spitting in an officer's face, attacking a fellow prisoner and other offences, Julia was forced back into the canvas dress and the straitjacket at night.[30] Six months later she was allowed to take the straitjacket off at nights, so long as two trusted female prisoners were in the cell with her at the time.[31]

The straitjacket did not stop Julia resisting the prison authorities and she was accused of resisting a male officer whilst being restrained in the straitjacket, and also of insulting the female matron. However, on this occasion she was not punished. Instead, the medical officer referred Julia to the attention of the prison director as she was, in his opinion, medically unfit to be punished.[32] There was further evidence of her mental anxiety in August 1878, when she was found to be trying to strangle herself with a piece of her cotton underwear. Indeed, she had tried to strangle herself several times that month. Again she was referred to the director.[33] It does not appear that any action was taken, for a few days later, Julia was found in her cell 'lying on the ground with a piece of calico twisted tightly around her neck'; there was also another piece passed through the perforated board at the end of her cell. Both pieces were particles of her cotton dress – ordered to be restrained in jacket by the medical officer – who regarded it as 'a feigned attempt in order to give trouble'.[34] The Roman Catholic priest stationed at the prison confirmed this view. He stated that, 'I am afraid that the prisoner is perfectly responsible for her actions and is simply wicked.'[35] This exchange reflects the interplay between medical power, which was second only to the authority of the prison director, and the power of the prison's religious bodies. It also reflects the considerable tension between modernism (medical knowledge) and traditional moral authority (the Church). However, a compromise of sorts seems to have been arrived at, since, following more threats to kill wardens and further destruction of prison property, Julia was sent away from Fulham Prison. The removal document stated that she was removed to Millbank 'for insubordinate conduct and suicidal tendencies'.[36]

The medical officer at the infirmary reported on 28 February 1879 that:

> Soon after her arrival in Millbank Julia 'broke out' and it was only after effectual restraint in jacket and ankle straps that she was subdued. For many weeks past she has been more manageable, although it has been necessary to grant her some indulgence in her diet. She is passionate, wilful, and impatient, and she complained much of pain in the top of her head. Her mental and physical disorders are aggravated if not caused by derangement in her uterine functions.[37]

Julia Hyland was moved to Woking Prison in May 1879, to be kept under further medical observation.[38] Woking prison served as a public works prison for women but also held those under medical observation. By this time she had committed over thirty prison offences and lost nearly one and a half year's remission. Her troubles had not ended. She was punished for yet another set of offences committed in her first months in Woking, and she continued to be treated for pains in her head and general debilities.[39] For instance, she was punished for feigning a suicide attempt and was yet again forced to wear the canvas dress.[40] Further 'feigned' suicide attempts followed, and her health started to fail. She was treated for pleurodynia (painful breathing) and cephalalgia (pains in the head).[41] Her requests to have the canvas dress removed were denied until August 1879 at which point she had been wearing it for three months.[42]

None of the punishments that were imposed on her, or the restraints that she endured, stopped Julia from getting in trouble with the prison authorities, however. She suffered more bouts of solitary confinement and a diet of bread and water over several months, until 1880. Julia was then discharged from invalid class because the authorities had decided that although that Julia may be 'excitable', she was otherwise 'sane'.[43] She committed ten more offences in 1881, some of which were extremely minor. On 19 May 1881, she was brought up for having extra items of wet clothing hanging on a line in the kitchen yard. She was removed from kitchen duties for this 'offence'. She also served another three days' close confinement in her cell merely for singing at night.[44]

Julia was removed to Woking where she was treated for bronchitis in the infirmary. Due to her aggression towards warders she was kept in a canvas dress during her treatment, which cannot have aided her recovery.[45] Nevertheless, she seems to have regained some of her strength as, in April, she 'rushed at the medical officer, stabbing him in the back of the neck, calling him disgusting names when he visited her cell'.[46] The medical officer reported that 'her general health is good but she is subject to occasional outbursts of violent temper during which she is dangerous. Her disposition is treacherous, so that in dealing with her it is well to be guarded'.[47] Subsequently, she was ordered to serve the remainder of her sentence at Millbank in Penal Class. However, her time in prison was coming to an end – she was released on expiration of her licence on 7 July 1882 and she immediately headed back up north to be with her husband, her son Cornelius and her sisters who all still lived in Manchester. Unfortunately for Julia, however, her reunion with her family at 56 Ridgeway Street lasted for only a few months.[48]

Julia Hyland was remanded to Manchester City Prison on 11 December 1882 and convicted of the theft of a frying pan in February 1883. Sentenced to seven years' penal servitude (again under the 1871 Prevention of Crimes Act), she found herself back in Millbank Prison.[49] Having now spent a considerable part of the last ten to fifteen years in prison, she seems to have been settled in the first years of this new sentence. During the whole of this phase of her incarceration history, she did get involved in some fighting, and she also made some threats to the lady superintendent, but considering her previous turbulent history of repeated aggression, fighting and violence, this was a considerable reduction in her prison 'offending'. In 1887, Julia was allowed to go to the East End Refuge in London prior to her formal release, and she was finally released on a conditional licence in January 1887.[50] She returned to Manchester with three years of her penal servitude 'unserved'.

Julia's life, so far as the official record is concerned, is a story of incarceration. We do not know much about her before she served her first prison sentence. Although she was first incarcerated at an early age, she had had time to grow into a teenager, have a baby, experience living in a poor area of town, work in a cotton mill and so on, and all of that experience receives little attention in the prison records. We also lack detail on Julia's life after she was released from prison. There is a death certificate for a Julia Hyland who died in Manchester in 1888, but this may or may not be the same woman.[51] If it is, then that might explain her sudden desistance from offending; it would also be a very sad end for a troubled woman, who spent the majority of her short life in prison, and who only had a few months of freedom before dying in the place of her birth. We do not know where Julia was buried. We do not even know whether she was buried in a Catholic or Protestant burial ground. Julia had entered prison in 1875 registered as a Protestant, but applied to change her religious affiliation to Roman Catholic.[52] Changes of affiliation were allowed, and in fact they were not uncommon, but they did require a good deal of bureaucratic investigation by prison authorities, as the following section explains.

This is the creative aspect of Julia's history - the unknown time

IV

Prior to 1774, there was little if any provision for religious instruction, either Protestant or Catholic, in local prisons. It was not until the passing of an Act of Parliament in 1773 which entitled Appointment of Chaplains to County Gaols (13 Geo. III c.58) that any progress was made. Moreover, this Act was only permissive rather than obligatory, as it stated that 'clergymen *may* (our emphasis) be provided to officiate in gaols'. The Act was amended during its passage through Parliament to also include Houses of Correction. However, as John Howard was to find as a result of his perambulations throughout the gaols of England, such provision was patchy at best. Bath Gaol, for example, did not appoint a Chaplain for another thirty years.[53] The reason for this was fundamentally financial – such chaplains were to be paid for out of the County Rate. It was therefore not until 1823, with the passing of the Gaols Act (4 Geo IV c 64), that local gaols were created in every county (and many major towns), paid for out of the local taxes. As part of this cost, provision was made for regular prison visits by chaplains. Whilst the vast majority of these chaplains were Church of England, some provision was made for Roman Catholic prisoners and members of minority faiths with guidance published by the Home Office in 1840 which stated that:

> Any prisoner of a religious persuasion differing from that of the established church may, on request to the governor and chaplain, be visited by a minister of his persuasion on Sundays, or any other days, at such reasonable hours as may not interfere with the good order of the prison; the name and address of such minister to be left in the governor's office, and to be communicated by him to the chaplain.[54]

In the 1878 Commissioners' Report, it was made clear that each convict prison could only accept convicts of one particular religion (presumably for two main reasons: to reduce possible religious tensions between convicts, and to save money and trouble by only employing one chaplain of a particular faith). Millbank Prison was designated as a Roman Catholic prison, whilst Pentonville only accepted Protestant convicts.[55] In his evidence to the commissioners, convict Henry Harcourt (who was born in Constantinople and raised as a Muslim) stated that his faith was not recognized by either prison, and that he had been forced to attend Roman Catholic services and was subsequently very badly treated when he resisted.[56] Convicts were well aware of the semi-official position of such prisons, and at least one convict, George Boreham, who was serving five years' penal servitude, tried to change prisons on numerous occasions, and admitted that 'his object in making application [to change his religion] is to change prisons'.[57]

Julia Hyland entered Millbank Prison as a prisoner who wished to convert to the Catholic faith in 1883. Indeed, she wished to convert back to Catholicism, as she had been brought up in that faith.[58] Julia was not alone in changing her declared religion whilst in prison. Many other convicts, both male and female, made similar requests throughout their incarceration. Their reasons were varied. Some applied to change religion following a misguided attempt to deceive, such as Patrick Madden, serving ten years' penal servitude from 1879 as the result of being found guilty of assault and robbery with violence at Wakefield Sessions. He applied to change from being a member of the Church of England to become a Roman Catholic in 1880 – but not through any religious conviction. Rather, on his prison record, it states that 'he entered his religion as C. of E. to avoid being recognised as a former convict'.[59] The Governor of Wakefield Prison wrote to the Chaplain of the convict prison stating that 'Madden has often been committed in his prison, always as a Catholic'.[60] Similarly, William Willcock, serving seven years in Millbank, requested to change religion from Roman Catholic to Protestant on 10 March 1883 – he stated that his father, who is now dead, was a Protestant, and that he (the prisoner) was previously convicted under another name and religion, as he did not want his relations to know that he had been convicted (his real name was Walter Harvey). Following a written request from prison to his wife, requesting her to state his religion, she plaintively replied that he was baptized as Church of England and wanted to know why he had 'not written for a considerable time?'[61]

Others, such as Mary Pearson, sentenced to seven years' penal servitude for larceny at Stafford Sessions in April 1880, applied in order to secure what they perceived to be better conditions. She petitioned twice in May 1880 to be recorded as a Protestant because, as she stated, 'four out of six other RCs do the same [i.e. change religion], as Protestants walk to their chapel every morning'.[62] Roman Catholics only received three visits during the week from a priest and two visits on a Sunday – just a simple opportunity to get out of her prison cell on a more regular basis was the catalyst for Mary's 'conversion'. Rather unusually, her request was granted. Normally, such a trivial and spurious reason would have been cause for denial.

Maud Percival, confined in Millbank Prison for a second time in 1880, also requested a change in religion from Catholicism to Protestantism, but once again not from any deep-seated religious conviction. The prison chaplain, Reverend Zanetti, stated in her prison file that:

There is no doubt that this woman is a Roman Catholic and of Catholic parents – she was before in Millbank under the name of Elizabeth Robinson. I remember her well. […] She said (like so many Catholics) that she was a Protestant, 'not to lose her privileges' i.e. principally not to be shut up in their cells when Protestants go daily to service.[63]

Similarly, Lucy Brent in 1883 requested to change her religion from Protestant to Roman Catholic, stating:

I am really a Roman Catholic. I am very unhappy having denied my religion and I was given to understand the Catholics was badly treated, another reason was I wished to go to Nine Elms Laundry at the expiration of my sentence. I'm very sorry to give this trouble.[64]

This is not to imply that conversions were never the result of serious and genuine doubts about their professed faith. Lydia Lloyd, serving seven years for larceny in Oxford, requested to convert from Protestantism to Roman Catholicism in 1875. The prison chaplain stated that 'prisoner was baptised and confirmed as a R.C. at Stafford but was persuaded to declare herself Protestant, regrets it and desires to return to the church in which she was brought up'.[65] Similarly, Ann Carney, a 64-year-old serving seven years in Millbank for a larceny conviction in 1881, requested to change her religion, as she did not enjoy good health and feared that her life was ending. On 25 of August 1881, she petitioned to change her religion and her prison file noted that she 'was brought up R.C. and all relatives R.C.'[66] The Roman Catholic chaplain, Reverend Zanetti, reported that she signed up as Protestant in Stafford Prison because they got more times out of cell than Roman Catholics. She 'did not care much about religion then, but is feeling old now, and fears much to be out of her religion'.[67] He supported her case and the change was granted nearly a month after her application had been submitted. Despite her morbid fears, Ann did not die until ten years later at the age of seventy-four.

With the development of convict prisons following the long and drawn-out ending of transportation from the 1840s onwards, a somewhat proscriptive system evolved to deal with convicts' requests to change their religion. The convict first had to petition the governor of the respective prison for a requested change in his or her religion, and the governor had the final say in the matter. For instance, the aforementioned Lydia Lloyd's attempts to change her religion from Roman Catholic to Protestant were dismissed by the governor of Woking Prison:

> There is no evidence as to the prisoner's religion beyond her own statement; under her former sentence she declared herself a protestant on reception and subsequently be allowed to be treated as Roman Catholic. Under her present sentence she declared herself Roman Catholic on reception, I can make no other further changes that she seeks.[68]

In 1878, Edmund Du Cane (Chairman of the Prison Commission) stated how the system worked:

> A prisoner when he comes into a convict prison states what his religion is; if after that he wished to alter that statement, he has to go through a certain process; he first of all records his name to be allowed to change his religion, and nothing is done upon that for a month; at the end of the month the chaplain of the religion to which he belongs is asked to report his opinion upon the point, and the chaplain of the religion to which the man wishes to change is asked to report his opinion. It then goes before the director [governor], who decides what shall be done. […] We send out to find from the convict's friends what religion he has been brought up in, and if he is recorded as of a different religion, he is allowed to go back to the religion in which his friends say that he has been brought up. If, on the other hand, he is already recorded as of the religion in which he was brought up, and wishes to change to another, we do not allow it.[69]

A few of the friends' or relatives' replies are preserved on record. A letter was written to 21-year-old John James Giblin's parents in January 1882, for instance, asking what religion he was brought up in. The parents replied that he was brought up a Roman Catholic, but also added 'but we think he is old enough to enjoy his own opinion'.[70] Annie Price, serving twelve years' penal servitude for manslaughter, requested to change from being recorded as a Protestant to a Roman Catholic in 1883. A letter requesting the religion of convict was sent to her friend, Mrs Mahar of Bradford, whose husband replied:

Sir Anne Lane is a Roman Catholic and a native of the citty of Cork. Dear anne we are all on good helth and I hope you enjoy the same and I hope you will come home when you are free. I remain yours James Mahar, Roman Catholic, Bradford.[71]

Remarks from the visiting Catholic priest stated that he had no doubt that Annie was a Roman Catholic, and that she had Roman Catholic parents. He further remarked that she was formerly under his care at Millbank and that she told him she had transferred to the Protestant faith in order to get away from the Roman Catholic priest and act as she liked. 'But she now really wishes to be better and to follow her own religion and she feels herself very unhappy […] I believe the prisoner to be sincere.'[72]

We do not know whether Julia's request to change her religion, and the subsequent granting of her request by the prison authorities, made her any happier. Her request could be taken to be a sign of her mental instability, although she was not unusual in wanting to make a change. More than one in ten (11.3%) of prisoners applied to change religion.[73] Of those approximately eight out of ten (81%) were granted.[75] There was clearly a multiplicity of reasons behind convicts' requests to change their recorded religion, ranging from genuine doubt or conversion, through to blatant attempts to achieve another objective. Whatever the reasons, as in Julia Hyland's case, many were successful. It would be heartening to think that Julia derived some pleasure and comfort from her change of religion.

V

Historical research has been greatly enhanced and expanded in recent years as more and more archival documents have been digitized. Reconstructing past lives has flourished into an earnest academic enterprise as a result. Such reconstructions provide a window through which we can begin to understand the past. Even the smallest of glimpses through this window can collectively provide understandings of the workings and effects of a past criminal justice system. Micro-histories, such as the featured micro-history of the criminal career of Julia Hyland, provide those glimpses and demonstrate the rich historical material that is available on people caught up in the criminal justice system of the past.

Through reconstructing Julia's criminal career, we can begin to piece together some of her experiences and see them with fresh eyes. Julia appears to have been reasonably typical of the female convicts in the latter half of the nineteenth century. She had an early entry into criminality with six minor summary convictions mainly for drunkenness and stealing before her appearance at the Quarter Sessions. The reliance on official sources for data means that there are certain details that have the appearance of being indisputable. For example, we are told that she was born in Wigan in 1845 and she was first imprisoned in 1868 for fourteen days for being 'drunk and riotous' aged fourteen with one child. We can also rely on the record that shows that she was sentenced to penal servitude for seven years in 1875 by Manchester Quarter Sessions for larceny of an oilcloth. These are more reliable pieces of information that we can gain. Other elements of Julia's micro-history are less certain.

Although she was repeatedly in trouble during her first sentence of penal servitude, as documented in the licence document, we have to apply an historian's gaze and 'interpret' her behaviour. We can interpret Julia's behaviour in one of two ways. We can see the repeated suicide attempts, regular infirmary stays for 'debility', repeatedly 'destroying her clothing' and 'prison property', the 'pains in her head' and 'derangement of her uterine functions', and the 'occasional outbursts of violent temper during which she is dangerous' as displays of mental instability and possible psychotic tendencies. But we are not doctors and cannot therefore judge for certain that this behaviour is evidence of psychiatric problems. Alternatively, we can see Julia's behaviour as a desperate and exaggerated reaction to a rigid and harsh environment. It is interesting to note that Julia was much more amenable to prison life when sentenced for a second time to seven years' penal servitude and was judged suitable for the care of the Catholic Sisters in charge of the East End Refuge. This was, one of a few refuges that took women released from penal servitude on conditional licence, usually for up to nine months. Such refuges would not have tolerated the behaviour Julia displayed whilst incarcerated in Millbank, Fulham and Woking prisons during her first sentence: they would simply have returned her to the prison. Nor would it have accepted a woman displaying signs of mental illness.

What we cannot determine, however, are the actions of prison officers that Julia might have been reacting to. Although Julia's behaviour and official judgements of that behaviour were intricately recorded, as could be expected, the words and actions that might have provoked her behaviour were not. Thus, the interpretation historians might make has to be careful not to see Julia's behaviour as unprovoked or triggered by the actions of others. Conversely, they must be careful not to imagine or attribute words or actions that cannot be verified or should not be assumed, or at least only do so with caution. Historians *do* have to make links between events; this is part of the historian's craft and without doing so history would just be a sequence of events. But in making the connections, correlations rather than causal links need to be suggested. This is especially important as Julia is not even privy to the history we have constructed for her, let alone able to correct us in any errors or misunderstandings that may have been made. Nor is Julia able to give or withhold consent for the dissemination of her history. She may, however, be particularly pleased that, as an 'invisible' subject who probably would never have thought of recording her life, her experiences have been brought to life and given a voice. Nevertheless, historians do have to be mindful of the ethics of their craft.

There is no doubt that micro-histories aid in understanding the past. They give us a unique, detailed insight into past lives as lived and, along with a macro-history, can provide a fuller, richer understanding of the past. The mass of data and the speed at which it can be collected through digitization can overwhelm the researcher, and concentrating on individual lives or experiences can bring some order to the research process. Although this micro-history is just one of many created during a larger research project, through trying to understand the criminal career of Julia Hyland, we have been able to consider the individual experiences of a convict's time during penal servitude. In so doing, we have been able to consider some broader questions regarding convicts and the convict system – such as whether the system helped or hindered those caught up in it, and what the cost, for example in terms of health and family may have been to the individual offender. Whether we suggest Julia was helped or hindered, it is clear that she did not find her time in prison easy and she suffered the consequences of that difficulty.

In creating the micro-history of Julia Hyland, though, we might not be able to give a conclusive answer to the question – was she 'simply wicked' or was she a victim of the convict system? However, we can suggest that Julia's violent conduct whilst in the convict system only appeared once committed to a convict prison, and even then, mainly during her first sentence of penal servitude. Prior to that, Julia had displayed no violent tendencies in her previous offending and none had been suggested during her previous prison committals (although we cannot know for sure whether none took place as we do not have access to those records). It was during her first sentence of penal servitude that Julia displayed the conduct that prison officers, prison doctors and prison chaplains all perceived to be 'wicked' behaviour. Given that it is difficult, even with contemporary research, to 'know' what people are thinking, this then is surely the importance of micro-history – that it can tell us about perceptions; especially the perceptions of those who had contact with those incarcerated on a daily basis. This information is crucial to our understanding of past events. It allows us to look at the detail and debate, with the benefit of hindsight, how those perceptions had been formed, how those perceptions affected those on the receiving end of the sanctions imposed because of them and what this means for our understanding of the past.

Julia Hyland's life was one mainly spent in prison, and our knowledge of how she lived is dependent on official sources. We do not know anything about her life after incarceration because there are few sources that would capture any detail of her life back in Manchester; even the date of her death is vague. The official source we have, the prison licence, is invaluable and is immensely detailed. However, we have to remember that these records are partial and do not capture the records of every convict passing through the system. We would not know very much about Julia's first period in prison, or her second, or indeed much about her life at all, if she had not been licenced at the end of her second period of penal servitude. She served the full period of her sentence for the first period of penal servitude, and therefore no licence record was created. If she had not been reconvicted, sentenced to penal servitude and been released on conditional licence, we would not know anything about the poor and disrupted life of Julia Hyland.

Notes

1. The National Archives (hereafter TNA) Prison Commission Records, Female Licenses (hereafter PCOM) 4/71/9. All subsequent details of Julia's prison records are taken from this source. The authors would also like to thank Dr David Cox (University of Wolverhampton) for his assistance with this research.

2. I. Szijártó (2002) 'Four Arguments for Microhistory', *Rethinking History: The Journal of Theory and Practice*, Vol. 6, No. 2, pp. 209–15.

3. Parliamentary Papers, Penal Servitude Acts Commission, *Report of the Commissioners Appointed to Inquire into the Working of the Penal Servitude Acts, Vol. I – Commissions and Report, 1878–79* [C.2368] [C.2368-I] [C.2368-II], pp. 7–10.

4. Ibid.

5. H. Johnston and B. Godfrey (2013) *The Costs of Imprisonment: A Longitudinal Study, ESRC End of Award Report, RES-062-23-3102* (Swindon: ESRC).

6. Parliamentary Papers, Penal Servitude Acts Commission, *Report of the Commissioners Appointed to Inquire into the Working of the Penal Servitude Acts, Vol. I*, pp. 11–13.

7. J. Davis (1980) 'The London Garotting Panic of 1862: A Moral Panic and the Creation of a Criminal Class in Mid-Victorian England', in V.A.C. Gatrell, B. Lenman and G. Parker (eds) *Crime and the Law: A Social History of Crime in Western Europe Since 1500* (London: Europa), pp. 190–213; P. Bartrip (1981) 'Public Opinion and Law Enforcement: The Ticket of Leave Scares in Mid-Victorian Britain', in V. Bailey (ed.) *Policing and Punishment in Nineteenth Century Britain* (London: Croom Helm), pp. 150–81 and R.S. Sindall (1987) 'The London Garrotting Panics of 1856 and 1862', *Social History*, Vol. 12, No. 3, pp. 351–9.

8. B. Godfrey, D.J. Cox and S. Farrall (2007) *Criminal Lives: Family, Employment and Offending* (Oxford: Oxford University Press) and B. Godfrey, D.J. Cox and S. Farrall (2010) *Serious Offenders* (Oxford: Oxford University Press).

9. TNA, Home Office, Criminal Registers (hereafter HO), HO26 and HO27, 1805–92.

10. Ibid.

11. Ibid.

12. Manchester Prison Records, 1872 (accessed via findmypast.co.uk).

13. Ibid.

14. Ibid.

15. TNA, HO26 and HO27, 1805–92.

16. *Edinburgh Evening News*, 4 July 1874.

17. Ibid.

18. TNA, PCOM 4/71/9.

19. Ibid.

20. Ibid.

21. Ibid.

22. Ibid.

23. Ibid.

24. Ibid.

25. Ibid.

26. Ibid.

27. Ibid.

28. Ibid.

29. Ibid.

30. Ibid.

31. Ibid.

32. Ibid.
33. Ibid.
34. Ibid.
35. Ibid.
36. Ibid.
37. Ibid.
38. Ibid.
39. Ibid.
40. Ibid.
41. Ibid.
42. Ibid.
43. Ibid.
44. Ibid.
45. Ibid.
46. Ibid.
47. Ibid.
48. Ibid.
49. Ibid.
50. Ibid.
51. Ibid.
52. Ibid.
53. Ibid.
54. C. Noble (2002) 'The New Gaol in Bathwick, 1172–1842', *Bath History*, Vol. IX, pp. 64–86 at p. 77.
55. (1840) *Home Office Regulations for Prisons in England and Wales* – Regulation 229 (London: Shaw & Sons), p. 37.
56. Parliamentary Papers, Penal Servitude Acts Commission, *Report of the Commissioners Appointed to Inquire into the Working of the Penal Servitude Acts, Vol. I*, pp. 335–8.
57. Ibid.
58. TNA, PCOM 3/769/31.
59. TNA, PCOM 4/71/9.
60. TNA, PCOM 3/770/10.
61. Ibid.
62. TNA, PCOM 3/762/207.
63. TNA, PCOM 4/71/17.
64. TNA, PCOM 4/69/13.
65. TNA, PCOM 4/69/19. The Nine Elms Laundry was founded in the 1860s by the Discharged Female Prisoners' Aid Society, a largely Protestant organization, in order to provide a home and paid work for female prisoners upon their release from convict prison.
66. TNA, PCOM 4/71/5.
67. TNA, PCOM 4/66/5.

68. Ibid.

69. TNA, PCOM 4/71/5.

70. Parliamentary Papers, Penal Servitude Acts Commission, *Report of the Commissioners Appointed to Inquire into the Working of the Penal Servitude Acts, Vol. I*, p. 54.

71. TNA, PCOM 3/764/146.

72. TNA, PCOM 4/70/2.

73. Ibid.

74. Johnston and Godfrey, *The Costs of Imprisonment, passim*.

75. Ibid.

CHAPTER 11
MAKING THEIR MARK: YOUNG OFFENDERS'
LIFE HISTORIES AND SOCIAL NETWORKS
Helen Rogers

I

Micro-history may focus on the small scale – 'the world in a grain of sand' – but invariably it investigates events that have generated large bodies of sources, comprising multitudinous words.[1] It is not surprising, therefore, that court cases have been the starting point for many of the ground-breaking works of micro-history.[2] Indeed, micro-history lends itself to crime history. The case study – its standard method – mirrors the trial process and coverage of it: the compilation and forensic scrutiny of evidence and deposition files; the adversarial claims of prosecution and defence; all poured over by the press before the court of popular opinion. Legal disputes can offer ample material for the 'thick description' micro-historians use to explore interactions and conflicts between individuals and the authorities.[3] They can also provide opportunities to 'hear' the voices of ordinary people, who rarely left first-person testimony. Media reporting, similarly, offers rich pickings for micro-historians. Sensational cases, which stoked the 'true crime' genre, have enabled historians to unravel the cultural narratives that inform legal and media treatments of defendants and witnesses and to show how these have worked to mythologize criminal individuals and events.[4] But cases that attract such attention are atypical of the vast majority of prosecutions and convictions.[5] Overwhelmingly, these were – and still are – for minor offences that pass with scarcely any media comment. How can crime history investigate the 'micro' in cases where sources are scanty and when the words of defendants, accusers and witnesses were largely omitted from the documentary record?

In this chapter, I outline strategies that micro-historians might deploy to investigate the lives of obscure, petty offenders and to reconstruct their social and cultural milieu. I focus on routine, everyday encounters with the criminal justice system in Great Yarmouth in the early Victorian years. Between 1839 and 1841, minor crimes and misdemeanours, heard summarily before a magistrate, led to 83 per cent of convictions at Great Yarmouth, but were seldom reported.[6] Even cases that went to trial at the Quarter Sessions received little more than half a line in the regional newspapers, except in a few extraordinary incidents that a reporter deemed comical or newsworthy.[7] To hear the voices of the labouring poor, who comprised the vast majority charged at Yarmouth, I turn instead to records produced in the prison, particularly the gaoler's admissions registers and disciplinary log, and the daily journal of the Christian visitor who voluntarily taught inmates to read, write and receive Biblical instruction. Records of quotidian life in nineteenth-century gaols have rarely survived in such detail, and yet, even here, inmates' voices are only briefly and occasionally reported, and always from the perspective of authority. By widening the scale to explore how individuals interacted in social space and the networks of familiarity they established, I seek to fuse micro and macro approaches and their respective viewpoints of proximity and distance.[8]

Since official documentation comprises the discourse and ideological perspectives of those who create them, Sigurður Gylfi Magnússon has argued recently that micro-historians should focus instead on first-person testimony or 'ego-documents' of the socially marginal, such as diaries and letters, and confine interpretation to the particular rather than the general.[9] To follow his approach, however, would mean overlooking the large majority of people who left no such testimony and also neglecting how subalterns interact with authority and, sometimes, resist it. As James C. Scott has claimed, 'the powerless are often obliged to adopt a strategic pose in the presence of the powerful'.[10] In the dock, as Zoe Alker has shown, defendants may work hard to conform to approved expectations of behaviour or, conversely, defiantly live up to stereotype.[11] Whilst subalterns 'ordinarily dare not contest the terms of their subordination openly', contends Scott, '[b]ehind the scenes they are likely to create and defend a social space in which offstage dissent to the official transcripts of power relations may be voiced'. This 'offstage dissent' marks 'a "hidden transcript" that represents a critique of power spoken behind the back of the dominant'.[12] Using ethnographic sources and techniques commonly deployed by micro-historians, Scott detects such 'hidden transcripts' in popular rituals, myths, folklore, rumours, and code and gesture, as well as in written and spoken words.[13] This is a useful insight, for the poor made their mark in their actions as much as in their words.

In this chapter, I investigate how inmates made their mark in gaol by examining the teacher's accounts of their responses to activities designed to improve their character, and the gaoler's punishment records for evidence of how they subverted these activities or broke prison regulations. Their reports of inmates' reactions to incarceration and instruction offer tantalizing glimpses of prisoners' attitudes and behaviour. However, to understand inmate responses from their own perspectives, rather than those charged with their discipline, we need to move outwards to reconstruct their family relationships and circumstances, and their peer networks inside and outside the gaol.[14] This involves examining their actions within social space, as well as their words. As David Green proposes, 'Excavating what was *done* rather than what was *said* is potentially a powerful way of understanding the complex relationships that underpinned social interaction, but it depends on the ability to ascertain how individuals were connected to each other and the wider community through their repeated, everyday actions.'[15]

If we are to locate individuals within this wider frame, it is necessary to supplement the close reading of primary sources that is the usual approach of micro-history. Green, for example, uses networking tools and data analysis to reconstruct peer associations amongst London paupers, forged in refractory conduct in and outside the prison and workhouse in the 1840s.[16] This method involves identifying multiple social relationships and behavioural patterns that are not observable through textual analysis alone. Many social and cultural historians have tended to be wary of macroanalysis and, indeed, micro-history developed out of critiques of large-scale, quantitative approaches to historical enquiry.[17] However, as Tim Hitchcock and Robert Shoemaker have claimed, to conduct a history from below out of the bureaucratic record we need 'to dismember the archives themselves, and reconstruct them with plebeian lives in mind'.[18] Through record linkage, group profiling and data analysis of multiple cases, it is possible, they show, to extrapolate patterns of shared behaviour and even how these vary and change by time and place. By reconstructing and comparing over three thousand London lives, drawn from various parish and criminal records, Hitchcock and Shoemaker have argued persuasively that plebeian Londoners drove changes in 'policing, justice and poor relief' in the eighteenth century, through the everyday tactics and survival strategies they adopted in their negotiations with governing actors and institutions.[19] 'Distant reading' techniques can expose, therefore, the agency of the poor and allow historians to detect the combined effects of their individual and collective actions.[20] Social and cultural historians have much to gain by integrating microscopic *and* macroscopic perspectives and techniques, as I demonstrate in this chapter.

Like much micro-history, my research began with close reading of printed records: the 1844 posthumous biographical sketch of the prison visitor Sarah Martin (1791–1843), a pioneer of prisoner rehabilitation who, unlike contemporary penal reformers, was a working woman – a dressmaker – who lived in close proximity with the labouring poor of Yarmouth.[21] Locating Martin's surviving journals, my biographical interest in the visitor shifted to her interaction with inmates and their relationships with each other.[22] Reduced to 'offenders' in the penal archive, I sought to recover their agency and humanity by examining their crimes and misdemeanours in the context of their 'whole lives' or what I can reconstruct of these from myriad sources. But can we derive historical meaning out of a single life plotted through the ten-yearly tabulations of the census returns or records of births, marriages and deaths? What interpretative weight can we place on incidental anecdotes and fragments of 'voices' found in the archive?

The strategy I have developed is to interweave biographical reconstruction with prosopography or group biography. By viewing individual lives in the context of their spatial location, social networks and the circumstances and characteristics they shared with others, we can speculate not only on the possible causes and outcomes of their actions, but also on what was probable. I call this approach 'intimate reading': getting up close and personal with our subjects through immersive reading and extensive contextualization. Record linkage lets us explore the relationships binding individuals and groups, and their interactions – no matter how unequal – with officialdom. Intimate reading is smaller in scope than the 'distant reading' methods practised in the digital humanities and is concerned with excavating 'deep' data on specific individuals rather than 'big' data on large aggregated groups. Whilst the voices of the convicted were only rarely recorded, intimate reading can reveal how they made their mark in other ways.

In this chapter, I focus on two brothers, their encounters with Christian philanthropy and the criminal justice system, and what these reveal about their social networks, behaviour and identities. Just as in the previous chapter, I use genealogical sources to conduct life-course analysis and investigate the brothers' particular family, occupational and offending histories but I also draw comparisons with the social profiles of young offenders like them, and with male youths as a cohort. To gain a wider perspective on the boys' journeys in and out of the penal regime, I draw on three related data sets: the prison population at Yarmouth (1839–41), comprising 724 admissions; inmates punished for disciplinary infractions (1836–45); and the life courses of twenty-six young, male convicts transported to Van Diemen's Land (1836–49), as well as transcripts of their tattoos.[23] Mapping the web of connections between the two brothers and their peers in this way gives us access to the 'hidden scripts' and 'offstage dissent' generated by the criminal justice process. It provides a framework to decode fragmentary scraps of evidence of words and actions, scattered across unconnected collections. Equally as important, it helps us interpret the gaps and silences in the archival trail.

II

The prison visitor Sarah Martin became acquainted with the Jenkins family in 1839 following the release of Abraham Jenkins, aged sixteen according to the gaoler, from his first three-month sentence for stealing a stone and a half of rope, a tin canister and a cork gender from the lugger *Ann*, a small fishing vessel. He was convicted with thirteen-year-old Joshua Artis, one of the lads subsequently transported with Abraham's younger brother, William, in 1845.[24] In October 1839, Sarah Martin reported approvingly on the conduct of Abraham and Joshua to the prison inspector, as examples of those who appeared 'reclaimed' in her Liberated Prisoners Book.[25] When Abraham arrived at the gaol, she had doubted his capacity for 'improvement'. His father was 'a sort of pedlar – a tinker' whose 'character is not correct' – and who, apparently, did not provide his son with a decent home and paternal supervision. Abraham's character was 'bad' but the teacher also observed his poor physical condition – 'dreadfully infested with vermin'.[26] (Likewise, the gaoler noted the boy was 'lousy', marked with small pox, and blind in the right eye.)[27] He had been living in 'hovels and outhouses' for two months, probably apart from his family, and making his way as a chip boy, hawking wood-chips from the shipyards, with his fellow accomplice Joshua.[28] Yet, like many prisoners, Abraham jumped at the chance of a brief education and, not knowing the alphabet, 'found great interest in learning to read and write', taking 'great care of his books' and saying proudly 'I am never lazy only when I am at my lessons.'[29] 'Only' lazy at his lessons: was this an error in the teacher's note-taking or an indication of the boy's ambivalence towards his instruction? Either way, his behaviour at trial convinced Sarah Martin he was not 'morally improved' for he appeared 'undaunted' and 'spoke improperly' to the witness giving evidence against him. After the teacher reprimanded the boy and denied him lessons for a day or two, he proved 'extremely diligent', repeating thirty verses and a hymn he had memorized.[30]

Invariably, the visitor's 'observations' of inmates' characters were exacting and judgemental, characteristic of the evangelical tone of contemporary prison philanthropy.[31]

Yet her assessments were also informed by over twenty years' experience of working with inmates and habitual offenders. Of the 'liberated prisoners' Sarah Martin believed 'reclaimed' in 1839, only two adults were subsequently reconvicted. By contrast, half the juveniles she included in her list were recommitted.[32] Young repeat offenders formed a sizable proportion of the gaol's average residency of about thirty inmates and, as the disciplinary record attests, they were its most troublesome residents.[33] Between 1839 and 1841, 41 per cent of prisoners at Yarmouth were eighteen or under. Juvenile offenders were the most likely to return to prison. Nearly two-thirds of repeat offenders were under twenty-one and, of these, 45 per cent were under eighteen. The mean age of lads transported to Van Diemen's Land when first imprisoned was fourteen.[34] On average, they had been imprisoned 4.2 times before the charge that led to their transportation, mostly before they were 21. Two-thirds of their convictions were for petty theft.[35]

The prison visitor's wary assessments of inmates' characters were balanced, nonetheless, by practical efforts to oversee their return to the community and continuing good behaviour. Martin, for instance, promised to support prisoners who seemed committed to going straight, inviting them to visit her or send letters about their progress. Robert Harrod, subsequently transported with William, was given a basket of herrings to hawk and a jacket when he found work aboard a ship. The prison visitor consulted his mother about his behaviour and was pleased to hear he 'was going on rightly'.[36] Surviving extracts from Martin's Liberated Prisoners Book indicate how former inmates and their relatives could react positively to this philanthropic intervention that tied many over till they found regular work. The responses of the Jenkins family hint at more instrumental approaches to Christian guidance and the limits of individual charity in preventing destitution.[37]

Sarah Martin told the inspector that, following his discharge, Abraham Jenkins had called on his former teacher three times and found work in a fish office whilst hoping 'to go to sea'.[38] She approved of this occupation, believing the disciplined life aboard ship helped many youths to settle down.[39] She visited his family, revising her estimation of Abraham's father. The tinker was ill 'with a wife and large family in the deepest poverty'.[40] The visitor seems to have tended to John Jenkins and was at his side when he died (apparently following his religious conversion), for she composed a poem, 'The Believer's Death', preserving the 'parting words' of this 'holy and good man':

He said, 'I suffer, but the God of heaven,
Has high support and boundless comfort given,'
The name of Jesus, to his spirit brought
A universe of joy beyond created thought.[41]

Perhaps his deathbed conversion was the tinker's insurance policy for the wife and children he left behind, but if Sarah Martin continued assisting his family it was not enough to keep them from the workhouse. When John's widow Elizabeth applied for poor relief she was removed to her parish of settlement with her children, including her youngest son, born shortly before her husband died.[42] This may explain why the family does not appear in the 1841 Census, but they made their way back to Yarmouth, where Elizabeth had raised her family and where William had been born in 1827.[43] When the two eldest brothers were committed to gaol together in February 1842, Abraham, then about nineteen, gave his occupation as fisherman. William had been working as a labourer and declared his age to be twelve, though christening records reveal he was fourteen years old.[44]

The brothers were arrested on suspicion of breaking into an unoccupied house and stealing brass bells, doorplates and tills with five other boys aged between twelve and fifteen. Re-encountering Abraham, Sarah Martin wearily noted her lengthy accounts of the lad, adding tersely: 'He has entirely learned to read and write in prison but fails in following the religious and moral instruction which has been imparted.'[45] The teacher's Everyday Book for 1842 has not survived, so we cannot know if Abraham knuckled back down to moral education but, in the month he spent in prison before acquittal at trial, he seems not to have attracted the attention of the gaoler or warranted punishment, for there are no references to him in the disciplinary log. After release he was never caught reoffending. Despite extensive searching in genealogical databases and online newspapers, I have been unable to find any information about his subsequent life or death. In other cases, tracking prisoners through parish and census documents can suggest the circumstances that facilitated desistance from crime. For young men, these tended to involve initiation into a trade and a degree of stability offered by regular employment and the responsibilities of marriage and family life.[46] By the 1851 Census, however, the Jenkins family was no longer in Yarmouth. Compromised by poverty and the loss of their father, the siblings seem to have gone their separate ways and cannot be located.

Sarah Martin's observations on William, the younger Jenkins brother she had met when visiting Abraham, cast doubt on the family's uptake of their father's purported Christian conversion. William possessed neither religion nor education, she recalled, finding him 'Remarkably quick in natural ability and clever but refractory, fearless and illdisposed [sic]. His bad behaviour in prison exposed him to frequent punishments.'[47] Like many first-timers, who Martin thought had yet to acquire the criminal traits of dissembling and concealment, William 'spontaneously' confessed the escapade that led to his conviction but she did not record the story.[48] When the case was heard at the Quarter Sessions a month later, he was the only boy convicted but neither the court records nor newspapers provide details of the trial. Examination of the offences and family circumstances of other juveniles, with whom William and Abraham associated, illuminate the challenges faced by poor boys as they negotiated the transition from childhood to manhood.

III

In the following discussion, information about juvenile boys in the gaol records (1842–4) is compared with the convict registers for twenty-six Yarmouth lads, sentenced to transportation (1836–49) and exiled to Van Diemen's Land where, on arrival, they answered questions on their former offences, occupations and family.[49] The names and whereabouts of their relatives can be cross-referenced with parish and census data. All had begun offending before the age of twenty-one.

Five boys were initially remanded with William and Abraham in 1842 for housebreaking and stealing. The two youngest had been committed before and would reoffend. Neither James Barnes (twelve) nor Henry Patterson (thirteen) appear to have been in school or employment. Only Richard Reynolds (fifteen), released after a few days, and William Creak (fourteen), acquitted at trial, would not be recommitted, though the latter's elder brother John became a repeat offender. The gaoler listed these two boys as labourers, like William Jenkins. Labouring jobs for boys were invariably irregular and low paid. Thomas Farrell (fourteen) had been an errand boy, probably for his parents who were listed as dealers in the 1841 Census.[50] Like most of his mates, Thomas hoped to go to sea. His subsequent offences occurred between fishing voyages, when boys had time on their hands and little money in their pockets, as was the case for Richard Reynolds and Abraham Jenkins, recently returned from sea.[51]

A common way of boys earning a little money was by scavenging: digging up manure, sand and soil, or scouring the docks for rope, wood and metal to sell on. Almost certainly this had been Abraham's intention when working as a chip boy and first arrested for stealing rope. On entering the gaol, he surrendered his property – 'a green bag with some small stumps of iron' – that he was collecting to sell or using to play games. Joshua Artis gave up a small bag, a knife and a halfpenny.[52] Similar patterns of irregular work are found in the criminal histories of the twenty-six convict lads, whose brushes with the law began after they had completed what little schooling their parents could afford. Joshua Artis, who could read and write at thirteen, was atypical; the majority had basic reading skills or knew only a few letters when they entered prison.[53] Most had yet to begin full-time work, though a third of the convicts had served some kind of an apprenticeship before transportation, usually in their father's or elder brothers' trade.[54]

Perhaps the most significant characteristic shared by boys who became repeat offenders or were transported is separation from parents, usually as a result of orphanage. Of the five boys arrested in 1842 with the recently bereaved Jenkins brothers, only Thomas Farrell and Richard Reynolds appear to have been living with both their parents at the time of the 1841 Census.[55] The four Creak siblings, aged between three and fifteen, were lodging with a young married couple and their infant children – the eldest boy and girl working respectively as labourer and female servant.[56] James Barnes appears to have been taken in by a tailor and his wife.[57] All these children may have had a parent working away, as did Henry Patterson when his mother died in 1839 and his father left his children in lodgings, with a woman Sarah Martin believed to be a prostitute. Most of the Patterson children began offending shortly after their mother's death, as did Henry, first imprisoned in 1840 for stealing apples from a garden. He was now in prison for the eighth time and was sentenced to transportation, a few months later, for stealing a pair of boots.[58]

Similarly, two-thirds of the convict lads had lost a parent, often shortly before their offending began. Over half (55 per cent) had lost their father, without whose wage most labouring families faced destitution. Moreover, fathers were the relatives best placed to introduce young males into the labour force. Thirty-nine per cent of convict lads had lost their mother, whilst a fifth had no surviving parent.[59] Nearly a third had been convicted as rogues and vagabonds, some of whom had been homeless or in the workhouse.[60] When William was released from gaol in April 1842, he was handed over to the parish relieving officer.[61] Some families were unable or unwilling to accommodate a son who failed to bring in regular income or brought shame on the household. Robert Harrod, transported with William, had been living in his stepfather's house. At the age of twelve, he was hauled before the magistrates by his mother for 'wandering from home'.[62] Robert was one of five convict lads who had been prosecuted by a relative: one measure of the strain evident on these families.[63]

With family support networks acutely compromised, friendships amongst peers were crucial for boys as they sought entry into the adult world of male labour and companionship. In these groups, they tried on and acted out the masculine identity codes that operated in the gender-segregated occupational structure of the port. Searching for employment on the peripheries of the labour market, work, play and offending segued into each other. In August 1843, recently returned from a sea voyage but without work, William Jenkins was sentenced to nine months for stealing rope from fishing boats with Charles Tunmore, another lad from a family of siblings who were repeatedly imprisoned.[64] In Van Diemen's Land, William attributed this conviction not to stealing rope, but to 'setting boats adrift'; had this been play, scavenging, pilfering or a mix of all three?[65] William was arrested only once on his own, suspected of stealing a child's frock, shortly after his first imprisonment.[66] Whilst all but one of the convict lads had stood trial alone, a third of their prosecutions were for joint offending and probably an even greater proportion of their undiscovered crimes and misdemeanours were carried out in groups.[67] Some knew each other through work but many met or firmed up acquaintances in prison. Their friendships and rivalries can be traced through the admissions register and the gaoler's list of their disciplinary infractions, a rich source for exposing 'hidden scripts'.

IV

Lacking control in the outside world, William Jenkins asserted himself in prison, notching up, like fellow inmate Joshua Artis, some eighteen punishments, which was far more than other prisoners accumulated. Of the other twenty-one convict lads whose full disciplinary record is known, for instance, a third were never punished during their imprisonment at Yarmouth. Two-thirds had been disciplined at least once, and together, they had averaged 3.6 punishments each.[68] As with other lads, William's infractions were associated with boisterous spirits and staking his place in the inmate pecking order; fourteen of his punishments were for larking about, being loud or jostling with other boys.[69] Within a week of his first confinement, William was deprived of cheese for being noisy at night and soon he would spend the day in solitary for noisy conduct with James Barnes.[70] Both lost their cheese allowance again, with fellow accomplice Henry

Patterson, for singing and calling out to each other in the early morning before cells were unlocked.[71] By far the greatest number of punishments doled out by the gaoler were for noisy behaviour (invariably singing, shouting or swearing), which signalled the determination of inmates to communicate with each other by calling to prisoners in other parts of the gaol.[72] Raucous behaviour was not only a challenge to the gaoler's authority, for it could also annoy inmates trying to sleep or work. In 1844, adult prisoners complained they could not concentrate on reading because of 'unnecessary talking' between William Jenkins and John Presant. The gaoler reprimanded the two lads and warned they would be punished for further disruptiveness.[73]

Playfulness frequently landed boys in trouble. During his first imprisonment, William Jenkins was sent to solitary for three days and deprived of cheese for blacking another boy's face with soot.[74] In subsequent confinements, he would be punished for climbing on the grating above the dayroom door and with another lad for 'wearing their dress in an unsightly manner'.[75] Whilst these minor infractions suggest youthful high spirits, larking about could quickly descend into conflict between boys as they jostled for status in the inmate pecking order. When still new to prison, for instance, William received a kicking from repeat offender James Bowles (age twenty-three), who was consequently confined for three days on bread and water.[76] Later, William served the same punishment for 'pushing and throwing things at Thomas Pyeman' and, again, for fighting with two boys.[77] In both play-acting and serious disputes, lads sought to prove the same physical 'hardness' they needed to demonstrate in the streets to hold themselves as men.[78]

Though most offenders were sentenced to 'hard labour', the gaol made little provision for employment and a treadwheel was not installed until 1845.[79] 'Useful work', however, supplied by the prison visitor, played a crucial part in keeping inmates occupied and orderly outside their lessons. Whilst Sarah Martin set female prisoners to needlework and adult men to various tasks, such as carving cutlery out of bone and straw-hat making, she employed boys in mending books and sewing patchwork of which 'they do not tire, but are every day asking for more pieces to sew together'.[80] In mending books for workhouse children and sewing items for the needy (one boy was employed making a quilt cover for a poor child), Martin hoped the juveniles would learn the value of thinking of and helping others.[81] Needlework, culturally associated with feminized labour, quiet contemplation and confinement, was one of the ways the visitor sought to educate boys in an evangelical model of Christian manliness, aimed at labouring boys and men. Also promoted by the religious tracts and magazines she gave them, this approved masculinity was the antithesis of the street-fighting, street-talking man: homely, industrious, dutiful and unassuming.[82] Sewing, however, had alternative meanings in the seaport, where it was a skill learned by mariners who needed to mend both nets and their own clothes whilst away at sea. During William's first imprisonment, Sarah Martin noted the boys enjoyed patchworking since 'it tends to secure order and quietness, as well as because it teaches them to sew, so that they may be able to mend their clothes and make some'.[83]

Evidence from the teacher's journals strongly suggests some lads welcomed the break from the loud posturing of inmate interactions that her quiet occupations, lessons and story-reading sessions afforded.[84] The men pleaded with the teacher to supply the boys more work since it kept them quiet and orderly, allowing the adults to concentrate on lessons, but she was reluctant to overindulge the juveniles in pleasurable labour, less they took it for granted.[85] Though it helped subdue her volatile scholars, she regretted this employment was not matched by more onerous tasks:

> these boys need some occupation here, of another character, and of a less amusing nature, viz. peremptory, engaged, fixed hours of labour. The greatest number of these boys are better fed than when out of prison; the cleanliness they are obliged to observe, and regular hours for sleep, if annoying at the first moment, soon promote comfort; so that in the absence of occupation of a deterring kind, these boys may well be always full of spirits, just like school boys on a play-ground.[86]

William Jenkins, however, was not content that his pleasure should depend on the good will of his teacher and perhaps baulked at the deferential manly ideal she advocated. Towards the end of his first imprisonment, he was found to have secreted a bag of patchwork and needles in his sleeping cell. Whilst the teacher saw patchwork and the provision of storybooks, and pens and paper as rewards for good conduct, to many inmates these were items of currency to trade in their illicit economy, or to keep for themselves for subversive use. When the turnkey and teacher discovered the missing bag, William attempted to burn his loot and, when prevented, was insolent to Miss Martin, for which he was locked up for two days on bread and water.[87]

The boy's insubordination on this occasion suggests that his refractory conduct was not just related to rowdy playfulness but marked his challenging stance towards authority and discipline, and perhaps to the domesticated ideal of Christian boyhood the teacher instilled. Already he had been punished for refusing to clean the day ward.[88] Towards the end of his last sentence at Yarmouth, he aggressively defied the gaoler, having already broken a pain of glass and been 'disrespectful' when the prisoners were reproved for the 'dirty state' of the ward. Instructed to take his 'night utensil' (presumably a chamber pot) to his cell, he rounded on the gaoler: "'you may take the tub yourself and be b——d for I will not take it'" and 'put his face in mine and in a rough tone of voice mocked me'.[89]

William Jenkins' punishment record illuminates how some inmates vociferously challenged official regulations governing conduct, communication and obedience, and the informal moral discipline enforced by the Christian teacher. It is only by placing these actions in the wider context of prisoner conduct, however, that we can appreciate the general responses of inmates to the disciplinary environment. The years 1842–4, during which William was confined, saw punishments doubling in number. These had risen steadily since the late 1830s (when a new gaoler was appointed who strove to implement recent statutory regulations governing prisoner conduct), only to fall by half following the introduction of the treadwheel in 1845.[90] Yet even in these more turbulent years, only a minority of inmates – typically juvenile boys – were disciplined. Most, it seems, kept their heads down so that, if they did not follow regulations to the letter, at least they avoided attracting the notice of their watchful teacher and the guards. Moreover, prisoners monitored and moderated each other's conduct to avoid conflict amongst inmates and the withdrawal of potentially profitable activities supplied by the teacher.

By contrast, acting up, throwing their weight around and filling the prison with their voices enabled the boys to exert control over their environment whilst demonstrating the toughness expected of men in the heavy and often dangerous occupations of the seafaring port. Larking about and tests of daring, in and outside gaol, were amongst the ways they gained entry into the convivial world of male labour, sport and pleasure. However, such unruly behaviour could also antagonize family and community members as well as land them in trouble with the authorities. By 1844, William Jenkins and his mates may have burned too many bridges, for they were picked up near Norwich for stealing from a dwelling house, having wandered from their native town. At trial, when they were sentenced to transportation for stealing £4 6s. from a public house, the court drew on the Yarmouth gaoler's testimony about their previous convictions: Joshua Artis (9 times), Robert Harrod (11 times) and William Jenkins (3 times at Yarmouth and a recent committal in Norwich).[91]

V

Convict records, compiled on each exile transported to Van Diemen's Land, often contain a 'hidden script' in the description of their tattoos. These 'embodied scripts' – as we might call them – provide an alternative perspective on the lads' antics and associations. In the marks they etched on their bodies, we see how convicts – rather than others – viewed themselves, their passions and close connections. Tattooing was one of the ways Yarmouth boys marked their passage into the rites of adult masculinity. At least twenty-four of the twenty-six convict lads were tattooed when they arrived in Van Diemen's Land. Probably most began adorning themselves long before they left Yarmouth. The tattooed ring worn by Robert Harrod when he was twelve (the youngest prisoner I have discovered with markings) no doubt symbolized his entry into the circle of night-time friends with whom he strayed from home.[92]

Tattoo parlours did not develop until the 1870s so the lads' tattoos must have been made by themselves or by companions. Some convicts will have begun making their marks in gaol and continued to embellish their body art aboard the transport ships, where tattooing was a major pastime and act of sociability.[93] In Yarmouth Gaol, where tattooing was prohibited, occasionally the gaoler caught prisoners in the act. Thomas Farrell, one of William's early accomplices, spent a day in the cells 'for endeavouring to make some marks on the Boy Bowles' arm by pricking it &c'.[94] We do not know if this was the first time these lads experimented with tattooing but when Thomas returned a year later for his sixth imprisonment, his initials, *T.F.*, had been scored on his left arm and *T* on his left hand. By then he had served his first berth at sea when, most likely, he proudly marked his initiation into life on the ocean with the anchor tattoo he was now sporting.[95]

William Jenkins may also have been discovered in the midst of a tattooing experiment when the gaoler interrupted a group of boys pricking the letter *H* into a piece of bread.[96] Possibly he had been sourcing do-it-yourself tattooing implements when he purloined the bag of needles from the prison visitor.[97]

Most boys began their tattoos with simple, easily achieved marks rather than elaborate designs, such as dots that probably signalled friendship groups. Sixteen convict lads sported dots, including William who had a row of dots on one arm and five dots between forefinger and thumb. Initials and names were the most common form of tattoo, often combined with a figure representing the person they named. Typically, sailors tattooed their names to ensure their bodies could be identified if drowned – a practice many convicts adopted.[98] William placed his initial *W* next to a man's head, perhaps symbolizing his dead father or the man he hoped to become. The man's face was illuminated by the sun and placed next to the anchor and cable, signs of faith and safe passage. The initials *HL* were repeated three times, either a love attachment or a companion. Apart from the self, initials usually represented lovers, relatives or friends, indicating the strength of these attachments despite the highly compromised circumstances of the boys' familial networks. Isaac Riches, prosecuted by his parents for stealing from his mother, portrayed all his family, including his father smoking and drinking and two men 'arm in arm', probably the brother with whom he was transported.[99] John Newstead tattooed the names of a group of boys with whom he was convicted and the one-time sweetheart he was imprisoned for assaulting.[100]

Their body art depicted the sports and pastimes enjoyed by Yarmouth's labouring men and boys. Probably the fouls (or cocks) on Thomas Bowles' left arm and hand signalled poaching, or cockfighting and gaming.[101] Robert Harrod had a dog on his right arm, a symbol of companionship that may also have denoted a passion for racing or poaching.[102] In prison, the boys devised their own blood sports by chasing mice and killing flies.[103] Gambling was an integral part of masculine culture. On admission, inmates handed over their gaming implements, but devised substitutes in gaol which were regularly confiscated from the wards. His tattooed draft board and snake conveyed John Newstead's game spirit in the battle of chance and his attachment to the fatalistic outlook of the labouring poor, as did the suns and half-moons, hearts and darts – the symbols of luck and ill fortune – many convicts wore.[104]

In their body adornment, the boys celebrated and commemorated their attachment and loyalty to family and friends, their town and its way of life. Maritime insignia depicted the seafaring trades many aspired to join. Only six convict lads described themselves as 'labourers' in Van Diemen's Land. Instead most gave the trade in which he had been apprenticed or that his male relatives pursued, thus linking him back to the life he had envisioned. William stated he was a seaman, like his brother and the man with the boat in his tattoos. Both the tattooed designs the convicts marked on their bodies during the voyage, and the statements they made about their occupations at its end, can be seen as the means of preserving self-identity in the face of banishment from the world they knew. How did these identities endure or change as they adapted to exile?

VI

After convicts left Yarmouth it becomes more difficult to sustain an 'intimate reading', when their actions and life choices can no longer be deduced from the circumstances and patterns of behaviour of a wider known cohort. On the transport ship *Theresa* the three Yarmouth lads – Jenkins, Artis and Harrod – encountered another evangelical teacher, Colin Arrott Browning, the ship surgeon responsible for their moral as well as physical welfare. Browning organized prisoners into small classes, each supervised by an orderly and literate man.[105] It is possible that Henry Lavery, who could read and write, was assigned responsibility for teaching William. Had the Yarmouth boy found an alternative father figure in this 45-year-old gardener and groom from Worcester, who had left behind a wife and four children? If so, this could explain the tattooed initials 'HL' with which the lad had marked himself three times.[106] At the end of the voyage, the surgeon described Jenkins' conduct as 'good', although despite nearly three years of prison schooling, the lad could only read on arrival in Van Diemen's Land. At 5 feet 3½ inches, and just shy of eighteen years old, he will have been near his full height.[107]

Few convicts, whatever their age or sex, served their sentence without getting into trouble with the authorities. In a penal colony considered a prison without walls, their movements were closely monitored.[108] Yet despite his turbulent history at Yarmouth Gaol, William Jenkins' disciplinary record is surprisingly light. Towards the end of his fifteen months' probation as a 'government servant' in a work gang, he was noted for 'disobedience' several times and had a month added to his probation for being 'absent without leave', one of the most common forms of misconduct. A couple of days later, he was sent to solitary for fourteen days for 'making threatening language to a fellow prisoner and ill-treating him'. But, after he was assigned to a sheep-farmer at Hamilton in the High Plains, north-west of Hobart, he was reprimanded just once for 'being in the township without a pass'. By July 1849 he received his ticket of leave and was free to find his own employment, provided he did not leave the colony. In January 1852 he received his Certificate of Freedom.[109]

Locating former convicts after they exited the penal system can be difficult, especially if they were not caught reoffending and had a common name. I trawled exhaustively through birth, marriage and death indexes for several William Jenkins, and through ship departures to see if he headed for the gold fields in Victoria, where most of his convict mates from Yarmouth chanced their luck when they obtained their freedom. Then finally I found him by reading every newspaper article including the name 'William Jenkins' because, like me, he searched for his family. Over four days in 1874 he placed advertisements in Tasmania's leading newspaper:

JENKINS, EDWARD AND ABRAHAM.
Information wanted as to the whereabouts of the above named parties, last heard of (being shipwrecked, but saved) at New Zealand, about thirty years ago.
Address, WILLIAM JENKINS, River Dee, 3736[110]

In my archival quests and digital searches I had missed William Jenkins, for he appears in the marriage register as 'Jenkings', wedded in 1863 at the minister's house in Bothwell, near Hamilton, where he had been assigned to sheep-farmers. He still had a hazy sense of his own age which was recorded as thirty-three. His bride, Mary Stock, was just seventeen.[111] Their first child, William, had been born in 1861.[112] In all they would have nine children, several bearing the names of William's birth family. Neither bride, nor groom, nor their witnesses, signed their names in the marriage register, their marks suggesting none could write.[113]

Mary had been born in Hamilton, the daughter of convicts who settled there in the 1830s. A labourer and ploughman from Essex, Joseph Stock had agricultural experience to turn his hand to cattle farming.[114] On arrival in the colony, Elizabeth Kepax from Worcester was listed as a house servant of washing and ironing, and a prostitute.[115] Arriving in Van Diemen's Land a few years before William, they will have been his near contemporaries. Almost certainly, they were amongst the former convicts who befriended the young man and helped him adapt to the rural life of the Central Highlands, where many emancipated convicts chose to remain. When William Jenkins married, he was listed as 'an eating house keeper', an occupation that suggests conviviality. Had young Mary been working as his servant when she became pregnant? He made a good catch. The year before Mary gave birth, William had purchased 838.5 acres overlooking the River Dee on the road between Hamilton and Marlborough. In 1871 he purchased a further 241 acres.[116] He may also have continued ducking and diving, however, for though never prosecuted after securing his freedom, he was named during his brother-in-law's trial for cattle rustling from one of the large landowners to whom William had been assigned.[117] Had he just got better at covering his tracks? When William died, of inflammation of the bowels at the house of his father-in-law in 1883, his occupation was recorded as farmer.[118] His death was reported in several newspapers. The funeral procession left from the Bridge Inn to the Church. The Hamilton correspondent recalled a man well known, liked and respected:

> Another old resident of the district, Mr. William Jenkins, who for many years resided at the Dee, New Country, has passed away amongst us. A large number of people yesterday followed his remains to their last resting place at the Ouse, where his body was interred in the Church of England Cemetery.[119]

Sometimes, one fragment can provide the missing link to connect a chain of otherwise isolated sources. In this case, it is an advertisement, placed in a newspaper, which links the middle-aged farmer back to the rowdy, gregarious boy who first entered gaol with his elder brother over three decades earlier. We cannot know if William Jenkins made contact with his brothers, and can only speculate how he had known of their shipwreck: Were they heading for New Zealand or Australia? Had they planned to join William when he was sentenced to exile? Had he stayed in occasional correspondence with family in England, despite his inability to write? What made William search in 1874? The man's experience as a convict servant, eating-house owner and farmer in the High Plains of

Van Diemen's Land was far removed from the seafaring life he had imagined, back in Yarmouth. But a connection had remained, if only in memory, with the family and life from which he had been forcibly parted. In its formal wording, the advertisement does not quite give us the old convict's 'voice' but, in its hopefulness, it conveys the strength of those attachments and his feelings.

VII

Reconstructing the outline of a life from scraps of evidence, made in different times and places, can yield more than isolated anecdotes and disembodied voices. Using record linkage, we can begin to interpret the experiences and subjective identities of boys and young men, cast by contemporary discourse as 'idle rogues' and 'artful dodgers'.[120] By plotting their movements, we can uncover their occupation of social space and the relationships and networks they forged there. In the penal records on their behaviour we may not hear the actual words spoken in their (not always) 'hidden scripts', but we can retrieve something of the tenor of their often loud and raucous 'off-stage (and on-stage) dissent' that disturbed and provoked authority. At Great Yarmouth, male juvenile offences closely correlated with the place of adolescent boys on the peripheries of the port's casual labour market and opportunities it afforded for unsupervised recreation and petty theft. Most convict lads had experienced parental loss and poverty – sometimes family conflict, too. Peer groups formed as supplements and alternatives to kinship ties and were cemented by male camaraderie and rivalries played out in the streets and prison wards. Most lads ceased offending as they approached their mid- to late-twenties, whether it was in Yarmouth or Van Diemen's Land, when they found the means to support themselves or formed families that stabilized them.

By intimately reading qualitative and quantitative data from multiple sources, we can begin to contextualize and interpret fragmentary surviving evidence on individuals, who were only briefly and occasionally noted by figures of officialdom and authority, and whose lives and behaviour they often dimly understood. It is uncommon for micro-histories to deploy quantitative analysis for, in current practice, most social and cultural historians focus on close readings of primarily textual and discursive evidence. Tracking the experience of individuals and their networks over time, however, reveals patterns in their behaviour and associations that rarely become apparent when tracing an individual in isolation through a single set of sources. Historians, suggests Hannu Salmi, citing Stephen Greenblatt, can 'give their work "the touch of the real" by tracing the situations, feelings, and reactions that were possible for contemporaries, even if their existence cannot be directly read from the sources'. Intimate reading, I would add, permits us to surmise not only what was possible, but also what was probable.[121] Characteristics and experiences shared by a distinct group or network, such as the prison and convict lads examined here, allow us to speculate on the gaps in the records that sketch out a life, whilst tantalizing traces of individual voices and actions can be used to speak for other hidden lives.

Acknowledgements

Versions of this research were presented at the European Social Science History Conference (Vienna 2014), the British Crime Historians Symposium (University of Liverpool 2014) and the 'Voices of the People' symposium (Birkbeck, University of London 2015). I thank participants for insights that helped me develop this chapter and the online conversations curated by the Many-Headed Monster Blog, July–August 2015, https://manyheadedmonster.wordpress.com/voices-of-the-people/, where 'Captured Voices', an illustrated short version of this chapter can be viewed (https://manyheadedmonster.wordpress.com/2015/08/07/captured-voices-2/). I am especially grateful to David R. Green for sharing his work on social networking and to Zoe Alker and Lucinda Matthews-Jones for their perceptive comments on an earlier draft.

Notes

1. William Blake (c. 1801–3) 'Auguries of Innocence'. On 'Microhistory and the Small-scale', see B.S. Gregory (1999) 'Is Small Beautiful? Microhistory and the History of Everyday Life', *History and Theory*, Vol. 38, No. 1, pp. 100–10 and D. Bell (2002) 'Total History and Microhistory: The French and Italian Paradigms', in L. Kramer and S. Maza (eds) *A Companion to Western Historical Thought* (Oxford: Blackwell), pp. 262–76.

2. C. Geertz (1973) 'Thick Description: Toward an Interpretive Theory of Culture', in his work *The Interpretation of Cultures: Selected Essays* (New York: Basic Books), pp. 3–30. For example: N. Zemon Davis (1983) *The Return of Martin Guerre* (Cambridge: Harvard University Press) and R. Darnton (1985) *The Great Cat Massacre and Other Episodes in French Cultural History* (New York: Vintage Books).

3. Geertz, 'Thick Description'.

4. See, for instance, readings of Jack Sheppard's celebrity in P. Linebaugh (1991) *The London Hanged: Crime and Civil Society in the Eighteenth Century* (London: Allen Lane) and M. Buckley (2002) 'Sensations of Celebrity: *Jack Sheppard* and the Mass Audience', *Victorian Studies*, Vol. 44, No. 3, pp. 423–64. For the cultural narratives surrounding Jack the Ripper, see J.R. Walkowitz (1992) *City of Dreadful Delight: Narratives of Sexual Danger in Late-Victorian London* (London: Virago).

5. Recent examples include investigations of Victorian women prosecuted for murder, whose trials exposed contemporary class and gender norms and influenced the rise of sensation in popular fiction and journalism: see K. Summerscale (2008) *The Suspicions of Mr. Whicher: A Shocking Murder and the Undoing of a Great Victorian Detective* (New York: Walker & Company); E. Gordon and G. Nair (2009) *Murder and Morality in Victorian Britain: The Story of Madeleine Smith* (Manchester: Manchester University Press) and K. Colquhoun (2014) *Did She Kill Him? A Victorian Tale of Deception, Adultery and Arsenic* (London: Little Brown).

6. Based on Norfolk Record Office, Great Yarmouth Gaol Registers, December 1838–December 1850 (Y/L2 9), for the three years 1839–41. Hundred and seven cases were heard at the Quarter Sessions out of 641 admissions for crime and misdemeanours. A further eighty-three admissions were on charges of debt. The total number of admissions in the period was 724. All extant records from Great Yarmouth Gaol are held at the Norfolk Record Office, Norwich (hereafter Norfolk RO).

7. For example, see H. Rogers (2012) 'Singing in Gaol: Christian Instruction and Inmate Culture in the Nineteenth Century', *Prison Service Journal*, Vol. 199, pp. 35–43, at p. 42.

8. For an insightful debate on scale and perspective in historical enquiry, see J. Brewer (2010) 'Microhistory and the Histories of Everyday Life', *Cultural and Social History*, Vol. 7, No. 1, pp. 87–109 and responses by P. Hudson (2010) 'Closeness and Distance', *Cultural and Social History*, Vol. 7, No. 3, pp. 375–85 and F. de Vivo (2010) 'Prospect or Refuge? Microhistory, History on the Large Scale', *Cultural and Social History*, Vol. 7, No. 3, pp. 387–97.

9. S.G. Magnússon (2015) 'Tales of the Unexpected: The "Textual Environment", Ego-Documents and a Nineteenth-century Icelandic Love Story – An Approach in Microhistory', *Cultural and Social History*, Vol. 12, No. 1, pp. 77–94, at pp. 77, 79 and 89.

10. J.C. Scott (1990) *Domination and the Arts of Resistance: Hidden Transcripts* (New Haven and London: Yale University Press), p. xii.

11. Z. Alker (2014) 'When High and Low Collide: Gender and Respectability in the mid-Victorian Courtroom – Street Violence in Mid-Victorian Liverpool' (Unpublished D.Phil thesis, Liverpool John Moores University), pp. 214–44.

12. Scott, *Domination and the Arts of Resistance*, pp. xi–xii.

13. For an insightful survey of the influence of ethnography and anthropology on micro-history, see W. Pooley (29 September 2015) 'Native to the Past: History, Anthropology and Folklore', *Past and Present*, No. 229 at http://past.oxfordjournals.org/content/early/2015/09/29/pastj .gtv038.short?rss=1 (accessed 25 March 2016).

14. Bruno Latour's actor-network theory (ANT) offers a useful way of conceptualizing agency through social networks; see B. Latour (2005) *Reassembling the Social: An Introduction to Actor-network Theory* (Oxford: Oxford University Press). For historical applications of ANT, see T. Bender (2006) 'History, Theory & the Metropolis', *CMS Working Paper Series*, No. 5 at http://www.metropolitanstudies.de/workingpaper/bender_005-2006.pdf.

15. D.R. Green (2014) 'Working the System: Pauper Communities and Plebeian Spaces in Mid-nineteenth-century London' (Unpublished Paper), p. 8. Crime historians are beginning to draw on scholarship on networking and space developed in cultural and historical geography, using GIS, visualization and networking tools. See Z. Alker's use of GIS in 'When High and Low Collide' and collaborative research in progress by *Founders and Survivors: Australian Life Courses in Historical Context, 1803–1920*, http://foundersandsurvivors.org/ as well as *The Digital Panopticon: The Global Impact of London Punishments, 1780–1925*, http://www.digitalpanopticon.org/.

16. Green, 'Working the System'. See also D.R. Green (2006) 'Pauper Protests: Power and Resistance in Early Nineteenth-century London Workhouses', *Social History*, Vol. 31, No. 2, pp. 137–59.

17. For an overview of these debates, see A.I. Port (2015 edition) 'History from Below, The History of Everyday Life, and Microhistory', in J. Wright (ed.) *International Encyclopedia of the Social and Behavioral Sciences – Volume 11*, pp. 108–13.

18. T. Hitchcock and R. Shoemaker (2015) *London Lives: Poverty, Crime and the Making of a Modern City, 1690–1800* (Cambridge: Cambridge University Press), p. 24.

19. Hitchcock and Shoemaker, *London Lives*, pp. 24 and 12.

20. The term is Franco Moretti's. See his collected essays in F. Moretti (2013) *Distant Reading* (London: Verso).

21. Anon (1844) *A Brief Sketch of the Life of the Late Miss Sarah Martin of Great Yarmouth, With Extracts from the Parliamentary Reports on Prisons; Her Own Journals &c* (Yarmouth: C. Barber). All subsequent references are to an expanded version, S. Martin (Undated) *The Prison Visitor of Great Yarmouth, With Extracts from Her Writings and Prison Journals* (London: Religious Tract Society); hereafter *Sarah Martin*.

22. Sarah Martin's surviving 'Everyday Books' are kept at the Tolhouse Museum (afterwards TM) by Great Yarmouth Museum Service. These are labelled: 'Prison School Journal 1836–8'; 'Everyday Book from November 7 1839 – April 6 1840'; and 'Copy Books written by prisoners under tuition of Sarah Martin. From April 12 1840 to August 12 1840'. Dated entries will be referred to as 'Everyday Book'.

23. Access databases were used to analyse: prisoner admissions 1839–41 based on Norfolk RO, Great Yarmouth Gaol Registers, December 1838–December 1850 (Y/L2 9); the gaoler's entries on discipline in Norfolk RO, Gaol Keeper's Journal, January 1836–December 1840 (Y/L2, 47) and January 1841–December 1845 (Y/L2 48); and individual convict records from the Tasmanian Archive and Heritage Office (TAHO), Convict Department (available online http://search.archives.tas.gov.au/default.aspx? detail=1&type=A&id=TA00060: Indents of Male Convicts, 27 July 1824 – 26 May 1853 (Con 19); Conduct Registers of Male Convicts Arriving in the Period of the Probation System, 1 January 1840–31 December 1853 (Con 33); and Description Lists of Male Convicts, 1 January 1828–31 December 1853 (Con 18). In subsequent notes, convicts' names are followed by their police number, ship, year of arrival and the record used.

24. Norfolk RO, Gaol Register, 24 May 1839 (Y/L2 9). Thomas Merryman was also remanded but not charged. Though listed as nine years old, baptism records show he was nearly eleven as he was christened on 27 October 1828 – see *England, Select Births and Christenings, 1538–1975*, Ancestry.com. Joshua Artis had spent his first time in prison earlier in the month, when remanded for three days on suspicion of stealing a watch; see Norfolk RO, Gaol Register, 3rd of May 1839 (Y/L2 9). He was listed as ten years old but his christening records indicate he was thirteen (birthdate 31 January 1826; baptized 12 February 1826); see *England, Select Births and Christenings, 1538–1975*, Ancestry.com.

25. Martin's 'Liberated Prisoners Book' has been lost. Extracts were included, however, in *Parliamentary Papers*, Inspectors of Prisons of Great Britain II, Northern and Eastern District, Fourth Report, Cmnd. 199 (1839), pp. 171–4 and ibid., Fifth Report, Cmnd. 258 (1840), 124–31, including Martin's reports on Jenkins and Artis, pp. 128–9.

26. 'A.J.' in Martin's table, 'A Glance at Some Persons who Seemed after their Imprisonment to have been Reclaimed or Improved', in *Parliamentary Papers*, Inspectors of Prisons of Great Britain II, Northern and Eastern District, Fifth Report, Cmnd. 258 (1840), pp. 128–9.

27. Norfolk RO, Index and Receiving Book from 25 December 1838 and 24 May 1839 (Y/L2 7).

28. For an evangelical story lamenting the abject state of such boys, see S. Canty (1855) *George Seten or the Chip Boy of the Dry Dock: A Tale of City Life* (New York: Garrett), available via the Internet archive. Thank you to the Sydney Jones Library, Liverpool University for this reference.

29. 'A.J.', *Parliamentary Papers*, Inspectors of Prisons of Great Britain II, Northern and Eastern District, Fifth Report, Cmnd. 258 (1840), p. 129.

30. Ibid.

31. W.J. Forsythe (1987) *The Reform of Prisoners 1830–1900* (London: Croom Helm) and M. Ignatieff (1978) *A Just Measure of Pain: The Penitentiary in the Industrial Revolution, 1750–1950* (London: Peregrine).

32. For detailed examination of these former inmates, see H. Rogers (2014) 'Kindness and Reciprocity: Liberated Prisoners and Christian Charity in Early Nineteenth-century England', *Journal of Social History*, Vol. 47, No. 3, pp. 721–45. See p. 733 for analysis of young liberated prisoners.

33. See table on the greatest, least and average number of prisoners held (1840–1843) *Parliamentary Papers*, Report of Prison Inspectors, Eighth Report, Cmnd. 517 (1843), p. 181.

34. Based on twenty-two convict lads whose age was confirmed by birth or christening records. Isaac Riches was the youngest at first imprisonment, just shy of twelve years old when summarily convicted as a rogue and vagabond, intent on stealing, though the gaoler recorded his age as fourteen; see Norfolk RO, Gaol Register, 26 May 1841. Christened on 13 June 1829, Isaac was 11 when he entered prison – see the online transcription of Baptism registers for St Nicholas, Great Yarmouth, 1813–1880 part of the Baptism Project Great Yarmouth St Nicholas, http://freepages.genealogy.rootsweb.ancestry .com/~tinstaafl/Church_Pages/yarmouth_gt_1829.htm#Top. This birthdate correlates with the age (seventeen years) he gave on arrival in Van Diemen's Land. See TAHO, Conduct Record Isaac Riches, 17982, per *Joseph Somes* (1) 1846, CON33/1/77. See also TAHO, Convict Indent CON14/1/35 and Description List CON18/1/45. Some historians have suggested prisoners lowered their ages in the hope of more lenient treatment; see J.J. Tobias (1967) *Crime and Industrial Society in the Nineteenth Century* (Oxford: B.T. Batsford), pp. 14–21, at p. 19 and V.A.C. Gatrell and T.B. Hadden (1972) 'Criminal Statistics and Their Interpretation', in E.A. Wrigley (ed.) *Nineteenth-century Society: Essays in the Use of Quantitative Methods for the Study of Social Data* (Cambridge: Cambridge University Press), pp. 336–96 at 379. Recorded variations in the convict lads' ages, however, do not indicate a clear effort to deceive, with as many overestimating as underestimating age at transportation. Since children were usually christened shortly after birth, baptism records are the best means of verifying the age of those born before compulsory birth registration was introduced in 1837.

35. Between them they had been committed 137 times at Yarmouth. In 120 of these admissions, the gaoler entered the offender as under twenty-one. Three-quarters of these committals (77) were for some kind of theft.

36. *Sarah Martin*, pp. 128–9. On arrival in Van Diemen's Land in 1845, William Jenkins listed his surviving family, resident in Yarmouth, as mother Elizabeth; brothers Thomas, Absolum, Edward; sisters Elizabeth and Mary Ann; see TAHO, Convict Indent, William Jenkins, 15933, per *Theresa*, 1845, CON14/1/29.

37. For example, see Rogers, 'Kindness and Reciprocity', *passim*.

38. 'A.J.', Inspectors of Prisons of Great Britain II, Northern and Eastern District, Fifth Report, p. 129.

39. TM, 'Everyday Books', *passim*.

40. 'A.J.', Inspectors of Prisons of Great Britain II, Northern and Eastern District, Fifth Report, p. 129.

41. (Sarah Martin) (1845) 'The Believer's Death', *Selections from the Poetical Remains of the Late Miss Sarah Martin of Great Yarmouth* (Yarmouth: James M. Denew), pp. 60–1. See also John Jenkins, *Death Index*, January–March 1840, Yarmouth, Norfolk, Vol. 13, p. 285 from Ancestry.com. John Jenkins was listed as a tinker when his youngest son, Henry, was baptized at Caister, 10 January 1840, shortly before he died. See Baptism Project Great Yarmouth St Nicholas (1840) http://freepages.genealogy.rootsweb.ancestry.com/~tinstaafl /Church_Pages/yarmouth_gt_1840.htm#Top.

42. TM, Sarah Martin's Prisoner Register, 1842, No. 120. Elizabeth Jenkins and her children were removed to Ayleburton, parish of Lydney Gloucester, 14 April 1840: Norfolk Record Office, Index of Examined Paupers, Y/L16/8 (1756–1844), MF/RO 597/6.

43. The Gaol Register states Abraham was born in Northampton but I have found no record of

his birth or his parents' marriage; Norfolk RO, Gaol Register, 24 May 1839 (Y/L2 9).

44. William was christened in Caister, 26 August 1827. Ancestry.com. *England, Select Births and Christenings, 1538–1975* (database online) (Provo, UT: Ancestry.com Operations, Inc., 2014), FHL Film Number 1278997.

45. TM, Sarah Martin's Prisoner Register, 1842, No. 119.

46. Rogers, 'Kindness and Reciprocity', pp. 729–32 and B.S. Godfrey, D.J. Cox and S.D. Farrall (2007) *Criminal Lives: Family Life, Employment and Offending* (Oxford: Oxford University Press), pp. 165–82.

47. TM, Sarah Martin, Prisoner Register, 1842, No. 120.

48. Ibid.

49. A similar number of Yarmouth lads were transported to other destinations in the same period.

50. Norfolk RO, Gaol Register, 7 January 1842 (Y/L2 9). See also 1841 Census, HO107/793/6, accessed from Ancestry.com. Thomas Farrell was wrongly included in the household for he is also listed as resident at the gaol.

51. Norfolk RO, Gaol Receiving Book, 22 October 1842 and 21 January 1843 (Y/D 41/28).

52. Norfolk RO, Index and Receiving Book, 24 May 1839 (Y/L2 7).

53. See H. Rogers (2012) '"Oh, What Beautiful Books!" Captivated Reading in an Early Victorian Prison', *Victorian Studies*, Vol. 55, No. 1, pp. 57–84.

54. See H. Rogers (2015) '"A Very Fair Statement of His Past Life": Transported Convicts, Former Lives and Previous Offences', *Open Library of the Humanities*, Vol. 1, No. 1, at http://researchonline.ljmu.ac.uk/2278/.

55. Thomas Farrell was wrongly included in the household for he is also listed as resident at the gaol in the 1841 Census, HO107/793/6, accessed from Ancestry.com. Reynolds senior was a labourer as we can also see from the 1841 Census, HO107/793/4 accessed from Ancestry.com.

56. 1841 Census, HO107/794/4, accessed from Ancestry.com.

57. 1841 Census, HO107/793/5, accessed from Ancestry.com.

58. Norfolk RO, Gaol Register, 27 July 1840; and 16 and 21 June 1842 (Y/L2 9). Mary Patterson, Free DMB Death Index, 1837–1915, April–June 1839, Yarmouth, Norfolk, Vol. 13, p. 287 accessed from Ancestry.com. At the 1841 Census, the Patterson children were living with their father in Yarmouth; see HO107/793/5, accessed from Ancestry.com. Following a stint in the juvenile reformatory, Parkhurst, Henry Patterson was transported per *Thomas Arbuthnot*, arriving Williamstown, Victoria on 4 May 1847; see Australian Joint Copying Project, Microfilm Roll 92, Class and Piece Number HO11/15, Page Number 149 (76).

59. It seems there were significantly higher rates of orphanage in this cohort of convict lads than in the wider population. In her analysis of autobiographies about working-class boyhood in the period 1800–78, Jane Humphries finds that by fourteen years of age, 16 per cent had lost their father, 13 per cent their mother and 27 per cent had survived both parents. See J. Humphries (2010) *Childhood and Child Labour in the British Industrial Revolution* (Cambridge: Cambridge University Press), pp. 61–72, especially at p. 65.

60. Three had convictions for being refractory paupers. See various Gaol Registers, *passim*.

61. Norfolk RO, Gaol Keeper's Journal, January 1841–December 1845, 14 April 1842 (Y/L2 48).

62. Norfolk RO, Gaol Register, 1808–November 1838, 26 September 1837 (Y/L2 8).

63. Rogers, 'A Very Fair Statement', *passim*.

64. Norfolk RO, Gaol Register, 27 August 1843 (Y/L2 9).

65. William Jenkins, TAHO, Conduct Record, CON33/1/67.

66. Norfolk RO, Gaol Register, 27 April 1842 (Y/L2 9).

67. Interestingly this proportion equates with the one-third of cases in Green's sample, where refractory paupers were sent to prison for jointly committing offences, compared with the two-thirds who were convicted as acting alone. See Green, 'Working the System', pp. 13–14.

68. Based on analysis of disciplinary log in Gaol Keeper's Journal, January 1836–December 1840 (Y/L2, 47) and January 1841–December 1845 (Y/L2 48). Three convicts, who served some of their imprisonment before or after the years 1836–45, have been excluded from this calculation.

69. Norfolk RO, Gaol Keeper's Journal, 11 June 1844 (Y/L2 48).

70. Ibid., 17 January and 1 February 1842 (Y/L2 48).

71. Ibid., 7 February 1842 (Y/L2 48).

72. Rogers, 'Singing in Gaol', pp. 39–41.

73. Norfolk RO, Gaol Keeper's Journal, 11 November 1844 (Y/L2 48).

74. Ibid., 6 March 1842 (Y/L2 48).

75. Ibid., 11 and 28 April 1844 (Y/L2 48).

76. Ibid., 27 January (Y/L2 48).

77. Ibid., 4 November 1843 and 12 February 1844 (Y/L2 48).

78. See C. Emsley (2005) *Hard Men: Violence in England since 1750* (London: Hambledon).

79. Norfolk RO, Gaol Committee 1836–50, 6 May 1844 (Y/TC 3/36) and 4 February 1845 (Y/TC 3/36).

80. TM, 'Everyday Book', 6 February 1842, cited in *Sarah Martin*, p. 126.

81. Ibid., 21 February 1842, cited in *Sarah Martin*, pp. 126–7.

82. Rogers, '"Oh, What Beautiful Books!"', pp. 60–76.

83. TM, 'Everyday Book', 6 February 1842, cited in *Sarah Martin*, p. 126.

84. Rogers, '"Oh, What Beautiful Books!"', *passim*.

85. TM, 'Everyday Book', 21 February 1842, cited in *Sarah Martin*, pp. 126–7.

86. Ibid., 6 February 1842; cited in *Sarah Martin*, p. 126.

87. Norfolk RO, Gaol Keeper's Journal, 28 March 1842 (Y/L2 48).

88. Ibid., 16 February 1842 (Y/L2 48).

89. Ibid., 11 June 1844 (Y/L2 48).

90. TM, 'Everyday Book', 15 May 1837; Norfolk RO, Gaol Committee 1836–50, 6 May 1844 (Y/TC 3/36) and 4 February 1845 (Y/TC 3/36).

91. Norfolk RO, Gaol Keeper's Journal, 20 December 1844 (Y/L2 48). See also TAHO, Joshua Artis, 15826, Robert Harrod, 15914, William Jenkins, 15933, per *Theresa*, 1845, Conduct Record CON33/1/67, Convict Indent CON14/1/29 and Norfolk RO, various Gaol Registers, *passim*.

92. Norfolk RO, Gaol Register 1808–November 1838, 7 July 1837 (Y/L2 8).

93. For convict tattoos, see: J. Bradley and H. Maxwell-Stewart (1997) '"Behold the Man": Power, Observation and the Tattooed Convict', *Journal of Australian Studies*, Vol. 12, No. 1, pp. 71–97; J. Bradley and H. Maxwell-Stewart (1997) 'Embodied Explorations: Investigating Convict Tattoos and the Transportation System' in I. Duffield and J. Bradley (eds) *Representing Convicts: New Perspectives on Forced Convict Labour Migration* (Leicester: Leicester University Press), pp. 183–203; D. Kent (1997) 'Decorative Bodies: The Significance of Convicts' Tattoos', *Journal of Australian Studies*, Vol. 53, pp. 78–88; L. Frost and H. Maxwell-Stewart (2001) (eds) *Chain Letters: Narrating Convict Lives* (Melbourne: Melbourne University Press); H. Rogers (2009) 'The Way to Jerusalem: Reading, Writing and Reform in an Early Victorian Gaol', *Past and Present*, No. 205, pp. 71–104; and Rogers, '"A Very Fair Statement"', pp. 27–32.

94. Norfolk RO, Gaol Keeper's Journal, 21 August 1841 (Y/L2 48).

95. Norfolk RO, Gaol Receiving Book, 22 October 1842 (Y/D 41/28).

96. Norfolk RO, Gaol Keeper's Journal, 11 May 1844 (Y/L2 48).

97. Ibid., 28 March 1842 (Y/L2 48).

98. I. Dye (1989) 'The Tattoos of Early American Seafarers, 1796–1818', *Proceedings of the American Philosophy Society*, Vol. 133, No. 4, pp. 520–54.

99. Isaac Riches, TAHO, Conduct Record, CON33/1/77.

100. Norfolk RO, Gaol Receiving Book, 8 June 1844 (Y/D 41/28) and John Newstead, 21025, per *Ratcliffe* (2), 1848, TAHO, Conduct Record, CON33/1/91.

101. Thomas Bowles, 10001, per *Asiatic*, 1843, TAHO, Conduct Record CON33/1/42.

102. Robert Harrod, 15914, per *Theresa*, 1845, TAHO, Conduct Record CON33/1/67.

103. 'Everyday Book', 24 September (1840 or 1841), cited in *Sarah Martin*, p. 125.

104. John Newstead, 21025, per *Ratcliffe* (2), 1848, TAHO, CON33/1/91.

105. C. Arrot Browning (1847) *The Convict Ship, and England's Exiles* (London: Hamilton, Adams & Co.), access via Internet archive.

106. No other convict aboard *Theresa* shared the same initials. Henry Lavery died at the end of the year at Port Cygnet, Van Diemen's Land (9 December 1845); see Henry Lavery, 15950, per *Theresa*, 1845, TAHO, Conduct Record, CON33/1/67.

107. William Jenkins, 15933, per *Theresa*, 1845, TAHO, CON33/1/67.

108. For an overview, see H. Maxwell-Stewart (2010) 'Convict Transportation from Britain and Ireland 1615–1870', *History Compass*, Vol. 8, No. 11, pp. 1221–42.

109. William Jenkins, 15933, per *Theresa*, 1845, TAHO, CON33/1/67.

110 *Mercury* (Hobart), 16–20 May 1874, p. 1, accessed via Trove.

111. 4 July 1863, TAHO, Tasmanian Names Index, Marriage Records – see https://stors.tas.gov.au/RGD37-1-22p6j2k

112. 4 June 1861, TAHO, Tasmanian Names Index, Birth Register – see https://stors.tas.gov.au/RGD33-1-39p205j2k

113. 4 July 1863, TAHO, Tasmanian Names Index, Marriage Register – see https://stors.tas.gov.au/RGD37-1-22p6j2k

114. Joseph Stock, 880, per *Marmion*, 1828 (TAHO) Conduct Record, CON 31/38, p. 296.

115. Elizabeth Kepax, per *Nautilus*, 1828 (TAHO) Conduct Registers of Female Convicts Arriving during the Assignment Period, 1 January 1803–31 December 1843, CON40/6.

116. *Mercury* (Hobart), 7 March 1860, p. 4 and *Mercury* (Hobart), 2 June 1871, p. 1.

117. *Mercury* (Hobart), 17 July 1874, p. 3.

118. TAHO, Tasmanian Names Index, Death Register, 22 February 1833, RGD35/1/52 no 376.

119. *Mercury* (Hobart), 1 March 1883, p. 3.

120. See H. Shore (1999) *Artful Dodgers: Youth and Crime in Early Nineteenth-century London* (London: Boydell).

121. H. Salmi (2011) 'Cultural History, the Possible, and the Principle of Plenitude', *History and Theory*, Vol. 50, pp. 171–87, at p. 182, quoting Stephen Greenblatt (1999) 'The Touch of the Real', in S.B. Ortner (ed.) *The Fate of 'Culture': Geertz and Beyond* (Berkeley: University of California Press), p. 14.

CHAPTER 12
REFLECTIONS ON THE CHAIN GANG AND PRISON NARRATIVES FROM THE SOUTHERN UNITED STATES
Vivien Miller

I

This chapter focusses on the seminal prison accounts of six inmates – five male and one female, three white and three African American – who served sentences between twenty-two days and twenty-four years in different chain gangs, penal camps and farms, and penitentiary-type prisons in the southern United States between the First World War and the 1950s. These classic works – Kate Richards O'Hare's *In Prison* (1923); Robert E. Burns' *I am a Fugitive from a Georgia Chain Gang!* (1932); Bayard Rustin's 'A Report on Twenty-two Days on the Chain Gang at Roxboro, North Carolina' (1949); Heywood Patterson and Earl Conrad's *Scottsboro Boy* (1950); Albert Ross Brown's *Freedom from Florida Chains* (1968); and Clarence Norris and Sybil D. Washington's *The Last of the Scottsboro Boys* (1979) – reveal much about the day-to-day lives of southern inmates and as fugitives evading the South's persistent carceral reach. Collectively, the works depict the unrelenting misery and cruelty of institutional life as well as illuminating individual acts of defiance, silent sabotage and overt protest, and survival and heroism.[1] Each narrative includes vivid ethnographic-like descriptions of two important social groups – prisoners and keepers – at the margins of society. This chapter emphasizes the key themes linking each account: food, sex, violence, racial oppression, hypermasculinity, labour exploitation and the futility of rehabilitation to underscore their significance as micro-historical studies for both southern historians' and prison historians' understanding of the social history of these institutions and their inhabitants, especially during the 'Jim Crow' period of *de jure* racial segregation and African American disfranchisement.[2]

II

O'Hare and Rustin were prisoners of conscience, anti-war and anti-segregation activists respectively, who were imprisoned as a direct result of their political actions. Burns, Brown, Norris and Patterson were 'ordinary criminals', although the latter pair were entirely innocent of the crime for which they were convicted. All became narrators and/or authors *because* of their prison experiences.[3] Further, O'Hare, Burns, Rustin and Brown were literate when they entered prison but Patterson and Norris could neither read nor write. Patterson was self-educated. He used a Bible to learn to read whilst on death row, as did Norris although less successfully, and later utilized the prison library to feed his interest in crime and detection stories.[4] Whilst the tone, language and narrative arcs of all six books would have been subject to editorial changes during the publication process, the relationship of narrator to professional writer is most explicit in the Patterson and Norris texts.[5] Indeed, historian James Miller describes *Scottsboro Boy* as the 'product of a sustained dialogue between a shrewd, wily, pragmatic survivor' (Patterson) and 'a veteran journalist and committed Communist' (Conrad) that resulted in a seminal critique of twentieth-century southern law, (in)justice and punishment.[6]

III

There was a flurry of convict autobiographies in the early twentieth-century United States, largely by imprisoned anarchists, socialists and labour union organizers as well as the so-called ordinary offender. They generated a stirring body of literature in which injustice and inhumane treatment, institutional corruption and the failure of the prison to reform or rehabilitate were major themes.[7] The dominance of white inmate experiences and white Anglo voices set these earlier accounts apart from what H. Bruce Franklin celebrated in the late 1970s as a 'coherent *body* of [prison] literature, not just works by individual criminals and prisoners' that reflected black political empowerment arising from the dynamic fusion of the Civil Rights/black freedom struggle, anti-Vietnam War protests, Black Power, prisoner rights movements and the urban and prison riots of the late 1960s and early 1970s.[8] The writings of George Jackson, Eldridge Cleaver, Angela Davis and others fused African American history, racial oppression, class struggle and prisoner consciousness to offer powerful critiques of the nation as prison. This expanding body of prisoner literature and growing carceral consciousness over the past forty years has shadowed the rise of the late modern *national* prison-industrial complex and mass incarceration, that is anchored in the Sunbelt region and which includes southern states such as Florida, Texas as well as California.[9]

More recently, the value and authenticity of the prisoner autobiography itself has been questioned. Caleb Smith opines that

> because the prisoner passes back and forth across the threshold between the ideal self and the abject other – and because so many people literally pass into and out of the modern prison – writings by inmates do not hold such a special status. Their authors are readers, often writing for audiences, in the outside world. They do not only record the lived experiences of abjection or struggle. They also engage the ideological and even imaginative dimensions of the institutions that hold them.[10]

However, very few of the many thousands of chain gang or industrial prison labourers in the pre-1960s southern region left extensive or complete written accounts of their penal lives. In the late nineteenth and early twentieth centuries, African American prisoners accounted for the vast majority of southern convicts – three-quarters in states such as Georgia and Florida. Southern penalty equated to the deliberate racial subordination and exploitation of the labour of captive black bodies. The black voice is heard in surviving convict work songs and in official records such as pardon applications and grand jury testimony on prison conditions for example, but complete autobiographical accounts are scarce.

The six works discussed here, by astute and resourceful ex-cons and survivors willing to tell their stories, are extraordinary, often intimate records that detail the inner workings and power structures of state penitentiaries and prison farms, 'Jim Crow' county jails, prison camps and chain gangs. That is not to say there are problems with authenticity, representativeness and the race, gender and class assumptions and prejudices of the authors. These prison autobiographies were ethically compromised in myriad ways – because of the processes of accommodation to the ideological dimensions of the penal institutions in which the narrators served their sentences and the disciplinary apparatuses therein. These in turn reflected the racial and gender oppression and class hierarchies of the Jim Crow period, as well as the complex interpersonal relationships between inmates and between the keepers and the kept. Further, as 'linguistic acts of self-presentation' they certainly cannot be read uncritically.[11] Yet they remain important windows – albeit distinctly personalized and individualized ones – onto the ideology and practice of punishment in the pre-Civil Rights southern region and penned by penal subjects who were deliberately and consciously 'bearing witness'.[12]

IV

An active member of the Socialist Party, Kate Richards O'Hare (1876–1948) was a prominent anti-war activist vehemently opposed to US participation in the First World War. Following US entry in April 1917, as chair of the party's Committee on War and Militarism, she travelled across the states to deliver impassioned speeches against the war. She was arrested following her address in Bowman, North Dakota, in July 1917, for violating the Espionage Act recently passed by the US Congress. Sentenced to five years in prison, O'Hare served only fourteen months as her sentence was commuted in May 1920 by President Woodrow Wilson after national protests and campaigns to secure her freedom by fellow socialists and civil libertarians, and she was later pardoned.[13] As there was no federal women's prison in the United States, O'Hare was boarded at the Missouri State Penitentiary at Jefferson City between April 1919 and May 1920, during which time *Prison Letters* (1919) appeared. The larger work *In Prison* (1920) was penned within two months of her release and attempted to incorporate her prison notes which had been lost or destroyed by prison officials. Looking back, O'Hare viewed her prison experiences as a powerful and necessary part of her social and political education as an agitator for penal reform.[14] She dedicated her book to fellow prisoners in 'cities of sorrow' and hoped her account would awaken 'the social conscience of the people of the United States to the duty we owe our weak and erring children' to demand changes to conditions and more importantly end the contract labour system.[15]

Albert Ross Brown (1896–?), formerly Al House and Florida inmate #16755, was an Indiana bootlegger who had travelled to Tampa, Florida, to purchase liquor at the height of the national prohibition when the manufacture, sale and distribution of alcohol was illegal. He was sentenced in January 1926 to a term of seventy years, later reduced to fifty, for a series of daring burglaries and armed robberies in and around Tampa.[16] He claimed he had been pressured into pleading guilty to these offences on the orders of a local crime lord and politician and to avoid being charged with the capital murder of a Tampa policeman. After his release from Florida's state prison farm at Raiford in November 1949, House produced an account of decades of brutality and mistreatment at the hands of corrupt, incompetent and callous officials.[17] He denounced Florida's 'cruel barbaric antiquated prison system – ill-administered by men who are incompetent ([except], in the art of cruelty) unsurpassed by Hitler's legions throughout'. He hoped 'that by recognizing these truths and facts – now made plainly evident [in the following 320 pages of his memoir] – a different and more humane system might be forced upon the Sovereign State of Florida'.[18]

When Warner Brothers released *I Am a Fugitive from a Chain Gang*, directed by Melvyn LeRoy and starring Paul Muni, in November 1932, the real fugitive from the Troup County chain gang was hiding in Newark, New Jersey. Robert E. Burns had secretly served as a consultant on the film that was based on his sensational best-selling account of brutality, mistreatment and daring escape that had been published eleven months earlier, but first appeared in serial form in *True Detective* magazine in 1931. The book, almost certainly narrated by Burns but written by his brother Vincent, chronicled the New Yorker's disaffection and rootlessness following demobilization, his arrest in Atlanta in February 1921 with two other men for an armed robbery that netted less than $6, and his sentence of 6–10 years on a Georgia chain gang.[19] Burns escaped first in June 1922 and reinvented himself as a respectable and successful magazine publisher in Chicago, but was rearrested in May 1929 when his estranged wife alerted the authorities to his whereabouts.[20] He returned to Georgia to serve what he thought was a one-year sentence with the promise of a pardon, but when it became clear that the Georgia governor and prison commissioners would renege on this, he escaped a second time in September 1930. He remained 'free' until he was eventually pardoned in 1945. His exposé was a direct assault on the chain gang system he had sworn to destroy.[21]

A Pennsylvania-born Quaker committed to non-violence, former Young Communist League member, youth organizer of the proposed 1941 March on Washington, and co-founder of the Congress of Racial Equality (CORE), Bayard Rustin (1910–87) was already a veteran social and civil rights activist when the United States entered the Second World War. As a conscientious objector, he spent more than two years from February 1944 to June 1946 in federal prison in Kentucky, during which time he also constantly pushed against the racial segregation and white hostility that was pervasive in that institution.[22] The June 1946 US Supreme Court decision *Irene Morgan v. Commonwealth of Virginia* had outlawed racial segregation in interstate travel, but states ignored the ruling.[23] Rustin was one of sixteen African American and white male participants in the 1947 CORE-sponsored Journey of Reconciliation, a non-violent direct action protest against segregated public transport. They travelled in small groups through North Carolina, Virginia, Kentucky, and Tennessee as test cases, and Rustin was one of three men sent to a North Carolina chain gang for violating segregation laws by 'sitting in a bus seat out of the jimcrow section'. He recalled, 'Late in the afternoon of Monday, March 21, 1949, I surrendered to the Orange County court in Hillsboro, North Carolina, to begin serving a 30-day sentence imposed two years before.' Rustin would serve twenty-two days in March–April 1949 (after earning eight days' good time or remission for good behaviour), during which he wrote his report on conditions in the notorious prison camps.[24]

Haywood Patterson (1912–52) and Clarence Norris (1912–89) were two of the 'Scottsboro Boys', nine African American teenage hoboes who stole a ride on a freight train in search of work during the early depression years and were arrested at the station at Paint Rock, Alabama, in April 1931 following a rape complaint by two young white women also taken from the train.[25] Like many other southern black defendants accused of the rape of a white woman, the explosive combination of race and sex meant they faced certain death – if not at the hands of a lynch mob, then in Alabama's electric chair. Two weeks after the initial incident, eight of the nine defendants were already under sentence of death. However, their cases caught the attention of the press and public outside the South. This, together with a wrangle between the NAACP and the Communist Party over who would represent the 'boys' in court – the CP's legal arm the International Labor Defense (ILD) won out – five different trials between 1931 and 1937, and two significant US Supreme Court reviews, meant that the defendants found themselves embroiled in one of the *cause célèbres* of the century.[26] Patterson was tried in Alabama four times and sentenced to death three times. His fourth and final sentence of seventy-five years imprisonment at hard labour was imposed in 1937. Historian James Miller observes,

> Defiant, sullen, wily, suspicious, and capable of sudden and violent mood swings, Haywood Patterson was arguably the central figure among the Scottsboro defendants. It was, after all, a sharp exchange between Patterson and a white hobo that triggered off the subsequent altercation on the train heading into Alabama ...[27]

Following a controversial 'settlement' of the Scottsboro case in summer 1937, five defendants had the rape charges dropped and four were released. Haywood Patterson, Clarence Norris, Andy Wright and Charlie Weems remained incarcerated for the rape of Ruby Bates and Victoria Price even though the former had recanted years previously.[28] The case then receded from the press reporting and public view for a while, until Patterson escaped from Alabama's notorious Atmore State Prison Farm in April 1943. He was recaptured after five days and sent back to Kilby Prison, but five years later he escaped again, headed for Atlanta, Chattanooga and Detroit, then onto Harlem, New York, and by spring 1949 had begun collaboration with Earl Conrad on *Scottsboro Boy*.[29]

Patterson's account was the first key source to appear for several years, and it reignited discussion over the rape case, Southern prison conditions before and after the Second World War, and whether there had been any significant changes or improvements to the 'racial situation', particularly as Patterson was rearrested by FBI agents in June 1950.[30]

Two years later he was dead.[31] Patterson's book is divided into three main sections that correspond to different phases of his penal life: 'The Big Frame' 1931–7 centres on the period of the trials; 'Murderers' Home' refers to the six years he spent at Atmore in southern Alabama; and then the last six-year period at Kilby, near Montgomery. In the absence of a complete published historical study of Alabama's prisons in the twentieth century, Patterson's account of the different institutions in which he was incarcerated remains an indispensable primary source.

Clarence Norris was similarly under sentence of death for five years: 'I had so many dates to die, I can't remember them all. Living that way, waiting, wondering and hoping is hell.'[32] Following commutation of his third death sentence in July 1937, he spent a further ten years in Kilby Prison. He and Andy Wright were paroled to a local lumber company in January 1944 to conditions not dissimilar to those of the prison camps, and so both broke parole nine months later. Norris headed for New York City. He was persuaded to return to Alabama by NAACP officials, then paroled again in September 1946 to dig ditches for gas lines, but fled again to Cleveland where he took his brother's identity and was employed in a series of unskilled jobs there and in New York City before eventually settling down there with his third wife in the 1960s.[33] In November 1976 the State of Alabama granted Norris, the last surviving 'Scottsboro Boy', an unconditional pardon on the grounds of innocence, based ironically on the same evidence that had been used to convict him seventy-five years previously. Norris' collaboration with Sybil Washington began prior to his receipt of the pardon from Alabama Governor George Wallace in 1976.[34]

V

All six works underline the miserable physical conditions of confinement: cramped, overcrowded and unsanitary bunkhouses and cells plagued with rats and cockroaches; filthy bedding and stinking clothing crawling with lice; constant noise and lack of sleep; scarce toiletries, writing paper and pencils thus inmates' reliance on outside financial and material assistance or the prison commissary's inflated prices; and the monotonous and limited prison diet that was heavy in beans and pork products but lacking in vitamin-rich fish, fruit and vegetables and frequently included rancid and stale food. Meals were eaten in silence at long wooden benches.[35] They detail also the exploitation of inmate labour and the range of methods used to discipline and punish inmates and to maintain racial and gender hierarchies. These included arbitrary corporal punishments, sexual and physical assault, as well as verbal abuse and solitary confinement.[36]

O'Hare declared that 'Food was one of the chronic sources of bitterness and friction in the prison, and, despite all protests and public scandals concerning it, no lasting improvements have resulted.' Inmates were aggrieved that milk and meat from livestock at the prison farm were sold for private profit rather than to feed the inmates. The undernourished women who had no outside sources of food supply were condemned to a 'process of slow starvation'.[37] Underfed male inmates in Florida road camps supplemented their weekend fare by trapping and skinning gophers, rabbits and possums and cooking them on a campfire with sweet potatoes purchased from a local 'cracker neighbour'.[38] Prisoners at Atmore similarly cooked and ate rabbits, squirrels, mud turtles, hogs and possums, or bought, with guard help, ham hock, eggs and occasional chickens also from poor farmers living near to the prison farm.[39] As a major prisoner grievance, poor food was thus at the centre of prisoner work stoppages, strikes and more serious riots, as at Kilby in the mid-1940s.[40] Inedible food also spurred a protest by black-and-white work squads at Atmore in the same period. This sit-down protest involved the agreement of both groups of inmates and was soon broken up by well-armed guards, but it highlighted the commonalities of prisoner experience and grievance in a system that privileged white over black, as discussed further below.[41]

Notoriety brought material advantages to the Scottsboro defendants. Patterson recalled that whilst on death row at Kilby Prison, 'From the mail we got we knew people were het up about us. It came to us in a flood, packages of cigarettes and candy; and in the letters was money, dollar bills and five-dollar bills, stamps and cheering words.'[42] Much to sheriff and prison officials' disgust, this included regular $5 per month payments from the ILD as well as more substantial amounts, such as $25 per month from heiress Nancy Cunard. Hundreds of dollars arrived for the 'boys' in the period between the second and third trials, and this made a substantial difference to their incarceration, including access to better food.[43] Patterson recollected,

> The way you bought from the commissary was this: when the convict waiters brought breakfast you gave them a written-out order for what you wanted at lunch; lunchtime he would bring you cakes, milk, candy, and canned goods – along with the regular prison slops you got anyway. You gave the convict a tip then and put in an order for the night meal.[44]

Most of the Scottsboro defendants moved back and forth between Jefferson County jail and Kilby Prison during the first three years of their incarceration in Alabama's penal system and likened the jail to 'a convict's paradise' where inmates 'could buy women, clothes, food, [and] liquor'.[45] A two-day protest and stand-off between the 'boys' and guards at Jefferson County jail in 1931 had led to better food there also. The irony of their situation was noted by Patterson:

> Sometimes we laughed about it, the ups and downs. Outside we were hobos; inside the prison we had some respect. By our being in jail we were getting the food there that our families never was able to buy us. It was a twist of the case we were in. We took advantage because we didn't know when we'd go back to death row.[46]

When Norris became part of the general Kilby prisoner population from 1937, he would pay the 'kitchen trusties three dollars a week to bring me the food I wanted. Ham and eggs, steaks, chicken, fish, desserts, and it would be cooked just the way I liked it'.[47]

O'Hare remarked that prisoners were always hungry for food and for love.[48] But sex rather than love dominated prison life and prisoner chat. Sex as a normal reaction to long periods of denial, as self-preservation, as perversion, as predatory or degenerating vice, and as prostitution features in all six works, most graphically in *Scottsboro Boy* and in passing in *I Am a Fugitive*. O'Hare denounced the 'negress trusty or stool pigeon' who oversaw the sale of sex in the women's ward at Jefferson City and the web of corruption that ensured sex commerce flourished: 'Only by deceit and lies, only by submitting to the most vicious forms of bribery and blackmail, could the clean women escape having the most unspeakable forms of sex perversions forced upon them.'[49] Both Patterson and Norris could regularly 'take their fun' with female prisoners at Jefferson County jail by paying guards three to five dollars each time. The women who were pimped by guards to service male inmates and the guards themselves receive little more than passing misogynistic comment from Norris and Patterson and scarce sympathy as they were 'Not what you would call good girls.'[50] Brown also detailed the sexual abuse of female inmates by officials and was outraged by the 1947 death of a black female inmate shot by a prison guard because she refused to have sex with him, as well as the cover story that she had assaulted the guard and was shot whilst attempting to escape.[51]

When Patterson was sent to the all-male Atmore prison farm, there were few opportunities for heterosexual relations, and inmates became either 'gal-boys' or 'wolves' and consequently enmeshed in violent and abusive bargains and systems. Gal-boys were commodities to be used and sold on, and so sex was just another prison racket which both fed into and promoted the aggression and hypermasculinism of prison survival. Within a short time of arrival, Patterson 'had taken a gal-boy, whupped a wolf, and set myself up as a devil.'[52] The inevitability of situational homosexuality is illuminated by a remark to Rustin by a long-time chain gang inmate: 'I hated punks when I came to jail. Now I turn over myself when I get the chance. And you-all would too if you had ten years to do in this hole.'[53] Norris was more circumspect than Patterson when discussing his own sexual profile but, like Brown, linked the violence of prison life directly to homosexual activities and rivalries.[54]

VI

The prison contract labour system's profiteering from the exploitation of inmates' labour is a dominant theme in *In Prison*. Private contractors paid the state for the prisoners' labour, the state provided the buildings and power sources, and each year Jefferson City's two thousand inmates produced millions of dollars of industrial goods and farm products, but each received a pittance in return. Along with the other 100 women, O'Hare was hired out to the Oberman Manufacturing Company to make overalls which bore free world labels, in an unventilated and badly lit prison factory and with sewing machines in bad repair.[55] The 'coarse, vulgar, egotistical, bigoted, intolerant' and sadistic twenty-year-old male overseer arbitrarily meted out punishments to women who failed to meet the volume of tasks that was impossible to achieve. All women worked, including syphilitic and tubercular inmates producing baby garments full of bacteria.[56] Similar themes of prisoner contamination of free world innocents appear in Brown's account.[57]

Long-term prisoners like Brown, Norris and Patterson were engaged in different forms of prison labour over time. After spending much of his early sentence in solitary confinement, Brown repaired roads, cleared swamps, cut down timber and worked in the prison canning and tobacco factories.[58] Norris lost a finger to a machine in the Kilby prison cotton mills, which continued to illegally churn out shirts that were sold on the open market with fake labels to disguise their prison origin.[59] At Atmore, Patterson cut rice in the prison rice fields, was a yardman tasked with keeping the prison camp clean and orderly, cleared farm ditches, and at Kilby was a sweeper in the cotton mill, cleaned out the death chamber after executions, and worked in the cannery.[60] As public interest in the Scottsboro case waned, Patterson and the others received fewer financial donations from well-wishers. Patterson became very active in the prison rackets at Atmore then Kilby, keeping dope or drugs for white inmates for a price, organizing prostitution with women visiting from outside and with animals, running card and dice games, dominating the trade in bootleg liquor, providing a pawnbroker service, and selling prison shoes, seed and fertilizer to outsiders, much of it with guard complicity and assistance.[61] Patterson's entrepreneurialism was boosted by his position as cell boy in both institutions. His most profitable racket was the prison store he ran from his Kilby cell that rivalled the official commissary in its range of merchandise and extension of credit to inmate customers, but came under attack in 1946–7 as a new warden arrived.[62]

Burns worked from dawn to dusk in chains in a quarry, on the public roads, as a camp yardman, in the soil-pit gang, and in gruelling road construction. As he explained:

> By sundown every prisoner is completely exhausted from the long hours of back-breaking toil in the terrific heat of a semi-tropical sun. Covered with a slime created of the mixture of human sweat and the dust of the dirt roads, we go back to camp, weary and fatigued of body; expressionless of soul and mind as men in a drug-induced coma.[63]

As road labourers, Burns and Rustin were part of small work crews transported from prison camps to worksites in prison trucks and under armed guard. Their labour was directed by the walking bosses, and they toiled at all times within sight of the guards. The prison camps varied in size, from 100 men in Georgia counties to 44 at Roxboro, North Carolina.[64] Newcomers had to be taught to handle picks and shovels by fellow convicts. Rustin was quickly advised to keep working and make no complaint, despite the unbearable pain racking through every part of his body: 'Quit cryin'; Quit dyin'; Give dat white boss; Sum'pin' on your time.'[65] Talking back to the bosses and not working hard enough in their eyes were sure ways to earn a beating.

Rustin witnessed one inmate who complained that he was not able to work even though the doctor said he was fine after being 'hung on the bars' for seventy-two hours.[66] Burns told of arbitrary and sickening floggings when he was on the Fulton County gang in the early 1920s. At Troup County in 1930 he recalled use of the 'jack', a form of stocks where convicts' hands and ankles were locked into holes and they were left there suspended in mid-air for up to an hour, 'pickshacks' or thirty-inch/10-pound bars of steel locked to convicts' legs whilst they worked, the 'La Grange' iron collars padlocked to inmates' necks and chained to the floor at night; and, sweatboxes for shirkers and escapees.[67] All six authors reported arbitrary beatings with straps, fists, blackjacks, kickings, sexual assaults, verbal abuse, forced drinking of castor oil (by inmates being sent to 'the hole' or solitary confinement) and medical neglect which were all utilized by guards and officials to punish, brutalize and degrade inmates. Patterson received twenty-one 'licks' after a knife was found on his person and was whipped again in the 1940s for stealing prison meat.[68] A bridle was included in the diet of punishments for women inmates at Jefferson City to be used for petty infractions.[69] Such methods often existed alongside approved sanctions such as solitary confinement on reduced rations, withholding of privileges, and forfeiture of gain or good time credits for early release. Information on prison discipline is also found in newspaper exposés, grand jury investigations, and inmate complaints to and by lawyers, but inclusion in the autobiographical accounts was clearly calculated to excite reader revulsion and public indignation.

Many of the guard-inmate confrontations and punishments meted out were racially motivated. Patterson and Norris recalled physical assaults by local deputies and National Guardsmen at Gadsden County Jail and being hit with big leather straps whilst on death row at Kilby 'just because I was a Scottsboro boy'. Norris survived at least one poisoning attempt by a white inmate. Consequently, they routinely carried knives concealed in the flies of their pants for self-defence.[70] Inmates often fought back, sometimes gaining concessions such as better food, more visitors and increased exercise privileges.[71] However, temporary prisoner power could invite further violence from officials, as in the 1935 general strike at Raiford. Brown described how prison 'rats' or snitches were targeted by some inmates and prisoners fired steel darts at the guard captain. There was considerable physical destruction of cell blocks. Once order was restored, Raiford guards beat the ringleaders with blackjacks; some of these prisoners were then sent out to different road prisons distributed around the state for additional working over by captains and guards there. Indeed, Brown's account is full of incidents of guards assaulting, even murdering, inmates and escaping sanction because of official collusion and cover-up.[72]

All six authors complained about the lack of professionalism amongst prison officials, captains, wardens, and the guard corps, and were contemptuous of the individuals whose own sense of powerlessness spurred a willingness to demean, humiliate and mistreat inmates, especially if they were 'Yankees' or non-white. The power of wardens, guards and jailers could be especially galling for individuals of higher education and who had social standing in the free world, such as O'Hare and Rustin. Guards and captains were lower-class white men, usually with little education and little training and no prospects for advancement. They performed a job that few on the outside were willing to do but many were willing to criticise. These men – 'the worst sort of redneck, ignorant, uneducated cracker' who 'were illiterate and trained only in the art of handling convicts and enslaved negroes [*sic*]' – were despised by inmates and outsiders alike.[73] Matrons were no better. O'Hare wrote:

> One of my most horrible memories is that of the voices of our keepers. They never spoke to us as normal humans speak; they either snarled at us, cursed us, or screeched at us, and those snarling, rasping, hateful voices still haunt my dreams.[74]

Like Brown, another long-serving inmate, Patterson offered several astute observations on the plight of the southern prison guard whose life 'wasn't much happier than a convict's'.[75] They also were better able to differentiate between the different personality types and mention the few more reasonable personnel who were less tolerant of convict bullying and abuse.[76] Patterson recalled the kindness of one prison guard who was sympathetic towards the Scottsboro defendants but committed suicide: 'That boy meant something to me and to the rest of us. The Guards knew that. That's why they told us [he killed himself]. He was like many nice Christian white folks there who didn't like what was going on.'[77] Drawing on his core philosophical and ideological principles and faith in the 'healing and therapeutic power of forgiveness and non-violence', Rustin went out of his way to avoid incurring the camp captain's hostility and disdain. He crafted an uneasy but more positive relationship with the captain, even communicating by letter his desire to achieve good conduct and acknowledging the captain's small kindnesses in providing cigarettes and soft drinks.[78] In his valorization of the innate humanity of keepers and inmates (something that is not repeated in the other five works), Rustin concluded,

> While one must recognize the real limitations for basic change in an authoritarian set-up such as the guard-inmate relationship, it is fair, it seems to me, to point out that our experiences do indicate that even in trying circumstances (for both the Captain and for me) it was impossible to reach a working solution without losing one's self-respect or submitting completely to outside authority.[79]

VII

Racial segregation, white supremacy, institutional racism and sexism, and differential treatment that privileged white southern inmates were embedded in all parts of southern criminal justice systems during the 'Jim Crow' period, and its legacy endures into the twenty-first century.[80] The authors here served their time in two-tier prison systems where race, class, gender and indeed sectionalism (including hostility towards and 'special punishments' for northern Yankee offenders) defined their treatment. Patterson described Morgan County jail as 'an old crumble-down place made of brick turning back into sand … condemned a couple of years before as not fitting for white folks – which meant it was fit for us'. Norris remembered,

> Time in Kilby was one gray day after another … I knew I was there because I was a 'nigger'. An animal to be locked up as in a zoo. Except the zoo animals are treated much better than the black men in Kilby Prison.[81]

Small acts of defiance could be as meaningful and important as more overt protests. African American inmates were expected to take their hats off in the presence of white folks. When Rustin was given a cap by the camp captain he resolved never to wear it:

> I had noticed the way men bowed obsequiously and lifted their hats off their heads and held them in the air whenever they spoke to the guard. I had decided I would rather be cold than behave in this servile way. I thanked the Captain for the cap and put it on my head and wore it until lunchtime. After lunch I put it in my pocket, never to wear it again in the presence of the Captain or the guards.[82]

Initially Patterson had embraced religion whilst in jail, but he later became increasingly angry at the ways in which prison ministers used it to exact deference and to reinforce racial subordination: 'Most of all I saw the white man wanted a black man to get down on his knees and be a pray-man. They just loved that. Then you were their "nigger". That alone taught me it couldn't be such a good thing for black folks to be so fetched up in all that Bible stuff.'[83]

O'Hare likened her imprisonment to chattel slavery but her tone was more of indignation than of sympathy for the degradations suffered by generations of African and African American slaves or their descendants trapped in the debt peonage, convict leasing and chain gang systems of the early twentieth-century South.[84] But O'Hare did lay bare the stark class disparities in the administration of US justice, particularly the non-existent or inadequate legal representation for people without means, the inability of elite male judges to understand lower or working-class lives, and the ways in which money and political connections enabled privileged offenders to avoid imprisonment altogether. According to O'Hare, the blatant primary role of prison was to discipline and punish the poor. As she explained, 'The whole system of criminal law has become a voracious cormorant that devours the bodies, brains, and souls of the poor.'[85]

The accounts also demonstrate that men and women could spend years together in captivity but in many ways they remained as strangers. Inmates referred to each other by nicknames, aliases or pseudonyms such as 'Purple', 'Easy Life', 'Softshoe', 'Shorty' and 'Buttercup'. Thus, like the guards discussed above, the authors frequently describe their fellow inmates in terms of caricature. Whilst each institution was a distinct community that provided support and survival networks for convicts and guards, as well as incidence of confrontation and resistance, inmate bonds of friendship were frequently based on temporary alliances and convenience, and collective acts of resistance could be undermined by participants who became 'snitches'.[86] Further, both Burns and

O'Hare viewed themselves as a breed apart from their fellow convicts – O'Hare's made no bones about her intellectual superiority – and their suspicion of and resentment towards non-white inmates is evident. Yet both relied on the prisoner networks and communities they so often despised in order to endure and survive the material deprivations and physical challenges of their penal lives, to avoid incurring the wrath of guards or captains and to ensure receipt of food or provisions.[87] Furthermore, Burns' 1922 escape was facilitated by a willing black inmate using his pick to loosen Burns' ankle chains.[88]

Similarly, masculine competitiveness infuses much of the narrative and tone of the works by Patterson, Norris, Brown and Burns. Getting one over on the guards was an important marker of manly courage, survival and bravado. For example, when Patterson became a successful racketeer at Atmore and Kilby (as noted above) and in the desire by Patterson and Norris to survive their prison ordeal rather than to submit to suicide or die at the hands of guards or other inmates. Survival meant victory. Patterson declared, 'If I didn't kill myself it was because I hated the state of Alabama more than I wanted to kill myself.'[89] Brown delighted in taunting the prison superintendent, threatening on one occasion to expose to the press the murders of inmates in 1929–30 that he claimed were being covered up, unless he was transferred to a road camp away from the prison farm. He was transferred but then returned to solitary confinement at Raiford two weeks later.[90] Enduring prolonged periods in solitary rather than capitulating to the regime or committing suicide therefore became a way of getting back at prison officials, like Patterson and Norris above. In their conversations with each other, male inmates often reconstructed past lives full of hypermasculine swagger and bravado. Rustin for instance noted that recreation time at Roxboro revolved around six main activities: 'dirty dozens' where two men tried to outdo each other with 'grossly offensive description of the opponent's female relatives'; telling exaggerated stories about sexual conquests and sexual relations; 'stealing "for the thrill of it"' from other inmates; gambling; and gossiping.[91]

Southern criminal justice systems and penal institutions were soaked in corruption. This took many forms: from inmates paying guards for favours or goodwill, to inmates running rackets and skimming from the state and fellow convicts, to the sale of paroles and pardons, to the use of cheap convict labour by private corporations, to the employment of 'snitches' and 'stool pigeons' by prison authorities to spy on fellow inmates and report back.[92] This meant reform and rehabilitation were largely impossible. Moreover, the central message of all six works was that the prison in all forms was a failing institution that contributed little towards crime prevention. Time spent in prison hindered rather than encouraged men and women to go straight. Rustin noted for example that,

> Neither this boy who reluctantly stole by compulsion … nor the homosexuals could be helped by life on the chain gang. Nor could society be protected, for in a short time these men and thousands like them return to society not only uncured but with heightened resentment and a desire for revenge.[93]

Recidivism and return were almost guaranteed for many inmates because at the end of their sentences they had no money, few clothes, and no jobs and were thus liable to be arrested for vagrancy.

For those who did not return, success in the free world remained difficult to achieve. As a fugitive living under his brother's name, Norris struggled with employment, relationships with women, and gambling, which in part was a legacy of 15 years of imprisonment. Yet none of the authors were prison abolitionists; they demanded the eradication of abuses and the implementation of meaningful reform, and each account (except that of Patterson) includes some optimism that prisons could be rescued from the webs of corruption and political neglect that surrounded them and that punishment should not be the domain of the poor, non-white and powerless.[94] Norris for instance visited his former ILD lawyer Sam Leibowitz, now a New York Supreme Court judge, in 1956:

> I told him I believed in capital punishment, used correctly. I can't see a thing wrong with it, if the person is guilty of a crime that merits the supreme penalty. But when whites deserve it, they should be executed just as the blacks are. In my time the system was lopsided. During the five years I was on death row, only one white guy went to the electric chair.[95]

VIII

Yet did the six books make any difference to prison conditions in the South? Each publication met with different public reactions. Burns' bitter denunciation of Georgia's chain gangs remains a classic text. It focussed attention on Georgia's brutal penal system whilst Hollywood did much to shape public opposition to southern penal practices.[96] In the period after the Second World War, the book and additional newspaper exposures of southern penal conditions led to successful opposition to extradition of southern fugitives found to be living in, or who had been arrested in, northern states.[97] Rustin's account led to an investigation into prison conditions in the North Carolina camps, similar to the investigations in Georgia in the early 1940s.[98] By contrast, Brown's exposure of conditions in Florida has been largely overlooked. O'Hare continued to agitate for prison reform following her release, investigated the abuses of the contract-labour system in US prisons and eventually became assistant director of the California Department of Penology in the late 1930s.[99] Her study had been ignored by professional criminologists in the 1920s, even though the first federal women's prison was opened in 1927, but warranted greater attention from federal prison administrators in the late 1930s.[100]

For Foucault, the prison's regimes of isolation and surveillance were to transform inmates into docile and submissive subjects.[101] For southern prison officials, the disciplinary power of the prison was geared towards labour exploitation, and the creation of a predominately black docile and submissive convict labour force which would produce farm and industrial products to offset the costs of their confinement.[102] Prison reports paid lip service to reform and rehabilitation but conditions in the prison farms, camps and chain gangs offered few incentives for reform and inadequate tools such as meaningful work, education, and skills to equip ex-offenders for their successful reintegration into free society.[103] Incarceration continued to carry a powerful stigma and these six individual accounts were socially, politically and penally constructed to challenge the stains of conviction and incarceration that were keenly felt by each author. They wrote to passionately affirm the value of their own identities and voices and to reject the penal identities imposed on them by others. For the non-white authors it was important also to reject the racial oppression and racial hierarchies embedded in the disciplinary apparatus of southern prisons. In reclaiming the self and individual identity, each account does therefore have crucial political and ethical impetus. Historians are often distrustful of autobiographies, viewing them primarily as acts of composition and performative views of the life and the self. All six accounts here offer distinctly personalized and individualized negotiations 'between events (the stuff of history) and what we make of them (the history we write)', but they are still valuable resources for studying the lives of inmates and for reconstructing the inner workings of early twentieth-century carceral institutions.[104]

Notes

1. K.R. O'Hare (1976 edition) *In Prison* (Seattle and London: University of Washington Press); R.E. Burns (1997 edition) *I am a Fugitive from a Georgia Chain Gang!* (Athens and London: The University of Georgia Press); H. Patterson and E. Conrad (1969 edition) *Scottsboro Boy* (Toronto: Collier Books); A.R. Brown (1968) *Freedom from Florida Chains Illustrated* (New York: Carlton Press) and C. Norris and S.D. Washington (1979) *The Last of the Scottsboro Boys: An Autobiography* (New York: G. P. Putnam's Sons). For this chapter, I used the PDF copy of the original manuscript of B. Rustin (1949) 'Report on Twenty-two Days on the Chain Gang at Roxboro, North Carolina' from the Document Collection Center at Yale University, available at: www.documents.law.yale.edu/sites/default/files/Official-report -chain-gang.pdf (accessed 14 May 2015). However, the report appears also in D.W. Carbado and D. Weise (eds) (2015 edition) *Time on Two Crosses: The Collected Writings of Bayard Rustin* (New York: Cleis Press Inc.).

2. Recent historical studies of southern prisons in the twentieth-century Jim Crow period include: E.W. Rise (1995) *The Martinsville Seven: Race, Rape, and Capital Punishment* (Charlottesville: University of Virginia Press); A. Lichtenstein (1996) *Twice the Work of Free Labor: The Political Economy of Convict Labor in the New South* (New York: Verso); M.J. Mancini (1996) *One Dies, Get Another: Convict Leasing in the American South, 1866–1928* (Columbia: University of South Carolina Press); D.M. Oshinsky (1997) '*Worse Than Slavery*': *Parchman Farm and the Ordeal of Jim Crow Justice* (New York: Prentice Hall); M.A. Myers (1998) *Race, Labor, and Punishment in the New South* (Columbus: Ohio State University Press); G. Williams O'Brien (1999) *The Color of the Law: Race, Violence, and Justice in the Post-World War II South* (Chapel Hill: University of North Carolina Press); D. Blackmon (2008) *Slavery by Another Name: The Re-enslavement of Black Americans from the Civil War to World War II* (New York: Random House); R. Perkinson (2010) *Texas Tough: The Rise of America's Prison Empire* (New York: Metropolitan Books); V.M.L. Miller (2012) *Hard Labor and Hard Time: Florida's 'Sunshine Prison' and Chain Gangs* (Gainesville: University

of Florida Press); E. Blue (2012) *Doing Time in the Depression: Everyday Life in Texas and California Prisons* (New York: New York University Press); S. Haley (2013) '"Like I Was a Man": Chain Gangs, Gender, and the Domestic Carceral Sphere in Jim Crow Georgia', *Signs*, Vol. 39, No. 1, pp. 53–77, and T.L. LeFlouria (2015) *Chained in Silence: Black Women and Convict Labor in the New South* (Chapel Hill: University of North Carolina Press).

3. H.B. Franklin (1977) 'The Literature of the American Prison', *The Massachusetts Review*, Vol. 18, No. 1, pp. 51–78 at p. 51.

4. Patterson and Conrad, *Scottsboro Boy*, pp. 40–2 and 208.

5. G.T. Couser (1989) *Altered Egos: Authority in American Autobiography* (New York: Oxford University Press), p. 20 and p. 248. These issues are long-standing and featured in the first reviews. See for example, G.L. Joughin (1950) 'Review of *Scottsboro Boy*', *Antioch Review*, Vol. 10, No. 3, pp. 422–4; J.L. Langhorne (1950) 'Review of *Scottsboro Boy*', *Journal of Negro History*, Vol. 35, No. 4, pp. 463–5. Similar concerns surrounded Alex Haley's collaboration with Malcolm X to produce *The Autobiography of Malcolm X*, first published by Gove Press in New York in 1965. See also, P.J. Eakin (1993) 'Malcom X and the Limits of Autobiography', in W. Andrews (ed.) *African-American Autobiography: A Collection of Critical Essays* (Englewood Cliffs, NJ: Prentice-Hall), pp. 152–61; R.B. Stepto (1991 edition) *From Behind the Veil: A Study of Afro-American Narrative* (Urbana and Chicago: University of Illinois Press) and K. Mostern (1999) *Autobiography and Black Identity Politics: Racialization in Twentieth-century America* (Cambridge: Cambridge University Press).

6. J.A. Miller (2009) *Remembering Scottsboro: The Legacy of an Infamous Trial* (Princeton and Oxford: Princeton University Press), p. 186.

7. T.S. Freeman (2009) 'The Rise of Prison Literature', *Huntington Library Quarterly*, Vol. 72, No. 2, pp. 133–46. Famous examples of radical prisoner life writing include A. Berkman (1912) *Prison Memoirs of an Anarchist* (New York: Mother Earth Publishing Co.) and E. Debs (1927) *Walls and Bars* (Chicago: Socialist Party Press). For the ordinary offender, see D. Lowrie (1912) *My Life in Prison* (London: John Lane, The Bodley Head).

8. Franklin, 'The Literature of the American Prison', pp. 51–2 and 73–6.

9. See, for example, G. Jackson (1970) *Soledad Brother: The Prison Letters of George Jackson* (Chicago: Chicago Review Press); G. Jackson (1990 edition) *Blood in My Eye* (Baltimore: Black Classic Press); A.Y. Davis (1974) *An Autobiography* (New York: Random House); E. Cleaver (1967) *Soul on Ice* (New York: McGraw Hill); E. Cleaver (1978) *Soul on Fire* (London: Hodder); E. Cleaver (2015) *Target Zero: A Life in Writing* (London: St. Martin's Press). White inmate accounts of southern prisons that appeared in the 1970s included G. Harsh (1971) *Lonesome Road* (New York: W.W. Norton); and A. Baker (1973) *Stolen Sweets* (New York: Saturday Review Press).

10. Couser, *Altered Egos*, p. 26. See also C. Smith (2009) *Prison and the American Imagination* (New Haven, CN: Yale University Press), pp. 20–1.

11. R. McLennan (2012) *American Autobiography* (Edinburgh: Edinburgh University Press), pp. 17–8 and 27.

12. P.J. Eakin (1992) *Touching the World: Reference in Autobiography* (Princeton, NJ: Princeton University Press), pp. 139–41 and 178–9.

13. 'Woman Sentenced Five Years in Pen for Opposing Draft', *Atlanta Journal-Constitution*, 15 December 1917, p. 1; 'Pardoned Woman Prisoner to Visit Candidate Debs', *Atlanta Journal-Constitution*, 30 June 1920, p. 4 and 'Seize Mrs. Kate O'Hare at Home of Friend; Party of Men Carry Off Socialist Pardoned by Wilson for Draft Law Crime', *New York Times*, 2 July 1921, p. 1.

14. O'Hare, *In Prison*, p. xxxviii; S.M. Miller (1993) *From Prairie to Prison: The Life of Social Activist Kate Richards O'Hare* (Columbia: University of Missouri Press). A selection of documents, including the prison letters, and other information on O'Hare, can be found on the Women and Social Movements in the United States, 1600–2000 project Web pages: see http://womhist.alexanderstreet.com/kro/intro.htm (accessed 15 May 2015). In 1920 there were only 150 federal women prisoners; 250 in 1922; 563 in 1923, and most were non-violent offenders, convicted of drug and alcohol offences under the Harrison Drug Act (1914) and Volstead Act (1919).

15. Preface to O'Hare, *In Prison*, p. v.

16. Brown, *Freedom from Florida Chains*, pp. 35–9.

17. Miller, *Hard Labor and Hard Time*, pp. 268–9.

18. Brown, *Freedom from Florida Chains*, p. 21.

19. 'A Fugitive from Georgia's Prison System', *New York Times*, 31 January 1932, p. BR4 and Burns (1997 edition) *I am a Fugitive*, pp. 38–46.

20. Burns (1997 edition) *I am a Fugitive*, p. 102; '"Fugitive" Author Arrested in Jersey', *New York Times*, 15 December 1932, p. 3; 'Chain-gang Convict Fights Extradition', *New York Times*, 16 December 1932, p. 3 and 'Georgia Sends North for Robert E. Burns', *Atlanta Journal-Constitution*, 16 December 1932, p. 1.

21. 'Arnall Asks Pardon for "Fugitive" Burns', *Atlanta Journal-Constitution*, 21 December 1943, p. 1. Additional accounts of the case were published by Burns' brother. See V.G. Burns (1942) *Out of These Chains* (Los Angeles: New World Books) and V.G. Burns (1968) *The Man Who Broke a Thousand Chains: The Story of Social Reformation of the Prisons of the South* (Washington: Acropolis Books). More details on Burns and the genesis of the book are found in M.J. Mancini (1997) 'Foreword to the Brown Thrasher Edition', of Burns, *I Am a Fugitive from a Georgia Chain Gang!*. See also V. Miller (2011) 'Films about Prison' in A.L. Wood (ed.) *The New Encyclopedia of Southern Culture: Volume 19 – Violence* (Chapel Hill: University of North Carolina Press), pp. 67–70.

22. D. Levine (2000) *Bayard Rustin and the Civil Rights Movement* (New Brunswick: Rutgers University Press), pp. 40–9.

23. *Morgan v. Virginia*, 328 U.S. 373 (1946) and G.N. Rosenberg (2nd edition, 2008) *The Hollow Hope: Can Courts Bring about Social Change* (Chicago: University of Chicago Press), pp. 64–5.

24. Rustin, 'Report on Twenty-two Days on the Chain Gang', p. 1. See for example, R. Arsenault (2004) 'You Don't Have to Ride Jim Crow: CORE and the 1947 Journey of Reconciliation', in G. Fellman (ed.) *Before Brown: Civil Rights and White Backlash in the Modern South* (Tuscaloosa: University of Alabama Press), pp. 21–67; M. Mollin (2006) *Radical Pacifism in Modern America: Egalitarianism and Protest* (Philadelphia: University of Pennsylvania Press); D. Catsam (2009) *Freedom's Main Line: The Journey of Reconciliation and the Freedom Rides* (Lexington: University Press of Kentucky) and J. Podair (2009) *Bayard Rustin: American Dreamer* (Lanham, MD: Rowman & Littlefield Publishers, Inc.).

25. The other seven defendants were Andy Wright, Roy Wright, Eugene Williams, Olen Montgomery, Willie Roberson, Charlie Weems and Ozie Powell.

26. The first full account of the case was D.T. Carter (1969) *Scottsboro: A Tragedy of the American South* (Baton Rouge: Louisiana State University Press). More recent studies include J. Goodman (1994) *Stories of Scottsboro* (New York: Pantheon). The US Supreme Court cases were *Powell v. Alabama* 287 U.S. 45 (1932) and *Norris v. Alabama* 294 U.S. 587 (1935).

27. Miller, *Remembering Scottsboro*, p. 170. Patterson and Norris were never friends and were frequently at odds. See Norris and Washington, *The Last of the Scottsboro Boys*, pp. 156–7.

28. Ozie Powell's rape sentence was curtailed, but he continued to serve a separate sentence of twenty years for cutting a sheriff's deputy. See Patterson and Conrad, *Scottsboro Boy*, p. 75 and Norris and Washington, *The Last of the Scottsboro Boys*, pp. 163–6.

29. Miller, *Remembering Scottsboro*, pp. 172, 186.

30. Ibid., p. 191.

31. 'Scottsboro Boy Patterson Dying of Cancer in Pen', *Atlanta Journal-Constitution*, 26 June 1952, p. 2 and Goodman, *Stories of Scottsboro*, p. 381.

32. Norris and Washington, *The Last of the Scottsboro Boys*, p. 51. Norris was 'hoboing' during the economic misery of 1931 when he was arrested for vagrancy and spent ten days on a city chain gang labouring in a quarry; this was several weeks before his Scottsboro arrest. See ibid., p. 36.

33. Norris and Washington, *The Last of the Scottsboro Boys*, pp. 198–207, 213–15.

34. M. Wazlavek, 'Norris Receives Pardon', *Atlanta Journal-Constitution*, 30 November 1976, p. 3A. For additional documents, oral interviews and historical commentary on Norris, see K. Mbiassi Kinshasa (1997) *The Man from Scottsboro: Clarence Norris and the Infamous 1931 Alabama Rape Trial, in His Own Words* (Jefferson, NC and London: McFarland and Company, Inc.).

35. See, for example, Burns (1997 edition) *I am a Fugitive*, pp. 47–57, 141 and 172–5; Rustin, 'Report on Twenty-two Days on the Chain Gang', pp. 14–15; Norris and Washington, *The Last of the Scottsboro Boys*, pp. 50–1 and Burns, *I am a Fugitive*, pp. 49, 52–3 and 143.

36. See, for example, Burns, *I am a Fugitive*, pp. 54–5 and 155–7 and Rustin, 'Report on Twenty-two Days on the Chain Gang', pp. 23–5.

37. O'Hare, *In Prison*, pp. 64 and 86–9. Norris and Washington, *The Last of the Scottsboro Boys*, pp. 50–1 and Burns, *I am a Fugitive*, pp. 49, 52–3 and 143.

38. Brown, *Freedom from Florida Chains*, p. 213.

39. Patterson and Conrad, *Scottsboro Boy*, pp. 101–3.

40. Norris and Washington, *The Last of the Scottsboro Boys*, pp. 188–9.

41. Patterson and Conrad, *Scottsboro Boy*, pp. 147–8. James Miller's more positive assessment of this incident emphasizes its 'the interracial solidarity' as 'an unmistakable salute to the contemporary interracial militancy of the CIO (Congress of Industrial Organizations)' union movement. But such incidents lacked the heightened politicization and radicalization of inmates that was so apparent in the late 1960s and early 1970s. See Miller, *Remembering Scottsboro*, p. 187.

42. Patterson and Conrad, *Scottsboro Boy*, p. 35.

43. Ibid., pp. 42–4 and 59.

44. Ibid., p. 44.

45. Norris and Washington, *The Last of the Scottsboro Boys*, p. 149.

46. Patterson and Conrad, *Scottsboro Boy*, p. 59.

47. Norris and Washington, *The Last of the Scottsboro Boys*, pp. 149 and 179.

48. O'Hare, *In Prison*, p. 125.

49. Ibid., pp. 112 and 130.

50. Norris and Washington, *The Last of the Scottsboro Boys*, pp. 149–50; Patterson and Conrad, *Scottsboro Boy*, pp. 58–9 and Miller, *Remembering Scottsboro*, p. 188.

51. Brown, *Freedom from Florida Chains*, pp. 267 and 333–4.

52. Patterson and Conrad, *Scottsboro Boy*, pp. 92–6, 98 and 135 and Miller, *Remembering Scottsboro*, p. 189. For similar observations on prison sexual relations, see Brown, *Freedom from Florida Chains*, pp. 165 and 284–5.

53. Rustin, 'Report on Twenty-two Days on the Chain Gang', p. 13. Homosexuality was illegal across the United States, and as a gay man in the mid-twentieth century, Rustin had first-hand experiences of hostility and backlash, for example, his forced resignation from the Fellowship of Reconciliation (FOR) in 1953, after his arrest and conviction on charges related to homosexual activity. See M.G. Long (2012) *Martin Luther King Jr., Homosexuality, and the Early Gay Rights Movement: Keeping the Dream Straight* (New York: Palgrave Macmillan), p. 77.

54. Norris and Washington, *The Last of the Scottsboro Boys*, pp. 182–3 and Brown, *Freedom from Florida Chains*, p. 131.

55. O'Hare, *In Prison*, pp. 99–103.

56. Ibid., p. 105.

57. Brown, *Freedom from Florida Chains*, p. 113.

58. Ibid., pp. 89, 113, 210 and 229.

59. Norris and Washington, *The Last of the Scottsboro Boys*, pp. 178 and 180.

60. Patterson and Conrad, *Scottsboro Boy*, pp. 86, 92, 99, 207 and 237.

61. Ibid., pp. 104, 124–7, 169 and 190 and Miller, *Remembering Scottsboro*, p. 189.

62. Patterson and Conrad, *Scottsboro Boy*, pp. 226–9.

63. Burns, *I am a Fugitive*, pp. 50, 59, 136 and 144.

64. Ibid., p. 50 and Rustin, 'Report on Twenty-two Days on the Chain Gang', p. 36.

65. Rustin, 'Report on Twenty-two Days on the Chain Gang', p. 6.

66. Ibid., p. 8.

67. Burns, *I am a Fugitive*, pp. 54 and 149–52. These punishments were also detailed in John L. Spivak's journalism and his novel about chain gang labour and racial and class oppression in early 1930s Georgia. See J.L. Spivak (1932) *On the Chain Gang* (New York: International Pamphlets) and J.L. Spivak (2012 edition) *Hard Times on a Southern Chain Gang: Originally Published as the Novel Georgia Nigger (1932)* (Columbia: The University of South Carolina Press).

68. Patterson and Conrad, *Scottsboro Boy*, pp. 115 and 198–9.

69. O'Hare, *In Prison*, p. 110.

70. Patterson and Conrad, *Scottsboro Boy*, pp. 26–8, 43 and 74 and Norris and Washington, *The Last of the Scottsboro Boys*, pp. 24–5, 163 and 187.

71. Patterson and Conrad, *Scottsboro Boy*, pp. 56–8.

72. Brown, *Freedom from Florida Chains*, pp. 152–4.

73. Norris and Washington, *The Last of the Scottsboro Boys*, 181–2 and Brown, *Freedom from Florida Chains*, p. 77.

74. O'Hare, *In Prison*, p. 115.

75. Patterson and Conrad, *Scottsboro Boy*, pp. 141–6 and Brown, *Freedom from Florida Chains*, p. 51.

76. Brown, *Freedom from Florida Chains*, p. 211.

77. Patterson and Conrad, *Scottsboro Boy*, p. 55.

78. Rustin, 'Report on Twenty-two Days on the Chain Gang', p. 31.

79. Ibid., pp. 31–2.

80. See the collection of articles in the 2015 Special Issue, 'Historians and the Carceral State' in the *Journal of American History*, Vol. 102, No. 1.

81. Patterson and Conrad, *Scottsboro Boy*, p. 49 and Norris and Washington, *The Last of the Scottsboro Boys*, p. 55.

82. Rustin, 'Report on Twenty-two Days on the Chain Gang', pp. 11–12.

83. Patterson and Conrad, *Scottsboro Boy*, p. 70.

84. O'Hare, *In Prison*, p. x and p. 102.

85. Ibid., pp. 38–48 and 52. For example, it was noted that judges were from the ruling classes so had little understanding of the lower or working classes. By contrast the white male southern judges in the Scottsboro cases had an acute understanding of the racial, gender and political hierarchies, and for the most part sought to shore these up. For example, Scottsboro defendants were questioned without having lawyers present and had little access to legal representation, so there were many initial attempts to railroad confessions from all nine defendants. See Patterson and Conrad, *Scottsboro Boy*, p. 45.

86. For example, Brown, *Freedom from Florida Chains*, pp. 69–70.

87. O'Hare, *In Prison*, pp. x, 61, 76.

88. Burns, *I am a Fugitive*, pp. 62–3.

89. Patterson and Conrad, *Scottsboro Boy*, p. 70.

90. Brown, *Freedom from Florida Chains*, pp. 88–9.

91. Rustin, 'Report on Twenty-two Days on the Chain Gang', pp. 18–19.

92. O'Hare, *In Prison*, pp. 57–8.

93. Rustin, 'Report on Twenty-two Days on the Chain Gang', p. 14.

94. O'Hare, *In Prison*, pp. 164–80.

95. Norris and Washington, *The Last of the Scottsboro Boys*, pp. 216–17.

96. See P. Sullivan (1996) *Days of Hope: Race and Democracy in the New Deal Era* (Chapel Hill, NC: University of North Carolina Press), especially chap. 3.

97. For example, *Johnson v. Dye*, 175 F. 2d 250, 253 (3d Cir. 1949); D. Fellman, 'Cruel and Unusual Punishments', *Journal of Politics* 19.1 (February 1957), pp. 34–42, at pp. 42–4 and Miller, *Hard Labor and Hard Time*, p. 170.

98. Arsenault, 'You Don't Have to Ride Jim Crow', p. 67.

99. Miller, *From Prairie to Prison*, p. 251; S.M. Kohn (1994) *American Political Prisoners: Prosecutions under the Espionage and Sedition Acts* (Westport, CN: Greenwood Publishing Group), p. 121.

100. See J.M. Holl (1976 edition) 'Introduction' to O'Hare's *In Prison*, p. xxii.

101. M. Foucault (1977) *Discipline and Punish: The Birth of the Prison* (New York: Pantheon Books), pp. 135–3.

102. Miller, *Hard Labor and Hard Time*, pp. 17 and 160.

103. Ibid., p. 70.

104. Eakin, *Touching the World*, p. 177.

CHAPTER 13

'NOTHING KEPT BACK, NOTHING EXAGGERATED': PIETY, PENOLOGY AND CONFLICT: JOSEPH KINGSMILL, PRISON CHAPLAIN (1842–60)

Neil Davie

> I may say that it would have been no difficult task to make the results of the experiments carried on here [at Pentonville] for the reformation of men appear more favourable, but I have kept back nothing on the one hand, nor exaggerated on the other ....[1]

I

Joseph Kingsmill (1805/6–65) belongs to that clutch of Anglican prison chaplains who rose to national prominence in the 1840s, a period often considered to represent the high watermark of the separate system as a guiding principle for Britain's prison regime. For its supporters, separate confinement was the penal equivalent of the silver bullet. It was capable of resolving not only a series of long-standing and intractable problems facing prison administrators, but also a whole raft of societal ills too. By the end of the 1830s, there were convinced separators in key positions in the Home Office, amongst the members of the new government inspectorate of prisons, and within a powerful and vocal section of expert opinion.[2] Prolonged cellular isolation was seen as possessing two major advantages compared with other prison regimes. Firstly, illicit communication within prison would be kept to a minimum thanks to a multitude of often ingenious architectural details and organizational arrangements. In this way, the moral contamination thought to be spread by what one contemporary called 'the evils of unrestricted communion'[3] between inmates could be thwarted. This would occur both whilst prisoners were locked in their cells and during the rare moments they spent outside them. Separation was also considered to fulfil a second important function, that of providing each prisoner with the solitude necessary to reflect on his or her crimes. Only such cellular introspection, it was argued, was capable of bringing the occupants of the significantly named *penitentiaries* to that state of self-awareness and contrition necessary for their ultimate reform and reintegration in the community.

The end of the previous decade had seen the country's two most senior Home Office prison inspectors, William Crawford and Whitworth Russell, both enthusiastic separators, consolidate their grip over the country's penal policy, aided by their ambitious recruit from the Royal Engineers, Captain Joshua Jebb. One result of that collaboration would be Pentonville Prison, the first national penitentiary in Britain to be designed and built solely on separate principles. The 'model prison', as it was dubbed, received its first inmates in December 1842.[4] Joseph Kingsmill was appointed as Pentonville's first assistant chaplain. Born in County Kilkenny, Ireland, Kingsmill had entered the Church a decade earlier, after studying classics and divinity at Trinity College, Dublin. He would only serve some twelve months in his new post, however. For, following the resignation of his colleague the Reverend James Ralph in 1843, he was promoted to the senior clerical position at the prison. Kingsmill would occupy the post until his retirement from the prison service in 1860.[5]

Although there has been little in-depth research on Kingsmill's career, he is regularly cited, along with John Clay of Preston House of Correction and John Field of Reading Gaol, as well as his own deputy at Pentonville, John T. Burt, as an example of how evangelical Protestantism wholeheartedly embraced the new penal philosophy of the mid-Victorian period and provided some of its most ardent and voluble defenders.[6] The conventional account sees this separatist doctrine as the unchallenged cornerstone of government penal policy in the late 1830s and 1840s – the object of mounting criticism in the 1850s – and effectively abandoned in the 1860s. The change in personnel at the top of the convict prison directorate following the sudden death of Joshua Jebb in 1863 is often placed in this context – a potent symbol that the era of unalloyed separation had come to an end. As chaplain of the country's flagship separate prison, and a close friend of Jebb's to boot, it might have been expected that the career of Joseph Kingsmill could be fitted smoothly into this narrative of 'the rise and decline of the separate system'.[7] We shall see in the following account that the reality is both more complex and more interesting. This is not to deny that the separate system could be the object of uncritical and unflagging support in some quarters during the 1840s. Indeed, William Crawford and Whitworth Russell provide striking examples of such a stance. Until their early deaths within a few months of each other in 1847, the two Home District inspectors drove forward the separatist agenda with impressive energy and single-minded determination.[8] However, two important provisos need to be borne in mind. Firstly, despite the best efforts of the Home Office and the inspectorate, and despite a favourable legislative and regulatory framework, the separators' grip over penal policy in Britain was never total. It was not just that they never managed to shake off the critics carping from the sidelines. Local studies of penal reform in this period reveal that alternative penal regimes remained in place up and down the country throughout the period.[9] The second, and for our purposes more significant, proviso is that the separate doctrine was not only repeatedly challenged from without, it was also riven by divisions from *within*.[10] In the case of Pentonville, the 'model prison' would survive in its original form for just seven years, and even during that period (1842–9), it was the scene of persistent conflict about just what should constitute the 'right' regime for the prison's 500 inmates.

II

On paper, 'separate confinement' seemed an unambiguous concept, rooted in the still highly respected theories of John Howard, Sir George Onesiphorus Paul and others, and developed in the last decades of the eighteenth century.[11] Since it was generally agreed that the contamination of prisoners by illicit communication was to be avoided at all costs (a key conclusion of Crawford's influential report delivered to the Home Office following his tour of American prisons in 1833–4[12]), then it seemed to many that cellular confinement was the obvious solution. However, that apparently straightforward premise had proven to throw up a whole raft of complex questions. Some of them were logistical: how to achieve veritable isolation when prisoners were known to communicate from cell to cell? How to manage separation *outside* the cell, for example, during exercise or at chapel? Engineer Joshua Jebb would devote his considerable skills and energy to seeking solutions to these problems at Pentonville.[13]

Even more intractable, however, were a range of other issues which could not be resolved by engineering alone, however ingenious. How long, for example, could inmates be safely left in total isolation? And what should 'total' isolation mean? Should prisoners be denied *all* human company (which smacked of *solitary* confinement, as reformers were well aware)? Or should they be the object of regular visits from senior prison personnel such as the governor, chaplain, medical officer and manufacturer – and if so, with what frequency? The question of labour in the prison raised its own set of questions: should prisoners be provided with some form of employment within their cells, or rather set to work in the company of other inmates in communal workrooms? The latter option presented certain practical advantages, but carried with it the danger of reintroducing the corrupting influence of illicit communication.

With little reliable empirical data on which to base policy, debate on these and other questions in the period tended to consist of a combination of recourse to moral dogma and/or the often tendentious use of what little empirical evidence was available. In a sense, the use of 'evidence' in this context was bound to be tendentious, since there was no agreed set of benchmarks against which it could be evaluated. Some argued that, for all their limitations, even imperfect statistics on crime or recommital rates were preferable to relying on doubtful claims of inmate 'reformation' or 'conversion' as these were based, it was alleged, on the selective use of prisoner case studies and correspondence. Prison chaplains were frequently charged with wishful thinking or even self-delusion in this area. They were apparently unwilling or unable to distinguish between genuine cases of prisoner reform and the contrived 'pattern penitence' of which Charles Dickens would famously complain in his 1850 article for *Household Words*.[14] But even assuming that reliable statistics of criminal activity could be collected, should this be considered to provide conclusive evidence that the rigours of the separate system had done, or not done, their work? Only an intimate knowledge of the spiritual state of individual prisoners, some argued, could provide an answer to that question, and who better to obtain such insights than the prison chaplain?

These were the kind of problems and issues, both theoretical and practical, with which prison chaplains, like other senior staff in the separate prisons, had to wrestle. It is not surprising that chaplains' appreciation of those problems and issues, and the solutions they proposed, turned out to vary according both to the particular circumstances in which each churchman exercised his profession and in line with the personal experiences and doctrinal stance he brought to bear on those circumstances. This is not to deny, of course, the existence of common patterns. With many Anglican prison chaplains of the period drawn from a similar cultural and doctrinal *milieu*, and confronted with a similar set of problems, linked to their presence in a highly structured, rule-bound professional working environment, any other state of affairs would have been extraordinary. However, what micro-histories of the kind offered in this book are perhaps particularly well placed to demonstrate, is the existence of a certain room for manoeuvre, for human agency in other words, in even the most structured of environments. In short, it needs to be recognized that rule-bound does not necessarily mean hidebound. In the case of Joseph Kingsmill and Pentonville, as will become clear, it is not only that there was room for *individual* interpretation of the rules, but that *the rules themselves* were in more or less in a constant state of flux.

Indeed, a close study of the surviving sources, including Kingsmill's private correspondence and personal journals from this period – many of which are discussed in detail for the first time here – reveals a situation of endemic conflict at the heart of the mid-Victorian prison system, with frequent clashes between the chaplain and other members of Pentonville's staff, as well as its management committee. What also emerges is a more fully rounded picture of Kingsmill himself than previous research has suggested and, by extension, of the pressures and challenges facing all prison chaplains in this period. Whilst the Pentonville chaplain's thinking remained firmly circumscribed by the tenets of mid-Victorian evangelical Anglicanism, he was evidently not unaware of the physical and mental dangers of cellular confinement and indeed clashed repeatedly with those at the model prison wishing to impose a more rigorous version of the separate regime on its inmates. He was aware too, as we shall see, of the danger of prison reformers being carried away by their own rhetoric. 'Separate confinement', he would observe in 1850, 'is no panacea for criminal depravity. It has been supposed capable of reforming a man from habits of theft to a lifetime of honesty, of vice to virtue. It has no such power. No human punishment has ever done this.'[15]

III

Although the model prison was not officially commissioned by the Home Office until early 1839, its intellectual origins can be traced back to the mid-1830s with the debate over William Crawford's *Report on the Penitentiaries of the United States*. As noted above, Crawford had returned from his transatlantic tour a convinced separator; writing in glowing terms of his impressions of Philadelphia's Eastern Penitentiary, where 'solitary imprisonment' acted 'not only [as] an exemplary punishment but a powerful agent in the reformation of morals'.[16] In their inspectors' reports of the late 1830s, Crawford and Russell would return time and again to the subject. In their *Third Report* of 1838, for example, they dwelt at length on the opportunities for spiritual reflection and guidance brought by separation:

> In the stillness and solitude of his cell, [...] the culprit is made to feel the reality of his condition, and the fearfulness of that prospect leads him to think of 'righteousness, temperance and judgment to come'. He has the opportunity and leisure to cherish these thoughts, and we may truly say that if ever there was a season in which advice and instruction would be profitably given – if any circumstances can be imagined calculated to impress with salutary effect the warnings and encouragements of religion upon the mind – it must be those of the convict in his cell, where he is unseen and unheard, and where nothing can reach him, but the voice which must come to him, as it were, from another world.[17]

There was no room for doubt or equivocation in this conception: 'let the prisoner's character be what it may, *he will, when thus circumstanced, at once reveal it; and the treatment which he experiences will exactly correspond with it, without difficulty and without failure*'.[18] These were highly ambitious claims, but as Pentonville passed from idea to blueprint and from blueprint to completed prison, this unalloyed confidence continued to suffuse every aspect of the project. Previous failures (including Whitworth Russell's own mixed record as chaplain at Millbank in the early 1830s[19]) were seemingly forgotten. Indeed, all of those closely involved in the design and conception of Pentonville assumed that the prison's cutting-edge architecture – including state-of-the-art cells specially designed to prevent communication between inmates and what have been called 'diabolically ingenious'[20] structures conceived by Jebb to isolate prisoners at chapel and during exercise – plus a hand-picked population of reformable convicts[21] would prove a winning combination.

Early signs were good, at least according to the first detailed report produced by the prison's management committee in March 1844. The commissioners emphasized, as had the Home District inspectors before them, that the prison's 'arrangements'[22] had 'divest[ed] the imprisonment of the injurious effects attendant upon solitary confinement', whilst noting that 'the utmost vigilance' was exercised to prevent communication between inmates.[23] The apparent success of the regime was attested both by the unusually low levels of punishment amongst the inmates, and what the commissioners described as 'unequivocal evidence that a moral reformation has begun in many of their minds'.[24]

However, this public image of unequivocal success belied a more troubling reality. By the time this second report of the Pentonville commissioners appeared in March 1844, the prison's chaplain James Ralph had been pressured to resign and Joseph Kingsmill had been promoted to take his place. It was alleged privately that Ralph's sermons and cell visits at the prison had resulted in several cases of 'religious mania' and other 'morbid symptoms' amongst the prison's inmates.[25] The cause, according to committee chairman Lord Wharncliffe, was Ralph's 'exaggerated estimate of his duty as chaplain' and 'a want of due consideration of the peculiar circumstances under which the inmates of Pentonville are placed'. This, he considered, had led to errors of judgement on the part of the clergyman, apparently unaware that prisoners undergoing separate confinement needed 'relaxation from the constant confinement of their minds' to religious subjects in the form of secular reading matter. The peer expressed his hope that the Reverend Ralph could be persuaded to 'alter his mode of communicating with some prisoners on religious subjects', but indicated that if he could not, the chaplain would have to be dismissed. 'I will not allow', he added, 'the mental health of the Prisoners to be risked, as it appears to be now'.[26]

Pentonville's committee chairman was supported in his view by the two external 'medical commissioners' on the prison board, Sir Benjamin Brodie and Dr Robert Ferguson, as well as by the prison's visiting medical officer, Dr George Owen Rees. Ranged against Wharncliffe and the trio of medical experts was another of the peers on the board at Pentonville, Lord Chichester, along with Home Office inspector Whitworth Russell and senior administrator, Joshua Jebb.[27] Kingsmill's own stance on the subject is not recorded, but as a lowly assistant chaplain, it is unlikely that his opinion would have weighed heavily in the balance. In any case, he may have been considered a less-than-impartial witness in the matter. Prior to his appointment, Pentonville's assistant chaplain had held the living of Longton near Stoke-on-Trent, just a stone's throw from Ralph's own parish church at Shelton. Indeed, according to Kingsmill's later account, it was on Ralph's 'suggestion' and 'solicitation' that he had followed his older colleague to the capital. In all, the 'brotherly' collaboration between the two churchmen would last some twenty years.[28] Ralph's defenders proved powerless to maintain him in his position, despite a vigorous attempt by the chaplain at the end of 1843 to defend his record before the board. It was decided to allow him to stay on until the following January, but only on condition that his ministry was limited to taking divine service. It was made clear that he was 'not to continue to give expositions of the scripture as hitherto any morning or evening or visit Prisoners in their cells'.[29]

Beyond its significance for Kingsmill's career, this episode, coming as it did barely a year after the arrival of Pentonville's first inmates, is also important for the way it reveals clear tensions, both structural and ideological, at the heart of the separatist project. There was widespread agreement in official circles, as we noted earlier, on the importance of the chaplain's role in the separate prison. Remove him from the equation, it was argued, and all you were left with was mere isolation and at best passive obedience. This was an improvement on the old associated prisons perhaps, but a regime shorn of any means of reclaiming criminal hearts, minds and souls, which for the system's supporters was its principal *raison d'être*. As historian W.J. Forsythe puts it,

[T]he long lines of cells and corridors, the masks which the prisoners had to wear when they left their cells, and the stalled chapels which were built in many prisons such as Reading and Pentonville, served to allow the freest flow of the work of redemption. Prisoners, humbled and thrown in upon themselves by isolation, reduced to sorrowing repentance, might turn avidly to the comforting kindness and consoling truths of the minister of God.[30]

Beyond those general principles, however, there was plenty of room for disagreement. For the reasons indicated earlier, there were differences of opinion about how best to ensure 'the freest flow of the work of redemption'. Clearly, some members of the management committee at Pentonville had their doubts about the wisdom of Ralph's programme of intensive religious exhortation and instruction. Indeed, some at the prison may have come to see Kingsmill's ministry in the same light, considering, – as a later virulent critic of his would put it – that he belonged to that group of 'narrow-minded chaplains of good intentions, but extreme Low Church views, who represent prisoners one day as "Hell deserving sinners" and the next [as] "converted saints"'.[31] What is clear, however, is that there was a view amongst members of the committee by late 1843 that 'the rigorous severity of separate confinement ... [had] proved too heavy a pressure on prisoners' minds'.[32] They called, as we have seen, for the diet of religious fare to be leavened with secular works; they also emphasized the importance of providing for prisoners what Dr Rees called 'real employment' – and not merely oakum picking – in order to combat 'mental distress'.[33]

The idea that the free flow of the work of redemption should be rationed or watered down was anathema, of course, to the evangelical mindset. Seen from this latter perspective, the prison chaplain represented, to use the words chosen by Kingsmill to describe Ralph, 'a Christian warrior ... [fighting] the good fight of faith, with all his armour on, his sword firmly grasped, and his face toward the enemy'.[34] Such a conception of the prison chaplain's ministry could be – and often was – used to justify clerical intervention in virtually every aspect of prison life. Where such a role was welcomed by the governor and other senior managers, this gave the prison chaplain a degree of power and influence over the inmates second to none.[35] However, with both job descriptions and chains of command rarely specified in detail, there was clearly room for friction and conflict; particularly when – as in the early days at Pentonville – senior staff were accountable to a management committee the members of which failed to agree amongst themselves as to how the prison should be run. The Reverend Ralph's 'proud and haughty spirit'[36] may not have helped matters. However, given Pentonville's competing structures of authority, clashes between the chaplain and other senior figures at the prison were all but inevitable.

Kingsmill was evidently profoundly affected by what he saw as the hounding out of his former colleague and friend. Indeed, there is evidence that the events of 1843–4 left the Pentonville chaplain with a lasting sense of rancour towards those on the prison's governing board and amongst the staff whom he held responsible for Ralph's demise. In a sermon given in 1855 at his colleague's funeral, Kingsmill referred with probably deliberate irony to 'the benevolent theorists who had suggested the [Pentonville] experiment to the British government, [and] who were also the most active members of the governing board' – an apparent reference to inspectors Crawford and Russell. It was when this active group became 'dissatisfied with the result' at the prison, Kingsmill told the congregation that Ralph had resigned. Pentonville insiders would no doubt have had no trouble filling in the gaps in the churchman's elliptical account.[37]

The Pentonville chaplain came to believe that those 'benevolent theorists' on the prison's governing board only *appeared* to be staunch defenders of separate confinement;

for in reality they were working actively to undermine the religious values on which the system was – or should be – based. An oblique reference to this view can be found in Kingsmill's first published work, *Prisons and Prisoners* (1849), where he accuses those 'who cry up extravagantly the separate system' of 'dishonour[ing] Christianity'. For them, he argues, the Christian faith

> is merely an adjunct, and not a very safe one sometimes,[38] and they speak of the reformatory process of the system, whilst they would shrink in general from acknowledging the power of the grace of God in turning the sinner from the error of his ways, if indeed they believe it.[39]

It is possible, as we shall see presently, that Kingsmill's determination to 'complete the vindication of poor Ralph's ministerial character' (as he put it in a letter to Joshua Jebb in the summer of 1850)[40] played a role in the chaplain's decision, taken shortly after his promotion, to begin illustrating his official reports with detailed, proto-criminological investigations of the physical and mental characteristics, educational level, and recommital rates of successive cohorts of the prison's population. In his report for 1849, for example, Kingsmill chose to examine in detail the one thousand offenders who had passed through Pentonville during that year.[41] On examining the criminal records and life histories of this group, he noticed that more than two-thirds of inmates over the age of twenty were single and almost all had left home. Kingsmill's conclusion confirms a point noted by Forsythe that for all the chaplain's emphasis on the role of environmental factors in the causes of crime, 'his distinctive contribution was the notion that the first link in the progressive chain was a choice made by the individual to reject Christ. This first step was the necessary precursor of the rest'.[42] Thus, argues Kingsmill:

> The causes of their first lapse into vice and criminality were generally these – not wishing to retain God in their knowledge, and therefore deserting or neglecting the house of God and the Sabbath – disobedience to parents and neglect of their counsel, combined with, consequently, separation from home. But a few had never a home, nor any one to guide them aright.[43]

The Pentonville chaplain clearly rejected the argument, advanced by some of his contemporaries, that descent into crime was the result of a lack of education per se:

> The distinguishing features of criminals from the honourable classes [of the 'honest and virtuous poor in our factories and fields' ...] are not, I am confident, their deficiencies either in intellect, or attainment in mere knowledge of elementary subjects, [...] nor even of the Bible itself as a book; but their terrible want of moral and religious principle, being destitute of the fear of God, and true religion, in which for the most part they were never in any degree instructed, or which they presumptuously and wickedly cast off, choosing the pleasures of sin, or the quickest mode to be rich, in preference to the pleasures of wisdom, the patient toils of honest industry, and that godliness which with contentment is great gain.[44]

Kingsmill had already touched on the theme of education, including religious education, in his previous report for 1848. On that occasion, he chose to concentrate on educational provision within the prison. Significantly, he examined the connections between religious instruction and insanity at Pentonville, with a view to comparing recent trends with those during the ministry of James Ralph. A peak in cases in insanity in the prison in 1848, Kingsmill argued, effectively 'remov[ed] whatever feeling of suspicion may have existed as to the dangerous influence of any particular manner of communicating religious instruction, upon the minds of the prisoners'. The cases of insanity observed at the prison clearly arose from other causes, he concluded, 'or the will of God alone'. Pentonville's chaplain proceeded to invite the members of the board to 'rejoice […] to do justice to the ministry of my honoured predecessor'.[45]

There was probably not very much in the way of 'rejoicing' on the Pentonville board at this news, as Kingsmill must well have known. In fact, by the time these words appeared in print, in May 1849, the prison's chaplain had publicly distanced himself from the ultra-separatist camp at Pentonville. This was a process which had begun with his official report for 1846 (published in March 1847) and was repeated in his testimony before the Lords' Select Committee on the Criminal Law the same month. In sharp contrast to his first two reports as chaplain at Pentonville, which had both been unequivocal in their praise for the disciplinary and reformatory capability of the regime of eighteen months' 'probationary' separation at the prison,[46] Kingsmill was now sounding a note of caution. His 1846 report notes that whilst 'the generality' of prisoners 'exhibit no undue depression of spirits', and indeed 'when they begin to take an interest in trade or education, are remarkably cheerful, […] there are cases where it is otherwise – i.e. where men take no interest in religion, or books, or trade, and having no confidence in any one, make their confinement one of almost absolute solitude'.[47]

Kingsmill went on to list four categories of prisoners whose 'conditions of mind' made them ill-suited to prolonged isolation: the sullenly obstinate (the largest category); the mentally deficient; those with 'active and energetic' minds frustrated at the lack of opportunities for progress; and finally those given to introspection and 'intentness of thought'.[48] It was presumably these groups which the chaplain had in mind when he told the Lords Select Committee that March that there were instances where six months' separate confinement would be 'enough to unhinge the mind'. For the majority of prisoners, he urged that the maximum period of isolation be reduced from eighteen months to between twelve and fifteen.[49]

Looking back on this period from the early 1850s, Kingsmill recalled how he had reached these conclusions. His account is worth quoting at some length:

Among the convicts of the first years, most carefully selected, as they were, in the matter of general health, age, crime, and sentence, there was an undue proportion […] of mental disturbance and excitement, from insanity down-wards to a sort of indescribable nervous or hysterical condition, which was partly observable in the prison, but much more so on board ship,[50] where a large proportion were seized with convulsions. […] It was reasonable to infer, that where no such actual result followed, there was yet an effect produced upon the system of an unfavourable character; and this I thought observable in the appearance of our convicts, viewed in comparison with the others around them. Could it be imagined that longer detention in such a state would not aggravate this mischief? [...] That result, [...] in my opinion, seemed consistent enough with the supposition of a gradual and perhaps imperceptible decline of the physical and mental energies of the mass of persons subjected to the trial. Active disease might be developed in the first stage of confinement, whilst general debility or prostration of spirits would mark the latter part of a long confinement in separation; and when released the sufferers would not be competent to work their way in the world like other men; and having this disadvantage, with the loss of character, would be doomed in too many cases to hopeless pauperism, vagrancy, or crime.[51]

The solution, Kingsmill came to realize, was to replace the original

probationary period of a lengthened term of separate confinement with a system of convict discipline [...] which secures whatever advantages belong to separate confinement, consistently with mental safety; is combined with active bodily exertion and training in out-door labour; incorporating all through the elements of a wholesome severity with those of humanity and religion.[52]

The Pentonville chaplain's 1846 report went on to make just such a proposal, stating that 'much additional good would be accomplished, after a period of separate imprisonment, by a well-regulated system of associated labour, instruction and worship'.[53]

Kingsmill was well aware of the likely impact of these words on the died-in-the wool separators who dominated the management committee and senior staff at Pentonville and included amongst their number his own assistant, John T. Burt. Indeed, Kingsmill confided as much to Joshua Jebb in a letter written a few months before the publication of the commissioners' report, noting that he had 'no expectation that every thing in my report will please every one'.[54] However, whilst increasingly isolated at the model prison, Kingsmill had a powerful ally in Jebb. In the space of a few short years, the former captain in the Royal Engineers had risen from architectural advisor to the Home Office inspectorate, to become the government's principal advisor on penal policy. He would soon assume control of a new, centralized convict prison directorate.[55] Evidence from Jebb's *Second Report of the Surveyor-General of Prisons* (1847), published that summer, along with his testimony before the Lords' Select Committee on the Criminal Law earlier in the year, reveal that by this period he had come to share many of Kingsmill's concerns about the potentially deleterious effects of the separate system. Significantly, Jebb's official reports from this period contain frequent and often lengthy quotations from the reports and published writings of the Pentonville chaplain, judiciously selected to back up his argument that separate confinement, if limited in duration, was generally effective, but that it needed to be followed by a period of 'well-regulated intercourse, in association of small parties'. Such a regime, Jebb argued, echoing Kingsmill, would 'afford a better opportunity of perfecting their training, and fitting them to meet the trials and temptations to which they would be exposed on their liberation, than a longer continuance of separation and absolute control'.[56]

As Jebb readily admitted,[57] this radical shift in official thinking had not been plucked out of the ether. As originally conceived back in 1842 (just five years previously, it will be recalled), the regime at Pentonville had been intended not as an alternative to transportation, as had been the case with the prison's ill-fated predecessor at Millbank, but as a complement to it, providing a period of reformatory probation for a hand-picked group of promising convicts before they were dispatched to Van Dieman's Land as more or less free 'exiles'.[58] By the mid-1840s, that policy was no longer tenable. Conditions in the penal colony were judged unacceptable and the Treasury was baulking at the spiralling costs involved.[59] Some government ministers remained confident that transportation to the Antipodes still had a long-term future. Others, from whom Jebb took his lead, preferred to devote their energies to exploring how convicts might be accommodated instead on British soil. This would entail a short period of separate confinement, followed by a longer term at one of the new 'public works' prisons. With a longer spell in isolation now ruled out on health grounds, and transportation, for the present at least, not an option either, Jebb concluded that a period of association had become 'a matter of *necessity* under present circumstances'.[60]

We quoted earlier in this chapter the candid admission made by Kingsmill in his official report for 1849 that separate confinement was not to be regarded as a 'panacea' and that in fact no penal system had proved 'capable of reforming a man from habits of theft to a life of honesty, of vice to virtue'. In his report for the following year, 1850 (the first to be published by the new three-man national Directorate of Convict Prisons chaired by Jebb), Kingsmill developed this 'no panacea' argument. He began by stating starkly that 'Cases of real change of heart in individuals may be found, when all are fully tested, to be rare in the ministry of the prison chaplain.' This was not to underestimate the value of religious teaching in prison, but Kingsmill implied that its value lay less in its ability to achieve the genuine 'conversion of the sinner to God' – a phenomenon he considered to be rare in practice, despite the 'evidence' offered up by some of his colleagues of the cloth – than as a tool for 'promoting among men of a degraded stamp the feelings of order, respect for authority and law, industrious habits, and regard for the rights of others'.[61]

However, at the end of the day there was only so much the prison could achieve, for was it not the case that '[t]he great work of the suppression of crime […] in the land belongs, less, practically viewed, to the law, the police, and the officials of prisons, than to society at large'? Like many Tory evangelicals of his day, Kingsmill considered that the priority was to combat the forces of irreligion, licentiousness and self-indulgence which were constantly threatening to overrun the country and undermine those political institutions which had assured 'the moral elevation of England and the surpassing grandeur of her wide-spread dominion'.[62] It was thus *outside* the prison walls, in Kingsmill's view, that the 'wisest sort of philanthropy' should concentrate its efforts.[63] Indeed, in 1856 he published a pamphlet with precisely this objective in mind. Aimed at the 'thinking men of the industrial classes', the pamphlet sought to steer its readers away from beer and Chartism and towards what he considered more wholesome pursuits.[64]

One way of interpreting Kingsmill's comments about the priority for the 'wisest sort of philanthropy' would be to deduce that some had been *unwise* to place so much faith in the reformatory power of the separate system, and by extension in the transformative potential of the prison chaplain's ministry. Kingsmill's new-found pessimism – or lucidity – may not be unrelated to the recently changed circumstances at Pentonville. In 1849, the prison was stripped of its status as an exemplary 'model' institution devoted to the scientific study of penal discipline. All of those connected with the prison were having to adjust to its – and their – newly diminished status. No longer could they see themselves as penal pioneers, venturing into uncharted territory in order to hammer out the principles of prison management and design for the benefit of the country's 'ordinary prisons'.[65] For, by this date, the model prison had *become* an ordinary prison – a small(ish) cog in Colonel Jebb's new three-tier convict regime. The prison population at Pentonville had also changed: its inmates were no longer hand-picked probationers, but merely run-of-the-mill convicts undergoing a standardized twelve-month sentence of separate confinement before being readied for dispatch to the public works prisons, the hulks, or the new penal colony established in Western Australia. For those who had placed their faith in the separate system, it was a doubly bitter pill to swallow.

The prison's management committee – now reduced to a three-man rump of professional prison administrators[66] – was, like Kingsmill, keen to lower expectations with regard to separate confinement. Indeed, they quoted the chaplain's 'no panacea' remarks at the end of their report for 1849.[67] The commissioners also stated in their report that the conduct of the prison's inmates during the previous year had been 'on the whole quite as good as could have been anticipated considering the descriptions of convicts which have been received'.[68] This was hardly a ringing endorsement for the new regime at the prison. Prospects for reform at Pentonville were evidently having to be revised downwards, as Kingsmill admitted, albeit guardedly, in his report for 1850:

> It is very obvious that so great a difference in the circumstances and character of our prisoners must very much increase the amount of anxiety and discouragement of those who are called to labour for their moral and religious improvement, and indeed of those whose duty it is to carry out the discipline.[69]

Kingsmill's assistant John T. Burt evidently shared his colleague's anxiety. In July 1850, standing in for Kingsmill (who had been suffering from intermittent bouts of ill health for some time), Burt made the point forcefully in the chaplain's personal journal:

> I entertain a deliberate opinion that that [moral] influence over the prisoners is greatly diminished. In the course of the last few days there will hardly be any prisoners here who have been here more than six months. There are forty five of the prisoners under sentence for life: some of the prisoners are degenerate characters and we do not know who or what they are.[70]

Burt would later go into print on the subject, expressing his profound opposition to the recent changes at the prison. Discipline, he argued, had been 'impaired'; reformation 'prevented and destroyed'; whilst insanity had 'increased'.[71] The governor, prison medical officer and former medical commissioners Brodie and Ferguson all added their voices to the criticism of the new regime.[72] Indeed, Governor Hosking went as far as claiming in October 1849 that Pentonville was no longer 'a proper or safe place of custody for a large class of the prisoners there, viz. those of them who are [of a] brutalised, desperate and reckless character'.[73]

Despite his reservations about the modified version of the separate system now in place at Pentonville, Kingsmill clearly had no wish to see the *ancien régime* re-established at the prison. On the contrary, he evidently gained satisfaction from the fact that his former critics had lost their former power and influence – a change indicated, as he put it, by their 'lowered tone and less confident step'. These words are taken from Kingsmill's 1850 letter to Jebb, referred to earlier, in which he expressed his hopes that the new insanity figures for the prison would vindicate the record of his predecessor. There were other positive signs for the Pentonville chaplain. A new governor had been appointed to replace Hosking, a man in whom, Kingsmill considered, 'authority and vigour and good sense combined with the manner of a gentleman'. All in all, he concluded jokingly, 'this place is beginning to grow comfortable'.[74]

IV

Kingsmill's comfort was only relative, of course. It was not just the ten- or twelve-hour days (reduced to four during his periods of ill health), the three Sunday services, each with a sermon; the 10,000 visits made yearly to inmates in their cells or in the infirmary in order to instruct, persuade and comfort; the supervision of the schoolmasters and library, or the requirement to advise (and correspond) on the individual and collective impact of the prison's reformatory effort.[75] More than that, like many of the more reflective prison administrators of the period, Kingsmill was constantly having to seek ways of extricating himself from the horns of a dilemma. On the one hand, he remained firmly convinced to the end that for all its faults the separate system was vastly superior to any of the penal alternatives. In a striking passage from the third and final edition of his most widely read work, *Chapters on Prisons and Prisoners and the Prevention of Crime* (1854), Kingsmill offers an eloquent paean to the benefits of isolation, confirming in the process that 'sentiment' and 'the desire to control' coexisted at the heart of the penitentiary reform project:[76]

> Separate confinement, relieved from the necessity of inflicting dis-proportionate punishment, admits also of the application, under the very strictest discipline, of much kindness. The stout-hearted can be kept down without brute force; all may be reasoned with, and every single prisoner experience the influence of that which Inspiration so beautifully calls the law of kindness. Now, of all things,

kindness most smoothes the ruggedness of temper, subdues antagonism, and clears the ground of impediments to the culture of right feelings and principle. If this be combined with firmness of purpose, and a superior mind in the Governor, discipline becomes a very valuable part of such reformatory means as can be used in a prison.[77]

However, as we have seen, Kingsmill acknowledged the rarity of genuine divine 'inspiration' on the prison cell block and was also keenly aware that the penal regime in which he set so much store could only be used safely in unadulterated form for a strictly limited period:

The severity of separate confinement consists in its opposition to the laws and impulses of our social nature, and in the pressure which it exercises on the mind. Hence may be derived some of its strongest recommendations as a mode of reformation; but to the same cause are due many of its difficulties in application, for mental sufferings cannot be measured nor adjusted.[78]

Kingsmill told the 1850 Select Committee on Prison Discipline that 'I do not think we are justified in carrying on a system which would materially injure the mind or body of persons who have lost their liberty.'[79] The problem, of course, as the Pentonville chaplain was only too well aware, was that given mental suffering amongst inmates could not be easily 'measured' or 'adjusted', it was never clear on whom, or for how long, separate confinement could be 'safely' imposed. The consequences for the ministry of the prison chaplain were profound:

Depression of spirits is not contrition; remorse is not repentance; resolutions and vows of amendment, made whilst suffering the penalty of transgression, imply no change of principle, – no real reformation of character. The weakening of man's physical and mental energies does not generate piety. Religion cannot be in a healthy state which originates in disturbance of the mental powers.[80]

Despite the best of intentions, then, there were clearly parts of separate prisons like Pentonville where Kingsmill's 'law of kindness' was unable to reach – spaces where the 'catacomb silence' and isolation of the prison cell were broken only by distant homilies and barked orders, and the occasional screams of inmates.[81]

Notes

1. *Parliamentary Papers*, Sixth Report of the Commissioners for the Government of the Pentonville Prison, Cmnd. 972 (1848), Appendix B, Chaplain's Report, p. 37.
2. W.J. Forsythe (1991) 'Centralisation and Local Autonomy: The Experience of English Prisons 1820–1877', *Journal of Historical Sociology*, Vol. 4, No. 3, pp. 317–45.

3. H. Mayhew and J. Binny (1862) *The Criminal Prisons of London and Scenes of Prison Life* (London: Griffin & Co.), p. 102.

4. Neil Davie (2015) *The Penitentiary Ten: The Transformation of the English Prison, 1770–1850* (Oxford: Bardwell Press), chap. 6–7.

5. B. Forsythe (2004) 'Kingsmill, Joseph (1805/6–1865)', *Oxford Dictionary of National Biography* (Oxford: Oxford University Press), available at http://www.oxforddnb.com/view /article/56015 (accessed 18 April 2014).

6. W.J. Forsythe (1987) *The Reform of Prisoners 1830–1900* (London: Croom Helm) and P. Priestley (1999 edition) *Victorian Prison Lives: English Prison Biography 1830–1914* (London: Pimlico).

7. U.R.Q. Henriques (1972) 'The Rise and Decline of the Separate System of Prison Discipline', *Past and Present*, No. 54, pp. 61–93.

8. E. Stockdale (1983) 'A Short History of Prison Inspection in England', *British Journal of Criminology*, Vol. 23, No. 3, pp. 209–28.

9. R.W. Ireland (2007) '*A Want of Order and Good Discipline': Rules, Discretion and the Victorian Prison* (Cardiff: University of Wales Press).

10. A key conclusion of Davie, *The Penitentiary Ten*, chap. 6–7.

11. See *Parliamentary Papers*, Third Report of the Inspectors Appointed under the Provisions of the Act 5 & 6 Will. IV. c. 38. to Visit the Different Prisons of Great Britain, I. Home District, Cmnd. 141 (1838) and *Parliamentary Papers*, [Joshua Jebb] Second Report of the Surveyor-General of Prisons, Cmnd. 867 (1847).

12. *Parliamentary Papers*, Penitentiaries (United States) – Report of William Crawford, Esq., on the Penitentiaries of the United States, Cmnd. 593 (1834).

13. *Parliamentary Papers*, [Joshua Jebb] [First] Report of the Surveyor-General of Prisons on the Construction, Ventilation and Details of Pentonville Prison, Cmnd. 594 (1844) and J. Jebb (1844) *Modern Prisons: Their Construction and Ventilation* (London: John Weale).

14. C. Dickens (1850) 'Pet Prisoners', *Household Words: A Weekly Journal*, Vol. 1, No. 5, pp. 97–103. On this point, see H. Johnston (2006) '"Buried Alive": Representations of the Separate System in Victorian England', in P. Mason (ed.) *Captured by the Media: Prison Discourse in Popular Culture* (Cullompton: Willan), pp. 103–21.

15. *Parliamentary Papers*, Eighth Report of the Commissioners for the Government of the Pentonville Prison, Cmnd. 1192 (1850), Appendix B, Chaplain's Report, p. 16.

16. *Parliamentary Papers*, Penitentiaries (United States) – Report of William Crawford, p. 12.

17. *Parliamentary Papers*, Third Report of the Inspectors, p. 16.

18. Ibid., p. 28 (author's emphasis).

19. See B. Forsythe (2004) 'Russell, William Whitworth (1795–1847)', *Oxford Dictionary of National Biography* (Oxford: Oxford University Press), available at http://www.oxforddnb .com/view/article/73632 (accessed 11 July 2010).

20. P. Steadman (2014) *Building Types and Built Forms* (Kibworth Beauchamp: Matador), p. 304.

21. All would be male, aged between eighteen and thirty-five and all first-time offenders, sentenced to a maximum of fifteen years' transportation.

22. Notably 'constant labour, the frequent visits of the prison officers and trade-instructors; the consciousness that he can, at any time, insure the attendance of an officer; daily exercise in the open air; attendance at chapel and school, and the means of instruction and relaxation placed within his reach'. See *Parliamentary Papers*, Second Report of the Commissioners for the Government of the Pentonville Prison, Cmnd. 536 (1844), p. 5.

23. Ibid.

24. Ibid., pp. 5 and 13.

25. Based on S. McConville (1981) *A History of English Prison Administration: Volume I 1750–1877* (London: Routledge), p. 207.

26. Quoted in ibid., pp. 207–8.

27. See Davie, *The Penitentiary Ten*, chap. 7.

28. J. Kingsmill (1855) *Faith's Triumph in Death: A Sermon, Preached in the Church of St. John, Horsleydown, Southwark, November 26, 1854, upon the Death of the Rev. James Ralph* (London: Longman, Brown, Green & Longman), pp. 11, 13 and 20.

29. Letter from Lord Chichester to Joshua Jebb, 13 December 1843, quoted in McConville, *A History of English Prison Administration*, p. 208, note 139. See also National Archives (hereafter NA), PCOM 2/84, Minute Book, Pentonville 1842–4, 16 December 1843, ff. 239–40.

30. Forsythe, *The Reform of Prisoners*, p. 47.

31. C.P. Measor (1861) *The Convict Service: A Letter to Sir George Cornewall Lewis […] on the Administration, Results and Expense of the Present Convict System* (London: Robert Hardwicke), p. 47. The author was deputy-governor of Chatham Convict Prison.

32. Kingsmill, *Faith's Triumph in Death*, p. 13.

33. NA, PCOM 2/84, Minute Book, Pentonville 1842–4, 2 September 1843, f. 179. For this point, see also Sir B. Brodie (1851) *Pentonville Prison* [privately published], p. 8.

34. Kingsmill, *Faith's Triumph in Death*, 19.

35. Forsythe, *The Reform of Prisoners*, pp. 44–51.

36. Kingsmill, *Faith's Triumph in Death*, p. 14.

37. Ibid., p. 13.

38. A guarded reference perhaps to the treatment meted out to James Ralph at Pentonville.

39. J. Kingsmill (1849) *Prisons and Prisoners* (London: J.H. Jackson), pp. 181–2.

40. London School of Economics, Jebb Papers (hereafter LSE Jebb), 3/9/19: Letter from Joseph Kingsmill to Joshua Jebb, c. August 1850.

41. The total number was in fact 1106; see *Parliamentary Papers*, Eighth Report of the Commissioners for the Government of the Pentonville Prison, p. 12.

42. Forsythe, *The Reform of Prisoners, passim*.

43. *Parliamentary Papers*, Eighth Report of the Commissioners for the Government of the Pentonville Prison, p. 14.

44. Ibid.

45. *Parliamentary Papers*, Seventh Report of the Commissioners for the Government of the Pentonville Prison, Cmnd. 1101 (1849), Appendix B, p. 16.

46. *Parliamentary Papers*, Third Report of the Commissioners for the Government of the Pentonville Prison, Cmnd. 613 (1845), Appendix C, Chaplain's Report, pp. 11–14 and *Parliamentary Papers*, Fourth Report of the Commissioners for the Government of the Pentonville Prison, Cmnd. 751 (1846), Appendix B, Chaplain's Report, pp. 26–30.

47. *Parliamentary Papers*, Fifth Report of the Commissioners for the Government of the Pentonville Prison, Cmnd. 818 (1847), Appendix B, Chaplain's Report, p. 41.

48. Ibid., pp. 41–2.

49. *Parliamentary Papers*, Second Report from the Select Committee of the House of Lords, Minutes of Evidence, Cmnd. 534 (22 March 1847), p. 218.

50. That is on the convict transport ships bound for Van Dieman's Land.

51. J. Kingsmill (1854 edition) *Chapters on Prisons and Prisoners and the Prevention of Crime* (London: Longman, Brown, Green & Longman), pp. 500–1. These extracts are taken from a report addressed by Kingsmill to the Pentonville commissioners, written in January of 1853.

52. Ibid., pp. 501–2.

53. *Parliamentary Papers*, Fifth Report of the Commissioners for the Government of the Pentonville Prison, p. 43.

54. LSE Jebb, 3/5/12: Letter from Joseph Kingsmill to Joshua Jebb, 24 February 1847.

55. On Jebb's connection with Pentonville, see Davie, *The Penitentiary Ten*, chap. 7 and E. Stockdale (1976) 'The Rise of Joshua Jebb, 1837–1850', *British Journal of Criminology*, Vol. 16, No. 2, pp. 164–70.

56. J. Jebb (1850) *Report on the Discipline and Construction of Portland Prison and Its Connection with the System of Convict Discipline Now in Operation* (London: William Clowes & Sons), p. 20.

57. *Parliamentary Papers*, Second Report from the Select Committee of the House of Lords, p. 220.

58. Letter from Sir James Graham to Pentonville Commissioners, 16 December 1842, reproduced in *Parliamentary Papers*, [First] Report of the Commissioners for the Government of the Pentonville Prison, Cmnd. 449 (1843), Appendix, 5.

59. P. Harling (2014) 'The Trouble with Convicts: From Transportation to Penal Servitude, 1840–67', *Journal of British Studies*, Vol. 53, No. 1, pp. 80–110.

60. Jebb, *Report on the Discipline and Construction of Portland Prison*, p. 20. For the context, see Davie, *The Penitentiary Ten*, chap. 7.

61. *Parliamentary Papers*, Reports of the Directors of Convict Prisons on the Discipline and Management of Pentonville, Parkhurst, and Millbank Prisons, and of Portland Prison and the Hulks for the Year 1850, Cmnd. 1409 (1851), Appendix B, Chaplain's Report, Pentonville, pp. 24–5.

62. *Parliamentary Papers*, Report from the Select Committee on Prison Discipline, Minutes of Evidence, Cmnd. 632 (July 1850), p. 144 and J. Kingsmill (1856) *The Sabbath the Working Man's True Charter: Thoughts for Thinking Men of the Industrial Classes, on the Sabbath Question* (London: Longman, Brown, Green, and Longmans), p. 14.

63. *Parliamentary Papers*, Reports of the Directors of Convict Prisons, p. 25.

64. Kingsmill, *The Sabbath, passim*.

65. The phrase had been used by Sir Benjamin Brodie in a letter to the Pentonville board – see NA, HO PCOM 2/88: Minute Book, Pentonville 1848–9, ff.243-5.

66. These were the three members of the newly formed Directorate of Convict Prisons: Jebb, Capt. Donatus O'Brien and Mr H.P. Voules – see McConville, *A History of English Prison Administration*, p. 216 and note 164.

67. *Parliamentary Papers*, Eighth Report of the Commissioners for the Government of the Pentonville Prison, p. 7.

68. Ibid., p. 5.

69. *Parliamentary Papers*, Reports of the Directors of Convict Prisons, Appendix B, Chaplain's Report, Pentonville, p. 22.

70. NA, PCOM 2/353: Pentonville Prison, Chaplain's Journal 1846–51, 27 July 1850, ff. 205–6.

71. J.T. Burt (1852) *Results of the System of Separate Confinement as Administered at the Pentonville Prison* (London: Longman, Brown, Green & Longman), pp. 247–8.

72. See Davie, *The Penitentiary Ten*, chap. 7.

73. NA, PCOM 2/88: Minute Book, Pentonville 1848–9, 6 October 1849, unpaginated. For more detail on this episode, and the reactions of Jebb and his colleagues, see Davie, *The Penitentiary Ten*, chap. 7.

74. LSE Jebb, 3/9/19: Letter from Joseph Kingsmill to Joshua Jebb, c. August 1850.

75. Based on Forsythe, 'Russell, William Whitworth (1795–1847)', *passim*. He cites Kingsmill's own calculation of the number of prison visits made during the period 1845–55.

76. P. Spierenburg (2013) *Violence and Punishment: Civilizing the Body through Time* (Cambridge: Polity Press), p. 81. For this point, see also H. Rogers (2009) 'The Way to Jerusalem: Reading, Writing and Reform in an Early Victorian Gaol', *Past and Present*, No. 205, pp. 71–104.

77. Kingsmill, *Chapters on Prisons and Prisoners*, pp. 117–8.

78. Ibid., p. 114.

79. *Parliamentary Papers*, Report from the Select Committee on Prison Discipline, p. 145.

80. Kingsmill, *Chapters on Prisons and Prisoners*, p. 501.

81. M. Ignatieff (1978) *A Just Measure of Pain: The Penitentiary in the Industrial Revolution* (London: Macmillan), p. 9 and Forsythe, *The Reform of Prisoners*, p. 65.

BIBLIOGRAPHY

Primary Sources

Unpublished Primary Sources

Archives Nationales, Paris
F7/13043 'Organisation de la Police, 1906–1936'.

Archives of the Préfecture de Police, Paris
BA 899, Plaintes Contre les Commissaries de Police et le Personnel des Commissariats 1907–1911.
BA 1554, Plaintes Contre les Commissaries 1896–1906.
KA 63, *Dossier du Personnel – Kien:*
  Anonymous complaints letter of February 1909.
  Career Summary No. 59.919.
  Complaint from M. Schwartz included in the report by Contrôle Général, 23 August 1898.
  Letter included in the report by Contrôle Général of 23 December 1897.
  Letter from Police Prefect Lépine to Kien, 7 January 1898.
  Letter of Complaint from Oscar Buttner, 14 November 1905.
  Letter from Kien to Police Prefect Lépine, 18 November 1905.
  Letter from Clemenceau to Police Prefect Lépine, 1 June 1909.
  Letter from Police Prefect Lépine to Kien, 20 June 1909.
  Letter from Police Prefect Lépine to Clemenceau, 29 June 1909.
  Letter by Police Prefect Fernand Raux to the Director of the Criminal Investigation
    Department (Police Judiciaire), 18 April 1918.
  Notice de Renseignement, 14 January 1916 and 17 January 1917.
  Report by Contrôle Général, 23 December 1897.
  Report by Contrôle Général, 4 November 1898.
  Report from Contrôle Général, 12 January 1904.
  Report by Contrôle Général, 30 June 1913.
  Report by Contrôle Général, 13 December 1915.
KA 90, *Dossier du Personnel – Mouquin*:
  Career Summary No. 54.941.
  Report of 26 March 1874.
Notes sur la Préfecture de Police (1880) (Internal Police Instructions).

London School of Economics
Jebb Papers
  3/5/12: Letter from Joseph Kingsmill to Joshua Jebb, 24 February 1847.
  3/9/19: Letter from Joseph Kingsmill to Joshua Jebb, c. August 1850.

Bibliography

National Archives (Kew, Surrey)
Home Office Records (HO)
  Criminal Registers, HO 26 and HO 27 (1805–1892).
  Home Office Registered Papers, HO 45/292, 14 June 1842.
Prison Commission Records (PCOM)
  Female Licenses, PCOM 3/762/207, PCOM 3/764/146, PCOM 3/769/31, PCOM 3/770/10,
    PCOM 4/66/5, PCOM 4/69/13, PCOM 4/69/19, PCOM 4/70/2, PCOM 4/71/5, PCOM
    4/71/9, PCOM 4/71/17.
  Minute Book, Pentonville 1842–4, PCOM 2/84.
  Minute Book, Pentonville 1848–9, PCOM 2/88.
  Pentonville Prison, Chaplain's Journal 1846–51, PCOM 2/353.
Records of the Metropolitan Police Office (MEPO)
  General Instructions (1829) MEPO 8/1.
  MEPO 7/11, 10 December 1845.
  MEPO 7/6, 11 February and 9 May 1830.
  MEPO 7/6, 1 July 1840.
  MEPO 7/9, 19 June 1844.
  MEPO 7/16, 21 February 1855.
  MEPO 7/20, 6 January 1859.
  MEPO 7/24, 25 May 1863.

National Records of Scotland (Edinburgh)
Process Papers, MSS JC26/78/1/12-13

Norfolk Record Office (Norwich)
Great Yarmouth Gaol
  Gaol Committee, Y/TC 3/36 (1836–1850).
  Gaol Receiving Book, Y/D 41/28 (1842–1843).
  Gaol Registers, Y/L2 8 (1808–1838).
  Gaol Registers, Y/L2 9 (1839–1843).
  Gaol Keeper's Journal, Y/L2 47 (1836–1840).
  Gaol Keeper's Journal, Y/L2 48 (1841–1845).
  Index and Receiving Book, Y/L2 7 (1838–1839).
  Index of Examined Paupers, Y/L16/8, 1756–1844, MF/RO 597/6.

Tolhouse Museum (Great Yarmouth)
Copy Books Written by Prisoners (1840).
Everyday Books (1837–1842).
Prison School Journals (1836–1838).
Sarah Martin's Prisoner Register (1842), No. 119 and No. 120.

Published Primary Sources

Official Documents and Publications (in chronological order)
Hansard, *House of Commons Debates*, 141, 3 April 1856: 414.
Hansard, *House of Commons Debates*, 145, 15 May 1857: 310–11.
Hansard, *House of Commons Debates*, 146, 8 June 1857: 1372.
Hansard, *House of Lords Debates*, 153, 24 March 1859: 686.

Hansard, *House of Commons Debates*, 178, 1 May 1865: 1286.

Hansard, *House of Commons Debates*, 278, 20 April 1883: 735–859.

Hansard, *House of Commons Debates*, 382, 4 August 1942: 860–931.

Hansard, *House of Commons Debates*, 408, 8 March 1945: 2207.

Parliamentary Papers, Charles II c. 21 (1661).

Parliamentary Papers, Charles II c. 11 (1665).

Parliamentary Papers, Will III c. 32 (1698).

Parliamentary Papers, 11 Geo. IV and 1 Gul. IV c. 64 (1830).

Parliamentary Papers, 4 and 5 W. IV, c. 85 (1834).

Parliamentary Papers, 2 and 3 Vict c. 47 (1839).

Parliamentary Papers, 2 and 3 Vict c. 71 (1839).

Parliamentary Papers, 3 and 4 Vict c. 61 (1840).

Parliamentary Papers, 17 and 18 Vict c. 79 (1854).

Parliamentary Papers, 18 and 19 Vict c. 118 (1855).

Parliamentary Papers, 23 Vict c. 27 (1860).

Parliamentary Papers, 32 and 33 Vict c. 27 (1869).

Parliamentary Papers, 35 and 36 Vict c. 94 (1872).

Parliamentary Papers, *Children and Young Persons Act*, 23 Geo. V c. 5 (1933).

Parliamentary Papers, *United States of America (Visiting Forces) Act*, 5 & 6 Geo. VI c. 31 (1942).

Parliamentary Papers, *Report from the Committee on the state of Police of the Metropolis 1816* (Cmnd. 510), Vol. V (1816).

Parliamentary Papers, *Third Report from the Committee on the State of Police of the Metropolis 1818* (Cmnd. 423), Vol. VIII (1818).

Parliamentary Papers, *Report from the Committee on the State of Police of the Metropolis 1822* (Cmnd. 440), Vol. IV (1822).

Parliamentary Papers, *Report from the Select Committee on the Police of the Metropolis 1828* (Cmnd. 533), Vol. VI (1828).

Parliamentary Papers, *A Return of All General Orders, Issued by the Magistrates Appointed under the Act of 1829, Since the Formation of the New Police: Instructions Part I, Police Constables* (Cmnd. 505), Vol. XXIII (1830).

Parliamentary Papers, *Report from the Select Committee on the Observance of the Sabbath Day* (Cmnd. VIII) (1831).

Parliamentary Papers, *Report from the Select Committee on the Petition of Frederick Young and Others* (Cmnd. 627), Vol. XIII (1833).

Parliamentary Papers, *Report from the Select Committee on Inquiry into Drunkenness* (Cmnd. 559) (1834).

Parliamentary Papers, Penitentiaries (United States) – *Report of William Crawford, Esq., on the Penitentiaries of the United States* (Cmnd. 593) (1834).

Parliamentary Papers, *Parliamentary Report on the Metropolis Police Offices 1837/8* (Cmnd. 578), Vol. XV (1838).

Parliamentary Papers, *Third Report of the Inspectors Appointed Under the Provisions of the Act 5 & 6 Will. IV. c. 38. to Visit the Different Prisons of Great Britain* (Cmnd. 141), Vol. I – Home District (1838).

Parliamentary Papers, *Report of the Royal Commission on the Constabulary Force (Constabulary Force Report)* (Cmnd. 169), Vol. XIX (1839).

Parliamentary Papers, *Inspectors of Prisons of Great Britain II, Northern and Eastern District, Fourth Report* (Cmnd. 199) (1839).

Parliamentary Papers, *Inspectors of Prisons of Great Britain II, Northern and Eastern District, Fifth Report* (Cmnd. 258) (1840).

Bibliography

Parliamentary Papers, *Report of Prison Inspectors, Eighth Report* (Cmnd. 517) (1843).

Parliamentary Papers, *(First) Report of the Commissioners for the Government of the Pentonville Prison* (Cmnd. 449) (1843).

Parliamentary Papers, (Joshua Jebb) *First Report of the Surveyor-General of Prisons on the Construction, Ventilation and Details of Pentonville Prison* (Cmnd. 594) (1844).

Parliamentary Papers, *Report from the Select Committee on Gaming* (Cmnd. 297) (1844).

Parliamentary Papers, *Second Report of the Commissioners for the Government of the Pentonville Prison* (Cmnd. 536) (1844).

Parliamentary Papers, *The Three Reports from the Select Committee of the House of Lords Appointed to Require into the Laws Respecting Gaming* (Cmnd. VII) (1844).

Parliamentary Papers, *Third Report of the Commissioners for the Government of the Pentonville Prison* (Cmnd. 613) (1845), Appendix C, Chaplain's Report.

Parliamentary Papers, *Fourth Report of the Commissioners for the Government of the Pentonville Prison* (Cmnd. 751) (1846), Appendix B, Chaplain's Report.

Parliamentary Papers, *Second Report from the Select Committee of the House of Lords, Minutes of Evidence* (Cmnd. 534) (1847).

Parliamentary Papers, *Fifth Report of the Commissioners for the Government of the Pentonville Prison* (Cmnd. 818) (1847), Appendix B, Chaplain's Report.

Parliamentary Papers, (Joshua Jebb) *Second Report of the Surveyor-General of Prisons* (Cmnd. 867) (1847).

Parliamentary Papers, *Sixth Report of the Commissioners for the Government of the Pentonville Prison* (Cmnd. 972), Appendix B, Chaplain's Report (1848).

Parliamentary Papers, *Seventh Report of the Commissioners for the Government of the Pentonville Prison* (Cmnd. 1101) (1849), Appendix B.

Parliamentary Papers, *Eighth Report of the Commissioners for the Government of the Pentonville Prison* (Cmnd. 1192) (1850), Appendix B, Chaplain's Report.

Parliamentary Papers, *Report from the Select Committee on Prison Discipline, Minutes of Evidence* (Cmnd. 632) (July 1850).

Parliamentary Papers, *Reports of the Directors of Convict Prisons on the Discipline and Management of Pentonville, Parkhurst, and Millbank Prisons, and of Portland Prison and the Hulks for the Year 1850* (Cmnd. 1409) (1851), Appendix B, Chaplain's Report, Pentonville.

Parliamentary Papers, 24 & 25 Vict c. 100 (1861).

Parliamentary Papers, *Report of Royal Commission upon the Administration and Operation of the Contagious Diseases Acts. Vol. 1 – The Report* (Cmnd. 408–10) (1871).

Parliamentary Papers, *Contagious Diseases Acts: Copy of Annual Report, for 1874, of Captain Harris, Assistant Commissioner of Police of the Metropolis, on the Operation of the Contagious Diseases Acts* (Cmnd. 97) (1875).

Parliamentary Papers, *Annual Report of Assistant Commissioner of Police of Metropolis on Operation of Contagious Disease Acts* (Cmnd. 351) (1881).

Parliamentary Papers, *Report from the Select Committee on the Contagious Diseases Acts* (Cmnd. 351) (1881).

Parliamentary Papers, *Report from the Select Committee on Contagious Diseases Acts* (Cmnd. 340) (1882).

Parliamentary Papers, 61 & 62 Vict c. 36 (1898).

Parliamentary Papers, *Return of Summary Convictions for Street Betting in the Metropolitan Police District during the years 1903, 1904, and 1905* (Cmnd. 179), Vol. XCIX (1906).

Parliamentary Papers, *Judicial Statistics, England and Wales, 1907. Part I – Criminal Statistics* (Cmnd. 4544), Vol. CIV (1909).

Parliamentary Papers, *Royal Commission on Capital Punishment, 1949–1953 – Report* (Cmnd. 8932) (1953).

Parliamentary Papers, Penal Servitude Acts Commission, *Report of the Commissioners Appointed to Inquire into the Working of the Penal Servitude Acts, Vol. I – Commissions and Report, 1878–79* (Cmnd. 2368, 2368-I and 2368-II), Vol. I (1979).
United States Court of Appeal, Third Circuit, *Johnson v. Dye*, 175 F. 2d 250, 253 (1949).
United States Supreme Court, *Powell v. Alabama* 287 U.S. 45 (1932).
United States Supreme Court, *Norris v. Alabama* 294 U.S. 587(1935).
United States Supreme Court, *Morgan v. Virginia*, 328 U.S. 373 (1946).

Newspapers and Periodicals

Aberdeen Weekly Journal,
   9 April 1879, Issue 7531
   15 July 1879, Issue 7615
Atlanta Journal-Constitution,
   15 December 1917
   30 June 1920
   16 December 1932
   21 December 1943
   26 June 1952
   30 November 1976
Baner ac Amserau Cymru (The Banner and Times of Wales), 16 July 1879, Issue 1168
Belfast News-Letter,
   29 March 1879, Issue 19832
   31 July 1879, Issue 20018
Boston Globe,
   3 February 1945
   21 February 1945
   24 February 1945
   26 February 1945
   6 March 1945
   8 March 1945
   9 March 1945
Birmingham Daily Post,
   29 March 1879, Issue 6466
   30 April 1879, Issue 6493
Bristol Mercury and Daily Post,
   31 March 1879, Issue 9632
   1 April 1879, Issue 9633
British Medical Journal, 16 December 1946
Cobbett's Annual Register, 3 April 1802
Collier's Weekly, 8 November 1924
Daily Express, 9 July 2011
Daily Gazette,
   29 March 1879, Issue 3675
   8 July 1879, Issue 3760
   10 July 1879, Issue 3762
Daily Mail,
   6 July 2011
   24 May 2012

Daily News,
    13 February 1879, Issue 10240
    29 March 1879, Issue 10278
    10 April 1879, Issue 10288
    4 July 1879, Issue 10361
Dundee Courier and Argus,
    18 July 1879, Issue 8110
    1 August 1879, Issue 8122
Edinburgh Evening News, 4 July 1874
Evening Express,
    5 December 1906
    14 December 1906
    15 December 1906
    23 April 1907
    24 April 1907
    22 March 1907
    24 April 1907
    26 April 1907
    27 April 1907
    29 April 1907
Freeman's Journal and Daily Commercial Advertiser, 4 August 1879
Hue & Cry,
    3 December 1773
    1 April 1809
    14 December 1816
    16 November 1822
Illustrated London News,
    9 August 1879, Issue 808
Illustrated Police News,
    1 March 1879, Issue 785
    12 April 1879, Issue 791
    19 April 1879, Issue 792
    26 April 1879, Issue 793
    3 May 1879, Issue 794
    10 May 1879, Issue 795
    17 May 1879, Issue 796
    24 May 1879, Issue 797
    12 July 1879, Issue 804
    19 July 1879, Issue 805
    26 July 1879, Issue 806
    2 August 1879, Issue 807
    9 August 1879, Issue 808
Jackson's Oxford Journal, 9 September 1826
John Bull,
    5 April 1879, Issue 3043
    19 April 1879, Issue 3045
    12 July 1879, Issue 446
La Lanterne, 7 October 1879
L'Aurore,
    2 July 1899

8 July 1908

4 February 1909

5 February 1909

7 February 1909

17 May 1909

Leeds Mercury,
   29 March 1879, Issue 12782

   8 July 1879, Issue 12868

   30 July 1879, Issue 12887

Le Journal, 15 August 1898

Liverpool Mercury,
   25 May 1866, Issue 5716

   1 August 1879, Issue 9844

Lloyd's Weekly Newspaper,
   14 December 1851

   30 March 1879, Issue 1897

   10 April 1879, Issue 1899

   4 May 1879, Issue 1902

   13 July 1879, Issue 1912

Manchester Times, 10 May 1879, Issue 1117

Mercury (Hobart),
   7 March 1860

   2 June 1871

   16 May 1874

   16 May 1874

   17 May 1874

   18 May 1874

   19 May 1874

   20 July 1874

   1 March 1883

Morning Post, 27 October 1818

New York Times,
   2 July 1921

   15 December 1932

   16 December 1932

   31 January 1932

   3 September 1989

Pall Mall Gazette, 28 September 1871, Issue 2067

Reynolds' Newspaper,
   30 March 1879, Issue 1494

   6 April 1879, Issue 1495

   13 July 1879, Issue 1509

The Blackburn Standard, 12 July 1879, Issue 2282

The Bury and Norwich Post and Suffolk Herald, 8 April 1879, Issue 5050

The Cambrian,
   1 February 1907

   26 April 1907

The Cardiff Times,
   4 May 1907

   27 April 1907

Bibliography

The Cheshire Observer, 12 July 1879, Issue 1405

The Daily Mirror,
   14 December 1906
   25 April 1907
   26 April 1907
   27 April 1907
   29 April 1907

The Daily News,
   13 October 1857
   6 April 1859

The Era,
   17 March 1839
   9 October 1859

The Graphic,
   24 May 1879, Issue 495
   19 July 1879, Issue 503

The Guardian, 10 April 2014

The Huddersfield Chronicle,
   4 April 1879, Issue 3639
   5 April 1789, Issue 3640

The Hull Packet and East Riding Times, 18 July 1879, Issue 4900

The Independent, 30 December 1994

The Lancaster Gazette, 16 July 1879, Issue 4946

The Manchester Guardian,
   24 May 1822
   5 January 1828
   25 April 1907
   27 April 1907

The Morning Post,
   21 November 1839
   10 December 1839
   21 August, 1866, Issue 28921
   19 March 1879, Issue 33299
   8 July 1879, Issue 33394
   31 July 1879, Issue 33414

The Morning Chronicle,
   4 January 1802
   2 December 1839
   4 August 1842
   25 October 1852
   6 October 1856
   8 November 1858

The Newcastle Courant, 18 July 1879, Issue 10672

The Penny Illustrated Paper and Illustrated Times,
   5 July 1879, Issue 936
   12 July 1879, Issue 937
   19 July 1879, Issue 938
   2 August 1879, Issue 940

The Sheffield and Rotherham and Independent,
   15 April 1879, Issue 7668

10 July 1879, Issue 7740
23 July 1879, Issue 7751
2 August 1879, Issue 7760
The Shield, 8 April 1876, Issue 255/46
The Standard,
    27 August 1839
    7 September 1839
    20 September 1843
The Telegraph, 5 July 2011
The Times,
    4 April 1800
    4 August 1811
    11 July 1815
    27 July 1815
    11 July 1816
    27 October 1818
    7 April 1825
    17 December 1825
    18 October 1839
    10 December 1839
    25 December 1839
    8 December 1842
    24 February 1843
    20 September 1843
    26 September 1843
    27 March 1844
    1 December 1847
    10 July 1865
    28 March 1879, Issue 29527
    29 March 1879, Issue 29528
    2 April 1879, Issue 29531
    3 April 1879, Issue 29532
    29 July 1879, Issue 29632
    30 July 1879, Issue 29633
    11 August 1881
    4 November 1881
    14 December 1906
    23 April 1907
    27 April 1907
    25 July 1917
    18 September 1924
    16 October 1944
    28 November 1944
    17 January 1945
    18 January 1945
    20 January 1945
    21 January 1945
    24 January 1945
    26 January 1945
    20 February 1945

Bibliography

7 March 1945
9 March 1945
4 May 1945
20 October 1956

The York Herald,
15 July 1879, Issue 6994
30 July 1879, Issue 7007
1 August 1879, Issue 7009
28 August 1879, Issue 7032

Weekly Mail,
27 April 1907
4 May 1907

Western Mail, 4 April 1879, Issue 3091

Y Genedl Gymreig (The Welsh Nation),
3 April 1879, Issue 113
17 July 1879, Issue 128

Online Sources

Agustín, L.M. (2005) 'Helping Women Who Sell Sex: The Construction of Benevolent Identities', *Rhizomes: Cultural Studies in Emerging Knowledge,* Issue 10 (Accessed via http://www .rhizomes.net/issue10/index.html)

Amirtha, T. (2015) 'Why Dark Tourism Is Thriving', *Motherboard,* 29 October 2015. (Accessed via http://motherboard.vice.com/en_uk/read/sightseeing-in-hell)

Bender, T. (2006) 'History, Theory & the Metropolis', *CMS Working Paper Series,* No. 5. (Accessed via http://www.metropolitanstudies.de/workingpaper/bender_005-2006.pdf)

Cox, D.J. (2010) 'Ruthven, George Thomas Joseph (1792/3–1844), Police Officer'.

Forsythe, B. (2004) 'Kingsmill, Joseph (1805/6–1865)'.

Forsythe, B. (2004) 'Russell, William Whitworth (1795–1847)'.

Lentin, A. (2004) 'Mathews, Sir Charles Willie, Baronet (1850–1920)'.

Manchester Prison Records – 1872. (Accessed via findmypast.co.uk)

Oxford Dictionary of National Biography Online. (Accessed from http://www.oxforddnb.com/)

Pooley, W. (29 September 2015) 'Native to the Past: History, Anthropology and Folklore' in *Past and Present* (Virtual Issue), No. 229. (Accessed via http://past.oxfordjournals.org/content/ early/2015/09/29/pastj.gtv038.short?rss=1)

Rogers, H. (2015) 'A Very Fair Statement of His Past Life: Transported Convicts, Former Lives and Previous Offences', *Open Library of the Humanities,* Vol. 1, No. 1. (Accessed via at http:// researchonline.ljmu.ac.uk/2278/)

Rustin, B. (1949) 'Report on Twenty-Two Days on the Chain Gang at Roxboro, North Carolina' from the Document Collection Center at Yale University. (Accessed from www.documents .law.yale.edu/sites/default/files/Official-report-chain-gang.pdf)

The Proceedings of the Old Bailey (Accessed from www.oldbaileyonline.org)

The Trial of Thomas Northem (1811) Ref. t18110529-42.

The Trial of George Sanders and Elizabeth Sanders (1846) Ref. t18460105-469.

The Trial of Elizabeth Hodges (1853) Ref. t18530404-511.

The Trial of Jane Haynes (1860) Ref. t18601217-78.

The Trial of Annie Vinten (1862) Ref. t18620106-199.

The Trial of John Metze (1863) Ref. t18630302-489.

The Trial of John Wainwright (1866) Ref. t18660409-378.

The Trial of Margaret O'Brien (1871) Ref. t18710403-342.

The Trial of Thomas Bryant (1873) Ref. t18730922-578.
The Trial of Ann Mills (1879) Ref. t18791020-950.
The Trial of Thomas Perryman (1879) Ref. t18790331-395.
The Trial of Catherine Webster (1879) Ref. t18790630-653.
The Trial of Eleanor Myers (1881) Ref. t18810228-308.
The Trial of Louis Wheeler (1885) Ref. t18850302-369.
The Trial of Susan Sophia Grant (1886) Ref. t18860913-977.
The Trial of Ellen Giles (1892) Ref. t18920111-178.
The Trial of Freeman Ellingham (1897) Ref. t18970524-415.
The Trial of Maria Abbott (1900) Ref. t19001210-74.
The Trial of Helen Nemetsclek (1900) Ref. t19000625-446.
The Trial of William Lilley (1906) Ref. t19060521-31.
The Trial of Frederick Parker (1906) Ref. t19060625-15.
The Trial of Louis Gold and Harry Cohen (1907) Ref. t19070422.
The Trial of Isaac Eidinow (1907) Ref. t19070422).
The Trial of Charles Laroche (1907) Ref. t19070422-38.
The Trial of Lilian Sarah Woodcock (1907) Ref. t19070528-46.
The Trial of John Lawrence (1909) Ref. t19090622-54.

Other Works

(1773) *The Bow Street Opera. In Three Acts. Written on the Plan of the Beggar's Opera. All the Most Celebrated Songs of Which Are Parodied and the Whole Piece Adapted to Modern Times, Manners and Characters* (London: Marriner).

(1774) *The Monthly Review*, Vol. 49, p. 346.

(1840) *Home Office Regulations for Prisons in England and Wales* – Regulation 229 (London: Shaw & Sons).

(1845) 'The Believer's Death', *Selections from the Poetical Remains of the Late Miss Sarah Martin of Great Yarmouth* (Yarmouth: James M. Denew).

(1879) *Trial, Sentence and Execution of Kate Webster for the Murder of Mrs Thomas at Richmond*, Bodleian Library, John Johnson Collection, Broadsides: Murder and Execution, 11 (18).

(1901) *A Century of Law Reform: Twelve Lectures on the Changes in the Law of England during the Nineteenth Century* (London: Council of Legal Education).

Acts of the Parliaments of Scotland, 1124–1707 (Twelve Volumes) (London: HMSO).

Angelo, H. (1830) *Reminiscences of Henry Angelo* (Two Volumes) (London: Henry Colburn and Richard Bentley).

Anon. (1811) *The Trial of the Reverend Robert Bingham, Taken in Shorthand by Mr Adams, by Order of the Directors of The Union Fire Office, London* (London: J.M. Richardson).

Anon. (1844) *A Brief Sketch of the Life of the Late Miss Sarah Martin of Great Yarmouth, With Extracts from the Parliamentary Reports on Prisons; Her Own Journals &c* (Yarmouth: C. Barber).

Anon. (1827) *Richmond: Scenes from the Life of a Bow Street Runner* (London: Henry Colbourn).

Anon. (c. 1845) *The Handsome Wife* (London: Ryle & Co).

Arrot Browning, C. (1847) *The Convict Ship, and England's Exiles* (London: Hamilton, Adams & Co.).

Babbington Macaulay, T. (1849–65) *The History of England* (Five Volumes) (London: John Wilson).

Baker, A. (1973) *Stolen Sweets* (New York: Saturday Review Press).

Baring Gould, S. (1880) *Mehalah: A Story of the Salt Marshes* (London: John Murray).

Bibliography

Bending, L. (2000) *The Representation of Bodily Pain in Late Nineteenth-century English Culture* (Oxford: Oxford University Press).

Berkman, A. (1912) *Prison Memoirs of an Anarchist* (New York: Mother Earth Publishing Co.).

Bleiler, E.F. (ed.) (1976 reprint of 1827 edition) *Richmond – Scenes from the Life of a Bow Street Runner* (New York: Dover Publications).

Brown, A.R. (1968) *Freedom from Florida Chains Illustrated* (New York: Carlton Press).

Bruce, A. (1995) *Blind Justice* (New York: Berkeley).

Buchan, J. (1924) *The Three Hostages* (London: Hodder and Stoughton).

Burns, R.E. (1997 edition) *I am a Fugitive from a Georgia Chain Gang* (Athens: University of Georgia Press).

Burt, J.T. (1852) *Results of the System of Separate Confinement as Administered at the Pentonville Prison* (London: Longman, Brown, Green and Longman).

Byron, Baron G.G. (1824) *Don Juan* (London: J. & H.L. Hunt).

Casserly, G. (1926) *The Desert Lovers* (London: Blackledge).

Charteris, L. (1928) *Meet the Tiger* (London: Ward Lock).

Cleaver, E. (1967) *Soul on Ice* (New York: McGraw Hill).

Cleaver, E. (1978) *Soul on Fire* (London: Hodder).

Cleaver, E. (2015) *Target Zero: A Life in Writing* (London: St. Martin's Press).

Cobbett, W. and T.B. Howell (eds) (1809–26) *A Complete Collection of State Trials* (Thirty-Four Volumes) (London: Hansard).

Cole, M. (2007) 'The FSA's Approach to Insider Dealing', Speech, American Bar Association, 4 October 2007.

Conan Doyle, A. (1887) 'A Study in Scarlet', *Beaton's Christmas Annual*, Vol. 28, pp. 1–95.

Conan Doyle, A. (1892) 'The Adventure of the Blue Carbuncle' in his *The Adventures of Sherlock Holmes* (London: George Newness)

Craig, M. (1697) *A Lie Is No Scandal, Or a Vindication of Mr Mungo Craig form a Ridiculous Calumny Cast upon Him by T.A. Who Was Executed for Apostasy at Edinburgh, the 8 of January, 1697* (Edinburgh: W. Bell).

Davis, A.Y. (1974) *An Autobiography* (New York: Random House).

Debs, E. (1927) *Walls and Bars* (Chicago: Socialist Party Press).

Dickens, C. (1850) 'Pet Prisoners', *Household Words: A Weekly Journal*, Vol. 1, No. 5, pp. 97–103.

Dickens, C. (1852) *Bleak House* (Four Volumes) (Leipzig: Bernhard Tauschnitz).

Ellis, S.M. (1927) *The Solitary Horseman* (London: The Cayme Press).

Falkirk, R. (1974) *Beau Blackstone* (New York: Stein & Day).

Fielding, H. (1988 reprint of 1751 edition) *An Enquiry into the Causes of the Late Increase of Robbers and Related Writings* (Edited by Malvin R. Zirker) (Oxford: Clarendon Press).

Fielding, J. (1755) *A Plan for Preventing Robberies within Twenty Miles of London, With an Account of the Rise and Establishment of the Real Thieftakers* (London: A. Millar).

Forrester, A. (2012 reprint of 1864 edition) *The Female Detective* (London: British Library).

Gissing, G. (1889) *The Nether World* (London: Dent).

Guyot, Y. (1879) *La Préfecture de Police par un Vieux Petit Employé* (Paris: La Lanterne).

Guyot, Y. (1884) *La Police* (Paris: Charpentier).

Haldane, A. and V. Madouros (2012) 'The Dog and the Frisbee' (Federal Bank of Kansas Economic Policy Symposium, Jackson Hole, Wyoming, 31 August 2012). http://www.bis.org /review/r120905a.pdf.

Hannam v FCA (2014) UKUT 0233 (TCC).

Harsh, G. (1971) *Lonesome Road* (New York: W.W. Norton).

Jackson, G. (1970) *Soledad Brother: The Prison Letters of George Jackson* (Chicago: Chicago Review Press).

Jackson, G. (1990 edition) *Blood in My Eye* (Baltimore: Black Classic Press).

James, G.P.R. (1833) *Delaware or The Ruined Family* [Three Volumes] (London: Cadell).

James, G.P.R. (1848) *Thirty Years Since: Or The Ruined Family* (London: Simpkin Marshall & Co.).

Jebb, J. (1844) *Modern Prisons: Their Construction and Ventilation* (London: John Weale).

Jebb, J. (1850) *Report on the Discipline and Construction of Portland Prison and Its Connection with the System of Convict Discipline Now in Operation* (London: William Clowes and Sons).

Johnston, H. and B. Godfrey (2013) *The Costs of Imprisonment: A Longitudinal Study, ESRC End of Award Report, RES-062-23-3102* (Swindon: ESRC).

Karstedt, S. and S. Farrall (2007) 'Law-abiding Majority? The Everyday Crimes of the Middle Classes', Third Briefing, Centre for Crime and Justice Studies, June 2007.

Kerr, D. (1936 edition) *Forensic Medicine* (London: Black).

Kingsmill, J. (1849) *Prisons and Prisoners* (London: J.H. Jackson).

Kingsmill, J. (1854 edition) *Chapters on Prisons and Prisoners and the Prevention of Crime* (London: Longman, Brown, Green and Longman).

Kingsmill, J. (1855) *Faith's Triumph in Death: A Sermon, Preached in the Church of St. John, Horsleydown, Southwark, November 26, 1854, upon the Death of the Rev. James Ralph* (London: Longman, Brown, Green and Longman).

Kingsmill, J. (1856) *The Sabbath the Working Man's True Charter: Thoughts for Thinking Men of the Industrial Classes, on the Sabbath Question* (London: Longman, Brown, Green, and Longmans).

Law Commission (1999) *Fraud and Deception: A Consultation Paper*, CP No. 155 (London: HMSO), para 1.4.

Lorimer, W. (1713) *Two Discourses: The One Setting Forth the True and Only Way of Attaining Salvation. The Other Shewing Why and How All Ought to Reverence Jesus Christ, the Son of God and Saviour of Men* (London: John Lawrence).

Lowrie, D. (1912) *My Life in Prison* (London: John Lane, The Bodley Head).

Martin, S. (undated) *The Prison Visitor of Great Yarmouth, With Extracts from her Writings and Prison Journals* (London: Religious Tract Society).

Mayhew, H. and J. Binny (1862) *The Criminal Prisons of London and Scenes of Prison Life* (London: Griffin & Co.).

Measor, C.P. (1861) *The Convict Service: A Letter to Sir George Cornewall Lewis […] on the Administration, Results and Expense of the Present Convict System* (London: Robert Hardwicke).

Metropolitan Police (1862) *General Regulations, Instructions, and Orders, For the Government and Guidance of the Metropolitan Police* (London: HMSO).

Norris, C. and S.D. Washington (1979) *The Last of the Scottsboro Boys: An Autobiography* (New York: G.P. Putnam's Sons).

O'Hare, K.R. (1976 edition) *In Prison* (Seattle and London: University of Washington Press).

Orwell, G. (2009) *The Decline of the English Murder* (London: Penguin).

Osborne, Rt Hon George MP (2015) Mansion House Speech (London), 10 June 2015.

Patterson, H. and E. Conrad (1969 edition) *Scottsboro Boy* (Toronto: Collier Books).

Pelantant, Commissaire L. (1906) *Rapport sur le Service de la Police* (Grenoble: Imprimérie Générale).

Pitcairn, A. (ed.) (1843) *Acts of the General Assembly of the Church of Scotland, 1638–1842* (Two Volumes) (Edinburgh: Ritchie).

Sayers, D.L. (1923) *Whose Body?* (New York: Boni & Liveright).

Smith, F.J. (ed.) (1910 edition) *Taylor's Principles and Practice of Medical Jurisprudence* (London: J.A. Churchill).

Stockton, K. (2012) *The Missing Heiress* (London: Knox Robinson).

Thorndike, R. (1927) *The Further Adventures of Dr Syn* (London: Rich & Cowan).

Bibliography

UNODC (2006) *The Integrity and Accountability of the Police: Criminal Justice Assessment Toolkit* (New York: United Nations).

United States of America War Office (1920) *The Articles of War* (Washington: Government Printing Office).

Wright, R. (1999) 'The Investigation and Prosecution of Serious and Complex Fraud towards the Twenty-first Century', ISRCL Commercial and Financial Fraud Conference, 12 July 1999.

Secondary Sources

Monographs and Key Edited Collections

Ager, A.W. (2014) *Crime and Poverty in Nineteenth Century England: The Economy of Makeshifts* (London: Bloomsbury).

Agulhon, M. (1990) *La République 1880–1932* (Paris: Hachette).

Allan, D. (2002) *Scotland in the Eighteenth Century: Union and Enlightenment* (Harlow: Pearson Education).

Altick, R.D. (1970) *Victorian Studies in Scarlet: Murders and Manners in the Age of Victoria* (New York: W.W. Norton and Co.).

Alwyn, R. (1945) *The Cleft Chin Murder* (London: Claude Morris).

Anderson, M. (2011) *In Thrall to Political Change: Police and Gendarmerie in France* (Oxford: Oxford University Press).

Andrew, D.T. (2013) *Aristocratic Vice: The Attack on Duelling, Suicide, Adultery, and Gambling in Eighteenth-century England* (New Haven and London: Yale University Press).

Armitage, G. (1932) *The History of the Bow Street Runners 1729–1829* (London: Wishart & Co.).

Ashe, T.M. and L. Counsell (1993) *Insider Trading* (Croydon: Tolley).

Babington, A. (1999 edition) *A House in Bow Street: Crime and the Magistracy, London 1740–1881* (London: Macdonald).

Baggoley, M. (2011) *Surrey Executions: A Complete List of Those Hanged in the County during the Nineteenth Century* (Stroud: Amberley Publishing).

Bailey, P. (1978) *Leisure and Class in Victorian England: Rational Recreation and the Contest for Control, 1830–1885* (London: Routledge and Kegan Paul and Toronto: University of Toronto Press).

Bailey, V. (ed.) (1981) *Policing and Punishment in Nineteenth Century Britain* (London: Croom Helm).

Ballinger, A. (2000) *Dead Women Walking: Executed Women in England and Wales 1900–1955* (Aldershot: Ashgate).

Bamford, S. (1964) *Passages in the Life of a Radical* (Oxford: Oxford University Press).

Beattie, J.M. (1986) *Crime and the Courts in England 1660–1800* (Oxford: Oxford University Press).

Beattie, J.M. (2001) *Policing and Punishment in London 1660–1750: Urban Crime and the Limits of Terror* (Oxford: Oxford University Press).

Beattie, J.M. (2012) *The First English Detectives: The Bow Street Runners and the Policing of London 1750–1840* (Oxford: Oxford University Press).

Bechofer Roberts, C.E. (1945) *The Trial of Hulten and Jones* (London: Jarrolds).

Bell, I.A. (1991) *Literature and Crime in Augustan England* (London: Routledge).

Benson, M.L. and S.S. Simpson (2009) *White-collar Crime: An Opportunity Perspective* (London: Routledge).

Bentley, D. (1998) *English Criminal Justice in the Nineteenth Century* (London: Hambledon Press).

Bequai, A. (1978) *White-collar Crime: A Twentieth Century Crisis* (Massachusetts: Lexington Press).

Berlière, J-M. (1993) *Le Préfet Lépine: Vers la Naissance de la Police Moderne* (Paris: Denoël).

Berlière, J-M. (1996) *Le Monde des Polices en France* (Paris: Complexes).

Berlière, J-M. and R. Lévy (2011) *Histoire des Polices en France de l'Ancien Régime à nos Jours* (Paris: Nouveau Monde).

Bernstein, S. and G. Bernstein (1987) *La IIIe République* (Paris: Seuil).

Black, J. (2001) *The English Press 1621–1861* (Stroud: Sutton).

Black, J. and D. McRaild (2002) *Nineteenth-century Britain* (Basingstoke: Palgrave).

Blackmon, D. (2008) *Slavery by Another Name: The Re-Enslavement of Black Americans from the Civil War to World War II* (New York: Random House).

Blue, E. (2012) *Doing Time in the Depression: Everyday Life in Texas and California Prisons* (New York: New York University Press).

Brooks, C. (1997) *Communities and Courts in Britain, 1150–1900* (London: Bloomsbury).

Brown, C. (2001) *The Death of Christian Britain: Understanding Secularisation 1800–2000* (London: Routledge).

Bruneteaux, P. (1996) *Maintenir l'Ordre* (Paris: FNSP).

Burns, V.G. (1942) *Out of These Chains* (Los Angeles: New World Books).

Burns, V.G. (1968) *The Man Who Broke a Thousand Chains: The Story of Social Reformation of the Prisons of the South* (Washington: Acropolis Books).

Canty, S. (1855) *George Seten or the Chip Boy of the Dry Dock: A Tale of City Life* (New York: Garrett).

Carbado, D.W. and D. Weise (eds) (2015 edition) *Time on Two Crosses: The Collected Writings of Bayard Rustin* (New York: Cleis Press Inc.).

Carrabine, E., P. Cox, M. Lee and N. South (2002) *Crime in Modern Britain* (Oxford: Oxford University Press).

Carter, D.T. (1969) *Scottsboro: A Tragedy of the American South* (Baton Rouge: Louisiana State University Press).

Carter Wood, J. (2004) *Violence and Crime in Nineteenth-century England: The Shadow of Our Refinement* (London: Routledge).

Catsam, D. (2009) *Freedom's Main Line: The Journey of Reconciliation and the Freedom Rides* (Lexington: University Press of Kentucky).

Clark, A. (1987) *Women's Silence, Men's Violence: Sexual Assault in England 1770–1845* (London and New York: Pandora Press).

Clarke, K. (2013) *Bad Companions: Six London Murderesses Who Shocked the World* (Stroud: The History Press).

Clerk, R. (2009) *Capital Punishment in Britain* (Hersham: Ian Allen).

Cockburn, J.S. and T.A. Green (eds) (2014) *Twelve Good Men and True: The Criminal Trial Jury in England, 1200–1800* (Princeton: Princeton University Press).

Coleman, C. (1996) *Understanding Crime Data: Haunted by the Dark Figure* (Buckingham: Open University Press).

Collins, P. (2013) *Duel with the Devil: The True Story of How Alexander Hamilton and Aaron Burr Teamed Up to Take on America's First Sensational Murder Mystery* (New York: Crown Publishers).

Colquhoun, K. (2014) *Did She Kill Him? A Victorian Tale of Deception, Adultery and Arsenic* (London: Little Brown).

Conley, C.A. (2007) *Certain Other Countries: Homicide, Gender, and National Identity in Late Nineteenth-century England, Ireland, Scotland and Wales* (Columbus: Ohio State University Press).

Couser, G.T. (1989) *Altered Egos: Authority in American Autobiography* (New York: Oxford University Press).

Bibliography

Cox, D.J. (2012) 'A Certain Share of Low Cunning': A History of the Bow Street Runners 1792–1839 (London: Routledge).

Cox, D.J. (2013) Crime in England 1688–1815 (London: Routledge).

Cox, D.J., K. Stevenson, C. Harris and J. Rowbotham (2015) Public Indecency in England 1857–1960 (London: Routledge).

Cressy, D. (2001) Agnes Bowker's Cat; Travesties and Transgressions in Tudor and Stuart England (Oxford: Oxford University Press).

Critchley, T.A. (1978) A History of the Police in England and Wales (Edinburgh: Constable).

Crone, R. (2012) Violent Victorians: Popular Entertainment in Nineteenth Century London (Manchester: Manchester University Press).

Darnton, R. (1985) The Great Cat Massacre and Other Episodes in French Cultural History (London: Vintage Books).

Daudet, L. (1934) La Police Politique, Ses Moyens et Ses Crimes (Paris: Denoël).

Davie, N. (2015) The Penitentiary Ten: The Transformation of the English Prison, 1770–1850 (Oxford: Bardwell Press).

D'Cruze, S. (1998) Crimes of Outrage: Sex, Violence and Victorian Working Women (London: Routledge).

D'Cruze, S. and L.A. Jackson (2009) Women, Crime and Justice in England since 1660 (Gender and History) (London: Palgrave Macmillan).

D'Cruze, S., S. Walklate and S. Pegg (2011 edition) Murder (Abingdon: Routledge)

De Beer, E.S. (1976–89) The Correspondence of John Locke (Eight Volumes) (Oxford: Clarendon Press).

Deluermoz, Q. (2012) Policiers dans la Ville: La Construction d'un Ordre Public à Paris, 1854–1914 (Paris: Sorbonne).

Devine, T.M. (1999) The Scottish Nation 1700–2000 (London: Penguin).

Donoghue, B. and G. Jones (2001) Herbert Morrison Portrait of a Politician (London: Phoenix).

Dyhouse, C. (2013 Kindle Edition) Girl Trouble, Panic and Progress in the History of Young Women (London: Zed Books).

Eakin, P.J. (1992) Touching the World: Reference in Autobiography (Princeton, NJ: Princeton University Press).

Eastwood, D. (1993) Governing Rural England: Tradition and Transformation in Local Government 1780–1840 (Oxford: Clarendon Press).

Emsley, C. (1983) Policing and Its Context 1750–1870 (London: Macmillan).

Emsley, C. (1996) The English Police: A Political and Social History (London: Routledge).

Emsley, C. (2005) Hard Men: Violence in England since 1750 (London: Hambledon).

Emsley, C. (2010 edition) Crime and Society in England: 1750–1900 (Abingdon: Routledge).

Evans, D.M. (1968 edition) Facts, Failures and Frauds Revelations: Financial Mercantile Criminal (New York: Augustus M Kelley).

Evans, D.M. (1970) The Commercial Crisis 1847–1848 (1848, reprinted New York: Burt Franklin).

Evans, R. (1998) Tales From the German Underworld: Crime and Punishment in the Nineteenth Century (Yale: Yale University Press).

Ferguson, E.E. (2010) Gender and Justice: Violence, Intimacy, and Community in Fin-de-Siècle Paris (Baltimore: John Hopkins University Press).

Ferguson, W. (1990) Scotland 1689 to the Present (Edinburgh: Mercat Press).

Fitzgerald, P. (1972 reprint of 1888 edition) Chronicle of Bow Street Police Office: With an Account of the Magistrates, 'Runners' and Police (Two Volumes) (Montclair, New Jersey: Patterson Smith).

Flanders, J. (2011) The Invention of Murder: How the Victorians Revelled in Death and Detection and Created Modern Crime (London: Harper Press).

Forsythe, W.J. (1987) The Reform of Prisoners 1830–1900 (London: Croom Helm).

Fosdick, R. (1969 edition) *European Police Systems* (Montclair, NJ: Patterson Smith).

Foucault, M. (1977) *Discipline and Punish: The Birth of the Prison* (New York: Pantheon Books).

Foucault, M. (2001) *The Order of Things: Archaeology of the Human Sciences* (London: Routledge).

Foucault, M. (2006) *Madness and Civilisation* (London: Vintage Books).

Fox, J.A. and J. Levin (2005) *Extreme Killing: Understand Serial and Mass Murder* (Thousand Okas, CA: Sage Publications).

Foyster, E. (2005) *Marital Violence: An English Family History, 1660–1857* (Cambridge: Cambridge University Press).

Friedman, L.M. (1993) *Crime and Punishment in American History* (New York: Basic Books).

Friedrichs, D.O. (2004) *Trusted Criminals: White-collar Crime in Contemporary Society* (Belmont CA: Wadsworth).

Frost, L. and H. Maxwell-Stewart (eds) (2001) *Chain Letters: Narrating Convict Lives* (Melbourne: Melbourne University Press).

Gammon, E.E. (2015 Kindle Edition) *A Fatal Pick Up* (London: Mereo Books).

Gatrell, V.A.C. (1994) *The Hanging Tree: Execution and the English People 1770–1868* (Oxford: Oxford University Press).

Gaute, J.H.H. and R. Odell (1980) *Lady Killers* (London: Panther).

Goddard, H. (1956) (with an introduction by Patrick Pringle) *Memoirs of a Bow Street Runner* (London: Museum Press).

Godfrey, B., D.J. Cox and S. Farrall (2007) *Criminal Lives: Family, Employment and Offending* (Oxford: Oxford University Press).

Godfrey, B., D.J. Cox and S. Farrall (2010) *Serious Offenders* (Oxford: Oxford University Press).

Goodman, J. (1994) *Stories of Scottsboro* (New York: Pantheon).

Gordon, E. and G. Nair (2009) *Murder and Morality in Victorian Britain: The Story of Madeleine Smith* (Manchester: Manchester University Press).

Gorn, E.J. (2011 edition) *Dillinger's Wild Ride: The Year That Made America's Public Enemy Number One* (Oxford: Oxford University Press).

Gottschalk, P. (2009) *Knowledge Management in Police Oversight* (Boca Raton, FL: Brown Walker Press).

Gottschalk, P. (2010) *Police Management – Professional Integrity in Policing: Criminal Justice, Corrections and Law Enforcement* (New York: Nova Science).

Graham, M.F. (2013 edition) *The Blasphemies of Thomas Aikenhead: Boundaries of Belief on the Eve of the Enlightenment* (Edinburgh: Edinburgh University Press).

Grant, J. (1837) *The Great Metropolis* (Two Volumes) (London: Saunders & Otley).

Gribble, L. (1957) *Famous Judges and Their Trials: A Century of Justice* (London: John Long).

Guillais, J. (trans. Jane Dunnett).(1990) *Crimes of Passion: Dramas of Private Life in Nineteenth-century France* (New York: Routledge).

Guinn, J. (2009) *Go Down Together: The True Untold Story of Bonnie and Clyde* (London: Simon & Schuster).

Haley, A. (1965) *The Autobiography of Malcolm X* (New York: Grove).

Harris, R. (1989) *Murders and Madness: Medicine, Law, and Society in the Fin-de-Siècle* (Oxford: Oxford University Press).

Harrison, B. (1971) *Drink and the Victorians: The Temperance Question in England, 1815–1872* (London: Faber & Faber).

Hartman, M.S. (1977) *Victorian Murderesses: A True History of Thirteen Respectable French and English Women Accused of Unspeakable Crimes* (London: Robson Books).

Harvie, C. (2014) *Scotland a Short History* (Oxford: Oxford University Press).

Hay, D. (ed.) (1989) *Policing and Prosecution in Britain 1750–1850* (Oxford: Oxford University Press).

Hilton, B. (1986) *Age of Atonement: The Influence of Evangelicalism on Social and Economic Thought 1785–1865* (Oxford: Clarendon Press).

Bibliography

Hitchcock, T. and R. Shoemaker (2015) *London Lives: Poverty, Crime and the Making of a Modern City, 1690–1800* (Cambridge: Cambridge University Press).

Hoeper, G. (1995) *Black Bart: Boulevardier Bandit – The Saga of California's Most Myserious Stagecoach Robber and the Men Who Sought to Capture Him* (Fresno, CA: Craven Street Books).

Hollow, M. (2014) *Rogue Banking: A History of Financial Fraud in Interwar Britain* (London: Palgrave).

Horder, J. (2007) *Excusing Crime* (Oxford: Oxford University Press).

Humphries, J. (2010) *Childhood and Child Labour in the British Industrial Revolution* (Cambridge: Cambridge University Press).

Ignatieff, M. (1978) *A Just Measure of Pain: The Penitentiary in the Industrial Revolution* (London: Macmillan).

Ireland, R.W. (2007) '*A Want of Order and Good Discipline': Rules, Discretion and the Victorian Prison* (Cardiff: University of Wales Press).

Irvine, W. (2007) *Between Justice and Politics: The Ligue des Droits de L'Homme, 1898–1945* (Stanford: Stanford University Press).

James, B. (2011) *Popular Crime: Reflections on the Celebration of Violence* (New York: Simon & Schuster).

Jenkins, R. (1991) *A Life at the Centre* (London: Macmillan).

Jewkes, Y. (2011 edition) *Media and Crime* (Los Angeles and London: Sage).

Jones, D.J.V. (1982) *Crime, Protest, Community and Police in Nineteenth Century Britain* (London: Routledge and Kegan Paul).

Joyce, B. (1999) *The Chatham Scandal: A History of Medway's Prostitution in the Late Nineteenth Century* (Rochester: Baggins Book Bazaar/Bruce Aubry).

Kelly, J. (2001) *Gallows Speeches from Eighteenth Century Ireland* (Dublin: Four Courts Press).

King, B. (1997) *Lustmord: The Writings and Artefacts of Murderers* (Burbank, CA: Bloat Books).

King, P. (2000) *Crime, Justice and Discretion in England, 1740–1820* (Oxford: Oxford University Press).

Kirk, D. and A. Woodcock (1996) *Serious Fraud: Investigation and Trial* (London: Butterworth).

Knelman, J. (1998) *Twisting in the Wind: The Murderess and the English Press* (London and Toronto: University of Toronto Press).

Kohn, S.M. (1994) *American Political Prisoners: Prosecutions under the Espionage and Sedition Acts* (Westport, CN: Greenwood Publishing Group).

Lad Panek, L. (2011) *Before Sherlock Holmes: How Magazines and Newspapers Invented the Detective Novel* (Jefferson, NC: McFarland & Co.).

Lambeth, Lord Morrison of (1960) *Herbert Morrison – An Autobiography* (London: Odhams).

Landau, N. (2002) *Law, Crime and English Society, 1660–1830* (Cambridge: Cambridge University Press).

Latour, B. (2005) *Reassembling the Social: An Introduction to Actor-Network Theory* (Oxford: Oxford University Press).

Lee, C. (2013) *Policing Prostitution* (London: Pickering & Chatto Publishers Ltd).

LeFlouria, T.L. (2015) *Chained in Silence: Black Women and Convict Labor in the New South* (Chapel Hill: University of North Carolina Press).

Lennon, J.J. and M. Foley (2010) *Dark Tourism: The Attraction of Death and Disaster* (Andover: Cengage Publishing).

Levi, M. (1987) *Regulating Fraud: White-collar Crime and the Criminal Process* (London: Tavistock Press).

Levine, D. (2000) *Bayard Rustin and the Civil Rights Movement* (New Brunswick: Rutgers University Press).

Levy, L. (1993) *Blasphemy: Verbal Offense against the Sacred from Moses to Salman Rushdie* (New York: Knopf).

Leyton, E. (1986 edition) *Hunting Humans: The Rise of the Modern Multiple Murderer* (Ontario: McClelland and Stewart).

Lichtenstein, A. (1996) *Twice the Work of Free Labor: The Political Economy of Convict Labor in the New South* (New York: Verso).

Linebaugh, P. (1991) *The London Hanged: Crime and Civil Society in the Eighteenth Century* (London: Allen Lane).

Lloyd, A. (1995) *Doubly Deviant, Doubly Damned: Society's Treatment of Violent* Women (Harmondsworth: Penguin).

Lock, J. (1982) *Tales from Bow Street* (London: Hale).

Lombroso, C. and G. Ferrero (trans. Nicole Hahn Rafter and Mary Gibson) (2004 edition) *Criminal Woman, the Prostitute, and the Normal Woman* (Durham, NC: Duke University Press).

Long, M.G. (2012) *Martin Luther King Jr., Homosexuality, and the Early Gay Rights Movement: Keeping the Dream Straight* (New York: Palgrave Macmillan).

López, L. (2014) *La Guerre des Polices n'a pas eu Lieu: Gendarmes et Policiers, Co-acteurs de la Sécurité Publique sous la Troisième République (1870–1914)* (Paris: Sorbonne).

Luddy, M. (2008) *Prostitution and Irish Society, 180–1940* (Cambridge: Cambridge University Press).

Machelon, J-P. (1976) *La République contre les Libertés* (Paris: FNSP).

MacKay, C. (1955 edition) *Extraordinary Popular Delusions and the Madness of Crowds* (London: Wordsworth Editions).

MacRaild, D.M. (2010 edition) *The Irish Diaspora in Britain, 1750–1939* (Basingstoke: Palgrave McMillan).

Magnusson, S.G. and I.M. Szijarto (2013) *What Is Microhistory? Theory and Practice* (Abingdon: Routledge).

Mancini, M.J. (1996) *One Dies, Get Another: Convict Leasing in the American South, 1866–1928* (Columbia: University of South Carolina Press).

Matthews, D. (2010) *William Marwood: The Gentleman Executioner* (Peterborough: Fastprint Publishing).

Maunder, A. and G. Moore (eds) (2004) *Victorian Crime, Madness and Sensation* (Aldershot: Ashgate).

May, A. (2006) *The Bar and the Old Bailey, 1750–1850* (Chapel Hill: University of North Carolina Press).

Mayeur, J.-M. (1973) *Les Débuts de la IIIe République 1871–1898* (Paris: Seuil).

Mbiassi Kinshasa, K. (1997) *The Man from Scottsboro: Clarence Norris and the Infamous 1931 Alabama Rape Trial, in His Own Words* (Jefferson, NC and London: McFarland and Company, Inc.).

McConville, S. (1981) *A History of English Prison Administration: Volume I 1750–1877* (London: Routledge).

McLennan, R. (2012) *American Autobiography* (Edinburgh: Edinburgh University Press).

McMillan, J.F. (2000) *France and Women, 1789–1914: Gender, Society and Politics* (London and New York: Routledge).

Metcalfe, A. (2006) *Leisure and Recreation in a Victorian Mining Community: The Social Economy of Leisure in North-East England, 1820–1914* (London and New York: Routledge).

Miers, D. (2004) *Regulating Commercial Gambling: Past, Present, and Future* (Oxford: Oxford University Press).

Miller, J.A. (2009) *Remembering Scottsboro: The Legacy of an Infamous Trial* (Princeton and Oxford: Princeton University Press).

Miller, S.M. (1993) *From Prairie to Prison: The Life of Social Activist Kate Richards O'Hare* (Columbia: University of Missouri Press).

Bibliography

Miller, V.M.L. (2012) *Hard Labor and Hard Time: Florida's 'Sunshine Prison' and Chain Gangs* (Gainesville: University of Florida Press).

Mollin, M. (2006) *Radical Pacifism in Modern America: Egalitarianism and Protest* (Philadelphia: University of Pennsylvania Press).

Montillo, R. (2015) *The Wilderness of Ruin: A Tale of Madness, Fire and the Hunt for America's Youngest Serial Killer* (New York: Harper Collins).

Moretti, F. (2013) *Distant Reading* (London: Verso).

Morland, N. (1955) *Background to Murder* (London: Werner Laurie).

Morrissey, B. (2003) *When Women Kill: Question of Agency and Subjectivity* (London: Routledge).

Mostern, K. (1999) *Autobiography and Black Identity Politics: Racialization in Twentieth-century America* (Cambridge: Cambridge University Press).

Mulcahy, L. (2011) *Legal Architecture: Justice, Due Process and the Place of Law* (Abingdon: Routledge).

Mullan, D.G. (2010) *Narrative of the Religious Self in Early-Modern Scotland* (Farnham: Ashgate).

Murphy, R.E. (2015) *The Three Graces of Raymond Street: Murder, Madness, Sex, and Politics in 1870s Brooklyn* (Albany: State University of New York Press).

Myers, M.A. (1998) *Race, Labor, and Punishment in the New South* (Columbus: Ohio State University Press).

Naquet, E. (2014) *Pour L'Humanité: La Ligue des Droits de L'Homme de L'Affaire Dreyfus à la Défaite de 1940* (Rennes: Presses Universitaires de Rennes).

Nash, D.S. (1999) *Blasphemy in Britain 1789 – Present* (Aldershot: Ashgate).

Nash, D.S. (2007) *Blasphemy in the Christian World* (Oxford: Oxford University Press).

Nash, D.S. (2012) *Blasphemy in Britain and America 1800–1930* (London: Pickering and Chatto).

Nash, D.S. and A.-M. Kilday (2010) *Cultures of Shame: Exploring Crime and Morality in Britain, 1600–1900* (Basingstoke: Palgrave).

Norrie, A. (1993) *Crime Reason and History: A Critical Introduction to Criminal Law* (London: Wiedenfeld and Nicolson).

O'Donnell, E. (1925) *Trial of Kate Webster in the Central Criminal Court, London, July, 1879, for the Murder of Mrs. Julia Martha Thomas* (Edinburgh: W. Hodge).

O'Neill, G. (2006) *The Good Old Days: Crime, Murder and Mayhem in Victorian England* (London: Viking).

Oshinsky, D.M. (1997) *'Worse Than Slavery': Parchman Farm and the Ordeal of Jim Crow Justice* (New York: Prentice Hall).

Palmer, S.H. (1992) *Police and Protest in England and Ireland 1780–1850* (London: Longman).

Perkin, H. (1969) *Origins of Modern English Society, 1780–1880* (London: Routledge and Kegan Paul).

Perkinson, R. (2010) *Texas Tough: The Rise of America's Prison Empire* (New York: Metropolitan Books).

Perry Curtis, L. (2001) *Jack the Ripper and the London Press* (New Haven and London: Yale University Press).

Philips, D. (1977) *Crime and Authority in Victorian England* (London: Croom Helm).

Podair, J. (2009) *Bayard Rustin: American Dreamer* (Lanham, MD: Rowman & Littlefield Publishers, Inc.).

Priestley, P. (1999 edition) *Victorian Prison Lives: English Prison Biography 1830–1914* (London: Pimlico).

Pringle, P. (1956) *Hue & Cry: The Birth of the British Police* (London: Museum Press).

Pringle, P. (1958) *The Thief Takers* (London: Museum Press).

Radzinowicz, L. (1956) *A History of English Criminal Law and Its Administration from 1750* (Two Volumes) (London: Stevens & Sons).

Raynaud, E. (1926) *La Vie Intime des Commissariats: Souvenirs de Police* (Paris: Payot).

Rebérioux, M. (1975) *La République Radicale 1898–1914* (Paris: Seuil).

Rise, E.W. (1995) *The Martinsville Seven: Race, Rape, and Capital Punishment* (Charlottesville: University of Virginia Press).

Robbins, M. (1998) *The Railway Age* (London: Mandolin Press).

Rosenberg, G.N. (2008 edition) *The Hollow Hope: Can Courts Bring About Social Change* (Chicago: University of Chicago Press).

Rosoff, S.M., H.N. Pontell and R. Tillman (2010) *Profit without Honor: White-collar Crime and the Looting of America* (New Jersey: Prentice Hall).

Rowbotham, J., K. Stevenson and S. Pegg (2013) *Crime News in Modern Britain: Press Reporting and Responsibility, 1820–2010* (Basingstoke: Palgrave).

Ryder, N. (2014) *The Financial Crisis and White Collar Crime – The Perfect Storm?* (Cheltenham: Edward Elgar).

Salomonsson, E.J. (2015) *Swedish Heritage of Greater Worcester* (American Heritage) (Clemson: History Press).

Saunders, J. (1989) *Nightmare: the Ernest Saunders Story* (London: Hutchinson).

Schmid, D. (2005) *Natural Born Celebrities: Serial Killers in American Culture* (Chicago: University of Chicago Press).

Scott, J.C. (1990) *Domination and the Arts of Resistance: Hidden Transcripts* (New Haven and London: Yale University Press).

Seltzer, M. (1998) *Serial Killers: Death and Life in America's Wound Culture* (New York: Routledge).

Sewell Jr., W.H. (2005) *Logics of History: Social Theory and Social Transformation* (Chicago: University of Chicago Press).

Shapiro, A.-L. (1996) *Breaking the Codes: Female Criminality in Fin-de-Siècle Paris* (Stanford, CA: Stanford University Press).

Sharpley, R. and P. Stone (eds) (2009) *The Darker Side of Travel: The Theory and Practice of Dark Tourism* (Bristol: Channel View Publications).

Shore, H. (1999) *Artful Dodgers: Youth and Crime in Early Nineteenth-century London* (London: Boydell).

Shpayer-Makov, H. (2011) *The Ascent of the Detective: Police Sleuths in Victorian and Edwardian England* (Oxford: Oxford University Press).

Smith, C. (2009) *Prison and the American Imagination* (New Haven, CN: Yale University Press).

Smith, G. (1987) *When John Bull Met Jim Crow* (London: I.B. Tauris).

Smout, T.C. (1969) *A History of the Scottish People – Volume I* (London: Collins).

Spierenburg, P. (2008) *A History of Murder: Personal Violence in Europe from the Middle Ages to the Present* (Cambridge: Polity Press).

Spierenburg, P. (2013) *Violence and Punishment: Civilizing the Body through Time* (Cambridge: Polity Press).

Spivak, J.L. (1932) *On the Chain Gang* (New York: International Pamphlets).

Spivak, J.L. (2012 edition) *Hard Times on a Southern Chain Gang: Originally Published as the Novel Georgia Nigger (1932)* (Columbia: The University of South Carolina Press).

Srebnick, A.G. and R. Levy (eds) (2005) *Crime and Culture: An Historical Perspective* (Aldershot: Ashgate).

Steadman, P. (2014) *Building Types and Built Forms* (Kibworth Beauchamp: Matador).

Stepto, R.B. (1991 edition) *From Behind the Veil: A Study of Afro-American Narrative* (Urbana and Chicago: University of Illinois Press).

Bibliography

Sullivan, P. (1996) *Days of Hope: Race and Democracy in the New Deal Era* (Chapel Hill: University of North Carolina Press).

Summerscale, K. (2008) *The Suspicions of Mr. Whicher: A Shocking Murder and the Undoing of a Great Victorian Detective* (New York: Walker & Company).

Summerville, C. (2006) *Regency Recollections: Captain Gronow's Guide to Life in London and Paris* (Welwyn Garden City: Ravenhall).

Sutherland, E.H. (1949) *White-collar Crime* (New York: Dryden Press).

Taylor, D. (1997) *The New Police in Nineteenth-century England: Crime, Conflict and Control* (Manchester: Manchester University Press).

Taylor, J. (2013) *Boardroom Scandal: The Criminalization of Company Fraud in Nineteenth-century Britain* (Oxford: Oxford University Press).

Thomas, D. (2003) *An Underworld at War* (London: John Murray).

Thompson, F.M.L. (1963) *English Landed Society in the Nineteenth Century* (London: Routledge and Kegan Paul Ltd).

Thurmond Smith, P. (1985) *Policing Victorian London: Political Policing, Public Order, and the London Metropolitan Police* (Westport: Greenwood Press).

Tobias, J.J. (1967) *Crime and Industrial Society in the Nineteenth Century* (Oxford: B.T. Batsford).

Tosh, J. (2010 edition) *The Pursuit of History: Aims, Methods and New Directions in the Study of Modern History* (Harlow: Longman).

Vincent, H. (1912 edition) *A Police Code and General Manual of the Criminal Law* (London: Butterworth and Co.).

Walkowitz, J.R. (1992) *City of Dreadful Delight: Narratives of Sexual Danger in Late-Victorian London* (London: Virago).

Walkowitz, J.R. (1999) *Prostitution and Victorian Society: Women, Class, and the State* (Cambridge: Cambridge University Press).

Waller, M. (2003 Kindle Edition) *London 1945: Life in the Debris of War* (London: Studio 28).

Walsh, B. (2014) *Domestic Murder in Nineteenth-century England: Literary and Cultural Representations* (Farnham: Ashgate).

Whatley, C. (2000) *Scottish Society 1707–1830: Beyond Jacobitism, Towards Industrialisation* (Manchester: Manchester University Press).

Wiener, M.J. (1990) *Reconstructing the Criminal, Culture, Law, and Policy in England 1830–1914* (Cambridge: Cambridge University Press).

Wiener, M.J. (2004) *Men of Blood: Violence, Manliness, and Criminal Justice in Victorian England* (Cambridge: Cambridge University Press).

Williams, G. (1983) *Textbook of Criminal Law* (London: Stevens and Son).

Williams O'Brien, G. (1999) *The Color of the Law: Race, Violence, and Justice in the Post-World War II South* (Chapel Hill: University of North Carolina Press).

Wilson, D. (2011) *Looking for Laura: Public Criminology and Hot News* (Sherfield-on-Loddon (Hampshire): Waterside Press).

Wilson, P. (1971) *Murderess: A Study of Women Executed in Britain since 1843* (London: Michael Joseph).

Wilson, S. (2014) *The Origins of Modern Financial Crime: Historical foundations and Current Problems in Britain* (London: Routledge).

Wood, W. (ed.) (1916) *Survivors' Tales of Famous Crimes* (London: Cassell and Company).

Woodward, E.L. (1938) *The Oxford History of England: The Age of Reform 1815–1870* (Oxford: Clarendon Press).

Worsley, L. (2013) *A Very British Murder: The Story of a National Obsession* (London: BBC Books).

Worthington, H. (2005) *The Rise of the Detective in Early Nineteenth-century Popular Fiction* (Basingstoke: Palgrave Macmillan).

Zedner, L. (1991) *Women, Crime and Custody in Victorian England* (Oxford: Clarendon Press).

Zemon Davis, N. (1983) *The Return of Martin Guerre* (Cambridge: Harvard University Press).

Journal Articles

Anon (S.H. Taunton) (1852) 'A Reminiscence of a Bow Street Officer', *Harper's New Monthly Magazine*, Vol. 5, No. 28, pp. 483–94.

Aubert, V. (1952) 'White-collar Crime and Social Structure', *American Journal of Sociology*, Vol. 58, pp. 263–71.

Bailey, J. (2006) '"I dye [sic] by Inches": Locating Wife Beating in the Concept of a Privatization of Marriage and Violence in Eighteenth-century England', *Social History*, Vol. 31, pp. 273–94.

Beattie, J.M. (1974) 'The Pattern of Crime in England 1660–1800', *Past and Present*, No. 62, pp. 47–95.

Benson, J. (2009) 'Calculation, Celebrity and Scandal: The Provincial Press in Edwardian England', *Journalism Studies*, Vol. 10, pp. 837–50.

Bentwich, N. (1942) 'The U.S.A Visiting Forces Act, 1942', *The Modern Law Review*, Vol. 6, No. 1/2, pp. 68–72.

Bevan, F. (2006) 'Criminals and Conspirators', *Ancestors*, Vol. 51, pp. 33–5.

Bowman, M.S. and P.C. Pezzullo (2009) 'What's So "Dark" About "Dark Tourism"? Death, Tours and Performance', *Tourism Studies*, Vol. 9, No. 3, pp. 187–202.

Bradley, J. and H. Maxwell-Stewart (1997) '"Behold the Man": Power, Observation and the Tattooed Convict', *Journal of Australian Studies*, Vol. 12, No. 1, pp. 71–97.

Brewer, J. (2010) 'Microhistory and the Histories of Everyday Life', *Cultural and Social History*, Vol. 7, No. 1, pp. 87–109.

Brown, B.J. (1963) 'The Demise of Chance Medley and the Recognition of Provocation as a Defence to Murder in English Law', *The American Journal of Legal History*, Vol. 7, pp. 310–18.

Buckley, M. (2002) 'Sensations of Celebrity: *Jack Sheppard* and the Mass Audience', *Victorian Studies*, Vol. 44, No. 3, pp. 423–64.

Carter Wood, J. and P. Knepper (2014) 'Crime Stories: Criminality, Policing and the Press in Inter-war European and Transatlantic Perspectives', *Media History*, Vol. 20, No. 4, pp. 345–51.

Chadwick, E. (1829) 'Preventive Police', *London Review*, Vol. 1, pp. 252–308.

Cockburn, J.S. (1991) 'Patterns of Violence in English Society: Homicide in Kent', *Past and Present*, No. 130, pp. 70–106.

Crook, T. (2008) 'Accommodating the Outcast: Common Lodging Houses and the Limits of Urban Governance in Victorian and Edwardian London', *Urban History*, Vol. 35, No. 3, pp. 414–36.

Dickens, C. (1850) 'A Detective Police-Party', *Household Words*, Vol. 1, No. 18, pp. 409–14.

Dinsmor, A. (2000) 'Glasgow Police Pioneers', *Journal of the Police History Society*, Vol. 15, pp. 9–11.

Dye, I. (1989) 'The Tattoos of Early American Seafarers, 1796–1818', *Proceedings of the American Philosophy Society*, Vol. 133, No. 4, pp. 520–54.

Eisner, M. (2001) 'Modernisation, Self-control and Lethal Violence – The Long-term Dynamics of European Homicide Rates in Theoretical Perspective', *British Journal of Criminology*, Vol. 41, pp. 618–38.

Emmerichs, M.B.W. (1993) 'Trials of Women for Homicide in Nineteenth-century England', *Women and Criminal Justice*, Vol. 5, No. 1, pp. 99–109.

Engel, A.J. (1979) '"Immoral Intentions": The University of Oxford and the Problem of Prostitution, 1827–1914', *Victorian Studies*, Vol. 23, No. 1, pp. 79–107.

Feeley, M.M. and D.L. Little (1991) 'The Vanishing Female: The Decline of Women in the Criminal Process, 1687–1912', *Law and Society Review*, Vol. 25, No. 4, pp. 719–57.

Fellman, D. (1957) 'Cruel and Unusual Punishments', *Journal of Politics*, Vol. 19, No. 1, pp. 34–42.

Ferguson, E.E (2006) 'Judicial Authority and Popular Justice: Crimes of Passion in Fin-De-Siècle Paris', *Journal of Social History*, Vol. 40, pp. 293–315.

Ferrari, R. (1918) 'The "Crime Passionnel" in French Courts', *California Law Review*, Vol. 6, pp. 331–41.

Forsythe, W.J. (1991) 'Centralisation and Local Autonomy: The Experience of English Prisons 1820–1877', *Journal of Historical Sociology*, Vol. 4, No. 3, pp. 317–45.

Foucault, M. (1978) 'About the Concept of the "Dangerous Individual" in Nineteenth-century Legal Psychiatry', *International Journal of Law and Psychiatry*, Vol. 1, No. 1, pp. 1–18.

Foyster, E. (2002) 'Creating a Veil of Silence? Politeness and Marital Violence in the English Household', *Transactions of the Royal Historical Society*, Vol. 12, pp. 395–415.

Franklin, H.B. (1977) 'The Literature of the American Prison', *The Massachusetts Review*, Vol. 18, No. 1, pp. 51–78.

Freeman, T.S. (2009) 'The Rise of Prison Literature', *Huntington Library Quarterly*, Vol. 72, No. 2, pp. 133–46.

Gigot, A. (1903) 'Des Garanties de la Libereté Individuelle', *Revue Pénitentiaire: Bulletin de la Société Général des Prisons*, Vol. 27, pp. 1070–82.

Green, D.R. (2006) 'Pauper Protests: Power and Resistance in Early Nineteenth-century London Workhouses', *Social History*, Vol. 31, No. 2, pp. 137–59.

Gregory, B.S. (1999) 'Is Small Beautiful? Microhistory and the History of Everyday Life', *History and Theory*, Vol. 38, No. 1, pp. 100–10.

Grey, D.J.R. (2015) '"Agonised Weeping": Representing Femininity, Emotion and Infanticide in Edwardian Newspapers', *Media History*, Vol. 21, No. 4, pp. 468–80.

Gurr, T.R. (1991) 'Historical Trends in Violent Crime: A Critical Review of the Evidence', *Crime and Justice: An Annual Review of Research*, Vol. 3, pp. 295–353.

Haley, S. (2013) '"Like I Was a Man": Chain Gangs, Gender, and the Domestic Carceral Sphere in Jim Crow Georgia', *Signs*, Vol. 39, No. 1, pp. 53–77.

Hamilton, M. (1978) 'Opposition to the Contagious Diseases Acts, 1865–86', *Albion: A Quarterly Journal Concerned with British Studies*, Vol. 10, No. 1, 14–27.

Hammer, C. (1978) 'Patterns of Homicide in Early Modern Europe', *Past and Present*, No. 78, pp. 3–23.

Handler, P. (2007) 'The Law of Felonious Assault in England, 1803–61', *Journal of Legal History*, Vol. 28, pp. 183–206.

Harling, P. (2014) 'The Trouble with Convicts: From Transportation to Penal Servitude, 1840–67', *Journal of British Studies*, Vol. 53, No. 1, pp. 80–110.

Harris, C.J. (2012) 'The Residual Career Patterns of Police Misconduct', *Journal of Criminal Justice*, 40, pp. 323–32.

Harris, R. (1988) 'Melodrama, Hysteria and Feminine Crimes of Passion in the Fin-de-Siècle', *History Workshop*, Vol. 25, pp. 31–63.

Harrison, B. (1968) 'Two Roads to Social Reform: Francis Place and the "Drunken Committee" of 1834', *Historical Journal*, Vol. 11, No. 2, pp. 272–300.

Henriques, U.R.Q. (1972) 'The Rise and Decline of the Separate System of Prison Discipline', *Past and Present*, Vol. 54, No. 1, pp. 61–93.

Hobbs, A. (2013) 'The Deleterious Dominance of *The Times* in Nineteenth-century Scholarship', *Journal of Victorian Culture*, Vol. 18, pp. 472–97.

Hudson, P. (2010) 'Closeness and Distance', *Cultural and Social History*, Vol. 7, No. 3, pp. 375–85.

Johansen, A. (2013) 'Defending the Individual: The Personal Rights Association and the Ligue des Droits de L'Homme, 1871–1916', *European Review of History*, Vol. 20, No. 4, pp. 559–79.

Joughin, G.L. (1950) 'Review of *Scottsboro Boy*', *Antioch Review*, Vol. 10, No. 3, pp. 422–24.

Kent, D. (1997) 'Decorative Bodies: The Significance of Convicts' Tattoos', *Journal of Australian Studies*, Vol. 53, pp. 78–88.

King, P. (1996) 'Punishing Assault: The Transformation of Attitudes in the English Courts', *Journal of Interdisciplinary History*, Vol. 27, pp. 43–74.

King, P. (1999) 'Locating Histories of Crime: A Bibliographical Study', *British Journal of Criminology*, Vol. 39, No. 1, pp. 161–74.

King, P. (2004) 'The Summary Courts and Social Relations in Eighteenth Century England', *Past and Present*, No. 183, pp. 125–72.

Lacey, F.W. (1953) 'Vagrancy and Other Crimes of Personal Condition', *Harvard Law Review*, Vol. 66, No. 7, pp. 1203–26.

Langhorne, J.L. (1950) 'Review of *Scottsboro Boy*', *Journal of Negro History*, Vol. 35, No. 4, pp. 463–65.

Lawrence, P. (2012) 'History, Criminology and the "Use" of the Past', *Theoretical Criminology*, Vol. 16, No. 3, pp. 313–28.

Levi, M. (1991) 'Sentencing White-collar Crime in the Dark? Reflections on the Guinness Four', *Howard Journal of Criminal Justice*, Vol. 30, No. 4, pp. 257–79.

Levi, M. (2002) 'Suite Justice or Sweet Charity? Some Explorations of Shaming and Incapacitating Business Fraudsters', *Punishment and Society*, Vol. 4, No. 2, pp. 147–63.

Lilly, J.R. and J.M. Thomson (1997) 'Executing US Soldiers in England, World War II', *British Journal of Criminology*, Vol. 57, No. 2, pp. 262–88.

Lobban, M. (1996) 'Nineteenth Century Frauds in Company Formation: *Derry v Peek* in Context', *Law Quarterly Review*, Vol. 112, No. 2, pp. 287–334.

Locker, J.P. and B. Godfrey (2006) 'Ontological Boundaries and Temporal Watersheds in the Development of White-collar Crime', *British Journal of Criminology*, Vol. 46, No. 6, pp. 976–92.

Magnússon, S.G. (2015) 'Tales of the Unexpected: The "Textual Environment", Ego-Documents and a Nineteenth-century Icelandic Love Story – An Approach in Microhistory', *Cultural and Social History*, Vol. 12, No. 1, pp. 77–94.

Maxwell-Stewart, H. (2010) 'Convict Transportation from Britain and Ireland 1615–1870', *History Compass*, Vol. 8, No. 11, pp. 1221–42.

McWilliam, R. (2000) 'Melodrama and the Historians', *Radical History Review*, Vol. 78, pp. 57–84.

Minto, D. (2014) 'Review of *Common Prostitutes and Ordinary Citizens: Commercial Sex in London, 1885–1960* by Julia Laite', *The Journal of the Historical Association*, Vol. 99, No. 335, pp. 347–9.

Morris, R.M. (2001) '"Lies, Damned Lies and Criminal Statistics": Reinterpreting the Criminal Statistics in England and Wales', *Crime, History & Societies*, Vol. 5, pp. 111–27.

Mumm, S. (1996) '"Not Worse Than Other Girls": The Convent-Based Rehabilitation of Fallen Women in Victorian Britain', *Journal of Social History*, Vol. 29, No. 3, pp. 527–47.

Noble, C. (2002) 'The New Gaol in Bathwick, 1172–1842', *Bath History*, Vol. IX, pp. 64–86.

Oldham, J.C. (1985) 'On Pleading the Belly: A History of the Jury of Matrons', *Criminal Justice History*, Vol. 6, pp. 1–64.

Pellew, J. (1989) 'The Home Office and the Aliens Act, 1905', *The Historical Journal*, Vol. 32, pp. 369–85.

Rock, P. (2005) 'Chronocentrism and British Criminology', *British Journal of Sociology*, Vol. 56, No. 3, pp. 473–91.

Bibliography

Rogers, H. (2009) 'The Way to Jerusalem: Reading, Writing and Reform in an Early Victorian Gaol', *Past and Present*, No. 205, pp. 71–104.

Rogers, H. (2012) '"Oh, What Beautiful Books!" Captivated Reading in an Early Victorian Prison', *Victorian Studies*, Vol. 55, No. 1, pp. 57–84.

Rogers, H. (2012) 'Singing in Gaol: Christian Instruction and Inmate Culture in the Nineteenth Century', *Prison Service Journal*, Vol. 199, pp. 35–43.

Rogers, H. (2014) 'Kindness and Reciprocity: Liberated Prisoners and Christian Charity in Early Nineteenth-century England', *Journal of Social History*, Vol. 47, No. 3, pp. 721–45.

Salmi, H. (2011) 'Cultural History, the Possible, and the Principle of Plenitude', *History and Theory*, Vol. 50, pp. 171–87.

Seltzer, M. (1997) 'Wound Culture: Trauma in the Pathological Public Sphere', *October*, Vol. 80, pp. 3–26.

Shapiro, S. (1985) '"The Road Not Taken": The Elusive Path to Criminal Prosecution for White Collar Offenders', *Law and Society Review*, Vol. 19, No. 2, pp. 179–217.

Shapiro, S. (1990) 'Collaring the Crime, Not the Criminal: Reconsidering the Concept of a White-collar Crime', *American Sociological Review*, Vol. 55, pp. 346–65.

Sharpe, J.A. (1985) '"Last Dying Speeches": Religion, Ideology and Public Execution in Seventeenth Century England', *Past and Present*, Vol. 107, No. 1, pp. 144–67.

Sindall, R.S. (1987) 'The London Garrotting Panics of 1856 and 1862', *Social History*, Vol. 12, No. 3, pp. 351–9.

Slater, S.A. (2010) 'Containment: Managing Street Prostitution in London, 1918–59', *Journal of British Studies*, Vol. 49, No. 2, pp. 332–57.

Smith, F.B. (1990) 'The Contagious Diseases Acts Reconsidered', *Social History of Medicine*, Vol. 3, No. 2, pp. 197–215, at p. 197.

Spierenberg, P. (2004) 'Punishment, Power and History: Foucault and Elias', *Social Science History*, Vol. 28, pp. 607–36.

Stockdale, E. (1976) 'The Rise of Joshua Jebb, 1837–1850', *British Journal of Criminology*, Vol. 16, No. 2, pp. 164–70.

Stockdale, E. (1983) 'A Short History of Prison Inspection in England', *British Journal of Criminology*, Vol. 23, No. 3, pp. 209–28.

Storch, R.D. (1975) '"The Plague of Blue Locusts": Police Reform and Popular Resistance in North England 1840–1857', *International Review of Social History*, Vol. 20, No. 1. pp. 61–90.

Storch, R.D. (1976) 'The Policeman as Domestic Missionary: Urban Discipline and Popular Culture in Northern England, 1850–1880', *Journal of Social History*, Vol. 9, No. 4, pp. 481–509.

Sutherland, E.H. (1940) 'White Collar Criminality', *American Sociological Review*, Vol. 5, No. 1, pp. 1–12.

Sutherland, E.H. (1945) 'Is "White Collar Crime" Crime?' *American Sociological Review*, Vol. 10, pp. 132–39.

Szijártó, I. (2002) 'Four Arguments for Microhistory', *Rethinking History: The Journal of Theory and Practice*, Vol. 6, No. 2, pp. 209–15.

Taft, H.B. (1905) 'The Administration of Criminal Law', *Yale Law Journal*, Vol. 15, pp. 1–17.

Tomasic, R. (2011) 'The Financial Crisis and the Haphazard Pursuit of Financial Crime', *Journal of Financial Crime*, Vol. 18, No. 1, pp. 7–31.

Various (2015) 'Historians and the Carceral State', Special Issue of the *Journal of American History*, Vol. 102, No. 1.

Vivo, F. de (2010) 'Prospect or Refuge? Microhistory, History on the Large Scale', *Cultural and Social History*, Vol. 7, No. 3, pp. 387–97.

Walkowitz, J.R. and D.J. Walkowitz (1973) '"We Are Not Beasts of the Field": Prostitution and the Poor in Plymouth and Southampton under the Contagious Diseases Acts', *Feminist Studies*, Vol. 1, No. 3/4, pp. 73–106.

Wheeler, S., D. Weisburd and N. Bode (1982) 'Sentencing the White-Collar Offender: Rhetoric and Reality', *American Sociological Review*, Vol. 47, No. 5, pp. 641–59.

Wiener, M. (1999) 'The Sad Story of George Hall: Adultery, Murder and the Politics of Mercy in Mid-Victorian England', *Social History*, Vol. 24, pp. 174–95.

Wolpin, K.I. (1978) 'Capital Punishment and Homicide in England: A Summary of Results', *American Economic Review*, Vol. 68, No. 2, pp. 422–27.

Zedner, L. (1991) 'Women, Crime and Penal Responses: A Historical Account', *Crime and Justice*, Vol. 14, pp. 307–62.

Chapters from Edited Collections

Arsenault, R. (2004) 'You Don't Have to Ride Jim Crow: CORE and the 1947 Journey of Reconciliation', in G. Fellman (ed.) *Before Brown: Civil Rights and White Backlash in the Modern South* (Tuscaloosa: University of Alabama Press), pp. 21–67.

Bartrip, P. (1981) 'Public Opinion and Law Enforcement: The Ticket of Leave Scares in Mid-Victorian Britain', in V. Bailey (ed.) *Policing and Punishment in Nineteenth century Britain* (London: Croom Helm), pp. 150–81.

Beattie, J.M. (2006) 'Early Detection: The Bow Street Runners in Late Eighteenth-century London', in C. Emsley and H. Shpayer-Makov (eds.) *Police Detectives in History, 1750–1950* (Aldershot: Ashgate), pp. 15–33.

Bell, D. (2002) 'Total History and Microhistory: The French and Italian Paradigms', in L. Kramer and S. Maza (eds) *A Companion to Western Historical Thought* (Oxford: Blackwell), pp. 262–76.

Berlière, J.-M. (1991) 'Professionalization of the Police under the Third Republic in France 1875–1940', in C. Emsley and B. Weinberger (eds) *Policing in Western Europe: Politics, Professionalism and Public Order, 1850–1940* (New York: Greenwood Press), pp. 36–54.

Berlière, J.-M. (2008) 'La Carrière Exceptionnelle d'un Commissaire Special', in D. Kalifa and P. Karila-Cohen (eds) *Le Commissaire de Police au XIXe Siècle* (Paris: Sorbonne), pp. 173–91.

Bradley, J. and H. Maxwell-Stewart (1997) 'Embodied Explorations: Investigating Convict Tattoos and the Transportation System', in I. Duffield and J. Bradley (eds) *Representing Convicts: New Perspectives on Forced Convict Labour Migration* (Leicester: Leicester University Press), pp. 183–203.

Cameron, J.K. (1982) 'Theological Controversy: A Factor in the Origins of the Scottish Enlightenment', in R.H. Campbell and A.S. Skinner (eds) *The Origins and Nature of the Scottish Enlightenment* (Edinburgh: John Donald), pp. 116–30.

Carter Wood, J. (2014) 'Drinking, Fighting and Working-Class Sociability in Nineteenth-century Britain', in S. Schmid and B. Schmidt-Haberkamp (eds) *Drink in the Eighteenth and Nineteenth Centuries* (London: Pickering and Chatto), pp. 71–80.

Davis, J. (1980) 'The London Garotting Panic of 1862: A Moral Panic and the creation of a Criminal Class in mid-Victorian England', in V.A.C. Gatrell, B. Lenman and G. Parker (eds) *Crime and the Law: A Social History of Crime in Western Europe since 1500* (London: Europa), pp. 190–213.

Eakin, P.J. (1993) 'Malcom X and the Limits of Autobiography', in W. Andrews (ed.) *African-American Autobiography: A Collection of Critical Essays* (Englewood Cliffs, NJ: Prentice-Hall), pp. 152–61.

Englemann, F. (1773) 'A Late-Eighteenth Century Ballad Opera and John Wilkes: The Bow Street Opera', in U Böker, I. Detmers and A. Giovanpolous (eds) *John Gay's The Beggar's Opera 1728–2004 Adaptations and Re-writings* (Amsterdam: Rodopi), pp. 169–92.

Ferguson, E.E. (2014) 'Emotion, Gender and Honour in a Fin-de-siecle Crime of Passion: The Case of Marie Biere', in C. Strange, R. Cribb and C.E. Forth (eds) *Honour, Violence and Emotions in History* (London: Bloomsbury), pp. 145–61.

Friedrichs, D.O. (2012) 'Wall Street: Crime Never Sleeps', in S. Will, S. Handelman and D.C. Brotherton (eds) *How They Got Away with It: White Collar Criminals and the Financial Meltdown* (New York: Columbia University Press), pp. 3–25.

Gatrell, V.A.C. (1980) 'The Decline of Theft and Violence in Victorian and Edwardian England', in V.A.C. Gatrell, B. Lenman and G. Parker (eds) *Crime and the Law: The Social History of Crime in Western Europe Since 1500* (London: Europa Publications), pp. 238–370.

Gatrell, V.A.C. and T.B. Hadden (1972) 'Criminal Statistics and Their Interpretation', in E.A. Wrigley (ed.) *Nineteenth-century Society: Essays in the Use of Quantitative Methods for the Study of Social Data* (Cambridge: Cambridge University Press), pp. 336–96.

Geertz, C. (1973) 'Thick Description: Toward an Interpretive Theory of Culture', in C. Geertz (ed.) *The Interpretation of Cultures: Selected Essays* (New York: Basic Books), pp. 3–30.

Grant, M. (2013) 'Citizenship, Sexual Anxiety and Womanhood in Second World War Britain: The Case of the Man with the Cleft Chin', in S. Nicolas and T. O'Malley (eds) *Moral Panics, Social Fears, and the Media: Historical Perspectives* (London: Routledge), pp. 177–90.

Hunter, M. (1992) '"Aikenhead the Atheist": The Context and Consequences of Articulate Irreligion in the Late Seventeenth Century', in M. Hunter and D. Wootton (eds) *Atheism from the Reformation to the Enlightenment* (Oxford: Clarendon Press), pp. 221–54.

Johnston, H. (2006) '"Buried Alive": Representations of the Separate System in Victorian England', in P. Mason (ed.) *Captured by the Media: Prison Discourse in Popular Culture* (Cullompton: Willan), pp. 103–21.

Kalifa, D. and P. Karila-Cohen (2008) 'L'homme de L'entre-deux: L'identité Brouillé du Commissaire de Police au XIXe siècle', in D. Kalifa and P. Karila-Cohen (eds) *Le Commissaire de Police au XIXe Siècle* (Paris: Sorbonne), pp. 7–26.

Miller, V. (2011) 'Films about Prison', in A.L. Wood (ed.) *The New Encyclopedia of Southern Culture: Volume 19 – Violence* (Chapel Hill: University of North Carolina Press), pp. 67–70.

Nash, D.S. (2010) 'Moral Crimes and the Law since 1700', in A.-M. Kilday and D.S. Nash (eds) *Histories of Crime in Britain 1600–2000* (Basingstoke: Palgrave), pp. 17–38.

Nelken, D. (1994 edition) 'White-collar Crime', in M. Maguire, R. Morgan and R. Reiner (eds) *The Oxford Handbook of Criminology* (Oxford: Oxford University Press), pp. 355–92.

Philips, D. (1980) 'A New Engine of Power and Authority: The Institutionalisation of Law Enforcement in England, 1750–1850', in V.A.C. Gatrell, B. Lenman and G. Parker (eds) *Crime and the Law: The Social History of Crime in Western Europe Since 1500* (London: Europa Publications), pp. 155–89.

Port, A.I. (2015 edition) 'History from Below, The History of Everyday Life, and Microhistory', in J. Wright (ed.) *International Encyclopedia of the Social and Behavioral Sciences – Volume 11* (Londan: Elsevier), pp. 108–13.

Rowbotham, J. (2000) '"Only when drunk": The Stereotyping of Violence in England, c. 1850–1900', in S. D'Cruze (ed.) *Everyday Violence in Britain, 1850–1950: Gender and Class* (Harlow: Longman), pp. 155–69.

Shpayer-Makov, H. (2006) 'Explaining the Rise and Success of Detective Memoirs in Britain', in C. Emsley and H. Shpayer-Makov (eds) *Police Detectives in History, 1750–1950* (Aldershot: Ashgate), pp. 103–33.

Stebbings, C. (2012) 'Benefits and Barriers: The Making of Victorian Legal History', in A. Musson and C. Stebbings (eds) *Making Legal History: Approaches and Methodologies* (Cambridge: Cambridge University Press), pp. 72–87.

Watson, K.D. (2009) 'Is a Burn a Wound? Vitriol-Throwing in Medico-Legal Context, 1800–1900', in I. Goold and C. Kelly (eds) *Lawyers' Medicine: The Legislature, the Courts and Medical Practice, 1760–2000* (Oxford: Hart Publishing), pp. 61–78.

Wilson, S. (2016) 'Financial Crises and Financial Crime "Transformative Understandings" of Crime – Past Present and Future', in N. Ryder, U. Turksen and J. Tucker (eds) *The Financial Crisis and White Collar Crime – Legislative and Policy Responses* (Abingdon: Routledge), forthcoming.

Unpublished Theses and Dissertations

Alker, Z. (2014) 'When High and Low Collide: Gender and Respectability in the Mid-Victorian Courtroom – Street Violence in Mid-Victorian Liverpool' (Unpublished D.Phil thesis, Liverpool John Moores University).

Carrot, G. (1984) 'Le Maintien de L'ordre: France de la Fin de l'Ancien Régime Jusqu'à 1968' (Unpublished Thesis, Université Nice).

Cox, D.J. (2006) '"A Certain Share of Low Cunning": The Provincial Activities of the Bow Street Runners 1792–1839' (Unpublished PhD thesis, Lancaster University).

Griffin, R. (2015) 'Detective Policing and the State in Nineteenth-century England: The Detective Department of the London Metropolitan Police, 1842–1878' (Unpublished PhD thesis, The University of Western Ontario).

Kass-Gergi, Y. (2012) 'Killer Personalities: Serial Killers as Celebrities in Contemporary American Culture' (Unpublished BA Dissertation (American Studies), Wesleyan University, Connecticut).

Tucker, K.A. (2013) '"Abominations of the Female Sex": Five Case Studies of Late Nineteenth Century Criminal Women' (Unpublished MA (By Research) Dissertation, University of Central Lancashire).

Key Websites

Ancestry: http://www.ancestry.com
Executed Today: http://www.executedtoday.com
The Herald Scotland: http://www.heraldscotland.com/news/
Oxford Dictionary of National Biography: http://www.oxforddnb.com/
Parliamentary Papers Online: http://parlipapers.chadwyck.co.uk/marketing/index.jsp
Tasmanian Archives Online: http://search.archives.tas.gov.au/default.aspx?
The Proceedings of the Old Bailey Online, 1674–1913: http://www.oldbaileyonline.org/

INDEX

Index

Evans, Richard 4
Evening Express 109, 110, 113
Executed Today 29–30

Ferguson, Dr Robert 276, 283
Ferguson, Eliza 110, 112, 117
Ferrero, Guglielmo 110
Fielding, Henry 152–54
Fielding, Sir John 153, 159–60
    Plan for Preventing Robberies 154
    Public Hue & Cry 154–55, 157
financial fraud 10, 37–59, 131
Flanders, Judith 125
Florida State Prison 254
forensics 164
Forsythe, W.J. 276
Foucault, Emilie 11, 107–23, 137, 141
Foucault, Michel 2, 128, 264
France 12, 110–12, 117, 173–90
Fraser (Frazer), John 26
Freethinker 30
Friendless Girls Association 72
Fulham Prison 213, 215

Gammon, Edna 90
    A Fatal Pick Up 85, 87
Gaols Act (1823) 217
Gaspey, Thomas 162
Gay, John 159–60
gender 83, 95–6, 107, 111, 119 n.13, 126, 129–30,
    134–35, 141, 142, 145 n.55, 147 n.94, 242 n.5
General Assembly of the Church of Scotland 23
Ginzburg, Carlo 26
Goddard, Henry 159
Godfrey, Barry 210
Godwin, William 162
Gottschalk, Petter 174–75
Graham, Michael 22–4, 27, 28, 30
Grant, Matthew 86
Great Yarmouth 13, 229, 230, 231, 232, 236,
    238–39, 241
Green, David 228
Greenblatt, Stephen 241
Gronow, Captain Rees Howell 158
The Guardian, digital archive 211
Guillais, Joëlle 110
'Guinness Four' 51
Guyot, Yves 177

Habitual Offender Act (1869) 212
Hall, Thomas J. 198
Hamilton, Margaret 61
Hannam, Ian 51
Harris, Captain William 62
Harris, Ruth 110

Hartman, Mary 110
Harvie, Christopher
    Short History of Scotland 29
Heath, George Edward 83, 87–8, 91, 93, 99
Henry, Leroy 89
Herald Scotland 31
heresy 27, 30
Heyer, Georgette 165
'high art' crime 40, 45, 46, 52
Hilton, Boyd 46
history 5
    of crime 37–9, 41
    cultural history 5–6, 8, 41, 42–3, 52
    early use of 10
    gender history 8
    history of material culture 8
    history of mentalities 9
    social history 8
Hitchcock, Tim 229
Hobbs, Andrew 118
Holmes, H. H. 129, 143 n.23
Home Office 272, 273
    and model prisons 274
Home Secretary
    powers of 83
homicide 11, 84, 89–90, 93, 119 n.11, 125–48
    media reactions to 125–48
    narratives of 11
    and popular culture 129
House of Lords Select Committee on the Criminal
    Law (1847) 279
Hone, Nathaniel 160
Howard, John 216, 273
Hudson, George 46
Hulten, Gustav 11, 83–103
    appeal against conviction 92–4
    conviction of 92–4
    execution of 97
    state of mind of 92
Humanist Facebook Page 30
Hume, David 27
Hunter, Michael 26
Hutcheson, Frances 28
Hyland, Julia 13, 209–24

illegal drinking 12, 192–93, 195, 200
illegal gambling 12, 198, 199–200, 201, 202
Illustrated Police News 139
imprisonment 12–13
Ines, Charles 92, 95
infanticide 5
Ingram, John 157
International Labor Defence (USA) 255, 257
Intoxicating Liquors Act (1855) 195
Irene Morgan v Commonwealth of Virginia 254

320

Index

Index